Unfold.

Unfoldings

Essays in
Schenkerian Theory
and Analysis

CARL SCHACHTER

Edited by Joseph N. Straus

New York   Oxford

Oxford University Press

1999

Oxford University Press

Oxford   New York

Athens   Auckland   Bangkok   Bogotá   Buenos Aires   Calcutta
Cape Town   Chennai   Dar es Salaam   Delhi   Florence   Hong Kong   Istanbul
Karachi   Kuala Lumpur   Madrid   Melbourne   Mexico City   Mumbai
Nairobi   Paris   São Paulo   Singapore   Taipei   Tokyo   Toronto   Warsaw

and associated companies in
Berlin   Ibadan

Published by Oxford University Press, Inc.
198 Madison Avenue, New York, New York 10016

Oxford is a registered trademark of Oxford University Press

Library of Congress Cataloging-in-Publication Data
Schachter, Carl.
Unfoldings : essays in Schenkerian theory and analysis /
Carl Schachter ; edited by Joseph N. Straus.
p.   cm.
Includes bibliographical references and index.
ISBN 0-19-512013-2
1. Schenkerian analysis.   I. Straus, Joseph Nathan.
II. Title.   MT6.S2824U6   1998
781—dc21   97-47308

1 3 5 7 9 8 6 4 2

Printed in the United States of America
on acid-free paper

Acknowledgments

Michael Sumbera worked extensively and expertly in preparing the manuscript, supported by a grant from the Research Foundation of the City University of New York. At Oxford University Press, Maribeth Anderson Payne and Jonathan Wiener saw the manuscript through from conception to publication with their customary enthusiasm and élan. It has been a pleasure to work with them.

"The Adventures of an F♯: Tonal Narration and Exhortation in Donna Anna's First-Act Recitative and Aria" from *Theory and Practice* 16 (1991). © 1991 by the Music Theory Society of New York State. All rights reserved.

"Bach's Fugue in B♭ Major, *Well-Tempered Clavier*, Book I, No. 21" from *Music Forum* 3, ed. William Mitchell and Felix Salzer. Copyright © 1973 by Columbia University Press. Reprinted with permission of the publisher.

"Chopin's Fantasy, Op. 49: The Two-Key Scheme" from *Chopin Studies*, ed. Jim Samson. Copyright © 1988 by Cambridge University Press. Reprinted with the permission of Cambridge University Press.

Contents

A Dialogue between Author and Editor   3

PART I   RHYTHM AND LINEAR ANALYSIS

ONE   A Preliminary Study   17

TWO   Durational Reduction   54

THREE   Aspects of Meter   79

PART II   SCHENKERIAN THEORY

FOUR   Either/Or   121

FIVE   Analysis by Key:
Another Look at Modulation   134

SIX   The Triad as Place and Action   161

SEVEN   A Commentary on Schenker's *Free Composition*   184

PART III   WORDS AND MUSIC

EIGHT   Motive and Text in Four Schubert Songs   209

NINE   The Adventures of an F♯: Tonal Narration and
Exhortation in Donna Anna's First-Act Recitative and Aria   221

PART IV   ANALYTICAL MONOGRAPHS

TEN   Bach's Fugue in B♭ Major,
Well-Tempered Clavier, Book I, No. 21   239

ELEVEN   Chopin's Fantasy, Op. 49: The Two-Key Scheme   260

Carl Schachter: List of Publications   289

Index   291

Unfoldings

A Dialogue between Author and Editor

Editor's Note: This book gathers a selection of Carl Schachter's most important and representative essays from the past thirty years. He and I have made some slight adjustments—to correct a very small number of minor errors, to create stylistic uniformity, and to supplement the notes with references to more recent publications, particularly English translations of Schenker—but, for the most part, these essays are reprinted in their original form. We begin with three essays on rhythm, because these represent arguably Schachter's most important and original work. The four essays that follow engage different aspects of Schenkerian theory, as does, indeed, all of Schachter's work. These are followed by two essays on musical text-setting and two extended studies of individual works. We have not attempted to arrange the essays into a pedagogical order—it is hard to imagine what a suitable one would be—but readers may approach these essays in whatever way seems congenial. Each is reasonably self-contained (although the three essays on rhythm form a single unit) and permeated by a shared set of concerns. Each takes Schenker's work as an indispensable point of departure, offers close readings of important works from the tonal literature of the eighteenth and nineteenth centuries, and engages questions of musical expression, meaning, and interpretation. Methodological issues are discussed and Schenker's theory is extended, most notably in the three essays on rhythm, but the focus is much more on the music than on the methodology. As Schachter says, "Though I'm deeply interested in Schenker, I'm still more interested in Mozart and Beethoven."

In lieu of the usual editor's preface and author's introduction, we offer the following dialogue. Second thoughts, recent revisions, and biographical, historical, pedagogical, and philosophical speculations are all contained herein.

JS: What was the nature of your early musical training?

CS: Well, it was very early, and it was studying the piano. I started taking piano lessons at the age of five, and supplemented that when I got into my teens with violin and viola, although not very seriously. At the same time as I was studying the violin and viola, I did have theory lessons—I studied the Piston book, so I had a basis in traditional harmony. Then, my piano teacher in New York, Isabelle Vengerova, sent me to Mannes for theory and ear-training. Eventually I became a full-time student there, with a major in conducting. It was quite by accident that I was introduced to Schenker—it was simply because I went to Mannes and worked with Felix Salzer, who was there.

JS: So your turn to music analysis came simultaneously with your exposure to Schenker.

CS: Yes, absolutely. And even that was somewhat accidental. That is, I was thinking of pursuing a career in conducting, but I was offered a job teaching at Mannes even before I had quite finished my studies there. I thought that was going to be a temporary thing, but I got really fascinated with it and decided that was what I wanted to do.

JS: What was the nature of your early work with Salzer?

CS: I studied counterpoint with him. He didn't like to talk about harmony as a discipline in itself, but we did all kinds of melody and bass settings and things of that sort, both written and at the keyboard. I had two years of analysis class with Salzer; I also studied music history with him. He was a very comprehensively educated musician, and so he taught everything other than subjects like orchestration or dictation or sight-singing. My basic musical training was with him.

JS: Did you have contact with proponents of Schenkerian theory other than Salzer?

CS: Not at that stage. Somewhat later, I was introduced to Oswald Jonas in Chicago. I didn't know him well, but he did invite me to have dinner at his house once. We had a very nice talk, but hardly about music at all. Quite a bit later than that, I became a close personal friend of Ernst Oster, and learned really a great deal from him without ever having had a lesson with him. We had many discussions about music, and that was an important part of my musical education. But this would have been in the late '60s or early '70s, so I would already have been in my thirties. We maintained a very close friendship; we talked almost every day on the phone.

JS: Were there any other members of the Schenkerian community who were particularly influential on your own development?

CS: Well, certainly William Mitchell, who was a friend of mine and who taught for a while at Mannes. He was an extraordinarily knowledgeable person too little remembered, in my opinion. I also got to know Allen Forte at that time—he was briefly at Mannes. When I first knew him, he was very much involved in Schenkerian theory, and was starting a translation of *Free Composition*. He was interested in twentieth-century theory at that time, too, but that really developed fully much later.

JS: There's been a lot of talk recently about developing an appropriate Schenker pedagogy. Since you've taught this subject for many years, how do you do it, and how do you think it should be done?

CS: Well, first of all, it shouldn't start too soon. I don't think students should begin work in Schenkerian analysis without having a thorough grounding in counterpoint, without being able to realize a figured-bass or set a chorale melody or a melody in some other style. All of those things are necessary to give students the capability of making analytical judgments, so I would say students should probably have at least two years of theoretical work before work in Schenkerian analysis begins.

I usually start with a big piece, sometimes a Beethoven sonata movement, most often the D-minor Fantasy of Mozart. I try to give the basic outlines of the approach through several class sessions devoted to discussing that piece. One can show, for example, the composing-out of chords; one can show linear as well as harmonic elements in a bass line; one can show large-scale melodic fluency in the upper voice; one can show really quite wonderful motivic parallelisms and hidden repetitions. Jonas had a brilliant analysis of the D-minor Fantasy in which he showed how the Neapolitan sixth chord in the introductory Andante is left out of the main idea of the piece, in the Adagio, so that the piece becomes a kind of search for that lost Neapolitan, which then comes back in the reprise just before the turn to D major. So, one can also show how resolution can be postponed and tension built up and then eventually dispelled in a piece.

The next thing I do is what I call figured-bass reduction. I take pieces in a kind of articulated chordal texture, such as some of the preludes from Book I of the *Well-Tempered Clavier*, possibly the Prelude from the G-major cello suite of Bach, maybe parts of some Chopin etudes or preludes, and have the students reduce them to a bass line with figured-bass symbols, or possibly a kind of four-part texture including the bass with the top voice that reproduces at least the main outlines of the melodic line. It's very useful for students to work bar by bar that way. That is, I do these figured-bass reductions in real-time, in the rhythm of the actual composition.

After that, one can start doing real graphs of parts of pieces. I usually start with phrases that have a kind of *Ursatz*-like structure—very often they might be themes from Mozart or early Beethoven sonatas. I concentrate on the bass first, but then get into the upper voice, showing its basic structure, then getting into all the different kinds of melodic prolongations, and then gradually increasing the analytical spans and getting to short entire pieces in different forms.

If one teaches a one-year or one-semester Schenker course, one has to try to get to some really big and complex pieces, but the problem is that the students aren't really ready to do them on their own. So, if one does that, then the teacher has to do a good deal of the work and give the students smaller tasks, let's say the bass line of the development section or something of that kind, and gradually build up the piece in that way. At Mannes, where there is a two-year undergraduate Schenker requirement for most students, one can eventually get to big pieces that the students can do on their own, and that's much more satisfactory. Of course, in a doctoral program, it is possible for students to go much further, and acquire much more fluency and self-confidence.

JS: Do you focus directly on specific technical issues—unfoldings, initial ascents, things of that kind or do you let them come out of the literature you study?

CS: They come out of the literature. I try not to get the students in the habit of looking for a specific device, but rather to respond to the music and try to derive from the music what seems to be a proper understanding. I will sometimes, after we've gone through a number of excerpts, give them a list of abstract possibilities of unfolding or reaching-over or transfers of register up and down and all the different kinds of linear progressions, but that's after they've already begun to acquire a technical vocabulary. It doesn't hurt for them to look at certain schemata of that kind.

JS: To what extent can or should a Schenkerian orientation percolate down to teaching the most elementary aspects of music theory?

CS: Well, very much, I think. That is, I think one should teach elementary harmony and counterpoint in a way that would be compatible with going on eventually into Schenkerian analysis. And I think students will learn the harmony and counterpoint better if they understand it in some kind of larger musical context rather than in a sort of watertight compartment. So in the two books that I'm co-author of, *Counterpoint in Composition*, with Felix Salzer, and *Harmony and Voice Leading*, with Edward Aldwell, my co-authors and I have certainly tried to teach these elementary things in a way compatible with Schenkerian insights.

Basic training in theory is certainly made more interesting and meaningful if the students are introduced to ideas of the linear functions of chords, of large-scale harmonic progression, and of modulation as the outgrowth of a basically monotonal structure. Simple bar-by-bar reductions of surface figurations are also useful and valuable exercises. But to attempt systematic training in reduction at an early stage is not only not useful—it can be quite harmful, in my view.

JS: Do you think of Schenkerian theory as a discipline for only the select few, or is it something that could be of value to musicians more generally?

CS: I think it's both. Really being able to do work on one's own requires first of all a certain talent for it and second of all a commitment, and those are not qualities that every professional musician or serious music student can be expected to have. So that aspect of the study is, I think, for the few, essentially a self-chosen few. On the other hand, I think that there's a great deal that any music student, or even music lover, could benefit from through exposure to these ideas, and they should at least be made available to musicians more generally.

JS: Including performers?

CS: Especially including performers. Again, it's not easy for a performer, who has to spend hours every day simply honing performing skills, to devote the time necessary to become really expert at the analysis, but having some idea of the principles I think is of benefit to any performer.

JS: Why study Schenker?

CS: Essentially for three reasons: to get a better hearing and understanding of specific pieces of music, to improve one's musical skills, and to learn about the structure of the tonal system at large. To go very far with the last of these requires a lot of rigorous and systematic thinking, and it's not for everybody. This is one of the things that really is for the few. It's mainly for graduate students with a specialist's interest in theory. To overemphasize *these* aspects of the theory at an early stage is to do more harm than good, I think. Of course, even at the earliest stages, students need to learn to avoid self-contradictory readings and confusions of levels—for example, analyzing an appoggiatura as being of greater value than its resolution—so there's a theoretical component even at the earliest stages. But at the early stages I'd rely as much as possible on the students' intuitive musicality and knowledge of voice leading and harmony.

JS: In some of your early articles in this collection, you have a rather pessimistic view of the status of Schenker and Schenkerian theory in the musical world at large. I wonder if your attitude toward that has changed in the intervening years.

CS: Well, Schenker's work is very much better known now than it was twenty years ago. Of course, there was the publication of *Free Composition* in 1979, which was probably the biggest single influence in a wider dissemination of Schenker's ideas, but now even his earlier works, including some that have not been translated into English, are getting much more attention. When I wrote in the second of my articles on rhythm that the rhythmic reduction that Schenker did in his analysis of Beethoven's Op. 2, No. 1, was an aspect of his work that hardly anybody knows, I was being quite accurate. It wouldn't be accurate now. Many people know *Tonwille* and *Meisterwerk*. So people certainly known more about Schenker now, and that includes his work on rhythm.

The whole field of rhythm has opened up really wonderfully in the last fifteen years or so. There's outstanding recent work by William Rothstein and Charles Burkhart. And there's work by people who are not, strictly speaking, Schenkerian, for example, Joel Lester, or Fred Lerdahl and Ray Jackendoff, whose work impinges also on Schenkerian thought and definitely belongs in any kind of dialogue about an analysis of rhythm. And then there are younger scholars who are doing really valuable work. So that's a big, big change.

JS: I want to ask you about some of the unfinished business that you see ahead of us. More than twenty-five years ago, Allen Forte set a five-part agenda that included constructing a theory of rhythm for tonal music, determining the sources and development of triadic tonality, getting information about compositional technique, improving theory instruction, and understanding the structure of problematic modern works. To what extent does that agenda remain unfinished, and are there items that you'd like to add at this point?

CS: First of all, the entire enterprise is unfinished and will always remain so. As long as there is an interest in tonal music there will be no end to inquiry and investigation and the development of ideas. We've gone quite far along some of the paths that Forte has indicated, including rhythm above all.

As for tracing the sources of the tonal system and the ways in which it developed, that of course requires a kind of connection between analysis and theory on the one hand and history on the other. That's gone less far than I think it ought to have. Salzer was the person who began that, and it was continued most notably by Saul Novack. There are a few younger scholars who are working along these lines, but there is a signal lack of interest on the part of most musicologists in analysis, James Webster being an outstanding exception. That's an area where I wish still more would be done.

As for gaining insight into compositional techniques, there has been a lot of work of that type: sketch and manuscript studies; some kinds of analytical monographs, either on specific pieces or on categories of pieces. But this is something that will be built up in increments—it's not something that you can do in a global way. I think it gathers to a greatness slowly, and that's something that makes it not so easy to see quite how far one has gone, but I think there has been good progress.

With regard to improving theory instruction, I think Schenker's influence has been a good one, beginning even before his death. There are German works of the pre-Hitler period where the notion of composing-out of chords is mentioned, and of course in this country long before Forte's article we had the harmony book of William Mitchell, and later Forte's own harmony book, and Roger Sessions's *Harmonic Practice*, which acknowledges it owes a debt to Schenker. There are some pedagogical trends influenced by Schenker that I don't like very much—the attempt at being too rigorous too early seems to me not a healthy thing—but on the whole I would say that a lot of progress has been made.

As for understanding problematic twentieth-century works, I may not be the right one to answer that. Nonetheless, good work has certainly been done on the transitional music that lies between tonality and atonality—music that I think Forte also had in mind. This is a controversial area, one about which there's not any general agreement, but very good people have published in this area.

I'd also say that there is some unfinished business that Forte didn't mention. I am thinking first of all of the study of Schenker's own work in historical context, that is, its development in itself, its relation to the history of music theory, and its relation also to wider intellectual and especially philosophical tendencies, traditions, and trends. A lot of important research has gone into that, and that's been augmented more recently by the availability of Schenker's *Nachlass*. Indeed, the study of Schenker's unpublished work has become a sort of sub-specialty.

Then there's the study of Schenker and performance, something which was a major preoccupation of Schenker himself, but which none of his followers until very recently have addressed themselves to very much. Building a bridge between performing musicians and analytical work is, I think, a very important thing, not easy to achieve, but something worthwhile achieving.

The relationship between Schenker and a possible tonal music of the future is also worth exploring. Schenker's approach never was and never can be a method of composition, but there are people currently writing some kind of tonal music, just as there have been all throughout the twentieth century, and just as representational painting never died out. If anything, the writing of tonal music, like the painting of representational pictures, has been on the increase in recent years, and I think for composers to gain some insights into the nature of tonality and into the way tonal materials were used by the great composers could conceivably have an impact on the way they write. I don't see that that influence has been a very important one, but maybe in the future it will be.

And there's yet another area that I think is worth exploring, and that is the combination of careful and rigorous studies of tonal structure with attention to other aspects of the composition, including the possibility of a kind of narrative structure, texture, orchestration, and other, you might say, secondary qualities of the music. It's something that I think is being done increasingly and that my own work does to some extent, and I think it's definitely worth following up.

JS: So you would not accept the characterization of Schenker as an unredeemable formalist?

CS: No, not at all. There is obviously a strong formalist component to his work, but something like his analysis of the Chaos music from Haydn's *Creation* shows a wonderful awareness of the expressive possibilities of a work of music, and there are other examples all throughout his writings.

JS: There's been a lot of talk in recent years about the status of the motive in Schenker's work, particularly its status in making analytical decisions. That is, to what extent should analytical choices be influenced by a desire to find a particularly interesting motivic relationship?

CS: Well, that's always a temptation, and sometimes it's a temptation that needs to be resisted, because if that structure that one would infer in order to show an interesting motivic relationship isn't confirmed in the harmony and voice leading of its own immediate context, then the connection of the motive to its purported derivative is dubious. Nevertheless, even though one has to exercise caution, it is a very important part of the analytical process. One just needs to use a little common sense and good judgment, and not get carried away with enthusiasm for one's own ideas.

JS: When there's a conflict between harmony and voice leading on the one hand, and the motive on the other, is that a conflict that always needs to be resolved? Is it a conflict that always has to be resolved in one direction?

CS: Sometimes it's resolved and sometimes not, as we can see when the intervallic contents of a motive are not quite congruent with the tonic chord of the primary or local key. Ernst Oster had a fascinating unpublished reading of Brahms's Intermezzo in A Minor, Op. 118, No. 1. The first large harmonic unit composes out C major, which is III in the A-minor key, but the initial melodic idea is C–B♭–A–E, and the C–A–E suggests an arpeggiated A-minor chord. The emphasized A creates friction with its C-major surroundings. Does it resolve? Yes! The key eventually confirms the motive, and the first big harmony is eventually understood as the beginning of an auxiliary cadence in A minor. The rather indefinite feeling of key at the beginning is supplanted by a really crystallized A minor, and the C–A of the opening melodic line is the first hint of that outcome, even before A minor is felt as a tonic.

In Chopin's Mazurka in G♯ Minor, Op. 33, No. 1, the conflict occurs in the B-major middle section of its ABA form, and I don't think it's resolved. The top voice states an almost note-for-note paraphrase of the main outlines of the opening four measures, whose G♯-minor features (specifically the fourth D♯–G♯) fit a bit uncomfortably into the B-major context. The motivic allusion clouds the brightness of the B major with a shadow of the opening G♯ minor, probably for narrative and expressive reasons. Chopin did not provide a tempo indication for the Mazurka, but called it "Mesto," "sad." Although the G♯ minor comes back, the reprise of the opening doesn't really resolve the tension between motive and harmony in the B-minor part. That's because the da capo takes us back to the "Mesto" opening state (and home key) of the piece rather than forming the culmination of a continuous process of key definition, as in the Brahms.

Now in my analysis of the Chopin Fantasy in Chapter 11 of this book, I show a resolution of harmonic/motivic conflict very different from the one in the Brahms. What I call "motive x," the descending fourth F–E♭–D♭–C, strongly expresses the F minor of the opening section, but conflicts with the culminating and primary key of A♭ major. When the same fourth appears over the final cadence, the F is reduced to a neighbor-note, thus adjusting the motive to the key of A♭. the motive's governing interval is now the third E♭–C. This resolution is exactly opposite in meaning to the one in the Brahms Intermezzo. Here the motive changes its structure to conform to the harmony; in the Brahms, the harmony changes its focus in conformity with the motive.

JS: Is there any need in your view for a standardized Schenkerian notation, or should we celebrate diversity in this area?

CS: Well, I much prefer diversity to uniformity in graphing, except for pedagogical purposes in the beginning stages of study. Schenker's own graphs are so expressive partly because he used his graphic symbols so freely.

JS: Are there any notational symbols that you would rule out of court? There are certain things that don't seem to be used anymore, like different stem lengths, for example.

CS: Informally, I do use them sometimes, but it's impossible to use them in a very systematic way. That's because it's not clear whether stem length should be understood as the length per se of the stem or the height to which the stem is drawn, since notes fall on different parts of the staff. But to give a kind of emphasis to something by giving it a longer stem does seem to me a valid expressive thing to do. For some years, I have tended not to use the dotted beam that Salzer used so often. I prefer the beam to convey a sense of forward motion, and therefore I'm not so fond of the breaks that the dots create. So I prefer the dotted tie to the dotted beam, but that's not too important.

JS: How committed are you to the three standard forms of the *Ursatz*?

CS: I'm interested in the *Ursatz* largely because Schenker's description in Part I of *Free Composition* reveals some of the fundamental characteristics of the tonal system. In other words, the three *Ursatz* forms would be the simplest pieces of tonal music, so simple that they have no artistic value at all, but still fulfill some of the basic needs of a tonal piece. I think that a two-part outer-voice framework is one of the fundamental characteristics of tonal music. I think that the notion that one achieves the strongest resolution to the tonic note through a descending melodic motion is another one. So I'm not in a rush to add new *Ursatz* forms.

Of course one can occasionally find a piece that seems anomalous in this way. For example, in the storm movement from Beethoven's Sixth Symphony, which I analyze in Chapter 6 of this book, I hear the top voice as an *Anstieg*, or initial ascent, F–G–A; in that sense the movement would be a kind of expansion of what one would normally get just in the opening part of a composition. I have, although not in this book, an analysis of the opening Prelude from Bach's Fourth Cello Suite, and there I see the *Urlinie* covered under a prominent rising fourth, essentially a middle-voice progression superimposed on the structural top voice. But the sense of large-scale resolution comes from the *Urlinie*, not the rising fourth, and I prefer to regard the fourth as appearing at a later level.

JS: There have been many attempts in recent years to revise Schenker and move beyond Schenkerism. To what extent do you see yourself as a Schenker revisionist?

CS: Any approach is going to change as different people practice it over time, or as the same person practices it over time. Schenker's own approach was in a constant state of evolution, and even those followers who are considered orthodox did things differently from Schenker himself. For example, Ernst Oster's explanation of sonata form movements with $\hat{5}$-lines and inner-voice progressions of $\hat{3}$–$\hat{2}$ permits much more convincing readings of some pieces than Schenker's standard interruption theory allows. The various attempts by Salzer, Travis, and Laufer to modify the approach in order to deal with later repertory are perfectly legitimate. I have to say that though I'm deeply interested in Schenker, I'm still more interested in Mozart and Beethoven, and I find that the approach of the later Schenker gives me a perfectly satisfactory framework for developing my ideas about the music. I have yet to see that drastic revisions of Schenker have led to analyses that are as good as his own best readings, and that for me is the proof of the pudding. And yet I would have to say that there are aspects of his theory that fail to convince me, some of which—his treatment of modulation, for example—I discuss in these essays. A general point: he tends to favor simple and unitary higher-level explanations for foreground phenomena. In a melodic line D–E–C over V–I in C major, he would call the E an anticipation, not a neighbor-note. But why not both? An anticipation of the following harmony and a neighbor, incomplete, of the preceding melodic tone. He seemed to want the higher levels to be a kind of Platonic realm of certainty; I'm willing to get my sense of security, much more contingent than his, from the whole panoply of levels in their interaction, and I'm willing to accept some uncertainty at the basis of things. Still, if I'm a Schenker revisionist, it's to a rather small extent and, I think, within the central tradition.

JS: I suppose in a sense we're all Schenker revisionists insofar as the process that Rothstein describes as "the Americanization of Schenker" has already radically transformed who and what Schenker appears to us to be. Do you feel that that's the case? That Schenker has been so thoroughly Americanized as to be in a sense unrecognizable?

CS: No, I don't feel that, but certainly the approach has changed through its transplantation to these shores. Here I think first of the vocabulary of the technical terminology. The German terms that Schenker used are basically normal German words, some of them cobbled together for Schenker's purposes, like *Untergreifen*. Unfortunately, there is no way that we could get an English equivalent to a word like *Zug*—it just doesn't exist in the English language. It's very similar to Freud's vocabulary. Freud speaks of "das Ich," which doesn't seem to make sense in English as "the I," so it has been translated as "ego," using a Latin word. Some years ago, Bruno Bettelheim criticized the English-language Freudian vocabulary for being too objective and quasi scientific, but I'm afraid that's a little bit in the nature of the English language. One solution, which some people prefer, involves using just the German terms, but even that distances them from an English-speaking person in a way that would not be the case for a German speaker. There's definitely a vitalistic component, quite a wonderful one, I think, of Schenker's language that becomes a bit denatured through the English vocabulary, and while that doesn't change the notational symbols in the graphs, it may change the way people hear them and think about them, and not for the better. As far as I'm concerned, the only way of counteracting that is by stressing as much as possible the aesthetic and perceptual components of the analysis rather than simply the concepts that are there, and I think the best teaching of Schenker in this country, in fact, does that. Apparently, Schenker taught at the piano and played the graphs in order to get people to hear what they meant.

JS: Schenker espoused political and social views that probably strike us as unattractive, to say the least. What has been the impact on Schenker's own theoretical work and its adherents of his dreadful politics?

CS: Of course they related to his theoretical work. His tendency to dismiss any music not composed by "geniuses" certainly connects to his anti-democratic stance. And his restricting his analyses to mostly German composers is at least compatible with his pan-German nationalism. But let's not forget that his eleven geniuses—nine of them German—wrote a large proportion of the eighteenth- and nineteenth-century music, other than opera, that has survived in the repertory. Tovey cast a wider net than Schenker, but if we removed

Schenker's composers from *Essays in Musical Analysis* there would be very little left. And Schenker himself wrote appreciatively, though not always in his published writings, about Tchaikovsky, Strauss, Bruckner, Rossini, Puccini, Smetana, Bizet, Gounod, and others. He was less narrow than one might think. Of course the organicism and idealism of his approach is more compatible with German intellectual traditions than with British empiricism, but I hesitate to say that that's why he delighted in tracing hidden motivic parallelisms that Tovey would certainly reject. Maybe, but I'm not sure. The first generation of Schenkerians whom I knew—Salzer and Oster especially—hated Schenker's chauvinism and reactionary politics, but their musical thinking was, in different ways, very much in his tradition.

js: In Chapter 3 of this book, you say that "the goal of analysis is to find the best reading one can, not merely to find a solution that somehow 'works.'" In this postmodern age, how firmly do you still cling to the notion that some readings are simply better than others? Are there correct and incorrect interpretations? Better and worse ones?

cs: Yes to both questions. First, as to "incorrect." Take a melodic line E–D–C–B–C: a reading that showed the first C as passing between D and B, probably over a V chord, and that simultaneously showed the two Cs structurally connected as a retained tone would be self-contradictory and incorrect. C can't be both a passing tone and a retained main tone at the same level. Now about "better and worse." A reading that failed to take into account the specific individual features of a work—its motivic design, formal idiosyncrasies, textures, and so forth—is worse than one that does account for such features. In *Free Composition*, the analysis of the first-movement development of Beethoven's Sonata, Op. 14, No. 2, is unsatisfactory because the salient thematic and harmonic event—the "false recapitulation" in E♭—is virtually ignored, and two arpeggiated bass progressions are posited which receive little confirmation in the design and in the harmony. I suspect that Schenker inferred a connection between his large-scale arpeggios and the left-hand accompaniment figure at the beginning of the movement, but that connection would only be valid if the arpeggios form a convincing middleground structure in their immediate context, and they don't.

I think one searches for the reading that will encompass all of the important aspects of the piece in a satisfactory way. Obviously, there's no end to such a search. One might think one has come up with the best reading and realize—sometimes because a student will point something out—that there's a whole dimension of the piece that one hasn't addressed. I also feel that not trying to achieve something more than just mere correctness or plausibility weakens one's work as an analyst.

js: This would seem to raise the issue of musical ambiguity. In Chapter 4 of this book, you say, "This is not to deny the possibility that ambiguity and multiple meanings might exist in tonal music; they certainly do exist. But their function, in my opinion, is more narrowly circumscribed than some analysts . . . believe." Are there musical situations that are ambiguous all the way down, that can never be resolved in a satisfactory way?

cs: There are two separate problems here, one having to do with the process of analysis and the other with ambiguous features in a composition. I do sometimes find situations where I can't quite decide whether one or another reading is appropriate. This can occasionally happen in that bugbear of beginning students: is it a $\hat{3}$-line or a $\hat{5}$-line. Even Schenker apparently had a file labeled something like "$\hat{3}$?–$\hat{5}$?–$\hat{8}$?" Curiously, when this decision is really difficult, it's often not so important to decide. Once one gets beyond the first middleground level, the significant features of a piece may well have the same meaning and function with either *Ursatz* form; if they don't, the decision is usually pretty clear. Schenker's very interesting reading of the "Haffner" Symphony slow movement is from $\hat{3}$. I prefer reading it from $\hat{5}$, but I don't think for that reason that my analysis is significantly better than his.

Schenker himself points to the possibility of confusing IV and II. For instance, should one infer two *Stufen*, IV and II, or simply IV with a contrapuntal 5–6 motion above the bass? Often it doesn't matter much. That's because a genuine kind of double meaning in tonal music is that some events are at once harmonic and contrapuntal structures. Roman I–VI–II–V–I can also be understood as Arabic 5–6–5–6–6 above a rising bass $\hat{1}$–$\hat{2}$–$\hat{3}$. I usually prefer to take the contrapuntal perspective as primary unless we are dealing with a cadential progression, but the harmonic one is not necessarily invalid. Ernst Oster used to say that ultimately you can't completely separate harmony and counterpoint, important though it is to make the separation as much as possible when teaching the disciplines.

And this brings us to ambiguities that are inherent in the compositional situation, above all, enharmonics. In Schubert's "Nacht und Träume" (discussed in Chapter 8), the prolonged G major is the outgrowth of an F✗ functioning as a chromatic passing tone. If we take the background meaning as primary, the ambiguity is resolved; the tone is really an F✗. But the interest of the passage arises out of the conflict between that background function and the foreground impression of a G-major chord. The transient chromatic passing tone appears to be the root of an extended consonant triad, much as the fleeting insubstantial world of a dream appears to the dreamer like the real world. Resolving the F✗–G ambiguity in favor of F✗ is a necessary part of understanding the passage, but it's only a part. A more comprehensive understanding involves the simultaneous contemplation of both meanings and an awareness of the transformation paths leading from the F✗ to the impression of a G-major triad.

JS: I want to ask you about your readings of specific pieces and passages in this book. Are there any that you would like to change, that you've had a chance to rethink over the years?

CS: There are two that immediately occur to me. The first is Beethoven's Sonata, Op. 14, No. 1, second movement (discussed in Chapter 2). In my discussion of the structural cadence just before the codetta, I pointed to the fact that the goal tonic chord appears in measure 51 at the beginning of a measure-group and therefore sounds metrically, or hypermetrically, strong, in contrast to previous examples, whose closing tonics fell in weak metrical positions. All of this I still believe. I went on, however, to ask whether one might understand measure 51 as an originally weak measure reinterpreted as strong. My answer was no, because it follows measure 50, which is itself a weak measure and which completes a group of measures. I now think this answer is incorrect. If one understands measures 49 and 50 as the expansion of one bar of dominant harmony—and the cognate cadential dominant measure 15 does occupy only one measure—then measure 51 would indeed count as a weak measure at the end of one phrase reinterpreted as a strong measure at the beginning of the next phrase. Such reinterpretations are frequent at codas and codettas, and are a way of securing a strong metrical position for a final tonic. There is an interesting relationship between levels in such cases. If we assume, as I do, that the background I–V–I implies a tonal rhythm of strong–weak–strong, then a weak final tonic at the end of a phrase—a very frequent state of affairs—contradicts that tonal rhythm. The reinterpretation of the final tonic as a first hyperbeat restores the background rhythm—an example of a foreground closer to the background than the middleground is.

In my discussion of the Schubert song "Dass sie hier gewesen" (in Chapter 8), I don't want to change anything, but there's something I'd like to add. I was concentrating too exclusively on motive, which was my central topic in that essay, and I failed to observe that the ambiguous opening chord, which eventually becomes understood as a diminished seventh on C♯ applied to D as II of C major, is itself an outgrowth of an unspoken C-major chord. In fact, when the opening returns, the diminished seventh chord follows a C-major chord, so that there's yet another musical response to the idea that the perfume in the air is a sign that the girl had been there. The diminished seventh is, you might say, the perfume of the C-major chord, which is not present. The diminished seventh is a sign of the C-major harmony. That, I think, strengthens my analysis of the passage and is definitely something that should be mentioned.

PART I

RHYTHM AND LINEAR
ANALYSIS

ONE

A Preliminary Study

Of all the criticisms occasioned by the work of Schenker and his school, one has been especially persistent. It is that Schenkerian analysis, whatever insight it may give in many respects, fails to do justice to rhythm, that crucial element without which there could be no music. One might tend to brush aside such an objection if it were expressed only by those unconvinced by Schenker's approach. However, musicians who subscribe to many of Schenker's views have also voiced this criticism.[1]

To be sure, mere repetition does not make a statement true. How often have we heard that Beethoven was weak at counterpoint or that the use of extreme registers in his late works was due to his deafness? But whether wholly, partly, or not at all true, any criticism of such staying power deserves our careful attention. By considering its implications, those of us working with the approach can consolidate what we already know and begin to explore areas that are still largely uncharted. In this essay I shall try to explain how this criticism of Schenker arose and to determine the extent to which it is valid. I shall then discuss attempts in recent years to establish a theory of rhythm. And finally I shall outline some of my own ideas about the analysis of rhythm in tonal music.[2]

Schenker's Treatment of Rhythm

What elements in Schenker's work have led to the view that he slighted rhythm?[3] I believe that there are several:

1. Schenker often excluded rhythmic notation from his graphic analyses, particularly those remote from the foreground of the composition.

Originally published in *Music Forum* 4 (1976), pp. 281–334.

2. This exclusion results from his conviction that the Fundamental Structure (*Ursatz*) is arrhythmic[4] and that each level of prolongation brings with it an increasing rhythmic activity.

3. Thus, in Schenker's view, tonal relationships generally take priority over rhythmic ones as determinants of musical structure.

4. In his analyses, Schenker would often assign a high structural level to a tone, a chord, or a tonal complex that the composer had not emphasized by stress or duration. On the other hand, elements that were so emphasized might be consigned to a lower level of structure. In as early a work as *Harmony* (1906) Schenker stated that the harmonic or contrapuntal function of a chord does not depend upon its duration.[5] This idea, clarified by the concept of structural level, extended to melodic analysis, and expanded to include whole sections of a composition, is implicit in many of his later (graphic) analyses.

5. And finally, Schenker's most devoted adherent must agree that he elaborated no systematic approach to rhythm comparable to what he achieved in the realm of voice leading and tonal organization.

Rhythmic Notation and Graphs

The first of these points—the absence of rhythmic notation from background-level graphs—is certainly the least important. The graph, after all, is a representation and as such is dependent upon the conception leading to it. It should be noted, however, that Schenker often took great pains to include durational values and important groupings (both of tones and of measures) in his foreground graphs, and that these include a wealth of fascinating rhythmic detail. Furthermore, his middleground graphs, even those that contain no rhythmic notation, can yield much valuable insight into the larger rhythms of a composition.

Priority of Tonal Relationships

The second and third points—the arrhythmic nature of the *Ursatz* and the priority of tonal over rhythmic relationships—represent a specific and a general expression of the same thought. For the present I would like to concentrate upon the third point, reserving a discussion of the Fundamental Structure for later treatment.

In considering Schenker's assumption that tonal events take priority over rhythm, we might well begin by determining whether we can even investigate the two aspects of music apart from each other. According to Charles Rosen, such a separation is not valid. One of his complaints about Schenker is that "his neglect of rhythm, too, has only accentuated the nonsensical separation in theory of the elements of music, as if a tonal melody could exist without a rhythmic contour."[6]

Of course no melody could exist without a rhythmic contour (has anyone ever suggested that it could?). But does it then follow that any separation of the elements of music must be "nonsensical"? Only, I think, if the separation plays no role in our perception of music; in music theory the nonsensical is the unhearable. In this connection let us study a few very simple examples from the literature, concentrating upon melody.

Example 1.1 consists of two "melodies" from *The Musical Offering*; the upper is the subject given Bach by Frederick the Great, the lower Bach's variation in the fourth movement of the

EXAMPLE 1.1: J. S. Bach, *The Musical Offering*

trio sonata. It is obvious that the two melodies, despite the differences in rhythmic contour, have much in common. Otherwise we could not hear the second as a variation of the first. It must follow as a logical consequence that something other than rhythm—some relationship among the tones—must cause the similarity. If this is so, it could hardly be "nonsensical" to separate, for the purpose of analysis, the tonal contour from the rhythmic.

Now it might be objected that the rhythmic contrast between Frederick's subject and Bach's variation lies mainly on the surface, the underlying pace being very similar (see the alignment of the two melodies in Example 1.1). In our next example, however, it is precisely the larger proportions that change. Example 1.2a is taken from Philip's great soliloquy that begins Act III of Verdi's *Don Carlo*.[7] It consists of two phrases, the second a variation of the first. In both phrases the basic melodic structure is a stepwise line through a falling fifth: A–G–F–E–D. The very simple graph of Example 1.2b shows the tones of these stepwise lines in durational proportion. The reader will note that just where the first phrase moves most quickly (measure 4), the second undergoes a tension-creating rhythmic expansion of the tones F and E (measures 8–9). As in Example 1.1, the similarity between the phrases is clearly evident. And here again the rhythmic alteration does not impede our perception of this similarity. It would seem, therefore, that although no melody can exist without a rhythmic contour, some melodic properties do remain at least partly independent of any specific rhythmic shape.

Now Examples 1.1 and 1.2 both contain variations and thus, one might argue, represent a special case. But central to Schenker's way of thinking is the idea that variation is not a special case, but a fundamental process of composition. In other words, certain tonal structures, like the progression through a fifth of the Verdi aria, function as compositional substrata, occurring in countless guises and transformations. And that whenever such structures occur—whether in the same piece or in different ones—they will embody at least some common characteristics. Of course the deeper levels of structure, by definition, are not as readily accessible to direct perception as are events of the foreground as shown in Examples 1.1 and 1.2. If they were, there would be no point to our analyzing music. But learning to analyze means learning to hear in depth; a good analysis is always verifiable by the educated ear.

EXAMPLE 1.2: Verdi, *Don Carlo*, Act III

The above statement holds true for another aspect of variation technique in tonal composition. Schenker's analyses often point out the disguised repetition of figures or motives; the individual physiognomy of a piece often depends in part upon such disguised repetition. Sometimes the figure will recur at the same structural level; sometimes a foreground motive will be expanded to cover a considerable stretch of middleground. Both possibilities are important to our discussion, for in both the rhythmic alteration of a tonal figure is frequently far more drastic than in Examples 1.1 and 1.2. I have chosen Examples 1.3 and 1.4, both drawn from piano sonatas of Mozart, to illustrate the two possibilities.

Example 1.3 comes from the first movement of the Sonata in G Major, K.283. The development section does not begin by directly quoting a theme or motive; instead Mozart pre-

EXAMPLE 1.3: Mozart, Sonata, K.283

sents a seemingly new melody of an improvisatory character (Example 1.3a). But this "new" melody is in fact a remembrance of, a musing upon, something heard earlier. It corresponds almost note for note with the opening measures of the second theme (Example 1.3b). Differences in register, ornamentation, and, above all, rhythm disguise the underlying relationship. And indeed it is because the passage is at once the same and not the same as the earlier one that it has such an intriguing charm.

Our next example consists of the D-major episode from the Andante of the Sonata, K.545 (measures 17–24). As Example 1.4a shows, the melodic line moves stepwise up from d^2 to $f\#^2$ and then descends, also by step, back to d^2. The ascending phase of the curve is segmented by descending groups of two notes (reaching-over), thus: d^2–$c\#^1$ (measures 17–18), e^2–d^2 (measures 19–20), $f\#^2$ (measure 21). Example 1.4b reveals that the melodic outline of the entire eight-measure phrase is contained in the figuration of measure 17; the episode grows out of its first measure like a plant from a seed.

The Schenkerian literature contains many examples similar to the two I have cited. (For a particularly subtle and fascinating one, see, in Schenker's analysis of the *Eroica*, his discussion of the relationship between the opening theme of the first movement and the E-minor episode of the development.)[8] This aspect of analysis is especially liable to abuse; it is only too easy to fabricate "thematic relationships" and to impose them upon the music. But to minimize its significance, as Tovey tends to do,[9] is just as wrong. If the analyst has the necessary mixture of common sense and imagination, and studies thematic design in its connection with linear–harmonic structure, such analysis provides an indispensable view of the individual features of a composition. To perceive such relationships we must separate, as in Examples 1.1 and 1.2, tonal events from their rhythmic contour. Unless we are prepared to do so, we must, I believe, reject Schenker's work altogether.

And not just Schenker's, but virtually any theory of tonal music. To speak of a "leading tone" or a "tonic chord," to point to a V–I progression or to parallel fifths—these imply the possibility of separating some tonal configurations from rhythm. To do so is an indispens-

EXAMPLE 1.4: Mozart, Sonata, K.545, Andante

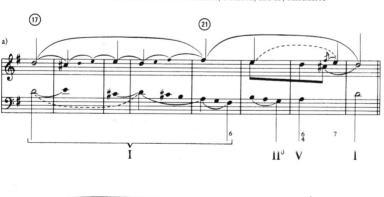

able procedure; it grows out of immediate musical perception and not out of some abstruse theory; there are very good reasons why we all do it.

What about the opposite procedure? Can one isolate rhythm and consider it apart from pitch? I believe that one can, but within narrower limits, for one crucial aspect of rhythm—grouping—depends in part upon tonal relationships. Without taking these relationships into account, we are often unable to arrive at even a primitive understanding of rhythm.

Let us examine the opening measures of a keyboard sonata by Domenico Scarlatti (Example 1.5a). How are we to understand the rhythm of this passage? Surely not as twenty-four eighth notes followed by a half note. Each of the first three measures shows a different rhythm, even though the note values are the same. In measure 1 (up to the downbeat of measure 2) the melody moves by step through a rising fifth at quarter-note pace. From the beginning of measure 2 to the end of the phrase, the melody descends to its starting point; the unit of pace is now the half note (Example 1.5b). In measure 1 the eighth notes occur in groups of two, thereafter, in groups of four (Example 1.5c). The falling fifth f^2–bb^1, unlike the rising one, is subdivided into two thirds, f^2–d^2 and d^2–bb^1. A change in design emphasizes this division; the melody becomes explicitly polyphonic (Example 1.5d). The melodic polyphony is thrown into relief by the most striking rhythmic development of the phrase, the syncopation in measure 3 caused by the placement off the beats of the main tones d^2 and c^1. One could say more about the rhythm of his phrase, but the foregoing discussion should suffice to show the reader how much our perception of rhythm depends upon tonal organization.

EXAMPLE 1.5: D. Scarlatti, Sonata, L.500/K.545

In view of this dependency of rhythm upon tone, Schenker's giving priority to the latter seems perfectly understandable. It is true, of course, that without time (hence some sort of rhythm) there can be no music, whereas one can create a kind of "music" without definite pitch. However, such music has played no role whatever in the Western world until very recent times (nor has it played a very prominent one in non-Western art music). The argument about which came first—pitch or rhythm—has persisted for years without anyone's having reached a satisfactory solution. A solution hardly seems possible; but is it really such an important problem? What is important is to understand how the two elements function in any composition or significant group of compositions. If it is true that, in Western art music, rhythm is more dependent upon pitch than pitch upon rhythm, then to place pitch at the core of musical structure, as Schenker does, is, I think, a perfectly logical procedure.

Structural Level and Rhythmic Emphasis

In any case, Schenker's results seem to me to be more convincing than those achieved in other ways. Which brings us to the fourth of our five points—the absence in many Schenkerian analyses of a correspondence between the structural levels of the graph and the rhythmic emphases of the composition. For it is here that Schenker's success in matching his analysis to the work analyzed has most often been questioned. Charles Rosen, for example, says, "It is not merely that one note of Schenker's basic line may last one second and another a full minute in the complete piece, but that Schenker often minimizes the salient features of a work."[10] (But when would the imbalance cease? Should the briefer tone last half a minute, or would ten seconds suffice?) And Arthur Komar, "I do not consider it inappropriate for a structural chord to have a brief duration in the foreground, but I do object to the structural chord which is *also* brief in the background."[11] But surely there are other ways of achieving rhythmic emphasis than through duration alone. Other factors might well outweigh in importance the brief or long duration of a tone or a chord.

One of these factors (in a broad sense also rhythmic) is *position*: where in the piece does the tone or chord occur? In this connection let us consider the three invariable constituents of a normal background progression: the opening tonic ($\hat{1}$, $\hat{3}$, or $\hat{8}$), the dominant ($\hat{5}$), and the closing tonic ($\hat{1}$).

The Closing Tonic   Let us begin at the end, with the closing tonic, for this is often the easiest of the three to locate in the actual music. Almost by definition it will occur toward the end of a piece, but precisely where depends upon individual circumstances. Two songs, Schumann's "In der Fremde," Op. 39, No. 1, and Schubert's "Erster Verlust," D.226, provide a useful comparison. In both of them the $\hat{1}$ symbolizes an element of the text. In the Schumann, it represents death and a kind of pantheistic union with Nature, longed for by the homeless stranger. In the poem this idea finds its fullest expression in the next-to-last line. Schumann, therefore, places the $\hat{1}$ not at the end of the vocal line (which would produce a more logical setting) but some four measures earlier, reserving the last line of text for a coda. All in all, the closing tonic extends to eight measures out of the song's twenty-eight (Example 1.6).

EXAMPLE 1.6: Schumann, "In der Fremde," Op. 39, No. 1, middleground graph

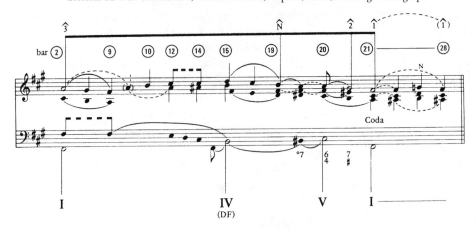

In the Schubert song, the tonic (F minor) represents the unhappy present; the mediant, the memory of a happier past. With matchless eloquence and simplicity, Schubert (who was all of eighteen when he wrote this song) has the singer end on $\hat{3}$ in the "illusory" mediant key; this occurs almost at the very end of the song. The brief closing cadence is given to the piano alone; the final tonic lasts for half a measure out of the song's twenty-two (Example 1.7).

In the Schumann song, the closing tonic occupies more than a fourth of the total duration; in the Schubert less than a fortieth. Could we therefore say that it is structural in the Schumann but not in the Schubert? Or more structural in one than in the other? To frame the questions is to be convinced of their absurdity. Certainly we might say that a final tonic gets more emphasis in one piece than in another. But here even that observation would be pointless. In connection with the text, Schubert's minimizing the $\hat{1}$ creates at least as much emphasis as Schumann's drawing it out.

The two songs, I believe, show that the closing tonic can assume widely divergent durations without changing its structural function. Before proceeding to the other background elements (the opening tonic and the dominant), I would like to discuss briefly an idea of

EXAMPLE 1.7: Schubert, "Erster Verlust," D.226, middleground graph

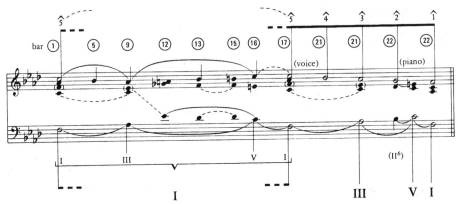

Arthur Komar's that bears directly upon the duration of a closing tonic and its implications. Komar develops the idea of a "structural time-span" subject to metrical division on several levels. About it he states that "the time-span of a final cadential chord(s) lies outside the structural time-span of a given unit, while still belonging to that unit." Thus for Komar a closing tonic—the final cadential chord of the background progression—may have a brief duration without its structural value coming into question.[12] (Komar's conception of background structure differs from Schenker's; but he states that his theories of meter and time span can be coordinated with a Schenkerian view.)

Komar explains the structural time span in connection with the opening eight measures of the variation movement of Mozart's Piano Sonata, K.331. The reader will recall that these eight measures are subdivided into two units of four measures each; the first ends with a half cadence in the middle of measure 4, the second with a full cadence in the middle of measure 8. Now the structural time span of the first unit would be three and a half measures; that is, one would subtract the duration of the final dominant chord from the four measures. Similarly, the structural time span of the eight measures would be seven and a half measures, the value of the final tonic being subtracted. But to arrive at the total of seven and a half measures one must add on the value of the dominant chord (of measure 4) that one had previously subtracted. This dominant chord, in other words, belongs to the structural time span of the eight measures but not of the four measures that form the first half of the eight. That a foreground prolongation of a fragment becomes structural within the whole seems a very doubtful proposition. But even if one could justify it logically, how is one to hear these subtractions and re-additions?

And there is another perceptual problem in this notion of a structural time span that continues only up to the "attack" of the final cadential chord. After all, *every musical event must occupy time*; none is consummated at the point of "attack." If the final cadential chord has no duration, there is simply no cadence. For the foreground, incidentally, one can specify fairly accurately the minimal duration of a final cadential chord—more accurately than most durational characteristics of tonal music. The rule is: the closing chord of a cadence will normally occupy at least a full metrical pulse (reckoning in rests, etc.). Exceptions are rather infrequent, and they sound like exceptions. See for example: Brahms's String Quartet, Op. 51, No. 2, first movement, measure 20; Beethoven's Piano Sonata, Op. 110, Scherzo, measure 36; Beethoven's String Quartet, Op. 135, Scherzo, measure 16. In all of these the "premature" disruption of the cadence becomes an important motivic element. Even in sections of great rhythmic freedom (such as recitatives) such exceptions sound abnormal if performed in anything approaching strict time. (See Example 1.8, where the abnormal effect is justified by the dramatic situation. Another exception: if the beginning of a phrase or section overlaps the final chord of the preceding one, the duration of that final chord cannot, of course, be specified; but there must be some duration or we could not hear an overlapping.)

The Opening Tonic   Now if we can admit the possibility of a "brief" final tonic (and if the reader will agree with me that the final tonic is not an exceptional case), why not the same for a tonic in another important position, perhaps at the beginning? Or for another harmony, the dominant, for example? Initial tonics, to be sure, announce the tonality and often must support a good deal of thematic material; therefore, they will often—perhaps

EXAMPLE 1.8: J. S. Bach, Cantata No. 60, *O Ewigkeit, du Donnerwort*: No. 4, Recitative and Arioso

usually—have a fairly long duration. But one does at times encounter a brief opening tonic whose structural value seems hardly open to question. One should examine, in this connection, the Scherzo of Schubert's Piano Sonata in A Minor, D.845 (Op. 42). In this fascinating piece the opening $\frac{3}{4}$ lasts only 5 measures out of 126. The piece is too long to quote here and I will present a fuller discussion of its proportions later. I should like, however, to quote the first five measures to show that within them there is more immediate emphasis on the V than on the I. And still I cannot imagine a convincing linear analysis of this piece that did not interpret these five measures as a structural tonic (Example 1.9). Certainly this tonic receives very little emphasis, and this is an extremely important characteristic of the piece. But the tonic, fleeting as it is, still forms the point of departure for

EXAMPLE 1.9: Schubert, Sonata, D.845, Scherzo

the subsequent harmonic and melodic movement. From this perspective—that is, from the perspective of background structure—it fulfills the same function as the opening tonic in the first movement of Mozart's Piano Concerto, K.491, which extends for more than a hundred measures.

The Dominant   In Schenkerian analyses, brief structural dominants ($\hat{\frac{2}{V}}$) figure frequently. A good example occurs in Mozart's Piano Sonata, K.310. The exposition and development of the first movement form a large-scale harmonic progression I–III–V (A minor, C major, V of A minor). The tonic area fills eleven measures (measures 1–11), the harmonic transition to the median another eleven (measures 12–22), the median *thirty-five* (measures 23–57), the transition to the dominant sixteen (measures 58–73), and the dominant only six (measures 74–79). On the basis of duration alone, one might conclude that the dominant is not emphasized enough to constitute a structural harmony. The manner in which it is reached, however, makes it clear that this chord forms the culmination of the development section and that it is not merely an interpolated, prolonging V.

Perhaps six measures—although only a thirteenth or so of the seventy-nine measures of exposition and development (and a still smaller fraction of the whole movement)—might not be brief enough to disqualify Mozart's dominant. But what about the chords that I have indicated as the $\hat{\frac{2}{V}}$ of Examples 1.6 and 1.7? They must surely be considered brief; yet I do not believe that their structural status can be open to doubt. For it is the stepwise melodic resolution of $\hat{2}$ to $\hat{1}$ together with the harmonic force of V moving to I that enables us to hear the $\hat{1}$ as the ultimate goal of motion in the two songs. In neither song does any extended dominant occur. Nor is it musically possible to group these cadential dominants with one or more chords earlier on, thus reading an area governed by V. And anyway, why should one feel impelled to do so? The position of these chords, immediately before the closing tonic, and their function, making it sound final—these alone justify our designating them as structural.

It is true that a foreground cadence does not necessarily coincide with a resolution in the background.[13] For example, a strong cadence early in the piece (as in the Schumann, measures 4–5) or one occurring after the motion to $\hat{1}$ would never function as a structural resolution. But in our two songs, how can we fail to hear the closing cadence as a background resolution? Only by excluding the top voice from the ultimate background progression.[14] But with that exclusion the distinction between opening and closing tonics ($\hat{\frac{5}{1}}$ or $\hat{\frac{3}{1}}$ and $\hat{\frac{1}{1}}$) is minimized; an important directional force disappears; the resulting picture of music is a curiously static one.

We have now considered the three invariable constituents of Schenker's *Ursatz* progressions. We have seen that all of them—the $\hat{\frac{2}{V}}$ and $\hat{1}$ especially often—can be of very brief duration in the actual music. I have tried to show that there can be compelling reasons, nonetheless, for regarding them as part of the fundamental progression of a piece. The *Ursatz*, it must be remembered, is not only the final reduction of the piece's linear and harmonic contents; it is also the expression, in the piece, of fundamental properties of major/minor tonality. Among these properties are: the origin in the tonic triad of melodic and harmonic progressions, the stepwise character of melody, the harmonic primacy of the fifth relationship, and progression to the $\hat{1}$ as final resolution.

Now these properties of the tonal system are among the elements of pitch organization that are, for the most part, independent of any specific rhythmic contour (although, as we shall see later, some of them do have rhythmic implications). It is in this light that one should view Schenker's arrhythmic *Ursatz* progressions. His exclusion of specific durations (absolute or relative), by helping to clarify the limits within which rhythm operates in tonal music, can also help us to clarify our ideas regarding rhythm.[15]

Duration and Form

I do not wish to draw out the subject of duration to unendurable lengths, but there is one further aspect that we must touch upon, at least briefly. This is the articulation of a piece of music into phrases, sections, and parts.[16] Although Schenker gave a great deal of attention to phrase rhythm and to the rhythmic aspects of motivic design (diminution), he did not concern himself much with the proportions of the larger sections. To be sure, the study of these proportions can be of great help in understanding some types of music. But, as Schenker himself pointed out, the matter ought not to be approached in a purely quantitative way, as if our perception of time could remain uninfluenced by the events that fill the time.[17]

Imagine, for example, three performances of the first movement of Beethoven's Piano Sonata in F Major, Op. 10, No. 2. In this movement, as in a binary piece, Beethoven calls for two repeats, one of the exposition, the other of the development plus the recapitulation. In most respects our imaginary performances are identical. However, Performance A contains no repeats, B only the first repeat, C both of them. That observing or not observing the repeats changes the performance is unquestionable. But the changes result at least as much from the sequence of events and from the total duration as from relative proportions. Performances A and C have the same proportions; yet they differ from each other at least as much as A and B—indeed, probably more, owing to the unfamiliar effect of the second repeat. (It was probably unfamiliar, or at least unexpected in a new work, when the piece was written, for by that time the second repeat in sonata movements was seldom called for.) And further: by omitting a single crucial measure (say measure 5) we can change the effect of the whole piece more drastically than by the large durational changes caused by disregarding the repeats. All of which is not to deny the importance of proportion, but to suggest that one responds to it in connection with other aspects of the music.

Schenker himself never arrived at a really comprehensive theory of rhythm (my fifth point at the beginning of this essay). His last work, *Free Composition*, contains a highly interesting section on rhythm,[18] and there are references scattered throughout his earlier works, but these do not constitute a systematic or exhaustive treatment of the subject. In themselves, however, they are extraordinarily interesting and valuable. Especially in his earlier writings, Schenker devoted a great deal of attention to rhythmic problems. But also in his later years, when he was more occupied with problems of voice leading, he never lost sight of the importance of rhythm, phrase rhythm in particular. This is shown by the section on rhythm in *Free Composition*, the *Five Graphic Music Analyses*, and the *Eroica* analysis. Now that more of Schenker's works are becoming available, both in the original and in translation, more and more musicians will become aware of how much he has to say about rhythm.[19]

Some Recent Theories of Rhythm

If Schenker never arrived at a comprehensive theory of rhythm, neither, to my knowledge, has anyone else. Theorists have been dealing with aspects of rhythm for centuries, sometimes with highly successful results.[20] In recent years many musicians have tried to come to grips with the problem of rhythm in tonal music.[21] Much of their work is interesting and helpful, but significantly enough, some of these writers themselves obviously consider their attempts to be merely preliminary excursions into a field still to be explored.

In view of its importance and the amount of attention it has received, rhythm has so far proved to be a rather intractable area of investigation. Why this should be so cannot be answered with certainty; if it could we should know more about rhythm. But the question is worth thinking about, even if the thought remains mere speculation. It is helpful, first of all, to understand that in using the term "music theory" we are lumping together a number of disparate elements. Just how disparate becomes evident if we compare works on orchestration by, say, Berlioz, Rimsky-Korsakov, or Strauss with those dealing with tonal organization: for example, Fux on counterpoint, C. P. E. Bach on thorough bass, or Rameau on harmony. In the first group we find factual information, practical advice, and many psychological judgments influenced in part by the stylistic tendencies of the author's period. While these elements are by no means lacking in the second group, they are overshadowed by an altogether different kind of thinking. In dealing with consonance and dissonance, voice leading, harmonic relationships, in short with the possibilities of tonal succession and combination, the authors of these works tend to relate a great variety of musical phenomena to a few fundamental organizing principles. Whether or not by the author's conscious intent, each of these works constitutes a kind of musical grammar and syntax.

The last few decades have seen a number of attempts at broadening the scope of music theory; not only theories of rhythm, but also theories of tone color and of thematic or motivic design have appeared. Now some of these "theories" are purely descriptive accounts of the musical surface, possibly decked out with mathematical trimmings. But others are attempts at discovering basic principles similar to those that govern tonal organization. In my opinion, the results of these attempts have not been completely convincing—certainly not in rhythm, the most important of these areas of investigation. Of course we can never prescribe in advance the content of a discipline; it is certainly conceivable that a future Schenker will develop a comprehensive theory of rhythm comparable in depth and scope to what Schenker achieved in the area of tonal organization.

But it is also conceivable that such a theory of rhythm is not a real possibility either at present or, perhaps, at all. Musicians tend to accept a theory of tonal relationships as a matter of course, not realizing that it represents a very special achievement without any close parallel in the other Western arts. The closest analogies to the tonal organization of music lie in linguistic structures. Rhetorical analysis in late antiquity and in the Renaissance and linguistic analysis in the twentieth century have had many adherents among writers and critics, but they hardly form a tradition of comparable magnitude or importance to, say, counterpoint in music of the past five hundred years or so.

That every aspect of music will lend itself to theoretical treatment in the manner of C. P. E. Bach or Fux (to say nothing of Schenker) is by no means a foregone conclusion. Furthermore, a comprehensive theory of rhythm, even if feasible in the long run, might well require a great deal of preparatory investigation. Schenker, after all, could draw upon a theoretical tradition reaching back thousands of years; and he did draw upon it, even though he rejected much of it. Furthermore, he was in touch with masters of the tonal language, with a world of great composers and performers that exists today only in memory. To arrive at a valid theory of rhythm in tonal music will require more, I am afraid, than just the will to do so.

Broad Rhythmic Organization

That we lack an adequate formulation of the principle of rhythm is most immediately evident, I think, in the problems that arise when we try to understand the larger rhythms of a piece. By now most musicians agree that tonal connections operate over large as well as small compositional spans, and the writings of such non-Schenkerians as Tovey, Schoenberg, and Hindemith frequently indicate broad tonal reaches. Many musicians feel that large-scale rhythmic progression also forms part of their experience of music; attempts to describe these larger rhythms go back at least as far as Alfred Lorenz. But what principles, if any, regulate broad rhythmic movement? Are they simply those that govern rhythmic detail expressed over greater spans?

It would seem that many who have written about rhythm believe the answer to the above question to be yes. This is so, I imagine, because accentual patterns do exhibit a hierarchical arrangement, at least up to a point. Thus the first part of a beat, the first beat of a measure, and (sometimes) the first measure of a phrase can all be termed strong. But just how far does this go? As far as with certain tonal relationships? Some tonal relationships, the progression from I to V, for example, can extend over almost any conceivable span: from the beginning to the end of a beat, a measure, a phrase, or a section; from one section to another; from the first tonic to the final cadential dominant almost at the end of the piece.

In a number of works on rhythm one finds such terms as "accent," "weak beat," "strong beat," "upbeat," "downbeat," and "afterbeat" used in reference to similarly wide spans of time. This usage stretches considerably the meaning of these terms, especially of "beat," which has had a long history of association with the human pulse. The association is musically significant, our feeling for tempo being closely bound up with it. But the extended usage may well be justified if the conception behind it is valid. And sometimes, at least, I think that it is.

To cite a well-known example, the first eight measures of Chopin's Etude, Op. 10, No. 12, seem to me to form a clear-cut instance of an extended upbeat. This impression arises from a number of factors working in combination. The first chord is played by the right hand alone; the lack of a bass prevents the opening from sounding like a strong downbeat. The hortatory character of the melodic line, with its broken-off exclamations, contributes to the impression of an upbeat; we hear the opening measures as preparatory to the "true" beginning of the tonal action. And above all, the sustained dissonance and the melodic tendencies of the main tones, b♮ and f, call for a resolution into something more stable.[22]

The impression of an extended upbeat, as in the "Revolutionary" Etude, occurs in many compositions, especially in those that begin with an introduction or away from the tonic. But we must avoid premature generalizations from such examples, which may turn out to be anything but models of normal rhythmic behavior. For very frequently—perhaps usually—the various compositional elements (melody, harmony, counterpoint, articulation, texture, dynamics, etc.) create a complex pattern with so many, possibly conflicting, emphases that no overarching structure of weak/strong or upbeat/downbeat emerges. In dealing with rhythm we must account for these conflicting emphases; otherwise we shall arrive at an oversimplified account of large rhythmic motion.

Among the most important recent attempts at explaining large-scale rhythm are those by Edward Cone, by Grosvenor Cooper and Leonard Meyer, and by Arthur Komar. Since all of these writers acknowledge the influence of Schenker, an investigation of rhythm and linear analysis must, perforce, deal with some of their ideas. I am not convinced that any of them has succeeded in accounting satisfactorily for broad rhythmic organization. Nevertheless, one can learn much by considering the problems they raise and the solutions they propose for them. These writers have performed a real service for musicians by venturing to build new paths through such slippery terrain.

Edward Cone   Cone's approach is the least systematized of the three and, perhaps for this reason, the most flexible. His best-known contributions are the idea of the "structural downbeat" and the notion that large rhythmic progression (of units ranging from the phrase to the whole piece) normally leads to a "structural downbeat." Cone explains his new term as follows: "By structural downbeat, of course, I do not mean the arbitrary accentuation of the first beat of every measure; I mean rather phenomena like the articulation by which the cadential chord of a phrase is identified, the weight by which the second phrase of a period is felt as resolving the first, the release of tension with which the tonic of a recapitulation enters."[23] And further: "It is just here [at the cadence] that the importance of rhythm to the establishment of tonality emerges, for the cadence is the point in the phrase at which rhythmic emphasis and harmonic function coincide."[24]

A structural downbeat, then, results when an important tonal event, such as a cadential tonic, coincides with a point of rhythmic emphasis; the emphasis, to a large extent, makes the listener aware of the importance of the tonal event—indeed, helps to create its importance. Cone is surely correct in calling attention to the possible coincidence of rhythmic and tonal emphases, for it constitutes an important compositional resource. In the "Revolutionary" Etude, for example, Chopin groups the opening eight measures in units of two measures which combine into larger, four-measure units; each segment of two or four measures begins with an accent. The tonic of measure 9, therefore, falls on a "downbeat" not only within the single measure but also in relation to these larger periodicities; the rhythmic emphasis certainly underscores the tonal significance.

Although I don't use Cone's term, I find no objection to its use for situations like the one in the Chopin. For there the tonic does indeed occur on the downbeat both of small and of larger metrical units. But Cone, although he concedes the possibility of large-scale meter (of measures within the phrase, for example), makes it clear that his structural downbeat is not metrical in origin.[25] And indeed his favorite example, a cadential tonic, would normally appear in a metrically weak measure (fourth or eighth)—weak, that is, unless the person scanning the phrase is a disciple of Hugo Riemann.[26] But if the structural downbeat is not metrical, what other aspect of rhythm makes it a downbeat? For me, at least, Cone does not provide a satisfactory answer to this question. He seems to come perilously close to regarding as a structural downbeat any stable tonal event that appears at a point of articulation and that resolves a preceding tension. Such events, of course, do receive some rhythmic emphasis from their position within the flow of the music. But not necessarily the character of a downbeat. To cite one example out of thousands, the Menuet of Haydn's Symphony No. 104 begins with an eight-measure phrase that leads to a perfect cadence. The closing tonic appears in measure 8, a metrically weak measure. It certainly serves as a goal of motion, as a release of the tension that generates it. But it sounds much less like a *downbeat* than does the dominant seventh of the preceding, metrically strong, measure. Near the end of the piece the initial phrase reappears in expanded form (measures 35–49). Here the V^7 is extended to two measures; the tonic, consequently, falls on a strong measure and, this time, sounds like a downbeat. I would maintain that some tonal goals (the tonic at the end of the Haydn Menuet, for example) are rhythmically strong and that others (the tonic in measure 8 of the Menuet) are weak. And that our conception of music is truer if we acknowledge this source of variety. In particular I would question Cone's rather Riemannesque conviction that a musical phrase, in principle, ends with an accent. A decrease in rhythmic emphasis—a diminuendo, so to speak—forms a natural and, indeed, a very frequent way to resolve tension. For me, therefore, many, perhaps most, of Cone's structural downbeats are not downbeats at all. And if large-scale rhythm is to prove accessible to musical analysis, it will not, I think, be mainly in terms of motion to a structural downbeat, useful as that idea may be for explaining some passages.

Grosvenor Cooper and Leonard Meyer   Unlike Cone, whose approach stresses the *continuity* of rhythmic progression, Grosvenor Cooper and Leonard Meyer take as their point of departure the *division* of musical motion into rhythmic groups. In *The Rhythmic Structure of Music* these authors maintain that five basic groupings (derived from the Greek metrical feet) organize musical spans ranging from the small detail to the complete piece. (However, Cooper and Meyer do not maintain that all complete pieces necessarily embody one of their basic rhythms.) Each group contains one or two unaccented impulses leading toward or away from a single accent; rhythmic structure consists of a hierarchical arrangement of such groups. Thus three quarter notes in a 3/4 measure might form a dactylic group; the whole measure (if strong relative to the next one) would be the first half of a two-measure trochee; and so forth.

Cooper and Meyer claim no ultimate validity for their approach; they make it clear that they do not regard their book as a definitive or even a comprehensive treatment of the subject, but rather as a starting point for further investigation.[27] And, in a way, the book has functioned as a starting point, for it has helped to create increased interest in rhythm as a field for investigation. I believe that reading *The Rhythmic Structure of Music* can make one more sensitive to the nuances of rhythmic organization. But I also believe that the analytic approach has serious flaws. Three of them, in particular, limit the usefulness of the authors' approach to large-scale rhythm.

1. The notion that, in principle, rhythmic groups cluster around a *single* accent creates a needlessly disconnected picture at every level of the analysis. Using the five basic groupings, we cannot view a motion from accent through non-accent to accent as a continuous rhythmic process unless we invoke such ideas as "ambiguity" or "fusion."
2. The approach is extraordinarily reductive. The analytic notation consists mainly of brackets to show groupings plus two diacritical signs, the macron ($-$) for accent and the breve ($\smile$) for non-accent; a few ancillary symbols supplement these. In moving

from the general picture to the detailed we find no increase in the richness and diversity of content; brackets, macrons, and breves simply split up into more brackets, macrons, and breves.

3. At the higher levels, long stretches of music—phrases, periods, and whole sections—function as "accents." Although the authors refrain from a rigorous definition of "accent," they make it clear that they regard the term as meaning a point of stability, a beginning of movement, or a punctuation in its flow.[28] But if this conception is true, the notion of an enduring accent contradicts an essential attribute of music: motion. (The idea of a long upbeat or afterbeat creates no such contradiction, for these terms imply a changing rate of rhythmic intensity.) To examine more closely this idea of a long-lasting accent, let us consider a sixteen-measure unit composed of two eight-measure groups in antecedent–consequent relation, perhaps the first part of the theme from the variation movement of Beethoven's Piano Sonata, Op. 26. At the highest level, the sixteen measures would form an iamb, measures 9–16 functioning as an accent relative to measures 1–8. This is because the tonic close of measure 16 resolves the tension created by the half cadence at measure 8. But are we to hear a phrase of eight measures as an "accent"—as a stable area—because the eighth measure contains the cadential tonic? What about the other seven measures with their movement toward the cadence? And Cooper and Meyer do not stop at eight measures. Their analysis of the first movement of Beethoven's Symphony No. 8 shows the development section (and, retrospectively, the exposition, too) as an upbeat to the recapitulation and coda. According to the analytic chart, these latter sections combine at the highest level to form an accent 183 measures long.[29]

In Cooper and Meyer's analyses, the large-scale accents, even apart from their duration, seem to be different in kind from the small-scale ones. The latter (accents on the level of beats within the measure) virtually always coincide with the strong pulses of the *meter*; they do not necessarily coincide with points of tonal stability. But the big accents tend to occur in (and, perhaps, to be equivalent to) areas of tonal stability.[30] In this respect (although not in some others) they resemble Cone's structural downbeats.[31] Both approaches, Cone's as well as Cooper and Meyer's, appear to operate on the assumption that tonal events, in themselves, produce a kind of rhythm. But neither approach makes headway against the central problem posed by this assumption: to distinguish between *rhythm as an active force* (helping to shape tonal events) and *rhythm as resulting* from the activity of tonal elements.

Arthur Komar   As its title indicates, Arthur Komar's *Theory of Suspensions* concentrates on a single element of musical structure, the suspension, rather than on rhythm in general. But in order to account for suspensions over long compositional spans, Komar develops an approach to large-scale rhythmic structure. His conception of strong and weak differs greatly from the Cooper/Meyer one. There are no accents of 183 measures in *Theory of Suspensions*, for Komar does not characterize durational spans as strong or weak, but only the initial attack points of analytically significant spans. And instead of rhythmic grouping, Komar makes metrical organization the basis of his method. Like the Cooper/Meyer groups, Komar's metrical divisions form a series of levels. Thus the normal division of a full measure of 6/8 time into six eighth notes would produce two such "metrical levels." The division of the measure into two dotted quarter-notes would produce the first level and the division of these into three eighth-notes apiece would produce the second. Within each level any new beat (i.e., one that does not occur in the next higher level) counts as weak. At the first level of our 6/8 measure the second dotted quarter note is weak relative to the first one; at the second level the second, third, fifth, and sixth eighth-notes are weak relative to the first and fourth.[32]

Komar believes that the same kind of metrical organization extends to larger musical spans. There, too, the "original" division is presumed to be into equal parts;[33] the "background" equality, however, can be obscured by such rhythmic transformations as extension or contraction. Over large as well as small spans, each new beat within a metrical level counts as weak. Let us imagine that a musical span of sixty-seven measures divides at the first level into two parts of thirty-two and thirty-five measures (the original equality having been modified by a cadential extension of the second part). At this level the attack point of measure 33 would be weak relative to the attack point of measure 1.

That meter does, in fact, operate over such long spans of time—that we can assume a metrical relationship of strong and weak between two downbeats separated by lines or even pages of music—is, I think, open to legitimate question. Komar does not attempt to prove the validity of his assumption and, indeed, one could hardly prove or disprove it. And the format of the book does not permit him to present a large enough number of analyses to show whether the idea of large-scale meter might be a productive working hypothesis. On the basis of the evidence that he does present it seems to me that Komar's approach, like Cooper and Meyer's, is least convincing at the more remote levels of structure. For the most part his analysis of meter within the measure (though it offers no important new insights) is accurate enough, except for an unsubstantiated assertion that the third beat of triple time is, in principle, stronger than the second.[34]

But what Komar does not take sufficiently into account is the fact that our perception of meter depends, in part, upon repetition. We cannot hear meter at all unless we hear two strong beats plus an indication of the intervening weak beat or beats. These are minimal conditions; in complex textures we may need more than two downbeats to "get" the meter. In such music, if we hear the first beat of the measure as strong, it is largely because of the cumulative effect of a repeated pattern underlying the varied rhythms of the piece. But at Komar's higher levels there may be just a very few strong and weak beats; at the highest level, just one of each. Over a long span, therefore, there will be little or even none of the patterned repetition upon which the normal perception of meter depends. How then are we to hear some of these beats as "strong" and others as "weak"? By Komar's definition, the strong ones have appeared in the next higher metrical level and the weak ones are new. But unless we adopt Humpty-Dumpty's view of the meaning of words, the terms of music theory should refer to what we can, or do, or should hear and not just to a theoretical formula. And Komar's approach seems to me to be at times very distant from the hearing of music.

Just how distant is shown by Komar's most ambitious example, a metrical analysis of the slow movement of Beethoven's Piano Sonata, Op. 13. Komar interprets the opening measure as an upbeat; therefore, he assumes as understood a suppressed downbeat measure ("measure 0") preceding the actual beginning. I do not agree that the first measure is an upbeat, but that is not an important issue. Some pieces, after all, do begin with an upbeat lasting a whole measure (the last movement of Mozart's String Quartet,

K.499, for instance). What is disturbing is the idea that the silent "measure 0" is supposed to function as a strong beat, not merely in relation to the following measure, but also in relation to larger spans at comparatively remote structural levels. But can we really hear a silent measure as "stronger" than some other measure much further along in the music?[35]

Analysis and Hearing

One might maintain that Komar is trying to explain background and middleground levels and that we ought not to expect to hear what his analysis reveals. But I should find such an argument utterly specious, and for reasons important enough to justify a brief digression. In the review mentioned earlier, Charles Rosen draws a parallel between Schenker's approach and those of Marx, Freud, and the structuralists.[36] In all of them an underlying pattern, made available through analysis, provides meaning for the data of direct experience. This parallel has some value, I think, as long as we keep in mind an important characteristic of music—the extraordinary, perhaps unique, transparency of its structure. Elsewhere in the same review, Rosen cites a large-scale registral connection in Schenker's analysis of Chopin's Etude, Op. 10, No. 8. He says about it, "This is a relationship that a pianist with a sense of line naturally sets in relief, *and is a direct part of musical experience*" (italics mine).[37] Rosen's observation hits the nail on the head. In tonal music the underlying pattern is not always hidden from immediate perception, but frequently "is a direct part of musical experience." And this is true of background relationships as well as of the middleground one that Rosen cites.[38]

The "surface" of tonal music, then, is by no means always an opaque cover concealing an underlying structure of an altogether different nature. The underlying structure (in its several levels of elaboration) is, often to a large extent, present in the surface. But the relationships in a great work are so many and so complex that the ear cannot possibly sort them out at once. Analysis, in part, is the process of sorting out, the clarification of, the various levels. In the course of analysis, discoveries often occur. One becomes aware of connections that one had not previously perceived even in a confused or not fully conscious way. But once aware of them, one hears them; if not heard, the analysis is meaningless. Schenker's approach begins and ends with direct musical experience, with hearing. If the analysis has been successful it leads to hearing that is incomparably clearer and more comprehensive than it had been before; it never leads to abstraction without sensory content.

For me this represents one of the greatest strengths of Schenker's approach. And I am, as a matter of principle, resistant to any modification or extension of his methods that leaves the realm of hearing. We are not, after all, anthropologists trying to reduce myths to underlying mental structures, or psychoanalysts uncovering patterns of repression in the imagery of dreams. For them, the myth or dream is less important than the structure concealed behind it. We are, after all, musicians trying to understand great works of art, works that conceal their structures much less than myths and dreams do for the structuralists and Freudians. And for us the work is incomparably more important than its structure; the latter is significant only insofar as understanding it—that is, hearing it—leads to an enhanced understanding (hearing) of the work which contains it.

Toward the Analysis of Rhythm

At this point I would like to suggest some of my own ideas about the analysis of rhythm. I shall indicate a few general principles and show their application to a few examples of compositional details. These principles do not constitute a coherent "theory of rhythm." As I mentioned earlier, I doubt whether such a theory is possible at present. In formulating these ideas I have been led by two fundamental considerations. The first is that rhythm is so bound up with tonal organization that the analysis of rhythm must be compatible with our clearest and deepest insights into tonal structure. For me, Schenker's approach provides such insights more readily than any other. The second consideration is that musical analysis has value only insofar as it helps us to hear.

How do we hear rhythm? As the organization of time, more significantly as organized movement in time. The word itself comes from a Greek verb meaning "to flow"; the word "stream" comes from the same Indo-European source. Quite apart from music we seem to experience time itself as movement; the imagery is deeply embedded in our cultural traditions and in our language (time passes, time flies, time goes by, etc.). Perhaps I am emphasizing the obvious, but many musicians writing about rhythm use a terminology that conveys anything but a sense of motion. There are two noteworthy exceptions, Edward Cone and Victor Zuckerkandl; in quite a different way, each of them emphasizes the kinetic aspect of rhythm.

Cone compares rhythmic motion to a ball thrown from one player to another;[39] Zuckerkandl compares one aspect of rhythm—metrical organization—to a succession of waves.[40] Each image expresses something important about musical rhythm, but Zuckerkandl's has one great advantage; it conveys the idea of differentiated, patterned movement, and this aspect, I believe, is of fundamental importance. (Cone would probably not disagree, for he is careful to state that "unlike the undifferentiated transit of the ball, the musical passage is marked by stronger and weaker points.")[41] To my way of thinking, some kind of patterning, of ebb and flow, is inherent in our conception of musical rhythm. And of other kinds of rhythm as well. Most musicians, I think, would immediately see the relation to their art of H. W. Fowler's beautiful little essay on prose rhythm in *Modern English Usage*, from which I have taken the following quotations:

> Rhythmless speech or writing is like the flow of liquid from a pipe or tap; it runs with smooth monotony from when it is turned on to when it is turned off, provided it is clear stuff; if it is turbid, the smooth flow is queerly and abruptly checked from time to time, and then resumed. Rhythmic speech or writing is like the waves of the sea, moving onward with alternating rise and fall. . . . Meter is measurement; rhythm is flow, a flow with pulsations as infinitely various as the shape and size and speed of the waves.[42]

The Two Sources of Musical Rhythm

What produces the patterned movement, the rise and fall of musical rhythm? I believe that there are two sources, one of them specifically musical, the other shared with other rhythmic phenomena. The purely musical one flows from the succession and combination of tones, *for the tonal system itself has rhythmic properties*. The recurrence of a tone after one or more different ones, the octave relationship, chordal and linear associations, consonance and dissonance, all of these create a "flow with pulsations as infinitely various as the shape and size and speed of the waves." In addition, of course, any tonal piece also reveals a complex pattern of durations, emphases, and groupings which do not arise from the tones; this is the second aspect of musical rhythm. We shall refer to the two types as "tonal rhythm" and "durational rhythm"; the second term is an acceptable oversimplification, duration being the most important although not the only constituent. Of course the two types are related, for both consist in the patterned flow of events in time. To understand the rhythm of a piece is, essentially, to understand how they combine into a single continuum, sometimes supporting, sometimes diverging from, sometimes even contradicting one another.

Tonal Rhythm   We have already seen an instance of tonal rhythm in the Scarlatti excerpt (Example 1.5), but we can get a clearer insight from simple melodic designs without durational organization. Example 1.10 comes from an exercise devised for pianists by Busoni, called by him "Scales in Spirals." The tonal rhythm of this passage has two principal agents; one is the recurrence of the central tone, c^2; the other, the scalar associations of the highest and lowest tones of the "spirals." The tonal motion oscillates between the fixed central point and the widening scales; intervening tones are heard as transitional. The contrast between the stable referential tones and the transitional ones produces an impression of patterned movement, in other words, an impression of rhythm. One might characterize the rhythmic impression as follows: one hears the repeated c^2s as strong, the turning points as relatively strong, and the intervening tones as weak. This impression does not depend upon accentuation; it arises even if the exercise is played without any stresses (though the rhythmic effect would be heightened by appropriate accentuation). Nor does it come from pulse or meter. The tonal rhythm persists through almost any conceivable pacing; we can play with equal duration for the single tones, with a gradual acceleration, or with equal duration for the groups beginning with c^2.

The rhythmic implications of tonal repetition and association make themselves felt in the most basic melodic structure, the scale. Play, for example, a major scale up or down a few octaves; you will hear that the recurrence of the tonic provides stable points similar to the repeated c^2s of Example 1.10 but, of course, at different registers. We experience the scale as a movement away from the starting point and toward the next higher or lower octave; in the tonal system, the turning point (where motion "away from" becomes motion "toward") occurs at the fifth tone of the scale (Example 1.11). The rhythmic character of the scale was, as far as I know, first pointed out by Victor Zuckerkandl.[43]

If we play our major scale with the right hand and hold the tonic triad with the left, we become aware of still another rhythmic consequence of tonal association. The members of the tonic chord function as stable elements in contrast to the other, "dissonant" tones; we hear the latter as transitional elements, as passing tones. The alternation of chordal and passing tones adds another layer of patterning to the melodic flow; again neither meter nor a steady pulse is required to produce the rhythmic effect (Example 1.12).

EXAMPLE 1.10: Busoni, "Scales in Spirals"

EXAMPLE 1.11: The rhythmic character of the major scale

Durational Rhythm   Tonal rhythm is most easily perceived where there is little or no durational patterning (as in the last few examples or, for that matter, Example 1.5); in the same way, durational rhythm makes itself most strongly felt where the tones have little or nothing to do. This is what occurs in the three excerpts shown in Example 1.13; each contains the patterned repetition of a single tone.

I would like to emphasize again that duration is not the only component of what I call, for the sake of convenience, durational rhythm. The composers of our three excerpts certainly had in mind a pattern of stresses as well as of durations. Stress and duration together give rise to clearly expressed pulse and meter (Examples 1.13a and 1.13b) and to subtler aspects of rhythm as well. The acceleration in Example 1.13a produces an increasing forward momentum; there are no longer notes or caesuras to act as a check (see arrows). The opposite effect occurs in Example 1.13b, measures 1 and 2, where the eighth notes block the development of a forward momentum; the first three notes, therefore, move away from the preceding strong beat rather than toward the next one. In the third measure, the steady sixteenth notes create a continuous motion from one downbeat to the next. At first they move away from the preceding downbeat; the absence of a longer note allows the development of a momentum forward, toward the next one. These two rhythmic directions, toward the next or away from the preceding strong beat, have their exact analogues in tonal rhythm, as I have indicated in discussing the scale (Example 1.11). To express them requires sensitivity to timing and dynamics on the part of the performer. The same holds true for the incredibly beautiful syncopation conceived by Beethoven for the last movement of the Piano Sonata, Op. 110 (Example 1.13c). Here the composer's fingering helps to produce not only the right touch and timing but also a visual gesture that will help to orient the listener.

Applications

Rhythm and Fundamental Structure   The distinction between tonal and durational rhythm will help us to deal with a problem that I posed near the beginning of this essay: is the *Ursatz* arrhythmic, as Schenker maintained?[44] My answer to this question is a qualified no. I believe that progressions in the Fundamental Structure embody tonal, but not

EXAMPLE 1.12: Chordal and passing tones in the major scale

EXAMPLE 1.13: (A) Handel, Concerto Grosso, Op. 6, No. 7

(B) Beethoven, String Quartet, Op. 59, No. 1

(C) Beethoven, Sonata, Op. 110

durational, rhythm. In Examples 1.14a and 1.14b, the recurrence of I in the bass and the chordal associations between the first and last tones of the top voice on the one hand, and the contrast effected by the $\hat{2}_V$ on the other, certainly create a rhythmic rise and fall, a "flow with pulsations."

The primary rhythmic implication of the *Ursatz*, therefore, results from the three invariable elements: the opening tonic ($\hat{8}_I$, $\hat{5}_I$, or $\hat{3}_I$), the dominant ($\hat{2}_V$), and the closing tonic ($\hat{1}_I$). In that the two tonics begin and end the motion, and in that the $\hat{2}_V$ has a transitional function, it would seem appropriate to characterize the rhythmic impression as strong–weak–strong. There is certainly an element of truth in this interpretation, but the idea can be misleading unless one keeps the following in mind: First of all, the rhythmic impression comes solely from the combination and sequence of tones; neither duration nor meter (both being aspects of durational rhythm) is implied. Second, in the actual composition the rhythmization of the *Ursatz* can assume many shapes, some of which can contradict the strong–weak–strong implication of the underlying progression. To understand the significance of this possibility, we must examine the ways in which tonal and durational rhythms interact with one another.

EXAMPLE 1.14: Tonal rhythm in the *Ursatz*

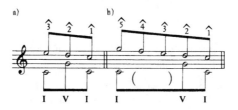

Rhythm and Meter   My distinction between tonal and durational rhythm cuts across different lines from the usual distinction between rhythm and meter. The relation between meter and the two aspects of rhythm is rather complicated. Obviously meter is much more closely bound to durational than to tonal rhythm. Without some kind of durational pattern, tonal motion cannot produce even a pulse, let alone meter, whereas durational rhythm can give rise to both. However, durational change can also produce a rhythmic pattern containing neither steady pulse nor meter—for example, the freely accelerating repeated notes in Bartók's Bagatelle, Op. 6, No. 12.

The designs of tonal rhythm often maintain a high degree of independence from any metrical scheme. Very frequently, however, aspects of tonal rhythm underscore the meter. The avoidance, in many styles, of bass repetitions from a weak to a strong beat, the related tendency to "change chord over the bar line," the normal practice of beginning the measure with the lowest tone in Alberti or dance accompaniments—all of these show how tonal movement can help to express the meter. From a broader perspective, the appearance of an important goal of tonal motion at a metrically accented place can be an important compositional resource.

Texture, Dynamics, Timbre, and Rhythm   Changes of texture, dynamics, and timbre can produce accents and groupings; they can, therefore, exert a significant influence upon the thythmic design of a piece. Sometimes one of these elements will create a pattern of independent significance, one whose rate of change helps to organize the flow of time.[45] Echo pieces of the Baroque period (e.g., the chorus "In our deep vaulted cell" and the dance that follows it in Purcell's *Dido and Aeneas*) show a consistent alternation of loud and soft. In Classical sonatas for piano and violin (in contrast to solo piano sonatas), important themes often appear twice, with the melodic line played first by one, then by the other, instrument. And in music of many styles one finds patterns of solo and tutti in alternation, for example, single voices against a whole chorus.

Ought one, then, to recognize the possibility of a rhythm of dynamic intensities, a timbral rhythm, or a textural rhythm independent of durational and tonal rhythms? Perhaps, but with one important reservation. As I mentioned earlier, the idea of motion is central to any conception of musical rhythm. Now a feeling of movement is immediately evoked by tonal successions. And over short spans of time, at least, the kinetic quality of durational rhythm, with its close analogies to physical movement, could hardly escape the ear. But the same is not true, at least to any significant extent, of timbre or texture. Thus we hear F moving to G, a group of eighth notes moving to a half note, a melodic line moving from the violin part to the oboe. But the violin sound does not move to the oboe sound; one simply follows the other. (In some recent music—especially in music for electronically produced sound—the increased control of timbral change perhaps makes possible the suggestion of movement through tone color. But this, to say the least, is not a very important resource of tonal music.)

Sometimes changes of loudness, even of a single tone, do give an impression of movement—think of a *fp*, a *messa di voce*, or a sustained crescendo. But the effect of patterned movement results in part from the pacing of the dynamic change and is, to that extent, a kind of durational rhythm. And when we hear, say, a crescendo over a long, sustained tone, we begin to expect another tone to appear; the dynamic change, therefore, may help to intensify a tonal rhythm. It would seem, then, that dynamic change—as well as timbral and textural—tends to articulate and clarify (or perhaps cloud) the rhythmic design of a piece, a design whose primary elements remain time and tone.

Accent and Tonal Stability   In the domain of durational rhythm, downbeats and other important accents would seem to correspond to stable tonal events in the domain of pitch organization and the tonal rhythm that arises from it. As we have seen, this correspondence figures in the explanations of large-scale rhythm by Cone and by Cooper and Meyer. We have also seen that Schenker's *Ursatz* progressions, in which durational rhythm plays no part, may suggest a pattern of strong–weak–strong. That the analogy has some significance seems evident. But how close is it, really, and what conclusions ought we to draw from it? First of all, we must remember that many of the indispensable words we use to describe our experience of music—words such as "tension," "stability," "motion," "energy"—are metaphors derived from our experience of physical nature. We cannot assume that the same metaphor applied to different aspects of music means exactly the same thing, although it is probably safe to assume that there is some overlapping of meaning.

In other words, the stability of the tonic and of the downbeat, or the tension of the leading tone and of the upbeat, may well differ from each other in some important respects. And indeed it seems to me that they do. A perceptually significant downbeat represents the culmination of a phase of increasing momentum; shortly afterwards there follows a relaxation which allows a new momentum to gather. The period of "stability" is very brief indeed. The timing of a stable tonal event is altogether different. First of all, it is by no means so transitory; a stable tone or tonal complex can last for quite a long time. Second, the relaxation often (probably usually) occurs at the impact rather than after it, as is the case with the downbeat. That this is so is borne out by the old rule that one must make a diminuendo into the resolution of a dissonant tone.

The analogy between metrical accent and tonal stability, then, ought not to be overdrawn. Despite certain obvious similarities, the two ideas are not completely congruent. Indeed, to reconcile their often conflicting demands can be among the most difficult tasks facing the performer. And in analyzing music we should be wary of facile comparisons, say, between a leading tone (or a chord containing one) and an upbeat. Of course the two frequently coincide and one can add to the force of the other. But contradictions are so frequent that we can hardly consider them abnormalities; they are a basic resource of the tonal system. In the three excerpts of Example 1.15, leading tones are strongly accented relative to their resolutions. And it is precisely from the conflict between accent and tonal stability that the rhythmic effect of the excerpts comes.

In one important respect a correlation between metrical accent and tonal stability can be demonstrated. When Fux stipulated that only the second of two half notes in his second species could be dissonant, he was, of course, following the practice of Palestrina. But that practice belonged to the final phase of a historical process dating back to the thirteenth century. Theorists and composers of the late Middle Ages and the Renaissance attempted to control and regulate the use of dissonance. One of the techniques that they learned was to place what we now call passing and neighboring tones in metrically unaccented positions. At first this tendency appears more consistently in theory than in practice, but that it represents an increasingly powerful trend seems hardly open to doubt. In music later than Palestrina (as in some earlier music) accented passing and neighboring tones appear fre-

EXAMPLE 1.15: (A) Mozart, Symphony No. 41, Trio of Menuetto

(B) Beethoven, Sonata, Op. 78

(C) Bizet, *Jeux d'enfants*, Op. 22, No. 7, "Les Bulles de savon"

quently. But why should we call them "accented" if we did not feel that the unaccented position represents the norm? Often such accented dissonances represent transformations of unaccented ones brought about through the techniques of displacement and contraction.[46] The relation between accent and tonal stability, then, is by no means a simple one. To understand it better will require much thoughtful and painstaking investigation.

Duration and Tonal Stability   By definition, stable tonal events will tend to persist for a longer time than unstable ones, but, as with accent and stability, the correlation is anything but absolute. Again we find the clearest evidence for such a correlation in the treatment of dissonance. In the late Middle Ages and the Renaissance, brief duration was one of the chief means used by composers to establish control over dissonance. Brief dissonances remained normal in later music, although exceptions become very frequent. To cite one instance out of many, in Chopin's Mazurka, Op. 59, No. 2, measures 45–59, we find a dissonant chord extended for some fifteen measures.

The treatment of modulation shows a parallel development. Kirnberger, for example, writes the following:

In particular we must guard against an opening section that is too brief. For the main key must so capture the listener's ear that throughout the whole piece he never completely loses touch with it. . . . According to the rules of modulation, the further removed the key of a section is from the main key, the shorter that section must be. For if we stay there too long, the impression of the main key is obliterated.[47]

Now Kirnberger, writing in the late 1770s, was describing with great accuracy and intelligence the normal practice of the early eighteenth century (there were exceptions even then, as in some of Domenico Scarlatti's music). But just as the great Baroque composers had developed a style of voice leading that could assimilate a prolonged treatment of dissonance, so the Classical masters created articulated but cohesive compositional designs that permitted them to dwell on remote tonal areas without "obliterating the impression of the main key" and thus destroying the balance of the piece. And with their work as models, the greatest composers of the nineteenth century were able to carry this practice even further (although not always so successfully, especially in large-scale works). Kirnberger's rule probably continued to represent the norm, but a norm increasingly often set aside.

The Schubert Scherzo cited earlier (Example 1.9) is an interesting and by no means extreme example of nineteenth-century practice in modulation. As we have seen, the opening tonic is prolonged for only five measures. This contrasts with a later section of twenty-four measures in A♭ major and minor. As a true enharmonic, A♭ is certainly "far removed from the main key." But its voice-leading function is so clear and so beautifully underscored by the motivic and phrase design that tonal balance is maintained. This despite the fact that the section in A♭ is almost five times as long as the opening section in the tonic. Example 1.16 shows the voice-leading function of the extended A♭ chord. The bass subdivides a motion from III to V into two major thirds, while the top voice moves from $\hat{3}$ to ♭$\hat{3}$ as an enharmonic preparation for $\hat{2}$. The tonal organization is certainly unusual (but compare it to the Menuetto of Schubert's String Quartet in A Minor). The amount of time given to the A♭ section is one of the unusual features of the Scherzo, but it is hardly unique; many equally striking examples could be found.

Tonal and Durational Rhythm in Context

The durational rhythmic design of a piece may contain very small figures (perhaps only two or three notes) which nonetheless function as significant elements. Patterns of tonal rhythm, on the other hand, usually require more time in which to unfold. Example 1.17a is drawn

EXAMPLE 1.16: Schubert, Sonata, D.845, Scherzo

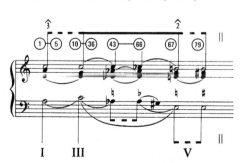

EXAMPLE 1.17: J. S. Bach, Suite for Lute in E Minor, BWV 996, Bourrée

from the Bourrée from Bach's Suite for Lute in E Minor. Aside from the clearly articulated meter, the most prominent element of durational rhythm is a three-note figure (characteristic of Bourrées) of two eighth notes moving to an accented quarter note. The guiding tonal progression is a melodic descending third, shown together with its harmonic support in Example 1.17b. The rhythmic aspect of this melodic fragment, the tonal rhythm, is the patterned movement caused by the chordally associated g^1 and e^1, on the one hand, and the transitional, conceptually dissonant $f\sharp^1$ on the other. How does this tonal rhythm interact with the durational rhythmic pattern? Example 1.17c shows how it relates to meter: g^1 appears in the strongest position, e^1 in the next strongest, the two statements of $f\sharp^1$ in the weakest. That e^1 appears on the second rather than the first beat underlines its function as a temporary and not very strong melodic goal; a melodic tonic on the downbeat comes only at the very end of the piece, where it forms a structural resolution. Note that the tones $d\sharp^1$ and b, although metrically strong, do not form part of the main melodic line.

Their function is shown in Example 1.17d; the $d\sharp^1$ forms part of a melodic unfolding; the b begins a motion out of the inner voice leading up to the e^1. While these diminutions have their own tonal rhythms, they are too fleeting to have much significance apart from the main melodic line. What is important, however, is how the tonal rhythm of the passage changes the effect of the bourrée figure of two eighth notes and a quarter note. I have shown this in Example 1.17e, hoping that the symbols are clear in themselves. I should like to point out, however, that the greatest conflict between meter and tonal rhythm occurs at the second downbeat where the metrically accented tone, far from serving as a melodic goal, is clearly on the way to the e^1.

In presenting this myopic view of a measure and a half of not very complicated music, my intention is primarily to give the reader a clearer understanding of the staggering complexity of musical rhythm. This example, after all, is merely a melodic fragment of twelve notes containing only a single durational figure; the explanation of this fragment has required three diagrams and quite a few words (and we have barely touched upon the bass). A similar study of an entire composition, embracing all formal articulations and structural levels, might require a whole book. Fortunately, musically talented people are usually responsive to many of these rhythmic implications without having to be fully conscious of all of their responses. A good performer would surely not play the bourrée figure with mechanical sameness; despite the quick tempo, he would find nuances to express the tonal rhythms. He would understand, in other words, that the rhythmic effect results from durational and tonal elements acting in combination, and that the same "rhythmic figure" can embody different rhythms, depending upon what the tones do.

The remaining few examples will be presented without elaborate descriptive detail, and my remarks will be confined to a few salient points that illustrate important principles. The first of these principles has been recognized by many musicians working with rhythm. It is that the patterns of what I call durational rhythm are—up to a point, at least—of a stratified, hierarchical nature. In other words, the music can contain inclusive durational patterns framing the succession of foreground durations. These larger rhythms are articulated by many forces, the most important being tonal associations and contrasts—in short, tonal rhythm. (We have already observed this in the Scarlatti fragment of Example 1.5.) Sometimes these larger durational patterns can become motivic elements. This occurs at the beginning of Beethoven's Piano Sonata, Op. 14, No. 2, first movement (Example 1.18a). Example 1.18b contains a rhythmic reduction of the first theme; the sixteenth-note figuration has been removed. The resulting rhythmic pattern, hidden behind the figuration in the actual music, comes to the surface in the transitional section (Example 1.18c); although the articulation differs, the relationship to the opening measures is undeniable. In view of it, I am inclined to regard the rhythmic figure of measures 6 and 7 (Example 1.18a) as a diminution of the same pattern.

In Mozart's Piano Sonata, K.310, first movement, the two main themes show a great deal of contrast in surface rhythm (Example 1.19a). But the tonal groupings of measure 23 create a background rhythm very similar to that of measure 1. The repeated tonal figure of measure 23 corresponds to the repeated tones of measure 1; the descending scale corresponds to the descending broken chord. Example 1.19b shows this similarity of larger rhythmic pattern.

In measure 23 of the Mozart Sonata, a small tonal figure of four sixteenth notes helps to articulate a larger durational pattern. This happens quite often; even more often, it would seem, patterns of tonal rhythm require more time for their unfolding than durational units.

EXAMPLE 1.18: Beethoven, Sonata, Op. 14, No. 2

EXAMPLE 1.19: Mozart, Sonata, K.310

Sometimes the latter are so palpably incomplete that their integrity as rhythmic groups comes into question. Such is the case with the three-note figure that begins the Schubert excerpt of Example 1.9. The half-note chord on the downbeat receives so much emphasis that in normal circumstances it would form a rhythmic goal. Just this emphasis, however, gives an unusual degree of tension to the melodic tone b^1, and to the V chord. And because the melodic and harmonic tension is so acute, one hears the rhythmic group as incomplete. The completion takes place, but only at the end of the phrase, after several frustrated attempts. Later on (for example, in the transition following the first double bar), the initial figure occurs in a tonal environment of much less tension; the rhythmic impression, consequently, becomes very different.

Example 1.20a, the subject of the Fugue in B♭ Minor from the *Well-Tempered Clavier*, Book II, shows a much subtler conflict between the groupings of durational and tonal rhythm. The subject is segmented by rests, the main division occurring in measure 2 where the rest, following a seeming resolution to the tonic, appears to split the subject into halves. A closer look reveals that the first three measures are built of a single motivic element, a stepwise line rising a fourth. The fourths can be seen in Example 1.20b; especially noteworthy are the diminutions (in both senses of the word) that produce fourths within a larger fourth in measure 3. Now the rest in the second measure (also the one in the first measure) occurs right in the middle of one of the rising fourths. In later entrances, the countersubject underscores the unity of this ascent and clarifies the meaning of the third tone in measure 2; it is not a functional tonic at all, but a passing tone. (To show the countersubject, I have included the second entrance in Example 1.20a.) From the perspective of tonal organization (including tonal rhythm), the division of the subject into two halves is illusory. This is,

EXAMPLE 1.20: J. S. Bach, *Well-Tempered Clavier*, Book II, Fugue 22

to be sure, a very complex fugue subject, but further discussion is not needed to bring out the principle exemplified: conflict between durational and tonal groupings can be of crucial importance in shaping a musical idea. Here the importance is such that one must question the validity of any approach to rhythmic analysis that would attempt to reduce such fascinating complexity to a single hierarchy of groupings.

The same conflict between the patterns of durational and of tonal rhythm can be observed over longer compositional spans: over phrases, phrase groups, and sections. My concluding discussion of the durational and tonal groupings in the opening phrase of Mozart's Piano Sonata, K.457, first movement, is by no means complete, but it should give the reader a glimpse of some of the problems that confront us when we attempt to understand the larger rhythms of a piece.

The phrase consists of eight measures; the durational grouping of these eight measures could hardly be clearer. There is a primary division into two balanced groups of four measures plus four. And each unit of four measures divides almost equally into two plus two— not quite equally, for the upbeats at the end of measures 2 and 6 prevent an absolute symmetry (Example 1.21a). This durational grouping is underscored by every important aspect of the music except the one that is perhaps the most important of all. Thus the motivic design of measures 5–8 repeats that of measures 1–4; the inner division of the four-measure units is emphasized by a change of motive. The motivic design of the entire phrase could be symbolized thus: a–b–a–b (see Example 1.21b). Changes of texture (unison versus several parts) and of dynamics (forte versus piano) accompany the motivic changes, thus helping to clarify the durational pattern.

How is it that this phrase, with such strongly marked inner articulations, does not sound overly segmented? It is because the patterns of tonal movement overlap the articulations and act as a counterforce to them. First of all, the diminished seventh chords of measures 4 and 7 are obviously related to each other and to the dominant of measures 5–6. From the point of view of chordal rhythm, these measures form a group and serve to connect the tonics of measures 1–3 and 8. The chordal group of measures 4–7 bridges the division at measure 5, which bisects the phrase. Similarly the dissonant neighboring tone, ab^2, of measure 4 finds its resolution to g^2 only in measure 8. (For reasons of motivic symmetry, the g^2

EXAMPLE 1.21: Mozart, Sonata, K.457

of measure 8 is immediately preceded by f^2 in measure 7. As seventh of the preceding dominant arpeggio and upper tone of a diminished fifth, f^2 would normally resolve down to $e\flat^2$. The appearance of the tone of resolution an octave lower in the left-hand part allows the f^2 to move up to g^2.)

In many eighteenth-century pieces, the opening phrase has a design like that of the Mozart Sonata. See, for instance, the three excerpts of Example 1.22; in all of them, as in the Mozart example, the chordal grouping counteracts the primary division of the phrase into two halves. Mozart's phrase, however, differs greatly from the others in the treatment of motivic elements, the ones that I have labeled "a" and "b." Mozart separates these ideas much more forcefully than the other composers; the rests in measures 2 and 6 and the above-mentioned contrasts in texture and dynamics set them apart. However, the chordal and melodic integration of the two ideas is much closer in the Mozart than in the other excerpts. Thus the tonic chord of measures 1 and 2 (idea "a") continues through measure 3 (idea "b"); the first tone of the ascending arpeggio functions as the bass for the entire three measures. And g^2, the culminating tone of the arpeggio and $\hat{5}$ of the structural line, does not appear in measure 1 or 2, as one might expect, but at the head of measure 3. This crucial tone enters without doubling or accompaniment in a piano made startling by its contrast with the energetic forte of the preceding measures. For once the overworked adjective "dramatic" seems appropriate.

EXAMPLE 1.22: (A) J. S. Bach, Organ Prelude, BWV 552

(B) Haydn, Sonata, Hob. XVI/34

(C) Beethoven, Sonata, Op. 2, No. 3

There would be little drama in this phrase were it not for the conflict between durational and tonal groupings. The former assert their independence in the face of the integrative tonal forces. And the latter strive to hold together widely different patterns of texture and intensity. The importance of this conflict can be seen if we attempt the old device of rewriting the passage (Example 1.21c). If durational and tonal patterns coincide, the musical tension is reduced immeasurably; the sudden changes in texture and dynamics lose all of their significance. The rewriting also shows the function of the rest in measures 2 and 6; by breaking off the unison passage before a strong beat, Mozart prevents the appearance of a rhythmic goal before the arrival of g^2 in measure 3 and f^2 in measure 7. (The rest also creates a fascinating rhythmic ambiguity, for the unison arpeggio could easily fit into a 3/2 meter. The cross-rhythms of measures 118–20 are a later consequence of this ambiguity.) The reduction in Example 1.21d shows the tonal and durational groupings as they relate to each other.

Notes

1. In the last few years, for example, Charles Rosen and Arthur Komar have done so, Rosen in a review of the reprint of Schenker's *Fünf Urlinie-Tafeln: Five Graphic Music Analyses*, new introduction by Felix Salzer (New York: Dover, 1969), in the *New York Review of Books* 16, no. 11 (17 June 1971), pp. 32–38 (hereafter referred to as Rosen Review), and in his book *The Classical Style: Haydn, Mozart, Beethoven* (New York: Viking, 1971), p. 36; Komar in a review of the first two volumes of the *Music Forum*, in *Perspectives of New Music* 9, no. 2–10, no. 1 (1971), pp. 314–22 (hereafter referred to as Komar Review).

2. I intend to develop these ideas further in future volumes of the *Music Forum*.

3. The view results in part from the fact that much of his work remains virtually unknown by most musicians. Schenker discusses rhythm to a far greater extent than many of his critics seem to realize.

4. See Heinrich Schenker, *Free Composition*, trans. and ed. Ernst Oster (New York: Longman, 1979), p. 15.

5. Heinrich Schenker, *Harmony*, ed. Oswald Jones, trans. Elizabeth Mann Borgese (Chicago: University of Chicago Press, 1954), pp. 151–52.

6. Rosen Review, p. 34.

7. Act IV in the original (Paris) version.

8. Heinrich Schenker, *Das Meisterwerk in der Musik*, 3 vols. (Munich: Drei Masken, 1925, 1926, 1930, reissued as 3 vols. in 1 in slightly reduced facsimile, Hildesheim: Georg Olms, 1974), vol. 3, p. 50, also pp. 100–101 translated as "Beethoven's Third Symphony: Its True Context Described for the First Time," trans. Derrick Puffett and Alfred Clayton, in *The Masterwork in Music*, ed. William Drabkin, vol. 3 (Cambridge: Cambridge University Press, 1997), pp. 30–31.

9. See, for example, Donald Francis Tovey, *A Companion to Beethoven's Pianoforte Sonatas* (London: Associated Board, 1931), p. 3.

10. Rosen Review, p. 34.

11. Komar Review, p. 320.

12. Arthur Komar, *Theory of Suspensions. A Study of Metrical and Pitch Relations in Tonal Music* (Princeton: Princeton University Press, 1971), pp. 51–54.

13. Komar Review, p. 320.

14. As Komar does in *Theory of Suspensions*, p. 51.

15. Thus, referring to "structural chords which are also brief in the background" implies a conception of the background fundamentally at variance with Schenker's. See Komar Review, p. 320 quoted in the text.

16. Probably among the "salient features" of a composition that, according to Rosen, Schenker minimized. See the quotation from Rosen Review in the text.

17. Schenker, *Free Composition*, p. 130.

18. Ibid., pp. 118–27.

19. To speak of Schenker's "neglect of rhythm" and "total disregard of proportions" is to perpetuate a misconception; it is simply not accurate. See Rosen Review, p. 34.

20. One example is Kirnberger's chapter on phrase rhythm, the earliest treatment of the subject I am familiar with. [When I first wrote this article I did not yet know the writings of Joseph Riepel.] See Johann Philipp Kirnberger, *Die Kunst des reinen Satzes in der Musik*, 2 vols. (Berlin and Königsberg, 1776–79, photographic facsimile bound in one volume, Hildesheim: Georg Olms, 1968), vol. 2, part 1, pp. 137–53. This has been translated as *The Art of Strict Musical Composition*, by David Beach and Jügen Thym (New Haven: Yale University Press, 1982), pp. 403–17. I shall refer to Kirnberger's chapter again later.

21. Among them are Victor Zuckerkandl, Edward Cone, Jan LaRue, Leonard Meyer and Grosvenor Cooper, Roy Travis, Peter Westergaard, Wallace Berry, Charles Rosen, and Arthur Komar. Most of these authors have been or will be cited and some of their ideas discussed in the course of this essay. Two whom I am not citing elsewhere I should like to mention here. They are Roy Travis, "Toward a New Concept of Tonality?" *Journal of Music Theory* 3, no. 2 (1959), pp. 257–84, especially pp. 274–75, which contain a "proportional rhythmic graph" of a Chopin etude; and Peter Westergaard, "Some Problems in Rhythmic Theory and Analysis," *Perspectives of New Music* 1 (1962), pp. 180–91.

22. The "upbeat" character is clearly implied in Schenker's beautiful reading of the piece; see in particular the "2. Schicht," *Five Graphic Music Analyses*, p. 54.

23. Edward T. Cone, "Analysis Today," *Musical Quarterly* 46 (1960), pp. 182–83, reprinted in *Music: A View from Delft*, ed. Robert P. Morgan (Chicago: University of Chicago Press, 1989), pp. 39–54.

24. Ibid., p. 183; reprint ed., p. 50.

25. Edward T. Cone, *Musical Form and Musical Performance* (New York: Norton, 1968), p. 26.

26. See Hugo Riemann, *Musikalische Rhythmik und Metrik* (Liepzig: Breitkopf and Härtel, 1903; reprinted, Niederwalluf: Sändig, 1971), p. 13. Riemann believed that all of the even-numbered measures of a phrase are metrically accented relative to the odd-numbered ones; Cone's conception of phrase rhythm is much more flexible. An account of phrase rhythm very similar to Cone's is sketched out in Roger Sessions, *Harmonic Practice* (New York: Harcourt, Brace, and World, 1951), pp. 83–84. Cone's "structural downbeat" corresponds very closely to Sessions's "accent of weight."

27. Grosvenor Cooper and Leonard B. Meyer, *The Rhythmic Structure of Music* (Chicago: University of Chicago Press, 1960), p. v.

28. Ibid., p. 61.

29. Ibid., p. 203.

30. See especially the analysis of Beethoven's Symphony No. 8, first movement, in ibid., pp. 188–203.

31. As Cone describes them, however, the structural downbeats are closer to the normal conception of beat; they do not last through whole sections.

32. Komar, *Theory of Suspensions*, pp. 51–54.

33. Ibid., p. 156.

34. Ibid., p. 54.

35. Ibid., pp. 151–61. The reference to "measure 0" occurs on p. 155.

36. Rosen Review, p. 34.

37. Ibid., p. 33.

38. By contrast, Freud's patients were by no means immediately aware of the latent content of their dreams or of the etiology of their neurotic symptoms.

39. Cone, *Musical Form and Musical Performance*, p. 26.

40. Victor Zuckerkandl, *Sound and Symbol: Music and the External World*, trans. Willard Trask (New York: Pantheon, 1956), pp. 168–200.

41. Cone, *Musical Form and Musical Performance*, p. 27.

42. H. W. Fowler, *A Dictionary of Modern English Usage* (Oxford: Oxford University Press, 1926), p. 504.

43. Zuckerkandl, *Sound and Symbol*, pp. 100–104. Zuckerkandl did not elaborate upon the idea of tonal rhythm, but he implied it in much of his writing. I have learned a great deal from his books, and I recommend them to the attention of thoughtful musicians.

44. I refer the reader to Schenker's diagrams in figures 9, 10, and 11 of *Free Composition*.

45. This idea was expressed by Wallace Berry in a review of Cone's *Musical Form and Musical Performance* in *Perspectives of New Music* 9, no. 2–10, no. 1 (1971), p. 276.

46. See Felix Salzer and Carl Schachter, *Counterpoint in Composition: The Study of Voice Leading* (New York: McGraw-Hill, 1969), pp. 178–88.

47. Kirnberger, *Die Kunst des reinen Satzes in der Musik*, vol. 2, section 1, p. 141, my translation. See also Beach and Thym, *The Art of Strict Musical Composition*, p. 407.

Durational Reduction

One of Beethoven's conversation books for the year 1824 contains the following entry in the hand of Anton Schindler: "The extended rhythms in your works do not result from computation, but rather from the nature of the melody and not infrequently from the harmony—am I right?"[1] I have not been able to find out if the entry is genuine or one of Schindler's later insertions.[2] But in either case, the remark holds considerable musical interest. In, Chapter 1,[3] I suggested that musical rhythm has two sources. One is the division of time, measurable by the motion of a physical body in space (clock or metronome) —Schindler's "computation." The other is the complex of periodicities inherent in the tonal system, in such phenomena as octave equivalence, scalar functions, dissonance resolving to consonance, and so on—in other words, "melody and not infrequently . . . harmony." I used the terms *durational rhythm* and *tonal rhythm to* refer to these two components. The earlier essay was of a very general, introductory nature, with few rhythmic analyses and none treating in detail examples more than eight measures long.

In this essay I shall try to develop further some of the ideas sketched out in the earlier one. I shall do so by demonstrating an analytic notation that can help to reveal connections between durational and tonal organization, at least in some types of music. This notation is based on *durational reduction* applied to and coordinated with significant structural levels of voice leading—in other words, durational reduction combined with a reduction, in Schenker's manner, of the tonal contents. In music with clearly defined measure-groups and phrases, the use of durational reduction frequently shows a "higher-level" metrical organization of measures, an organization of "hypermeasures," to use Edward Cone's term.[4] By indicating tonal events in durational proportion and by specifying the larger metrical divisions, such an approach can sometimes clarify aspects of rhythmic organization not directly revealed by graphic analyses that deal mainly with voice leading and harmony.

Originally published in *Music Forum* 5 (1980), pp. 197–232.

The examples that I shall discuss are, for the most part, short, relatively simple works. This will help the reader (and the writer!) to verify the analyses by ear, always an important consideration and one of overriding importance when the analytic procedure is, in some respects, a new one. If the analyses presented here are convincing—if, in some significant manner, they are true to the way the music sounds—then the approach will have demonstrated at least a limited utility, even though the pieces analyzed are comparatively short and simple ones.

Durational Reduction in Composition

That one might gain insight into some aspects of rhythmic organization by reducing note values and by grouping measures into larger metrical units is hardly a new idea. First of all, reduced note values and hypermeasures sometimes appear in compositions and in composers' sketches in a way that can clarify the rhythmic shape of an idea. Thus Beethoven's compression of the opening theme in the coda of the "Waldstein" Rondo (Example 2.1a) makes notationally explicit the theme's strong/weak metrics, though, to be sure, they are clear enough at the opening of the movement (Example 2.1b). On the other hand, a sketch of Beethoven's for the Allegro molto of the Piano Sonata, Op. 110, sheds light on a passage whose rhythmic shape is anything but obvious, having eluded some excellent musicians, among them Artur Schnabel.[5] This sketch does not employ reduced note values, but it is written, in part, in hypermeasures of 4/4 time instead of the 2/4 meter of the movement. The position of the bar lines shows that Beethoven heard the rhythm as syncopated; the chords appear off the main beats. Compare Example 2.2a (the upper voice of the passage as it appears in the composition) with Example 2.2b (the sketch).[6]

Durational Reduction in Analysis

Recently, some musicians and writers have used reduced note values, hypermeasures, or the two combined as analytic tools; among them are Roy Travis,[7] Grosvenor Cooper and Leonard B. Meyer,[8] and Wallace Berry.[9] Years earlier, Schenker used such tools in a particularly interesting way in one of his *Tonwille* monographs: the study of Beethoven's Piano Sonata, Op. 2, No. 1. At the end of his discussion of the first movement, Schenker presents a rhythmic reduction of the first twenty measures of his graph (*Urlinie-Tafel*) of the movement. Since this is a facet of Schenker's work that hardly anyone knows, I should like to reproduce the rhythmic reduction (Example 2.3a) together with the first twenty measures of the voice-leading graph (Example 2.3b).

EXAMPLE 2.1: Beethoven, Sonata, Op. 53, Rondo

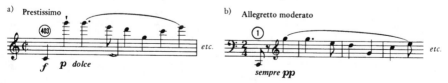

EXAMPLE 2.2: Beethoven, Sonata, Op. 110, Allegro molto

a)

b)

Schenker writes the following about his rhythmic reduction: "To deepen the reader's understanding of the sketch, it is warmly recommended that he picture its contents according to the following reduction of note values. This provides valuable insight, particularly into the reinterpretation of weak measures as strong ones."[10] (The final, normally weak measure of a phrase will be reinterpreted as strong if the beginning of a new phrase overlaps the cadential goal, as in measure 20 of the Beethoven movement.)[11] After showing the rhythmic reduction, Schenker continues: "In addition one might derive a metrical schema from the notes of the reduction:

$$- \cup \ | - \cup \ | - \cup \cup \ | - \cup \smallsmile \text{ etc.}$$

In so doing, one will derive still further insight into the rhythmic freedom of the whole."[12]

As far as I know, Schenker did not continue (or, at least, did not continue to publish) this kind of rhythmic reduction in any of his later analyses, those worked out after he had found clearer ways of indicating the various levels of voice leading than are found in the early *Tonwille* studies. (The reader will note that the durational reduction of Op. 2, No. 1, applies only to the foreground.) And the later writers whom I have cited, even those influenced by Schenker, have not attempted to coordinate their rhythmic reductions with the deeper levels of tonal structure. This, I think, has been a drawback. For one thing, details—rhythmic as well as tonal—often reveal their meaning only when perceived as part of a larger whole; to understand the foreground at all, one must take the middleground into account. In addition, larger considerations of rhythm almost inevitably escape a rhythmic analysis

EXAMPLE 2.3: Beethoven, Sonata, Op. 2, No. 1, Allegro, measures 1–20

a) Schenker's rhythmic reduction

b) Schenker's voice-leading sketch

that concentrates upon the foreground alone. The analyses that I shall present in the remainder of this essay (imperfect as they probably are) represent an attempt to understand rhythmic movement in its relation to large as well as to small tonal progression.

Analyses: Durational Graphs

Chopin, Prelude, Op. 28, No. 3

The Analytic Notation   Example 2.4 contains four graphs (Examples 2.4a–2.4d), vertically aligned, of the first piece that I shall discuss: the G-major Prelude from Chopin's Op. 28.[13] In these graphs, note values do not correspond to structural levels. Instead, they have a purely durational meaning: each quarter note equals a full measure ($\mathfrak{C}$) of the actual composition. Thus, the graph of Example 2.4d, which represents the foreground, contains thirty-three quarter notes, corresponding exactly to the thirty-three measures of the Prelude. Examples 2.4a, 2.4b, and 2.4c, which show three levels of middleground, contain fewer quarter notes than Example 2.4d: Example 2.4a contains sixteen; both Examples 2.4b and 2.4c contain twenty-four. These discrepancies do not result from different scales of reduction; the quarter note equals a measure on all four levels. They indicate, rather, that some of the prolongations go together with durational expansions. Thus the two introductory measures of the Prelude, the six measures of coda, and measure 11, which extends a four-measure group to five measures, all belong to the foreground and are represented only in Example 2.4d. Note that Example 2.4 does *not* include a graph of the background; more about this omission in the last part of this essay.

EXAMPLE 2.4: Chopin, Prelude, Op. 28, No. 3, durational reductions

Bar lines occur in all four graphs; they demarcate measure-groups (hypermeasures) in the composition. In these graphs most of the measures contain four quarter notes and, consequently, represent groups of four measures in the original piece. Since the Prelude also contains smaller hypermeasures of two measures—they are particularly clear in the introduction and coda—it might seem possible to place the bar lines after every two quarter notes instead of every four. Such a procedure, however, would give a distorted picture of the piece, for most of the two-measure groups form part of larger, four-measure units. In making durational reductions, it is advisable to show graphically the largest groupings of measures that recur more or less consistently throughout the piece or section. The reasons will be increasingly clear as we proceed. But it should be apparent already that the two-measure groups are easily discernible in Examples 2.4c and 2.4d, whereas the four-measure groups would be largely obscured if one doubled the number of bar lines.

In graphic analyses that use durational reduction, the measures in the graphs may represent phrases in the piece. They do not do so here if by "phrase" we understand a unit of tonal motion as well as of duration. Measures 3–6, for example, do not form a phrase, for they contain no tonal progression. The complete phrase includes the succeeding five measures (measures 7–11); it is a phrase of eight measures extended to nine.

Other symbols that occur in Example 2.4 have the same meanings that they would have in any graphic analysis.

Since the analytic technique I am using here is not a familiar one, I shall comment upon the graphs of this first example in rather considerable detail. I believe that the implications of the analysis will be understood most readily if we proceed from Example 2.4a to Example 2.4d. The reader should compare each of the four graphs with the actual composition, for each of them views it from a somewhat different perspective.

Example 2.4a   This graph shows the level of middleground closest to the piece's Fundamental Structure. In it the background progression ($\hat{3}$–$\hat{2}$–$\hat{1}$ over I–V–I) is divided and extended by the familiar technique of *interruption*, producing the progression $\hat{3}$–$\hat{2}$‖$\hat{3}$–$\hat{2}$–$\hat{1}$ over I–V‖I–V–I.

Whenever an interruption divides the Fundamental Structure, it is decisive for the piece's form. In our Prelude, the form-making power of interruption is particularly apparent. Like several of the Op. 28 Preludes, this one has a form more usually characteristic of a section than of a whole piece. In essence it consists of a single period of two phrases in antecedent–consequent relation. Of course a piece that was simply a period of, say, sixteen measures would be a virtual impossibility; it would sound incomplete. Chopin avoids this difficulty by modifying the consequent phrase; most often, as in our Prelude, he enlarges it and, by delaying the final tonic, creates a stronger ending. Many of the Preludes—and especially those written in period form—have a character different from almost anything else in the literature: they sound like stylized fragments and, because they are stylized, they are satisfying and complete in themselves. Unlike some of Schumann's fragmentary pieces, which are often true fragments, even the shortest of the Chopin Preludes makes sense when played alone.

When one compares this graph with the piece, two apparent discrepancies immediately stand out. The first has already been mentioned: the graph indicates a total duration of only sixteen measures while the piece contains thirty-three measures. A related discrepancy is that the sixteen beats of the graph divide equally into eight plus eight, whereas the piece is divided asymmetrically: even disregarding the introduction, the coda, and the "extra" measure 11, the second part of the piece is considerably longer than the first. By showing the main body of the piece with an equal duration for its two parts, I indicate that its asymmetrical proportions grow out of an underlying symmetry.

I don't believe that all rhythmic and metric irregularities in tonal music necessarily derive from an underlying regularity. But some surely do. And in the case of our Prelude we have excellent grounds for assuming that the tonal organization implies an equal division of time. For in hearing the consequent phrase of a period, we are guided by the expectations created by the antecedent. And one of these expectations is that the consequent will resolve the tonal tension produced by the antecedent *and that it will do so within the same amount of time.* Were this not so, expansions or contractions of the consequent phrase would lose much, if not all, of their effect. (To attempt to explain the grounds for this durational expectation would take us too far afield. I believe that most musicians will agree with me that it exists; besides, most consequent phrases do, in fact, have the same length as their antecedents.)

I should like to call attention to one other feature of this graph: the final tonic (measure 26) enters in the second half of a hypermeasure—in a metrically weaker place, therefore, than the dominant that precedes it. In my earlier essay, I discussed the rather prevalent view that phrases are normally end-accented, that the final cadential chord falls on an accent or downbeat.[14] I disagree with this view and follow Schenker in assuming that the final tonic of a phrase does not normally receive a metrical accent.[15] I see no reason to believe that the metrical organization of a group of measures differs in principle from that of a single measure and assume that both are beginning- rather than end-accented. Within a group of measures, just as within a measure, rhythmic organization can contradict the meter and produce a stress on a normally weak place. In the Chopin piece, however, the goal tonic of the soprano line falls at the end of a legato slur—a notation that suggests that it is rhythmically, as well as metrically, weak. The metrical position of the final tonic, incidentally, registers in the graph only if we show groups of four rather than two measures, another reason for barring the graph in fours.

Example 2.4b   The most striking feature of this graph is, of course, the enlargement of the consequent phrase; here it contains sixteen beats (sixteen measures in the piece) as against eight in Example 2.4a. Part of the added time is filled with an extension of tonic harmony (measures 16 and 17); reference to the score (or to Example 2.4c) will show that this expanded tonic becomes a V^7 of IV. A subdominant chord, supporting a neighboring tone in the soprano, occupies the rest of the time. It would be wrong to maintain that the extra measures serve merely to provide space for the IV chord; Chopin could easily have accommodated a IV–V–I cadence within the framework of an eight-measure phrase. By extending (and, consequently, emphasizing) the subdominant for as long as he does, however, Chopin adds immeasurably to the force of the cadence and gives the goal tonic a finality it would altogether lack if it came at the end of a symmetrical, sixteen-measure period. Thus we see an element of durational rhythm—pacing—serving to clarify a tonal function.

Chopin continues to group the measures of the consequent phrase into fours; the expansion does not disturb the larger meter. Note that the I and IV chords (of measures 12–23) occupy six measures apiece. The change of chord, therefore, overlaps the four-measure groupings and helps to prevent an excessive segmentation. Incidentally, the fact that the I becomes an applied dominant to the IV in measures 16 and 17 does not mean that the prolongation of IV begins in measure 16. The contents of measures 16 and 17 are not heard as IV, but as I directed toward IV. Therefore, it would be incorrect to assume that the "harmonic rhythm" of six measures (I) plus six (IV) has as its basis the division of four plus eight measures of the larger meter, as in Example 2.5. Here again, as in some of the examples from my previous essay, the conflict between tonal and durational groupings is built into the deeper fabric of the composition.[16]

Example 2.4c   From the point of view of rhythmic implication, this level offers more of interest in the consequent phrase than in the antecedent. A primary question is whether we even ought to regard it as a single phrase expanded to sixteen measures or rather as a group of two phrases of eight measures apiece (measures 12–19 and 20–27). At first hearing, the cadential effect of measures 16–19 (they suggest V^7–I in C major) and the long halt in measures 18–19 on the soprano's e^2 might lead one to hear two phrases. The "C major," however, is the IV of a I–IV–V–I progression; it moves on without a break to the V and I. In a deeper sense, therefore, the sixteen measures contain a single cadential progression, I–IV–V–I, and constitute a single phrase.

This graph sheds light on the contrapuntal meaning—and also, therefore, on the harmonic status—of the $^6_5$ chord (apparently a II$^6_5$) interpolated in measures 22–23 between the IV and V. (The b^1 in the soprano of measure 22 is a passing tone and does not affect the status of the chord.) In a true II$^6_5$, the sixth above the bass ($\hat{2}$) is a consonant tone; it represents the root of the chord. The foreign, dissonant element is the fifth; usually, it is a suspension resolving into the third of V. As the graph indicates, however, the a^1 in the Prelude is not a chord tone; it anticipates the fifth of dominant harmony. The chord, therefore, is not really a II; it is a IV with an anticipation added. Only an awareness of the larger metrical pattern enables us to perceive the a^1 as an anticipation and to hear the chord succession correctly.[17] Here, again, organizing the graph in small hypermeasures of two beats apiece would obscure this larger meter.

One other feature of this graph deserves mention. The main melodic tones b^2 (measures 5 and 14) and a^2 (in the graph, measure 9; in the piece, measures 8 and 10) now fall in the middle of the hypermeasures rather than at the beginning. Such displacements often result from melodic arpeggiations and unfoldings. Here they also help to give the right-hand part the same contours as the ostinato figure of the left hand.

Example 2.4d   This graph represents the foreground of the piece; only the rapid figuration is omitted. The most obvious "new" features are, of course, the introduction and the coda. But some of the rhythmic implications of the main body of the piece, viewed from

EXAMPLE 2.5: Chopin, Prelude, Op. 28, No. 3, measures 12–23

this perspective, are just as interesting. In the second half of the antecedent phrase (measures 7–11), the melodic progression e^2–a^2 appears twice, together with its harmonic accompaniment. (A seventh, $c\natural^2$, is added to the second statement of the D chord.) This is a simple example of prolongation by repetition. Its purpose here is twofold. First, it continues the larger metric groups of four measures begun in measures 3–6; the extra, fifth measure is heard so clearly as an extension that it does not at all disturb the hypermeter. Second, the repetition fills the four measures without retarding the melodic pace; compare Example 2.4d, where quarter-note motion prevails, with Example 2.4c, where half notes appear. In the second part of the consequent phrase, in contrast, the larger melodic progression does in fact slow down (see the half notes in Example 2.4d). How appropriate that it should do so just at the place where the phrase begins to expand and where the final tonic becomes a more distant goal.

No sooner has Chopin established a hypermeter of four (measures 3–6 and 7–10) than he playfully contradicts it with the "extra" measure 11. Here the rhythmic quirk calls attention to a beautiful tonal development: the enlargement of the motivic neighboring-tone figures e^2–d^2 and c^3–b^2 (see Example 2.6).

The most remarkable features of the introduction and coda lie in the sixteenth-note figuration—in the most immediate level, therefore, of the foreground—and are not registered in this graph. (For the sake of completeness, and because they are so beautiful, I shall describe them briefly a bit further on.) This graph does shed light, however, on the large metric organization of the introduction and coda. Note that the four-measure hypermeter continues into the coda (measures 28–31) and that the piece ends, as it begins, with a two-measure group. I doubt that this symmetry is accidental, though I can't prove that it is not.

Some Features of the Immediate Foreground

Some Features of the Immediate Foreground   Example 2.7 shows how the right-hand melody grows out of the accompaniment. The connection is so apparent that it hardly requires demonstration. One rhythmic aspect of the relationship, however, is perhaps not so obvious. The emphasized tones of the accompaniment form a rhythmic pattern (as well as a melodic one) very similar to that of the right-hand part; particularly striking is the appearance of the neighboring e^2 on the fourth sixteenth of a weak beat (Example 2.7a). The right-hand part of measures 3 and 4 has the same rhythmic contour "stretched apart," so to speak (Example 2.7b). In measures 16 and 20, Chopin uses the rhythm of measure 3 for the reiteration of a single note (Example 2.7c). Thus we find that the tonal rhythm concealed in the figuration of the opening measure gradually evolves into a purely durational pattern.

EXAMPLE 2.6: Chopin, Prelude, Op. 28, No. 3, measures 10–14

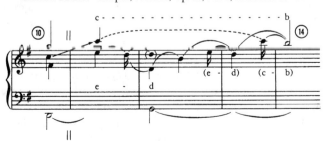

EXAMPLE 2.7: Chopin, Prelude, Op. 28, No. 3, relationship of melody and accompaniment

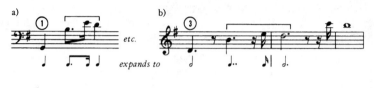

The progressive shortening of rhythmic groups in the coda (whole measures, half measures, quarter measures) is easy to recognize from the score and does not require an illustrative example. Less easy to see, but immediately apparent to the ear, is the way the two final chords indistinctly echo the accompaniment pattern and, indeed, the opening phase of the melodic line.

Mozart, Symphony No. 35, K.385, Trio of Menuetto

Graphic Notation   Example 2.8 contains graphs of the next piece we shall discuss, the Trio of the Menuetto from Mozart's "Haffner" Symphony. In addition to the durational graphs (Examples 2.8a–2.8e), there is a voice-leading graph of the foreground, not in rhythmic reduction (Example 2.8f). As with the Chopin Prelude, each measure of the original becomes a quarter note in the proportional reductions; groups of four measures in the piece become measures of four quarters each in the graphs. I have used an alla breve signature rather than one of 4/4 in order to represent the subdivision of the four-measure groups into smaller hypermeasures of two measures each. The two-measure groupings are even more strongly marked in the Trio than in the Chopin Prelude.

Examples 2.8a and 2.8b: Phrase Structure and Form   The Trio has the usual A:‖:BA:‖ form. The two A sections are identical; in the autograph, in fact, the second one is not written out but merely indicated by a da capo.[18] Each main section consists of a single phrase: one of eight measures in the A sections and one of twelve measures in the B section. (As in the Chopin Prelude, the four-measure groups are not complete units of tonal motion; therefore, they are not really phrases.) In Examples 2.8a and 2.8b, the twelve measures of the B section are represented by only eight quarter notes. This apparent contradiction indicates that the twelve measures must be regarded as the expansion of an eight-measure phrase. More about this expansion below.

Like the Chopin Prelude, the Trio is based on interruption; but here the technique leads to a three-part form. The first A section and the B sections make up the first phase of the interrupted progression; the second A section provides the second, closing phase. Three-part forms based on interruption occur frequently, a well-known example being the second song of Schumann's *Dichterliebe*, analyzed by Schenker in *Free Composition* and commented upon by Allen Forte in a widely quoted essay.[19] In such three-part forms, the two A sections function differently within the whole piece even when—as in the Trio—they contain identical material. The difference in function is not "theoretical"; it can be confirmed by direct musical perception. No one with any experience in music would hear the first part of the Trio as a complete piece, despite the strong harmonic cadence and the $\hat{3}$–$\hat{2}$–$\hat{1}$ progression of the top voice. It is too short, too lacking in articulation, development, and contrast. But when the same material recurs after the B section, the tonal resolution creates a definite impression of closure.

In the Trio, a *three-* part form grows out of a tonal structure divided into two parts by the technique of interruption. This relationship bears upon the most striking feature of Example 2.8a: the disproportion in duration between the two segments of the interrupted progression. In particular, the melodic $\hat{2}$ and the harmonic II^6–V (measure 26) of the second A section seem dwarfed by the long duration of the preceding structural chords and top-voice tones. (In the graph, the duple division of measure 26 is purely a notational convenience.) The disproportion is in marked contrast to the Chopin Prelude, in which the large-scale structure proceeds at a much more even pace (compare Example 2.8a with Example 2.4a). It is, perhaps, too early to draw conclusions from the lopsided proportions of Example 2.8a, but a few ideas suggest themselves:

In *Free Composition*, Schenker maintained that the first $\hat{3}$–$\hat{2}$ over I–V in an interrupted progression had greater structural weight than the second.[20] At least for pieces like our Trio— those where the first structural V forms the basis for an entire section—Schenker's contention is confirmed by the durational values.

Even within the A sections themselves, however (see Example 2.8b), there is a marked disproportion between the duration of the extended initial tonic and that of the closing cadential progression—so much so, in fact, that by itself the progression sounds most unconvincing. One is reminded of Schenker's comment that the masters tried to avoid the juxtaposition of sharply contrasting rhythmic values, and that they would adjust the rhythms of a piece so as to prevent such contrasts.[21] A glance at Example 2.8c will show how the adjustment takes place here; similar adjustments take place in the countless other cases where the opening tonic has a much longer duration than the cadential dominant. As Example 2.8c shows, the cadence continues the rhythmic values of the prolongational motions within the I rather than the extended duration of the prolonged I itself. Thus the pacing of middleground or background progressions may be partly determined by the rhythms of the foreground—a very frequent possibility, evident in the Trio but not in the Chopin Prelude, where the foreground rhythms of the top voice move at an unusually slow pace.

Examples 2.8c, 2.8d, and 2.8e: The Expansion of the B Section   Without a doubt, the most interesting rhythmic feature of the Trio is the expansion, in measures 16–20, of the B section, an expansion that produces a phrase of twelve measures from an "original" (in the middleground) of only eight. (That the phrase is to be heard as an expanded eight measures seems unquestionable, if only because of the varied repetition, starting in measure 13, of measures 9–12, a four-measure group; one expects the repetition to reach its goal in measure 16.)

This expansion is very different from the one in the second part of the Chopin Prelude. In the Prelude, the expansion coincides with a new harmony (IV) and a new melodic diminution; in the Trio, no new tonal material appears. In the Prelude, the extended phrase di-

EXAMPLE 2.8: Mozart, Symphony No. 35, K.385, Trio of Menuetto

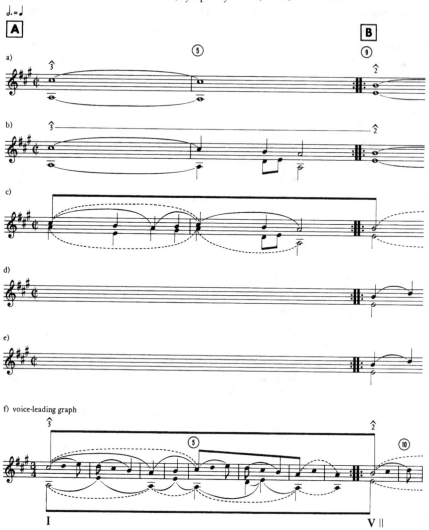

f) voice-leading graph

vides into regular four-measure groups; in the Trio, the expansion produces a metrically irregular grouping: the twelve measures do not divide evenly into three groups of four. Finally, the five-measure expansion in the Trio (measures 16–20) sounds like the enlargement of a single measure of the middleground (measure 16)—a clear and simple example of what Schenker calls a *Dehnung* (expansion).[22]

Examples 2.8d and 2.8e show very clearly the inner rhythmic organization of measures 13–20, far more clearly than the voice-leading graph (without rhythmic reduction) of the foreground. Note, first of all, that measure 16—in the listener's expectation a weak (fourth) measure—is reinterpreted as a strong (first) one.[23] Mozart emphasizes measure 16 by placing Great E in the second bassoon. The low bass note provides an accent that defines the

measure as the beginning of a new rhythmic unit. This new unit would also contain four measures (measures 16–19), except that rhythmic activity stops at the onset of measure 19 (note especially the viola part); once more a weak measure becomes reinterpreted as strong. A brief two-measure group (measures 19–20) restores metrical equilibrium and leads to a normal reprise that begins on a strong measure.

Beethoven, Sonata, Op. 14, No. 1, Allegretto

Graphic Notation   The graphs of Example 2.9 deal with the second movement of Beethoven's Piano Sonata, Op. 14, No. 1, with the E-minor part only, not with the Maggiore.

EXAMPLE 2.9: Beethoven, Sonata, Op. 14, No. 1, Allegretto, durational reductions

In these graphs, unlike the earlier ones, I have represented a full measure in the original by an eighth note. A measure of 4/4 in the graphs, therefore, is equivalent to eight measures of the original, not to four. And in these graphs, the measures coincide with complete phrases in that each of them ends with a clear cadence (except the last one, which closes into the codetta). I have chosen this different scale of reduction for two reasons: In this piece, for the most part, the eight-measure phrases divide much less clearly into two groups of four measures each than in the Chopin Prelude or the Mozart Trio. And, more important, the chief rhythmic feature of this piece—syncopation—is not conveyed clearly by a reduction of whole measures to quarter notes.

Overview of the Piece: Some Details of Voice Leading   The Allegretto is written in ABA[1] form and shows simple but effective use of registral contrasts. Each of the three sections contains two phrases in antecedent–consequent relation. In the first A section, the two phrases form a normal sixteen-measure period, all within an extended tonic. The B section also consists of a sixteen-measure period, based harmonically on a prolonged VI that moves (through an augmented sixth chord) to a dividing V. As in the Mozart Trio, the A and B sections together form the first segment of an interrupted structural progression. The final

A section is not an exact repetition of the first one; the consequent phrase is changed by the introduction of a strong IV, by new diminutions, and by an expansion from eight to ten measures. There is a codetta of twelve measures on I♯.

Though it is fairly simple in its tonal organization, the Beethoven piece is certainly more difficult to understand than the two other pieces I have analyzed. It would take us too far from our main subject if I were to discuss in detail every aspect of voice leading. However, I feel I must mention three important ones, especially since the rhythmic reductions do not reveal their meaning as clearly as voice-leading graphs would.

1. The entire piece is permeated by the initial neighboring-tone figure and related fig-ures derived from it. Example 2.10, a voice-leading sketch of the first eight measures, indicates the figure by means of brackets. In measures 17–24 (see Examples 2.9c and 2.9d), the right hand part, a polyphonic melody, contains two neighboring-tone motions, each extended over several measures. The first, e¹–f♯¹–e¹, belongs to the lower "voice" of the implied polyphony; the second, g¹–f♯¹–g¹, belongs to the upper (and main) "voice." These figures are expansions of the opening motive.
2. Example 2.10 also clarifies the meaning of the strange descending bass line of measures 1–5. The underlying idea is a downward transfer of the tonic (e–E), achieved by means of an arpeggiation. The unusual feature is that one tone of the arpeggiation, B, is

EXAMPLE 2.10: Beethoven, Sonata, Op. 14, No. 1, Allegretto, measures 1–8

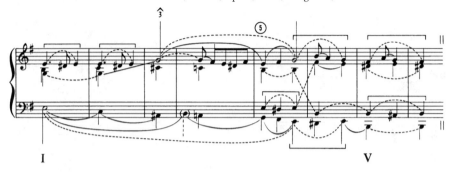

omitted; through this elision, A♯ (which would normally ascend to B) proceeds directly down to A♮ (compare Example 2.9d).

3. Measures 41–45 are difficult. As Example 2.11 indicates, the c² of measure 43 is a suspension resolving to b¹. The opening I moves to IV through a passing diminished seventh in ⁴₃ position (measures 43–44). The main top-voice motion is e¹–b¹–a¹; the bass passes from e through d to c.

Examples 2.9a and 2.9b   As in the Mozart Trio, the disproportion between the rapid structural cadence at the end and the prolonged harmonies earlier on is a striking feature of the first graph. A similar disproportion, involving the intermediate cadence that closes the first A section, can be observed in the second graph. Prolongational motions, on levels closer to the foreground, prepare the cadential rhythms—just as in the Mozart example.

However, this piece differs from the Mozart and Chopin examples in that the final tonic enters in a very strong metrical position—at the beginning of the twelve-measure codetta (measure 51). It is very instructive to compare the rhythmic effect of the final tonic, which falls on a true "downbeat," with that of the tonic that closes the first A section on a metrically weak measure (measure 16). Yet this significant difference would be minimized (or even ignored altogether) by an approach that in principle regards cadential tonics as "downbeats," no matter what the actual metrics might be.

Some readers might perhaps wonder whether measure 51, the beginning of the codetta, ought not to be heard as a weak measure reinterpreted as strong, for the tonic chord that begins there functions both as the goal of the preceding cadence and as the beginning of a new grouping. However, a necessary condition for such a reinterpretation is lacking here: the preceding phrase does not sound metrically incomplete, for it has a final (weak) mea-

EXAMPLE 2.11: Beethoven, Sonata, Op. 14, No. 1, Allegretto, measures 41–45

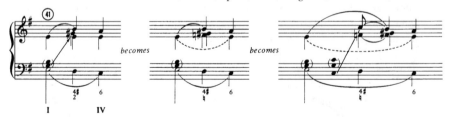

sure—measure 50. It would, therefore, require a mental contortion to understand measure 51 as weak and as belonging to the preceding group of measures.

One brief further comment about Examples 2.9a and 2.9b. In measure 30, I have shown the A♯ in the bass rather than the middle voice (where it occurs in the music) simply to be able to fit the graphs on a single staff. Example 2.9d shows the actual disposition; in any case, the two versions share more or less the same meaning, so the rearrangement changes nothing fundamental.

Examples 2.9c and 2.9d   The character of this Allegretto is, to a great extent, influenced by the numerous sforzandi that occur in measures 3, 18, and 45 and parallel places. They produce an unusually powerful effect and, perhaps, might bear out Schindler's otherwise surprising statement that Beethoven performed the piece almost as if it were an Allegro furioso.[24] A study of the music reveals that all of the sforzandi have at least one thing in common: they accentuate weak beats or measures and produce syncopated rhythms.

In the first eight-measure phrase, for example, rhythmic and textural changes produce strongly marked groupings of two measures. The two-measure hypermeasures, in fact, project so clearly as almost to create the impression of a 6/4 meter. I say "almost" advisedly, for actually writing the piece in six would create a very different (and much weaker) notational picture. There are, of course, four two-measure groups in the phrase; as my graphs indicate, I hear the phrase as metrically analogous to a measure of 4/4. The third measure of the phrase, therefore, would be equivalent to the second beat of a 4/4 measure; though strong in relation to the immediately preceding and following measures, it counts as weak within the larger metrical scheme (four "beats" of two measures each). In relation to this larger scheme, the sforzando in measure 3 creates a syncopation (see especially Example 2.9c).

The meaning of this sforzando relates to the tonal organization as well as to the meter. Example 2.10 indicates that g^1 ($\hat{3}$) of the main top-voice line is shifted away from the tonic chord to which it belongs and into a dissonant relation with the A♯ of the bass. The displacement of g^1, therefore, produces a syncopation that is not only rhythmic, but contrapuntal as well.[25]

The motivic connection of measures 17–24 with measures 1–8 is obvious. As a consequence, we hear the sforzandi of measures 18 and 20 as related to the one in measure 3. Nevertheless, the new sforzandi have a partly different character and meaning. First of all, they produce syncopations within a smaller time span, for they stress the second measure of a two-measure group. This contraction is reflected in the graphs; these syncopations appear at a later level (Example 2.9d) and stress eighth notes, not quarters. And second, the displaced g^1s now form only rhythmic syncopations, not contrapuntal ones. Reference to the score (or to Example 2.9e) shows that the shifted tones are consonant with the G chords against which they sound, as well as with the C chord that governs the section.

The sforzandi in measures 45–46 (Example 2.9d) produce syncopations within a still narrower metrical framework, for they fall on the second beat of a 3/4 measure. These syncopations, too, are purely rhythmic, not contrapuntal. Yet the drastic rhythmic effect results, in part, from the contradiction of a tonal implication. As Example 2.9d indicates, measures 45–47 (first beat) count as the expansion of a single measure; the expansion arises out of the repetition of the eighth-note figure of measure 44 and of the downbeat chord to which it leads. Now the beginning of the eighth-note figure (in measure 44) contains the resolution of a dissonant suspension; such a resolution, of course, must be played more softly than the preceding dissonance. But when the figure repeats in measures 45 and 46, the sforzandi fall on repetitions of the very note that had previously taken the resolution. This sudden reversal in dynamic "gesture" gives these syncopations an almost violent character.

All of these syncopations that we have cited fall on the *second* unit of a metrical group. The syncopation in measure 3 falls on the second of four hypermeasures within an eight-measure phrase. The one in measure 18 falls on the second measure of a two-measure hypermeasure. And the one in measure 45 falls on the second beat of the measure. As the piece moves forward, each "new" syncopation occurs on the same "beat" as the preceding one, only measured against a faster pulse. This compression, if one can call it that, contributes greatly to the developing momentum of the piece.

Schubert, "Valse Sentimentale," Op. 50, No. 13

Graphic Notation   The last piece that I shall discuss will be the A-major Waltz from Schubert's Op. 50 (Example 2.12). I have used the same scale of reduction for these graphs as

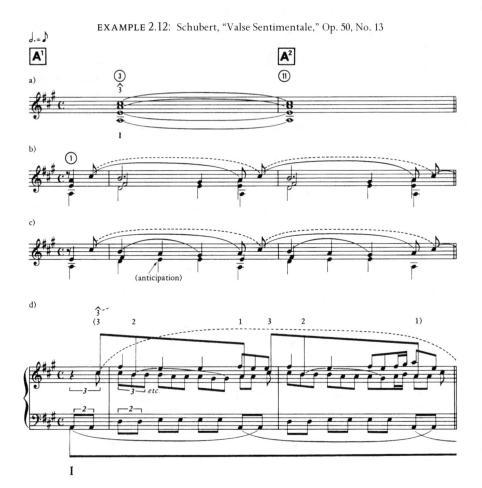

EXAMPLE 2.12: Schubert, "Valse Sentimentale," Op. 50, No. 13

for those of the Beethoven example: a 3/4 measure in the piece becomes an eighth note in the graphs; more important, a hypermeasure of two measures becomes a quarter-note beat. Such hypermeasures occur very prominently in this piece—more so than in any of the other three I have discussed. This is partly because the bass moves almost every two measures, and where it does not (measure 7 and parallel places), a $^6_4$ moves to a V^7. The most striking rhythmic feature of the piece, the cross-rhythm of the right-hand part, also emphasizes two-measure units: the right hand sets up a secondary meter of 3/2 against the 3/4 pattern of the left-hand part.

Texture and Form   The right hand plays two melodic lines written in free imitation: The lower of these lines (starting on c♯² in measure 2) carries the main melodic motion and is, in general, more active than the upper one. The upper line, therefore, functions as a secondary part placed over the main one. A curious feature of the upper line is its beginning on f♯², a tone foreign to tonic harmony (the f♯², of course, is the upper neighbor of e²). A glance at the Waltz that precedes this one helps to explain the emphasis on f♯² in our piece; Op. 50, No. 12, is in D major, with f♯² as its most prominent melodic tone. The f♯² forms a link between the two Waltzes; such links occur fairly often in a chain of short pieces.

The Waltz is written in ABA form with varied repeats of the A section. Taking the repeats into account, we might represent the form as A¹A²‖:BA³:‖. The varied repetitions of the A section change it only very slightly, but where so much repetition takes place, even slight changes assume significance. Of these changes, perhaps the most important occur at or near the cadences. Thus, at the first cadence (measures 8–9), the main melodic line settles on its goal, a¹. However, the secondary line above it remains immobilized on e². At the second cadence (measures 16–17), both lines lead to the tonic; the cadence, therefore, is stronger. And at the end of the piece (measures 34–37), both lines resume their original registers after a sojourn in the higher octave; again, as at the second cadence, the two lines move to the tonic. The final cadence, therefore, is the strongest of all.

Example 2.12a   The first of the graphs represents a level of middleground very close to the background of the piece. I regard the twelve measures of the B section as resulting from the expansion of an eight-measure phrase, as we shall see when we discuss Example 2.12d. Therefore, the B section is represented by one measure of 4/4 (eight eighth notes, equivalent to eight measures of 3/4 in the piece). The first complete phrase begins in measure 3. I have therefore left out of the graph the opening two measures, whose rather special meaning becomes clear only from a perspective slightly closer to the foreground of the piece.

One aspect of the tonal structure must be mentioned here. The B section is based upon a prolonged c♯-major chord: III♯³ in A major. As the graph indicates, I hear this chord as passing to the II⁶ of measure 29, which belongs to the final A section. Example 2.13 adds some explanatory detail and shows that the bass tone, c♯, supports and makes consonant a passing G♯ in the middle voice. It might seem plausible, at first, to understand the C♯ chord as the main connection between I and V, thus: I–III♯–V; in that case, the II⁶ would assume the status of a passing chord. But such a reading would contradict a chief feature of the Waltz: the fact that the II⁶, most unusually, occurs at the "downbeats" of all three A sections.

Examples 2.12b and 2.12c   At the level of prolongation shown in Example 2.12b, the meaning of the first two measures begins to become clear. In order to understand them, let us compare the opening of the Waltz with the Chopin Prelude. Both pieces begin with tonic harmony in the left-hand part alone. In the Prelude, the tonic persists beyond the introductory measures and continues through the next four-measure group. To leave out the two introductory measures, therefore, would not change the tonal structure at all, though it would disfigure the Prelude in other ways. In the Waltz, on the other hand, I moves to II⁶ at measure 3. To omit the first two measures would be to suppress the opening tonic altogether; more than that, it would make the whole piece pointless and nonsensical. For a basic

EXAMPLE 2.13: Schubert, "Valse Sentimentale," Op. 50, No. 13, II⁶ as a goal of motion

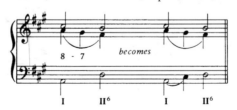

premise of the Waltz is a version of the age-old musical paradox, "ma fin est mon commencement." Schubert places the tonic in the two measures before the first strong downbeat; in the light of subsequent events we might say that the tonic falls in measures 7 and 8 of an incomplete phrase. The closing tonics of all three A sections also fall in measures 7 and 8; by analogy with the beginning, therefore, the cadential tonics also function as the initial chords of the subsequent phrases.

The first two measures also determine the end of the B section (measures 29–30), for a convincing reprise requires two introductory measures and the eighth-note upbeat figure of the right hand. But here a problem arises. At the beginning of the piece (and also at measures 9–10) the two measures in question contain a structural tonic. At the reprise, however, this would be an impossibility; the main connection in the bass, C♯ to D, excludes a structural return to I at this point. Luckily, an alternative solution exists. A 5–6 motion above C♯ (together with a return from E♯ to E♮) produces an A chord (Example 2.12b). This chord, solely a product of voice leading, takes on more stability if the root, A, occurs in the bass (Example 2.12c). Even in root position, however, the A chord does not function as a true tonic, as a beginning or goal of motion. It is clearly "on the way" from the C♯ chord to the II⁶. But it is close enough in sound to the beginning, and especially to measures 9–10, to lead convincingly into the reprise. Incidentally, the seventh, G♮, derives from the last eighth note of measure 10.[26]

Example 2.12c helps to explain the $^6_4$ chord of measures 5–6 and parallel places. This $^6_4$ seems to be of the familiar cadential type, with V in the bass and normal stepwise motion to tones of V⁷ in the upper parts. Rhythmically, however, the $^6_4$ is anything but normal, for it occurs in a weaker metrical position than the V⁷ to which it resolves. The weak metrical position of the $^6_4$, is not immediately evident from *looking* at the music, for the larger meter is, of course, not notated. But it is easily heard. As the graph indicates, this $^6_4$ arises out of an *anticipation* in the bass that counterpoints the passing fourth in the main melodic part. In the normal cadential $^6_4$, by contrast, the bass tone is stable; the fourth functions as a *suspension* (sometimes an accented passing tone) in one of the upper parts. In the Waltz, the metrically weak $^6_4$ allows the final tonic of the phrase also to fall in a metrically weak position (fourth hypermeasure)—a necessity here, since this tonic represents the two introductory measures. In *Free Composition*, Schenker cites a metrically weak $^6_4$ in measure 38 of Chopin's Waltz, Op. 64, No. 2; there, too, the $^6_4$ permits a weak final tonic.[27] Anticipating $^6_4$s are not frequent, but they occur from time to time, especially in music of the nineteenth century. Schubert and Chopin probably use them more than any other great composers, though examples can also be found in music by Schumann, Mendelssohn, and others. They are hardly ever mentioned in theory books.[28]

Example 2.12d   This graph shows the foreground of the piece, including the secondary, "covering" voice of the right-hand part and the changes in register effected by this secondary voice. For the most part, the graph is self-explanatory. However, some explanation must be given of the B section, with its expansion of eight measures to twelve. That the twelve measures do, in fact, grow out of eight measures in the middleground is borne out by examining how they built. Note that measures 24–27 repeat measures 20–23 and that measure 23 has a double meaning: the goal of the preceding four measures, it is also (exactly like measure 19) the beginning of the next motion. The listener, so to speak, goes over the same ground twice; when he arrives at measure 27, he is visiting measure 23 for the second time. Without this repetition, the section would contain eight measures, as shown in Examples 2.12a, 2.12b, and 2.12c.

Example 2.12d also points to other interesting features of this section. Note, first of all, that the C♯ triad—the main chord of the section—always appears in a strong metrical position, on an odd-numbered "beat." This is in marked contrast to the A sections, where the tonic chord is always metrically weak. The strong position of the C♯ chord furthers the coherence of the piece, for it permits measures 29–30, which represent the first two measures, to fall in a weak hypermeasure.

A curious feature of the melody accompanies the metrically strong C♯ chord. For the most part, measures 20–23 are an almost exact transposition of measures 14–17, the cadential measures of the A² section. But, as the graph shows, the metrics are reversed: measures 20–23 reach their goal on a strong measure, whereas measure 17, the goal of the A² section, is weak. Because of the rhythmic alteration, the melodic figure becomes almost a new motive. And this at least partly explains the repetition and the consequent expansion of the section. For to present a striking new idea once only would make it sound arbitrary and unconvincing. At least one repetition (exact or disguised) is required to make the idea a "motive," that is, an element in the compositional design. Incidentally, the abrupt tonal contrast between the C♯ triad (measures 27–28) and the seventh chord on A (measures 29–30) can easily mislead the listener into hearing measure 29 as a downbeat. The performer must take care to project measures 29–30 as an upbeat to the II⁶ in measure 31.

Some Implications of Durational Graphs

The Fundamental Structure

I should like to conclude with a few general observations about the durational graphs. The first has to do with leaving the Fundamental Structure out of the graphs; each of the four analyses begins with a level of middleground, specifically with that level of middleground where the form of the piece first becomes apparent. As I explained in my earlier essay, I believe that the Fundamental Structure does have some rhythmic implications, but that these arise out of tonal function only and have nothing to do with duration.[29] To include the Fundamental Structure in durational graphs, therefore, would make little sense. To be sure, one might show the *pacing* of the structural progression in these graphs. One would first establish a "basic duration" for the piece, that is, the number of measures it would contain without expansions (or elisions) that belong to the middleground or foreground. (If the piece is short and clearly articulated, we do, I think, measure its flow against such a basic duration, though not usually in a fully conscious way.) We could then coordinate the structural progression with this basic duration.

But to do so would be misleading, for the basic duration takes on meaning only in relation to the groupings of measures and to the form. In the Schubert Waltz, for example, the basic duration is thirty-two measures: four phrases of eight measures each. Example 2.14 shows the background progression of the Waltz distributed over this duration, using the same scale of reduction as in Example 2.12. Since the C♯ chord of the B section is not part of the structural framework, I have not included it in the graph. But the omission obliterates any

EXAMPLE 2.14: Schubert, "Valse Sentimentale," Op. 50, No. 13, Fundamental Structure

trace of the piece's form. For without the contrast between A and C♯, there is no B section, no ABA (or A¹A²BA³) form, no inner necessity for four phrases or for a basic duration of thirty-two measures. The graph shows the pacing of the structural progression, but it does so too abstractly to demonstrate a convincing connection with the thirty-two measure time span. Only when we take the C♯ chord into account—only with the middleground, therefore—does the basic duration have meaning.

Since the form of a piece always relates to the prolongation, segmentation, or repetition of its structure and never simply to the structure itself, we can safely assume that we would find similar difficulty in applying durational proportion to the background level of any piece.

Larger Metrical Organization

In discussing the rhythmic features of the four pieces that I have analyzed, I have proceeded on the assumption that a *metrical* relation of strong to weak exists between the downbeats of successive measures. And that a similar relation exists between the downbeats of successive hypermeasures, if such hypermeasures are clearly in evidence. I assume that such a relation exists because I hear it in these pieces (and in many others). Some readers may be skeptical about the possibility of metrical organization on so large a scale. If they are, I would ask them to consider the syncopated effect of the sforzando in measure 3 of the Beethoven example and the upbeat character of the first two measures of the Schubert Waltz, as well as the unusual sound of the ⁶₄ chords throughout the Waltz. How are we to understand such phenomena if not in relation to a larger metrical scheme? If we understand "meter" as "measure," then the durational graphs show metrical organization on a scale still larger than that of measures or hypermeasures within a phrase. For each of the pieces analyzed, the level nearest the background (Examples 2.4a, 2.8a, 2.9a, and 2.12a) shows a division into two, three, or four *equal* segments of time, thus:

Chopin	two segments of eight measures
Mozart	three segments of eight measures
Beethoven	three segments of sixteen measures (plus codetta)
Schubert	four segments of eight measures (perhaps two segments of sixteen measures: A¹A²‖:BA³:‖)

Each of these large segments is, in turn, subdivided into two equal spans of four or eight measures. And the listener "measures" the music's flow quite as much against these large periodicities as against the smaller ones of measures, beats, and fractions of beats. As the graphs approach the foreground of the piece, the smaller metrical units become more and more prominent, as do the tonal and durational features that contradict and modify the large symmetries.

When we speak of "meter" we normally mean something more than the division of time into equal (or equivalent) segments; we mean a pattern composed of strong and weak impulses in some kind of regular alternation. That a metrical relation of strong and weak exists over the very large subdivisions of time seems doubtful to me, for reasons that I explained in my earlier essay.[30] And even if we were to assume that, say, measure 33 of the Beethoven example is "weaker" than measure 1, the assumption would lead to no further insights into the music, at least none that I am aware of. But at our present state of knowledge, it would be premature—and, therefore, wrong—to close our minds even to such seemingly doubtful possibilities.[31]

For this essay, I selected pieces in which groups of measures exhibit clearly defined metrical organization. To forestall possible misunderstandings, I should perhaps mention that there are pieces—indeed, whole categories of pieces—where the groupings are less regular. I have sometimes found that durational reduction can reveal interesting aspects of the free rhythmic structure of such pieces. But they are more difficult to understand than the ones that I have presented and, therefore, are less suitable for an introductory discussion.

The Utility of Durational Reductions

This essay has shown, I hope, that durational graphs can be a useful analytic tool. The analysis of the Chopin Prelude, for example, demonstrated that the "II$^6_5$" of measures 22–23 is not a harmonic entity—a fact that eluded even Schenker. The anticipatory character of the $^6_4$ chords in the Schubert Waltz, the syncopated entrance of the $\hat{3}$ in the Beethoven Allegretto, the rhythmic structure of the expanded B section in the Mozart Trio—all these and many other rhythmic features are conveyed by the durational graphs with great clarity. The pacing of tonal events with respect both to phrase structure and to form also emerges more clearly from durational than from voice-leading graphs.

At the same time, certain inescapable disadvantages limit the usefulness of these graphs. As I mentioned earlier, the rhythmic notation makes it more difficult to show structural levels and, in general, makes the voice leading harder to perceive. This problem is minimized in simple pieces, such as the four analyzed here. With longer and more complicated works, the deficiencies of the notation would soon make themselves felt. In addition, at or near the foreground of the piece, the reduced durations suggest a tempo several times faster than the real one, and, consequently, produce a distorted picture. (This drawback, incidentally, does not exist in Schenker's rhythmic graphs of the foreground, for they use the actual time values of the piece.) And finally, the smaller details of rhythm, those at the most immediate level of foreground, do not show up at all in these reductions.

The solution to these problems seems simple and obvious. It is to use the durational reductions only where they reveal important features of the piece more clearly than other methods would. And, where necessary, to offset their deficiencies by using them together with voice-leading graphs. The rhythmic reductions will probably prove most useful as an adjunct to graphs of the voice leading and harmony, used to clarify some otherwise obscure aspect of the rhythmic organization.

Notes

1. Ludwig van Beethoven, *Konversationshefte*, vol. 5, ed. Karl-Heinz Köhler, Grita Herre, and Peter Pötschner (Leipzig: VEB Deutscher Verlag für Musik, 1970), book 57 (end of February to mid-March 1824), p. 198, also cited in Hans Kann's preface to J. B. Cramer, *21 Etüden für Klavier* (Vienna: Universal, 1974), p. vii. The original German reads as follows: "Die verlängerten Rhythmen in Ihren Werken liegen nicht in der Berechnung, sondern in der Natur der Melodie und öfters sogar in der Harmonie—habe ich Recht?" At that time, the word "rhythm" was often used to mean a group of measures or, broadly speaking, a phrase; Schindler probably employed it in this sense.

2. Recent investigation has shown that many of Schindler's entries in the conversation books were added by him after Beethoven's death.

3. Carl Schachter, "Rhythm and Linear Analysis: A Preliminary Study," *Music Forum* 4 (1976), pp. 281–334, and reprinted as the first essay in the present collection, hereafter referred to as Rhythm I.

4. Edward T. Cone, *Musical Form and Musical Performance* (New York: Norton, 1968), pp. 79–80.

5. Ludwig van Beethoven, *32 Sonatas for the Pianoforte*, ed. Artur Schnabel (New York: Simon and Schuster, 1935), vol. 2, p. 804, footnote *a*.

6. The sketch is transcribed by Karl Michael Komma in Beethoven, *Die Klaviersonate As-Dur Opus 110: Beiheft zur Faksimile-Ausgabe* (Stuttgart: Ichthys Verlag, 1967), p. 11.

7. Roy Travis, "Toward a New Concept of Tonality?" *Journal of Music Theory* 3, no. 2 (1959), pp. 274–75.

8. Grosvenor Cooper and Leonard B. Meyer, *The Rhythmic Structure of Music* (Chicago: University of Chicago Press, 1960), pp. 83–87.

9. Wallace Berry, *Structural Functions in Music* (Englewood Cliffs: Prentice-Hall, 1976), chapter 4, especially pp. 334, 352, and 395–96. Also see his review of Cone's *Musical Form and Musical Performance* in *Perspectives of New Music* 9, no. 2–10, vol. 1 (1971), pp. 280–81.

10. Heinrich Schenker, *Der Tonwille*, vol. 2 (Vienna: A. Gutmann Verlag, 1922), p. 30.

11. Heinrich Schenker, *Free Composition*, trans. and ed. Ernst Oster (New York: Longman, 1979), pp. 125–26.

12. Schenker, *Der Tonwille*, vol. 2, p. 30. Each 2/4 measure of Schenker's durational reduction (Example 2.3a) becomes a strong or weak *beat* in the metrical schema. Thus the first grouping $(-\ \smile)$ represents measures 1–4 of the piece.

13. My analysis of the tonal events of the Prelude is based on Schenker's in *Free Composition*, figure 76/2. My reading differs from Schenker's in a few details.

14. Rhythm I, p. 305; this volume, p. 32.

15. Schenker, *Free Composition*, p. 121.

16. Rhythm I, pp. 329–34; this volume, pp. 47–49.

17. In *Free Composition*, p. 114, Schenker cites this passage (in his Figure 76/2) as one where we might hear either a single harmony (IV^{5-6}) or two harmonies (IV–II). But if we take the hypermeter into account, we cannot infer a functional II.

18. See W. A. Mozart, *Symphony No. 35 in D, K.385, "Haffner" Symphony*, facsimile ed., with an introduction by Sydney Beck (New York: Oxford University Press, 1968).

19. Schenker, *Free Composition*, figure 22b. Forte's comments are found in "Schenker's Conception of Musical Structure," *Journal of Music Theory* 3, no. 1 (1959), pp. 9–14, reprinted in *Readings in Schenker Analysis and Other Approaches*, ed. Maury Yeston (New Haven: Yale University Press, 1977), pp. 12–18.

20. Schenker, *Free Composition*, p. 37 and figure 21b.

21. Ibid., p. 122.

22. Ibid., pp. 124–25.

23. As in measure 20 of Beethoven's Sonata, Op. 2, No. 1, first movement, discussed on p. 56.

24. Anton Schindler, *Biographie von Ludwig van Beethoven*, 2d ed. (Münster: Aschendorff, 1845), p. 234.

While it appears in this and the first edition (1840), as well as in Ignaz Moscheles's translation (1841), this statement is absent from the third edition (1860), on which Donald MacArdle based his English edition, *Beethoven As I Knew Him* (Chapel Hill: University of North Carolina Press, 1966; reprinted, New York; Norton, 1972).

25. In the Chopin Prelude, the $\hat{3}$ is also shifted to the third measure of the phrase. But the effect of syncopation does not arise in the foreground, partly because there is no unusual dynamic stress and partly because tonic harmony continues—the b^2 is a locally consonant tone.

26. A similar apparent tonic that results from a 5–6 over III (in this case, ♭III) occurs in Brahms's Waltz, Op. 39, No. 8, measures 21–24.

27. Schenker, *Free Composition*, p. 121, in a reference to figure 137/1. Schenker does not call the bass of the $^6_4$ an anticipation; I believe that it is one, just as in the Schubert Waltz.

28. But see Edward Aldwell and Carl Schachter, *Harmony and Voice Leading*, 2d ed. (New York: Harcourt Brace Jovanovich, 1989), pp. 298–99.

29. Rhythm I, pp. 317–18; this volume, pp. 38–39.

30. Rhythm I, pp. 308–9; this volume, pp. 34–35.

31. I plan to discuss meter—including large-scale meter—more fully in the subsequent essay.

Aspects of Meter

Measurement began our might

(W. B. Yeats)

Meter is a problem. Theorists investigating rhythm have reached no consensus about such fundamental issues as the nature of the metrical accent, the possibility of meter over large spans of time, and the status of discrepancies between the meter as notated and some of the obvious rhythmic emphases in a piece. When different theorists attempt a metrical analysis of the same piece or passage, the divergent results can be striking indeed. The classic instance is that most overanalyzed piece of music, the theme for the variations that open Mozart's Piano Sonata in A Major, K.331. Hugo Riemann maintains that Mozart failed to notate the true downbeats, and he "improves" the notation by putting bar lines in the middle of Mozart's measures. Joel Lester also sees a contradiction between Mozart's notation and the actual metrics, but his interpretation involves changes from 6/8 to 12/8 to 6/8 to 9/8 and back to 6/8. Schenker accepts Mozart's 6/8 time; in addition he infers metrical organization over four-measure spans. But Edward Cone and Robert Morgan refuse to accept a four-measure hypermeter and opt instead for a rhythmic pattern that encompasses a beginning accent, a transitional segment, and an end accent.[1]

To be sure, K.331 is an extreme case; the number of its tribulations among the analysts calls to mind the fate of Lavinia in *Titus Andronicus*. But if K.331 is an extreme, it is an extreme that illuminates the norm. After all, the theme's metrical structure is not unusually complex and its divergent—sometimes diametrically opposed—analyses must result less from particular difficulties of the piece than from more general problems in dealing with meter. One would probably find as many discrepancies among analyses of other pieces if one could find other pieces that had been analyzed as much. (The published analyses of K.331 also disagree about tonal structure, but these disagreements involve rather more rarefied judgments; to the best of my knowledge nobody has yet proposed that E, rather than A, should be regarded as the tonic.)

Originally published in *Music Forum* 6/1 (1987), pp. 1–59.

Theorists are not the only musicians who have problems with meter. The greatest composers will sometimes change their minds, perhaps more than once, about the number or the location of notated downbeats. Mozart and Schubert, to cite two, have rebarred otherwise finished compositions.[2] And metrical problems can be among the most serious difficulties that confront the conscientious performer. He must decide what to do when the time signature seems not to correspond to the actual meter of a passage. He must decide how much emphasis he wants to give to the metrical schema, he must know what unit of meter (beat, measure, group of measures) he ought to bring out most strongly, and he must reconcile—or at least adjudicate—conflicts between the metrical and the tonal or durational emphases of a passage.

As the title of this essay suggests, I am going to concentrate on a few crucial aspects of meter rather than attempt an exhaustive survey of the subject. I do not propose to offer solutions to all of the analytic problems associated with the aspects of meter that I shall discuss; indeed, I shall try to show that a problematic character is inherent in metrical organization. Although I shall present some new ideas, my conception of meter is more traditional than that of many recent writers. In particular I am more reluctant than some of my colleagues to dismiss the composer's notation (the ghost of Riemann seems to be walking abroad these days). The core of the essay lies in the analysis and discussion of the musical citations. As in my two previous essays, my point of departure will be perception.[3] But some of the pieces that I shall cite are difficult, and we shall reach a point with them where hearing will require thought as a companion and guide.

The Metrical Accent

Equal Divisions of Time

Every piece of music is, among other things, a pattern of durations—or better, a complex of such patterns. For duration to become even a moderately important issue in a piece, the pattern must become intelligible to the listener, who must be able to compare one span of time with another and thus intuit relationships among the various durations that make up the pattern. In many kinds of music, including Western tonal music, such comparison is made possible by the articulation of regularly recurring equal segments of time.[4] Some of these time spans arise directly out of the pacing of sounds; others—most obviously the larger ones—must be inferred by the listener out of patterns of long and short, of loud and soft, of repetition and change, of voice leading and harmony, of all of these elements and others, singly and in any imaginable combination.

The equal segments of time that arise in these ways participate directly in a piece's rhythmic design. Everyone will agree that the awareness of beats, measures, consistent divisions of beats, and consistent groupings of measures forms part of the normal experience of listening to music. In addition, the equal time spans provide a standard of measurement for some of the divergent, non-recurring durations that might appear in a piece, and thus they help to integrate them into the larger rhythmic pattern. No listener could relate a lone five-measure group to the four-measure groups that preceded it were it not for the persistence of the measure as a common unit.

To the extent that we hear spans of time, the boundaries that articulate them must necessarily attract our attention, for it is at these boundaries that the durations themselves become available to our consciousness. Let us say that we are listening to a succession of six eighth notes:

♪ ♪ ♪ ♪ ♪ ♪

If for any reason we infer three quarter-note spans:

1 & 2 & 3 &
♪ ♪ ♪ ♪ ♪ ♪

then the time points marked "1," "2," and "3" will attract a measure of attention solely because they articulate the quarter-note spans. The points marked "&" will attract no such attention, though the notes that occur at these points might attract special attention on other grounds.

If one condition is met, the listener's awareness of time spans automatically produces accents that punctuate his experience of the music; *these accents result from the heightened attention attracted by the boundary points of the spans.* The necessary condition is the presence of non-accents, for a thing is accented only in relation to a comparable thing that is not. In our succession of six eighth notes, the non-accents are provided by the boundary points of the second, fourth, and sixth notes. Accents produced by the awareness of time spans differ from all others in that they arise out of temporal position alone and not from any special emphasis in the composition or its performance. Of course some kind of emphasis is required initially in order to make the listener aware of the spans, but *equal divisions*, once established, can persist in the listener's consciousness without special sensory reinforcement. Indeed, they can persist for a time in the face of strongly contradictory signals. And even when sonic emphases coincide—as they often will—with these accents, the emphasis and the accent produced by perceived time spans are two separate events. Once the listener becomes aware of recurrent durational units—beats, measures, and larger periodicities—that awareness, in and of itself, adds another layer of accentuation to the musical image. The accents thus produced are true *metrical accents*—metrical because they arise directly out of the listener's awareness of the equal divisions of time that measure the music's flow.

Levels of Pulse

It is a truism that meter arises out of the interaction of strong and weak beats. That means that meter will never result from a single string of equal time spans. At least two series must be present, coordinated so that all points that demarcate the longer spans at higher levels simultaneously mark off shorter spans at all lower levels. Thus in a passage in 9/8 time, the beginning of each measure also begins the first dotted quarter-note span within the measure. Any boundary that marks off only a single level counts as "weak" compared to one that marks off two levels, and one that marks off two levels will be weak compared to one that marks off three. In our 9/8 passage, the weakest boundaries are those that demarcate only eighths (one level); those that demarcate dotted quarters as well as eighths are stronger; those that demarcate whole measures, dotted quarters, and eighths are the strongest of the three. This aspect of musical meter has been explained in detail by several writers, among them Arthur Komar, Maury Yeston, and Fred Lerdahl and Ray Jackendoff.[5] I recommend their writings to the attention of any reader for whom my explanation has been too sketchy.

A listener who becomes aware of this layered patterning of time spans will necessarily hear metrical accents at the intersections of all but the lowest-level (shortest) spans. Since they result from the listener's awareness, metrical accents might seem to inhabit a realm of pure subjectivity. Such a view would be only partially true, however, for the listener's response is conditioned by signals built into the composition. In an approximate way the effect of metrical accents resembles the effect of round numbers. The number fifty stands out because it forms a multiple focus of orientation for the person counting: it completes a group of ten and (among other things) also completes half a hundred. Any merchant would agree that $50.00 is an "accented" price compared with $49.99. That the psychological difference is so much greater than the monetary one is, in a sense, a subjective response of the purchaser, but it is a response to important properties of the decimal number system.

The Metrical Accent Accrues to the Compositional Event

A point in time can never receive an emphasis; only an event that occurs at the point can. The metrical accent, therefore, always colors the event—tone, harmony, occasionally even silence—that falls on the favored point. Conceptually the accent is localized at the boundary point, but the accent as embodied in the compositional event must shade off through time. This bears directly on one of the most obvious aspects of metrical organization: the emphasis on beginnings. The accent occurs on the boundary between two time spans, an old one and a new one. If only because of its novelty, the beginning of the new span attracts more attention than the end of the old one, and the emphasis accrues to the event that the new span brings to the listener.

Metrical Accentuation over Long Spans

An emphasis on beginnings is in seeming contradiction to the directional, goal-oriented character of most tonal motion. It is perhaps for this reason that so many writers on musical rhythm insist that phrase rhythm is end-accented and view with distaste the notion that a phrase of four measures might have a metrical organization similar to that of a measure containing four beats. The differences, of course, are important. A span of four measures can accommodate a complete harmonic progression or diminutional entity and thus can contain a complete motion to a significant goal. Very seldom can the same be true for a brief span like a measure. Within long time spans, therefore, meter may very well recede in importance compared to tonal motion and the tonal rhythm associated with it.

Yet if the long span is a durational unit that recurs, and if it is articulated by a network of regularly recurring smaller spans, it has a metrical organization which in principle is no different from that of a measure. A simple piece discussed in Chapter 2, the Trio of the Menuetto from Mozart's "Haffner" Symphony, provides a convenient example.[6] The piece divides into three phrases: of eight measures, twelve (representing an expanded eight), and eight. The first phrase divides into four and four; each four-measure segment divides into two twos; each two-measure segment divides into one plus one. Now the spans of two and four measures form important durational elements that are articulated by recurring spans at lower levels. Therefore the beginning of each two-measure segment is metrically stronger than any subsequent point within the segment, and the beginnings of measures 1 and 5 (which demarcate four-measure spans) are stronger than any subsequent point within the four measures. Finally, since the eight-measure span of the phrase is itself an important and recurring durational unit, the downbeat of measure 1 is metrically stronger than any other point in the phrase, including the downbeat of measure 5.

What about extending this kind of metrical evaluation to still larger units? In the Mozart Trio, for example, might we infer a metrical relation of strong–weak between the downbeats of measures 1 and 9? The answer must be no. Time spans of twenty measures (the sum of the first two phrases) or of sixteen (the first phrase plus the eight measures that underlie the second) do not function as durational elements in the piece; there are no recurrent sixteen- or twenty-measure spans. Of course a special emphasis accrues to the downbeat of measure 1, partly because it is the first downbeat and partly because it carries the opening tonic. In a sense, therefore, the downbeat of measure 1 may indeed be "stronger" than that of measure 9. But its priority is not metrical; it results from what Lerdahl and Jackendoff call a "structural accent."[7] In another piece analyzed in Chapter 2, however, the Allegretto from Beethoven's Piano Sonata, Op. 14, No. 1, the sixteen-measure period is a recurrent durational unit.[8] In that piece the downbeat of measure 9 forms an interior punctuation within the sixteen-measure span, and it would make sense to regard the downbeat of measure 1 as stronger than that of measure 9. Between measures 1 and 17, though, there would be no strong–weak relation, at least no metrical one.

Do the large metrical spans of the Mozart and Beethoven examples (and countless other pieces) weaken the effect of goal-oriented tonal progression? Far from it. Directed tonal motion gains in intensity if it plays against the resistance, so to speak, of beginning-accented metrical patterning, for tension always requires the play of opposing forces. It is certainly no accident that the greater forward drive of Baroque tonal procedures, compared with those of the Renaissance, goes together with a greater insistence on beats and consistent groupings of beats, or that the music with the most highly developed control of large form (that of Haydn, Mozart, Beethoven, and Brahms) should be the music with the most elaborate and strongly articulated phrase structure.

An advantage of the way of conceiving the metrical accent that I have sketched here— deriving it from the perception of equal time spans—is that it provides a starting point for finding the largest metrically divided spans in a given piece or passage. The task of applying this principle can be far more challenging than it is in connection with the Mozart and Beethoven pieces that I have discussed. I should like therefore to cite at this point a piece which offers greater problems in metrical interpretation.

Beethoven, Sonata, Op. 27, No. 1, Allegro molto vivace, measures 1–41

I shall discuss here only the opening, C-minor, section of this movement, a scherzo in all but name; later in the essay I shall present a reading of the middle, A♭-major, section of the movement. The forty-one measures divide into three strains (ABA¹) of sixteen, eight, and seventeen measures; the seventeen measures are actually a sixteen-measure unit with a one-

EXAMPLE 3.1: Beethoven, Sonata, Op. 27, No. 1 (*Sonata quasi una Fantasia*), Allegro molto vivace, measures 1–41

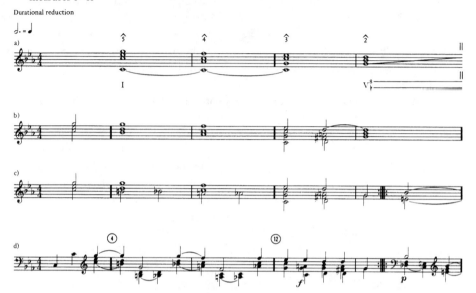

measure extension at the end. These divisions are clear and obvious; what is less obvious is the location of the strong (downbeat) measures. At first glance the piece might seem to scan in two-measure hypermeasures starting with a strong first measure. Contrasting registers (see measures 3–12), the change of the right hand's pattern in measure 3, and the sudden forte of measure 13 could easily suggest such a partitioning. In his discussion of this Sonata, Tovey, however, insists that measure 2, not measure 1, marks the first large-scale accent, and he points to the position of the repeat sign before measure 2 as evidence that Beethoven scanned it in this way.[9] I agree with Tovey's reading, which is also strongly supported by the tonal rhythms, especially the descending chromatic bass and diatonic soprano, whose steps coincide with Tovey's downbeat measures. In this piece the quasi-unison texture and the surface rhythms are so undifferentiated that tonal motion becomes the principal agent of metrical partitioning. The emphasized odd-numbered measures, then, would be interpreted as counterstresses that conflict with the metrical scheme rather than as downbeats.

Tovey does not discuss the possibility of inferring metrical groupings larger than two-measure units, but it seems to me not merely desirable but necessary to hear groups of at least four measures. This is because the reprise of the opening strain is not exact; it introduces 7–6 suspensions where the first part had only $^6_3$ chords (compare measures 28–35 with 4–11). The suspensions (mentioned by Tovey, incidentally) surely add another level of metric patterning to the two-measure groups, for each suspension and each resolution occupies two measures. Measure 28 must be stronger not only than measure 29, which continues the suspension, but also than measure 30, which contains the resolution. Except for the upper voice with its suspensions, the first twelve measures of the reprise correspond exactly to the opening strain, and the two strains surely scan in the same way. As a consequence, the very first downbeat on the four-measure level occurs in measure 4, measures 1–3 forming an extended upbeat. (Schnabel, in his edition of the Beethoven sonatas, scans this movement

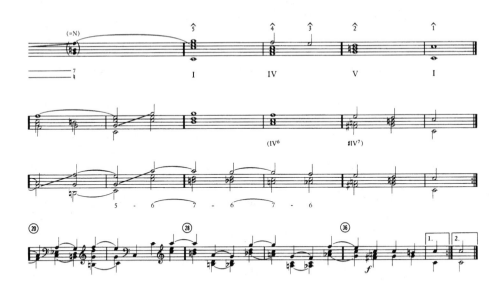

incorrectly, reading measures 2–5 as a four-measure group and indicating no scansion in the suspension passage of the reprise.)[10]

The three-measure upbeat is depicted in level d of Example 3.1, which is a durational reduction of the C-minor section. In this reduction I represent the 3/4 measure of the piece by a quarter note and the four-measure hypermeasure by a 4/4 measure. The analysis indicates that I do not regard the four-measure hypermeasures as the largest metrically organized spans; the heavy bar lines demarcate eight-measure groups. Measures 4–7 and 8–11 obviously combine into a single unit passing to the G-minor cadence at the end of the strain. The next four-measure group (measures 12–15) leads into a cadential measure that is complemented by the repetition of measures 1–3 and (at the *seconda volta*) by the three measures of preparation for IV (measures 17–19), so that an eight-measure periodicity is continued. Comparison of Example 3.1d with the score will show that this periodicity is maintained virtually without modification throughout the C-minor part of the movement (the only change is the expansion of measure 40 into a two-measure unit, measures 40–41).

Recognition of the eight-measure groups sheds light on the strangest tonal-rhythmic feature of the piece: the "premature" arrival on I in measure 24, one measure before the reprise. This occurs because the reprise, like the beginning, starts with a three-measure upbeat—starts, that is, with the *second* measure of a four-measure group. Unlike the opening strain, however, the reprise cannot start out of nowhere; something has to occupy the first measure of the group. That "something" cannot be anything but I if the parallelism between measures 17–20 and 21–24 is to be carried out. (The parallelism is a virtual necessity here, for the new idea of measures 17–20 demands some kind of repetition.) Very significantly, the I of measure 24 occupies the beginning of a four-measure group but *not* the beginning of an eight-measure one. Because the premature tonic is not in the strongest metrical position, its return carries with it something of the upbeat character of the opening.

Example 3.1 shows many interesting rhythmic features of the piece, many more than I have space to discuss here. We shall return to some of them later in the essay; the rest I leave to the interested reader to find out for himself. I must, however, comment briefly on one important feature that bears directly on our present discussion. Level a shows that the opening section and the reprise form an antecedent–consequent pair brought about through the interruption of the Fundamental Structure; the brief B section (see levels b and c) crystallizes around the seventh above V as preparation for the reprise. Since the two A sections occupy sixteen-measure spans (extended to seventeen in the reprise), and since the symmetry of their antecedent–consequent relation forms such a striking element in the foreground design, I regard the sixteen-measure span as a metrically organized unit—the largest such unit in the piece. I would therefore infer a metrical relation of strong–weak between the downbeats of measures 4 and 12. The sixteen-measure unit, obviously, does not carry over into the B section and hence does not pervade the entire form, as it does in the Allegretto of Op. 14, No. 1. In my view this fact does not invalidate the idea that the sixteen-measure span functions as a metrically organized unit. It suggests, rather, that the form is not so much a fully developed ABA[1] as it is an antecedent–consequent pair (AA[1]) separated by a brief extension that adds a seventh to the interrupting dominant.

Durational Levels

The Inference of Intermediate Levels

The long and short time spans that make up a metrical schema act upon each other in different ways: the long ones *group* the short ones and the short ones *subdivide* the long ones. Describing these functions in relation to perception, we might say that hearing the long spans makes us *differentiate* the short ones by means of strong and weak attacks, while hearing the short spans allows us to *measure* the temporal distance between the larger beats. In his interesting discussion of meter, Maury Yeston points out that a listener can transform a series of undifferentiated pulses into a metrically organized succession by mentally supplying the necessary larger groupings.[11] Related to this possibility is a fundamental component of the experience of meter: the inference of an intermediate level (or perhaps more than one) between a series of short and a series of long spans. Inferring intermediate levels makes it possible to "get" the meter in passages that do not literally articulate the beats.

In the first measure of *Eine kleine Nachtmusik* (Example 3.2a) the quickest notes produce a level of eighth notes, while pattern-repetition and tonal rhythm articulate a level of half notes. Nothing in the music articulates a level of quarter notes, but any competent listener would infer this missing level, for the quarter note is the only span that would fit together with the eighths and halves in a single metrical schema.[12] In the Chopin excerpt of Example 3.2b, two levels—eighths and quarters—are missing between the constant sixteenth-note motion and the half measures articulated by registral contrast and dynamic accents. Here pattern-repetition produces an unequal, syncopated division of each half note into three, three, and two sixteenths. In order to hear the syncopated effect of the repeated figure, the listener would have to supply the missing two levels by inference.

There are limits to the extent to which one can infer missing levels. Between any series of slow pulses (e.g., ♩·♩·♩·) and another moving six times as fast (♩ ♩ ♩ ♩ ♩), there is room

EXAMPLE 3.2: (A) Mozart, *Eine kleine Nachtmusik*, K.525, first movement

(B) Chopin, Etude, Op. 25, No. 12

for only one missing level. Since six is the product of two and three, the missing level will either divide the long pulses in two and group the short pulses in threes:

or divide by three and group into twos:

If the short pulses remain undifferentiated, the listener has no clue as to which intermediate pulse "ought" to be inferred. This ambiguity, of course, extends to multiples of six, only there will be more than a single missing level.

Such is the case in the first measure of Schubert's Piano Sonata in G Major (Example 3.3); the movement's 12/8 meter becomes evident only in measure 2. Aside from the ambiguity inherent in subdivisions of six and its multiples, the ratio between the long spans of measure 1 (dotted halves) and the short spans (sixteenths) is so great that the quick pulses cannot function as an adequate measure of the slow ones.

EXAMPLE 3.3: Schubert, Sonata, D.894, Op. 78, first movement

As part of what one might call the composing-out of meter, one can observe a definite tendency to realize explicitly those intermediate levels that had been missing or present only inferentially. In measure 2 of the Schubert Sonata, for example, both the dotted quarter-note beats and their eighth-note subdivisions become fully evident. Quite often the realization of missing levels takes on an important role in the elaboration of a piece's design. This is not always the case, however. In the Chopin Etude, quarter-note motion becomes an important element in measure 7, but eighth-note motion is never a very significant issue.

Duple Meter at Higher Levels

One might imagine a passage in which a recurrent unit of sixteen measures had no inner articulations longer than one measure; in other words, there would be no spans larger than one measure and smaller than sixteen. The durational pattern of our imaginary passage would be extremely difficult to hear, for it would spread over long spans of time the disproportion between long and short pulses found in the first measure of the Schubert Sonata; the disproportion would be so great that the succession of short pulses could not very well serve as a measure of the long ones. It follows as a logical consequence that passages in which higher-level meter plays an important part will tend to articulate the levels between the measure and the large group. In the excerpt from Beethoven's Op. 27, No. 1 (Example 3.1), the sixteen-measure spans divide into eight-measure units that subdivide further into units of four, two, and one. In other words, the entire panoply of levels from the measure to the sixteen-measure group is articulated. The intermediate levels serve to link the small and large units and help the listener estimate the distances between accented points.

This process, however, contains a built-in limitation, for each larger span results from *multiplying* the durational units of the next smaller one. In the Beethoven, the large-scale meter is duple, resulting from multiplication by twos: 1 measure x 2 = 2 × 2 = 4 × 2 = 8 × 2 = 16. Although the ratio between successive levels remains a constant 1:2, the increment in duration increases with each level from one measure to two to four to eight. This increasing disproportion eventually reduces the effectiveness of the next-to-largest unit as an aid in measuring the largest one—particularly as each increase in duration also represents an increase in musical contents. Over very long spans of time, therefore, meter ceases to be directly available to the listener, who receives little or no help in determining whether the time intervals are really equivalent.

Metrical organization by numbers larger than two rapidly produces a far greater disproportion between successive levels. If we start with one measure and proceed to group by threes, we arrive at spans of three, nine, twenty-seven, and eighty-one measures—the eighty-one at a level equivalent to a span of sixteen measures organized by twos. Large-scale triple meter, operating over several levels at once, is obviously harder for the listener to take in than duple. Triple hypermeter typically occurs at comparatively low levels (3 × 1 or 3 × 2 measures). At higher levels, triple organization would normally occur just once in the array of levels between the measure and the largest span, as when a twelve-measure phrase divides into 3 × 4 measures. Multilevel grouping by fives or sevens is a virtual impossibility.

Because it can proliferate over many levels, duple hypermeter brings an important advantage to music where large-scale metrical organization is a significant issue. This advantage, of course, is over and above the "naturalness" that so many theorists—Schenker among them—have rightly ascribed to duple meter. Schenker relates duple meter to the heartbeat.[13] Another basis is surely the bilateral symmetry of the human body, which has profoundly influenced musical meter through dance patterns and probably in other ways as well.

"Hidden" Periodicities: Schubert, "Wanderers Nachtlied"

There are pieces whose rhythms seem to be free from the constraints of any large periodicities. Such is the case in Schubert's song "Wanderers Nachtlied," D.768 (Op. 96, No. 3). The poem by Goethe to which it is composed is itself extraordinarily free, with varied lengths of line, shifting patterns of accent, an asymmetric rhyme scheme, and a sentence structure that frequently overlaps the division into lines. The song has only fourteen measures, a duration that obviously provides no scope for elaborate patterns of hypermeter, but one might expect units of, say, two measures to recur with some frequency. In keeping with the metric freedom of the poem, however, Schubert does not permit even the 4/4 measure to punctuate the flow of the music with any consistency.

Note for instance how new metrical units seem to start in the middle of measures 4 and 5 and how, as a consequence, the first beats of measures 5 and 6 lose their downbeat character. Even more striking is Schubert's setting of the lines "Warte nur, balde / Ruhest du auch." Both text and music repeat (compare measures 9–11 and 11–13); the second time around Schubert begins in the middle of the measure, shifting the entire musical content by half a measure. In a highly interesting discussion of this song, Thrasybulos Georgiades maintains that the largest metrical unit is the half note rather than the notated 4/4 measure. [14]

The notion that the song is "really" in 2/4 is surely not without foundation, but one wonders why Schubert should have written it in 4/4 if a 2/4 notation might have conveyed the metrics with greater accuracy. Example 3.4, a durational analysis of the song, is intended to shed light on the reasons for Schubert's notation. Since there is no consistent hypermeter, an analysis could use the actual durations of the song, but I find that a reduction of whole measure to half note gives a clearer picture of the proportions. The durational analysis contains only three levels, but each level appears in two forms, the lower one following the notated meter and the upper showing the unequal groupings produced by the design, by textural changes, and by the tonal rhythms. Above the durational graphs is an arrhythmic middleground sketch of the song.

Note how the bar lines of each pair of graphs (a_1–a_2, b_1–b_2, and c_1–c_2) move out of and into phase as the notation departs from and returns to the actual metrics. They begin in phase, diverge in the middle of measure 4, and converge again in measures 7 and 8. The beginning of measure 9 sounds like a downbeat, but the beginning of measure 10 does not. Only in the last two measures does the notation once again accord with the sound. Now the various departures from and returns to the notated meter are anything but arbitrary or random; they coordinate wonderfully with the inner form of this through-composed piece and—hardly a coincidence—with the sense and syntax of the poem. The main subdivisions are:

Introduction	measures 1–2
"Über allen Gipfeln . . ."	measures 3–6
"Die Vöglein . . ."	measures 7–8
"Warte nur, balde . . ."	measures 9–13
Postlude	measure 14

EXAMPLE 3.4: Schubert, "Wanderers Nachtlied," D.768, middleground graph and durational reductions

These subdivisions are marked in the graphs by heavy bar lines. In every case, the beginning of a new subdivision is both a notated and a felt downbeat. In addition, the final descent of the upper line, at the second "Ruhest du auch," occurs within a notated measure (measure 13), just like measure 2, which prefigures it, and measure 14, which echoes it. At the very least, then, Schubert's 4/4 notation conveys the form of the piece far better than would a notation in 2/4 or one alternating 4/4 and 3/2 along the lines of levels a_1, b_1, and c_1 of my graphs.

As it happens, however, the 4/4 notation has another and more important meaning as well. Each subdivision of the song contains a multiple of whole measures (two measures, four measures, two measures, five measures, one measure), as the heavy bar lines in Example 3.4 indicate; the 4/4 measure, therefore, is the largest recurrent unit that can be inferred from the rhythmic foreground. Furthermore, the introduction presents and confirms the 4/4

measure as a primary durational unit. And finally even the deviations from the notated 4/4 measure serve to keep its memory alive. They are of two kinds: groups of four quarter notes starting on the third beat of the notated measure (measures 4–5 and 10–11) and groups of six quarter notes, all of which can be scanned as a 4/4 unit extended by half a measure (measures 3–4, 5–6, 9–10, and 11–12). No deviant passage lasts long enough to obliterate entirely the force of the notated meter, which in any case is confirmed at the beginning of each new subdivision. This song shows that a metrical unit can withdraw from the foreground but can continue to exert a controlling influence at deeper levels. Though hardly available to uninformed perception, the metrical structure of "Wanderers Nachtlied" becomes accessible to a perception deepened by reflection.

Although there is much about this song—including its most significant aspects—that I cannot discuss here, I must mention briefly two features that relate directly to its meter.

The first feature is the development in measures 3–7 of the neighbor-note figure of measure 1. As Example 3.5 shows, this motive first fits into a single measure. When it is taken up in the voice part of measure 3, however, it stretches over six beats; indeed, it is this very enlargement of the motive that brings the first departure from the notated meter. When the figure reappears a step higher, starting in the middle of measure 5, the third note (c^2) does not enter where expected, but it is replaced by an inner-voice f^1 (painting the word "Hauch"). The expected c^2 arrives only at the downbeat of measure 7, so that the figure now occupies a span of eight beats; the further enlargement bridges over the beginning of the new section at measure 7.

The second feature connects directly with the enlargement of the neighbor-note figure. In its original form (measure 1) the three-note figure d^1–$e♭^1$–d^1 has the following underlying rhythm: ♩ ♪ ♪. The unequal note values reconcile the conflict between the *three* notes of the figure and the *duple* metric division of the time span it occupies. The enlargement of the figure in measures 3–4 equalizes the note values, and precisely this equalization produces the conflict between the song's basic 4/4 time and the free rhythmic groupings that obscure it. A glance at levels b_1 and b_2 of Example 3.4 will suffice to show how much the pacing of the song is governed by equal durations; see especially the groups of five notes at the two statements of "Warte nur" (measures 9–13). Although the rhythmic structure of this song is highly unusual, it points up an idea of general importance. The clear expression of the equal time spans that produce meter often requires the unequal pacing of the tonal events that fill those time spans. We shall return to this idea later in this essay.

Unequal Partitioning: The Quasi-Metrical Effect

As we have seen, a fully developed metrical schema requires an array of at least two coordinated series of equal time spans. The element of repetition is fundamental to meter, for it alone sets up expectations definite enough to cause the awareness of metrical accents as they were described above. Therefore, non-recurrent time spans—measure-groups of constantly changing length, for example—do not function as true metrical units. Nonetheless, a quasi-metrical effect can sometimes accrue to such a measure-group; that is, because of some special emphasis built into the composition, it can sound like one unit of a metrical schema. In the Schubert song, for example, the two-measure groupings (measures 1–2 and 7–8) do not recur often or consistently enough to add a layer of hypermeter to the array of durational levels. Nonetheless, the quasi-metrical effect of these two-measure groups is undeniable, at least to my ear. It arises partly out of tonal rhythm (the third-progression of measures 1–2; the dominant pedal of measures 7–8), partly out of the strong downbeat effect at the beginning of

EXAMPLE 3.5: Schubert, "Wanderers Nachtlied," D.768, neighbor note figure in different rhythmic settings

"Hauch"

measures 3 and 9. Although the two-measure groups do not continue, one might well expect them to continue, and in some obscure way they serve as a measure of the free rhythmic groupings that follow them.

Quasi-metrical effects occur particularly strongly with three-measure groups. In speaking of such groups, Schenker often used the German term *Takttriole* (triplet of whole measures). In so doing he tacitly acknowledged their quasi-metrical effect even where the group in question does not form part of a repetitive pattern. There is an interesting example in the second movement of Beethoven's Piano Sonata, Op. 110, where Schenker infers a "triplet of whole measures" at measures 33–35, a lone three-measure group.[15] As with the two-measure groups in the Schubert song, the quasi-metrical effect arises out of the tonal rhythm combined with the particularly strong downbeat character of measure 36.

Syncopated Time Spans

A quasi-metrical effect will sometimes accompany a time span syncopated within a larger time span. Syncopated time spans arise out of various factors in combination; one of these is usually a tonal event displaced from its normal metrical position. In particular, if a tonal unit containing *three* elements articulates the first, second, and fourth beats of a *four-beat* span, the suppression of beat 3 can easily produce a syncopated effect. In the excerpt from Mozart's Sonata for Piano and Violin, K.378, given in Example 3.6a, the two-measure spans divide into fours at the half-note level. The harmonic rhythm and melodic emphases create a strong segmentation at the midpoint of the first and third measures compared to which the following first beats recede in importance; this creates a syncopated division more or less like 2/4 . . . 4/4 . . . 2/4. The reduction in Example 3.6b shows the tonal events in a normal, that is, unsyncopated, metrical setting.

Syncopated time spans can encompass longer durations. Example 3.7, the opening of the "Dies irae" from Mozart's Requiem, consists of a four-measure phrase whose second and third measures form a syncopated span. Here the syncopation is made possible because e^2, the second note of a rising linear progression d^2–e^2–f^2, occupies measures 2 and 3. In addition, the sharp surface rhythm and the importance of the word "irae" give a special emphasis to measure 2. At the same time, the repeated motive and aspects of the orchestration (especially the trumpets and timpani) articulate a metrical division of the four measures into two plus two. In this passage the acute listener will hear two conflicting divisions at once: the two measure groups partitioned by the motivic design, and the syncopated time span of measures 2–3 formed by the emphasis on e^2 in measure 2.

In both Mozart excerpts, dissonances appear at the beginnings of the syncopated time spans. There seems to be no general agreement about the proper evaluation of such dissonances; some analysts hesitate to read them as suspension formations (which they obviously resemble) because the dissonances are metrically weaker than their resolutions. Might I offer the following suggestion? The syncopated time spans form quasi-metrical structures within which the dissonances fall on strong pulses. Inside these time spans, therefore, the dissonances represent perfectly normal suspensions even though they occur on weak pulses of the larger metrical schema. One might speak here of the foreground transformation of metrical values.

EXAMPLE 3.6: Mozart, Sonata for Piano and Violin, K.378, first movement, Allegro moderato

b) Unsyncopated setting

Incommensurable Levels

Sometimes a durational span might be punctuated by two incommensurable levels of quicker pulsation. Such effects occur frequently at the foreground when a beat is divided by two and three or three and four at the same time; some authors (e.g., Charles Seeger and Maury Yeston) have used the not inappropriate term "rhythmic dissonance" to cover these situations.[16] Rhythmic dissonances will occasionally occur over long spans of time; the

EXAMPLE 3.7: Mozart, *Requiem*: "Dies irae" (choral parts only)

Menuetto from Mozart's String Quartet, K.590, offers an astonishing case in point. As Edward Lowinsky points out in a justly celebrated article, the Menuetto is ruled by the number seven.[17] Its forty-two measures divide into three strains of fourteen measures each, one before the double bar and two following it. Example 3.8 shows the opening strain, which subdivides into two seven-measure phrases of different harmonic focus but parallel motivic design. Although each phrase has an asymmetric, seven-measure structure, the pairing of the two phrases seems to create a compensating symmetry of higher order. Lowinsky regards the maintenance of a balance between symmetry and asymmetry as a distinguishing mark of Mozart's rhythmic style.[18]

a)

EXAMPLE 3.8: Mozart, String Quartet, K.590, Menuetto

b) Durational reduction

But perhaps the symmetry is more disingenuous than it might at first appear to be. Close study of Example 3.8a will reveal that the two phrases, though similar in design, are in some ways opposite in rhythmic shape. In the first phrase, the opening measure is clearly an extended upbeat. But the initial measure of the second phrase (measure 8), though it contains the same melodic figure, is just as clearly a downbeat. The cadential measure of the first phrase (measure 7) is weak; the corresponding measure of the second phrase (measure 14) is strong. These discrepancies arise because, starting in measure 2, the entire strain is divided into two-measure hypermeasures so that all the even-numbered measures count as strong. The articulation into hypermeasures results from a combination of many factors: instrumentation, dynamics, tonal rhythm, and the diminutions of the first-violin part. (Note especially how the material of measures 2–3 is compressed into a single measure—measure 9—in the second phrase.)

What Mozart is doing here is to partition the fourteen measures in two different and incommensurable ways. The hypermeter divides them into seven twos; the tonal contents and design divide the fourteen into two sevens. As tonal configurations the two phrases are equal in length. Measured from initial downbeat to initial downbeat, they are unequal; the first contains six measures preceded by one measure of upbeat, while the second has eight measures, the eighth measure completing the hypermeasure begun by the final measure of the phrase. This eighth measure is represented, the first time around, by the repeat of the opening upbeat measure and, after the double bar, by the first measure of the next strain, which also forms an upbeat. These events are depicted in the durational reduction of Example 3.8b, where each 2/4 measure of the reduction represents a two-measure hypermeasure of the original.

"Motivic Durations"

In the second and third strains of the Menuetto an important event occurs after the first seven measures, though neither strain subdivides into two parallel phrases. At the midpoint of the second strain, the first violin reaches c^3, the culminating note of a rising octave-progression and the initial note of a descending one—what Schenker, in his early writings, would have called a *Knotenpunkt* (nodal point). In the third strain, the eighth measure brings striking changes in surface rhythm and motivic design. In both strains the beginning of the eighth measure forms the durational midpoint, but it does not form a metric division in a strict sense. This is because both strains, like the first, begin with upbeat measures so that the eighth measure is closer to the preceding than to the following big downbeat.

In the Menuetto, the fourteen-measure strains and their seven-measure subdivisions obviously articulate equal spans of time, but they do not form part of a metric schema. Because of the two-measure groupings, the sevens do not divide the fourteens metrically. And the sevens themselves are not subdivided by consistent groupings—say of two, two, and three—that might give at least a quasi-metrical effect. The recurrent durational spans of this piece remind me of Schenker's "hidden repetitions," but repetitions of a segment of time rather than a tonal figure. They are not immediately discernible through the complexities of the foreground, but for the knowing listener (and player) they give a heightened sense of order to the large formal divisions of the piece.

In this Menuetto, the large spans of fourteen and seven measures are clearly articulated by the musical foreground; they are accessible to anyone who can read a score and count measures. Yet how many listeners, including trained musicians, would become conscious of their presence without consulting the score? By contrast, in the excerpt from *Eine kleine Nachtmusik* with which we began this section of the essay (see Example 3.2a), the primary, quarter-note, pulse of the movement is missing. Though not composed directly into the music, the quarter-note level would be inferred more or less automatically by most listeners. Thus the listener's ease in processing rhythm does not depend solely on the acoustical signals he hears. I would conclude from this that the durational aspect of music—including meter in even its simplest manifestations—will be slow to give up its secrets to a literal-minded approach.

Alternative and Conflicting Metrical Patterns

Schumann, Davidsbündlertänze, Op. 6, No. 1

"The" Meter   Most writers on rhythm agree that equal pulses are in some way fundamental to meter. This notion, whether one finds it valuable, trivial, or even wrong, is at least not difficult to grasp. Yet its application to analysis is by no means always straightforward. One difficulty arises from the very real possibility that different compositional elements might articulate different, and perhaps contradictory, time spans within the same passage. By "contradictory" I do not refer to rhythmic dissonances like the one between the two- and the seven-measure groups in the first strain of the Mozart Menuetto. There the music clearly articulates both spans; the problematic aspect is the incommensurability of the two spans within a single metrical schema. I refer rather to alternative metrical schemata *at a single level*, as in the movement from Beethoven's Op. 27, No. 1 (Example 3.1), where changes in register articulate spans that begin with the *odd-numbered* measures, whereas the tonal rhythms (and a notational clue of Beethoven's) suggest that the *even-numbered* measures should be the strong ones. In such cases, can one speak at all of "the" meter of the passage? Perhaps several metrical patterns are going on at once. Or perhaps the different interpretations of different listeners are equally valid.

The first piece of Schumann's *Davidsbündlertänze* offers an extreme example of the possibility of alternative metrical interpretations. Example 3.9a shows the five-measure introduction and the first four measures of the opening strain. The introduction is not metrically problematic, but in the strain that follows, at least three plausible alternatives to the notated meter come to mind. Examples 3.9b, 3.9c, and 3.9d show these possibilities in simplified (reduced) notation. Example 3.9b follows the left-hand entrances and the changes of harmony. Example 3.9c follows the time spans articulated by the right-hand part. Example 3.9d follows the left- and right-hand parts in combination. In all three interpretations, notes that Schumann writes as upbeats are reinterpreted as downbeats. All of the reinterpretations produce typical dance rhythms.

Listeners who hear any of the alternative metrical patterns shown in Example 3.9 are responding to relationships composed into the music. These relationships are spans of time marked off by bass notes, by the beginnings of the right hand's melodic figures, and by a

EXAMPLE 3.9: Schumann, *Davidsbündlertänze*, Op. 6, No. 1, conflicting metric interpretations

a)

b) Conflicting metric interpretation following left-hand part

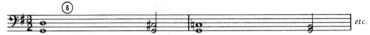

c) Conflicting metric interpretation following right-hand part

d) Conflicting metric interpretation, left- and right-hand parts combined

combination of the most prominent notes of the left hand and the right. Nevertheless, I believe that there is "a" meter that governs this passage, and that it is the one that Schumann notates. Both the upbeat beginnings of the left hand and the anticipations of the right grow directly out of Clara Wieck's motto (measures 1–2), which expresses the notated 3/4 quite clearly; the motto is also the basis for the two-note melodic figure that forms the piece's main motivic element.[19] The connection between the motto and the main body of the piece would be lost (or at least seriously weakened) if the meter were conceived according to the alternative patterns of Example 3.9.

In addition there is the indisputable fact that Schumann notates the meter as he does, and not in some other way. In evaluating the notation of meter, the analyst should accord a great composer something like the presumption of innocence that obtains in a court of law; one ought to presume that he means what he writes unless there is strong evidence to the contrary. (Here the placement of the crescendo signs also speaks for the validity of the notated meter.) Of course the upbeat beginnings conflict with the metrical pattern and will suggest to some listeners one or more of the alternatives shown in Example 3.9. And the possibility of hearing the meter in more than one way is, I think, one of the main issues of the piece. But in a successful performance the alternative possibilities will strive against the notated meter without ever quite supplanting it.

"The" Hypermeter   Identifying patterns of hypermeter is almost always more difficult than identifying measure meter, if only because there is almost never a "hypermeter signature" to provide at least a first clue. The Schumann piece obviously goes in four-measure groups starting in measure 6 (measures 1–5, too, represent a unit of four measures—extended to five by a written-out fermata). What is not obvious, however, is the scansion of the four-measure units. Any of the four measures could serve as downbeat; of the four possibilities only the one with measure 3 as downbeat is really unlikely. The seeming ambiguity of phrase meter relates to the rather equivocal way in which measures 6ff. project the smaller meter; the lack of strongly articulated measures makes it difficult for a strongly articulated hypermeter to emerge.

That four different scansions might be possible does not mean that all four are equally good. In my view the main downbeat of each group falls on the *first* measure. The motivic two-note figures b^1–a^1 and a^1–g^1 (measures 6–9) should certainly scan strong–weak, strong–weak—again the connection with Clara Wieck's motto. The large rhythm of this passage cannot be read literally from the immediate foreground, where the melody is shifted away from the bass and the bass itself anticipates the measure. These foreground rhythms represent the transformation of a simpler pattern at a prior level, a pattern more or less like Example 3.10. It is from this prior level that one would infer the strong–weak scansion of the two-measure figure.

There is confirmation for my reading in a characteristic notational quirk of Schumann's found in the first edition, where he marked off sections with double bars. These are not repeat signs (as in the second edition) and are therefore purely interpretive marks. They occur before measures 6, 14, 26, 34, 42, and 66; *every one* precedes the first of a four-measure group, suggesting that Schumann heard it as a "1." (Only the last two of these double bars are retained in the second edition, where the added repeat signs made it necessary to remove most of them.)[20]

I do not mean to suggest with this example that the notation always gives a true picture of the metrical structure of a passage or that meter is always unambiguously expressed at every level. And I certainly acknowledge the possibility that in some passages meter might not be a very significant issue; the scansion, especially at the higher levels, might not greatly influence how one hears the passage in other respects. But in general I think that something is gained from assuming at first that each passage has "a" metrical schema that regulates its rhythmic progression. The goal of analysis is to find the best reading one can, not merely to

EXAMPLE 3.10: Schumann, *Davidsbündlertänze*, Op. 6, No. 1, underlying metric pattern

find a solution that somehow "works." In my experience, there is often one interpretation of the meter that gives a clearer and more comprehensive account of the piece's important features (in their conflicts as well as correspondences) than any other.

Simultaneous Meters   In measures 42–61 of the Schumann piece, the two-note motive is used again and again to "reach over" the top voice and in so doing to achieve an ever higher register. The reaching-over occurs on the second quarter of measure 43 and assertively projects a cross-meter of 3/2 that almost obliterates the basic 3/4 time of the piece. I say "almost" because the earlier associations of the left-hand figure keep the 3/4 alive in the listener's mind. Example 3.11a quotes the beginning of this passage; Example 3.11b makes explicit the cross-meter of the right hand and shows it against the continuing 3/4 background provided by the left hand.

Example 3.12 contains a durational reduction that explains the hypermeter of this fascinating passage. Just as with the smaller meter, two different and conflicting patterns are projected: in this case, four-measure units starting in measure 42 (Example 3.12a) and four-measure units starting in measure 43 (Example 3.12b). Since measure 42 is the same as measure 6, it counts as a "1." The sequential repetitions built into the rest of the passage maintain four-measure groups; these groups continue the hypermeter that begins in measure 6 and that goes on without modification to the very end of the piece. At the same time, however, the melodic design and the harmonic rhythm articulate four-measure groups starting one measure later, in measure 43. This scheme of partitioning comes across much more

EXAMPLE 3.11: Schumann, *Davidsbündlertänze*, Op. 6, No. 1, metric conflict

EXAMPLE 3.12: Schumann, *Davidsbündlertänze*, Op. 6, No. 1, conflicting metrical schemata

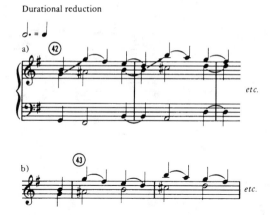

strongly than the other and constitutes a kind of metrical foreground syncopated against the background hypermeter. (A three-measure group in measures 69–71 brings the foreground meter into phase with the background meter.)

Although this passage is of unusual metrical complexity, the principle it follows can be seen at work in many other passages as well. Two conflicting metrical schemata are projected simultaneously, one of them continuing a previously established pattern and the other contradicting it. Usually, as in the Schumann piece, the new pattern is the stronger of the two, but it is not necessarily "the" meter of the passage, for it can often be heard as struggling against the prevailing meter rather than supplanting it. In the Schumann piece, the effect of the rhythmic shifts becomes very tame if the listener does not feel the almost violent transformation of weak (second) beats and weak (second) measures into strong ones. This sense of transformation is produced only if the listener hears the previously established meter as basic.

An irreducible residue of personal opinion remains in any metrical analysis of a piece which, like the Schumann example, lends itself to more than one plausible interpretation. There is no way that I (or anyone else) can "prove" the correctness of my reading to someone who is convinced that one of the alternative schemata of Example 3.9 represents the basic meter or, for that matter, to someone who thinks that there is no one basic metrical pattern. Perhaps the government might one day appoint a Commissar of Metrics who will decide such matters for us. Before that day arrives, however, we shall have to live with these disagreements as best we can. The important thing is to make our evaluations of the meter in the light of the clearest and most comprehensive understanding we can achieve of all the significant aspects of the piece.

Incidentally, there are interesting rhythmic dissonances in the Schumann piece, measures 35–36. The right hand divides each 3/4 measure into 6/8 (3 × 2♪ = 2 × 3♪), while the left hand groups the two measures into a large hemiola pattern of 3/2 (2 × 3♩ = 3 × 2♩). For a brief span of two measures, three different metrical (or quasi-metrical) units occur simultaneously: two measures of 6/8, one measure of 3/2, and, underlying these, the unit of two 3/4 measures, which persists in our memory. Example 3.13 illustrates.

EXAMPLE 3.13: Schumann, *Davidsbündlertänze*, Op. 6, No. 1, rhythmic dissonances

The Transformation of Metrical Structures

Prototype and Transformation

As a composition unfolds, it manifests a constant process of self-reflection. Foreground elements reappear in exact repetition or in variation. And of course the foreground also reflects—sometimes quite literally—the tonal structures of higher order whose elaboration and transformation it represents. In the course of foreground variation or of prolongation from level to level, a tonal prototype might be transformed into something of different or even seemingly opposite character; a stepwise progression, for example, might become a leap of a seventh or ninth. Yet the prototype and its variant have enough in common to enable a skilled listener to sense their connection. To a more limited but still significant extent, metrical structures can undergo a similar process of elaboration. In an excerpt from Haydn's "Clock" Symphony (Example 3.14), the motivic upbeat figure of measure 24 continues to precede the metrically parallel four-measure groups. As a result, the big downbeats occur every five measures rather than every four. Nonetheless, the four-measure groups retain both their integrity as hypermeasures and their continuity from one to the other. The upbeat measures function as insertions and are clearly heard as "extra"; to infer organic five-measure units here would be to misconstrue the passages altogether.

Since the eighteenth century, theorists have maintained that a metrical schema can accommodate a good deal of stretching and compression without losing its identity. Such a notion might make literal-minded people uncomfortable, but it seems to me to follow almost inevitably from the very nature of music as a temporal art. To the extent that music is an image of our experience of events in time, succession and duration must be appropriate subjects for artistic elaboration. The enlargement of metrical units—especially of hypermeasures—plays a particularly important role in tonal composition, for it can provide a place for the prolongational expansion of tonal contents. The shortening of metrical spans can create a more continuous succession of events by fusing the end of one span to the beginning of the next. Of course when metrical groups are altered, equal time spans often cease to appear literally on the musical surface; the listener must arrive at the idea of equal spans—and consequently of an underlying metrical structure—through a process of inference. Sometimes, as in the Haydn excerpt, the process is a simple, almost automatic, one; sometimes it requires attentive and repeated hearings. And sometimes the difficulties are such that some listeners may never be able to draw the right inferences, just as some readers and

EXAMPLE 3.14: Haydn, Symphony No. 101, first movement

theatergoers may miss the subtler nuances of language and characterization in a play of Shakespeare.

Among the theorists who relate at least some asymmetric time structures to simpler, usually duple, models is Heinrich Schenker; indeed, this is one of the facets of his theory that most directly reflects the work of his predecessors. The chapter on rhythm in *Free Composition* contains illuminating, though very brief, discussions of metrical alteration such as extra upbeat measures (demonstrated in Example 3.14) and the reinterpretation of a weak measure as strong. He also allows for the possibility of an extra *downbeat* measure that follows a complete unit of hypermeter but that does not initiate another complete unit.[21] This last device seems not to be very widely acknowledged, so an example of it at this point might be of some value.

The beginning of Schubert's song "Der Wegweiser" contains two downbeat measures that appear in immediate succession (Example 3.15, measures 5 and 6). Measures 1–4 could easily constitute a perfectly balanced four-measure unit, one that could very well close on the dominant chord of measure 4. That the four measures make a complete rhythmic unit is

EXAMPLE 3.15: Schubert, *Winterreise*, No. 20, "Der Wegweiser"

underscored by the way Schubert composes the beginning of the vocal line: he sets the first complete sentence of the poem to a four-measure idea that is essentially a repetition of measures 1–4. In both the piano introduction and the song proper, a tonic resolution uncharacteristically appears at the end of the phrase, extending it to five measures. Since the scansion of measures 1–4 and 6–9 must be strong–weak, strong–weak, the tonally emphasized fifth measure sounds strong; indeed, it sounds like a "1." And since measures 6 and 10 are, in fact, "1s," two strong measures come together without an intervening weak one.

The phenomenon of the added downbeat measure is connected with the fact that an odd-numbered measure easily produces an accent if it follows a series of clearly articulated groupings by twos; the reason, of course, is that the measure comes where a new "1" would be expected. The strength of the accent thus produced depends on whether the expected "1" would begin an important unit (hypermeasure, phrase, or section) or only a subgrouping within a larger unit. In scanning measure-groupings, difficulties can arise in deciding whether to read, say, 1 2 1 or 1 2 3, 1 2 3 4 1 or 1 2 3 4 5. Often the two readings are equally good as long as one realizes that the "3" or "5" carries downbeat implications or that the "1" connects to the preceding unit, not the following one.

Expansions

In Chapter 2 I referred briefly to (and made use of) the notion of expansion (*Dehnung*)—probably Schenker's most important contribution to the understanding of rhythm.[22] Unfortunately, Schenker's explanation of this idea is as compressed and cryptic as the idea itself is important. To appreciate the scope of Schenker's concept, one must study how he applies it in his analyses; his theoretical description, taken by itself, is of limited value. In this connection I should like to recommend the excellent dissertation by William Rothstein, who has worked out an admirably clear and intelligent interpretation of Schenker's approach to rhythm. Rothstein gives a particularly good explanation of Schenker's *Dehnung* concept. I shall try as much as possible to avoid duplicating it, but some duplication will be unavoidable if I am to present my own ideas in a coherent manner.[23]

In *Free Composition*, Schenker distinguishes between expansions and other rhythmic phenomena, such as extra upbeat measures (discussed above). The extended upbeat is not an expansion in Schenker's sense because it forms an insertion between two measure-groups rather than an integral part of either group. An expansion, by contrast, represents the durational enlargement of a measure (or perhaps a hypermeasure) that does form an integral part of a measure-group. The group that serves as the basis of the expansion is called a "metric prototype."[24] The excerpt from Verdi's *Don Carlo* cited in Chapter 1, for example, contains a true expansion: the next-to-last measure of the first phrase (the prototype) becomes two measures in the second, where it extends the cadence in a kind of composed ritardando.[25]

Schenker makes another distinction: "The concept of expansion does not include those 6-, 10-, and 12-measure groups which serve a diminution organically."[26] This distinction rests on another basis and, in fact, reflects a difference of a more radical kind. As I view it, a group of measures serves a diminution organically if the *tonal rhythm* of the diminution determines the number of measures. This will happen if the elements of the diminution maintain an even pace, thereby restricting the role of durational rhythm to an irreducible minimum.

The number of elements will then determine the number of measures (or other metrical units). In "Wanderers Nachtlied," for example, the even pacing in half measures of the neighbor-note figure and of the rising third-progression, both containing three notes, creates groupings of one and a half measures (see Example 3.4).

A more familiar example: measures 1–6 of the Menuetto of Mozart's G-minor Symphony contain two third-progressions, bb^1–a^1–g^1 and d^2–c^2–bb^1. At a pace of one note per measure, the tonal succession creates a grouping of six measures divided into two threes.[27] Incidentally, many pitch structures of fundamental importance contain an odd number of elements, especially three. Such tonal patterns will frequently—indeed usually—have to adjust to a duple metrical schema; cases such as "Wanderers Nachtlied" and this Mozart Menuetto represent the exception, not the norm. These adjustments probably constitute the ultimate source for the *necessity of unequal pacing* in metrically patterned music.

The basis of an expansion is not the tonal rhythm of a diminution but the contents of a metrical unit, usually a measure, belonging to a larger unit or "prototype." The expansion transforms the unit into a longer span, quite possibly one with an elaborate metrical structure of its own. The expansion would then form a measure-grouping within a larger measure-grouping. Example 3.16, taken from the last movement of Mozart's "Hoffmeister" Quartet, K.499, shows both the prototype and the expansion; the prototype is itself based upon a still earlier passage (measures 44ff.). Here the prototype takes the form of a six-measure antecedent phrase, subdivided into three two-measure hypermeasures (measures 309–14). The expansion acts upon the second of the three hypermeasures; it transforms its two-measure model into a ten-measure span (measures 317–26). Because of the expansion, the consequent phrase contains fourteen measures, not including the tonal resolution, which arrives only with the first measure of the next group. The ten-measure expansion, like the prototype, divides into very clear two-measure hypermeasures.

The conceptually simplest kind of prototype—and the only one that Schenker discusses in *Free Composition*—is one that appears earlier in a piece than its expanded variant. Sometimes, as in the excerpt from *Don Carlo*, the variant is a modified repetition of its model.[28] At other times, as in the "Hoffmeister" Quartet, the model and its variant form an antecedent–consequent pair. In the Quartet excerpt the two phrases differ significantly in bass line and harmonic structure as well as in duration. The connection between the prototype and its expanded reproduction can be still looser. Schenker sees measures 10–21 of the first movement of Mozart's G-minor Symphony as an expanded eight-measure group—or, more accurately, a group of four two-measure hypermeasures.[29] Yet it is in no way a repetition of its prototype (measures 3–9), which relates to it only through general features of tonal rhythm, lower-level meter, and motivic design.

The excerpt from the G-minor Symphony resembles closely another type of expansion—one that occasionally appears in Schenker's analyses but that he leaves unexplained in *Free Composition*. In these expansions no earlier passage serves as the prototype. Schenker's well-known reading of the C-major Prelude from the *Well-Tempered Clavier*, Book I, shows measures 1–4 as an expanded first measure within a hypermeasure transformed by the expansion from a four- to a seven-measure span.[30] Obviously there is no prototype before measure 1 that might form the basis for this expansion. A particularly interesting example in *Free Composition* shows the very beginning of the Allegro vivace from the first movement of Beethoven's String Quartet, Op. 59, No. 3; here the thirteen measures represent a four-

EXAMPLE 3.16: Mozart, String Quartet, K.499, fourth movement, Molto allegro

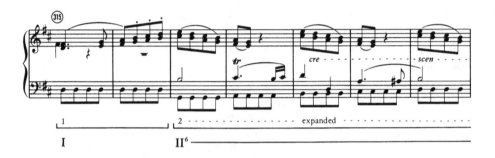

measure group expanded by cadenza-like interpolations. Here again a literal prototype is out of the question.[31]

In an important footnote to the translation of *Free Composition*, Ernst Oster suggests that expansions without literal models earlier in the composition derive from prototypes at prior structural levels.[32] This would mean that expansions divide into two main types: those with literal models in the foreground and those whose models must be inferred from events at a deeper level of structure. Rothstein's discussion of this issue is particularly good; among other things, he points out that the two types of expansion tend to merge into each other.[33] A prototype that occurs earlier in the piece need not be an exact model, and one occurring only at a relatively deep level will almost necessarily conform to the prevailing metrical structure of the piece or passage. In both the Bach Prelude and the Beethoven Quartet, for example, the expansions act upon four-measure prototypes. It should be noted that the Prelude continues to the end in four-measure hypermeasures and that the Quartet establishes a four-measure norm in the passage immediately following the one that Schenker cites.

Central to Schenker's notion of expansion is the assumption that metrical organization can take place at levels prior to the immediate foreground, that entities such as measures and hypermeasures exist at higher foreground or even middleground levels. If the expansion has no actual model in an earlier passage, its underlying metrical structure exists "only at some higher level that is not literally expressed."[34] A literal prototype, of course, announces its metrical structure more directly, but in the expanded variant, the meter of the prototype no longer occurs in the immediate foreground. It, too, withdraws to a higher level, though the listener's memory of the earlier passage helps him draw the necessary inferences.

By connecting the idea of expansion to his theory of levels, Schenker made it a far more powerful analytic tool than the old and familiar notion of "phrase extension," which it obviously resembles and from which it almost certainly derives. The superiority of Schenker's approach lies first of all in his taking into account the levels of tonal structure and diminutional content that are associated with the prototype and the expansion; it is never simply a question of counting extra measures. In addition, Schenker brings a new perspective to the study of purely metric phenomena. An expansion—especially a large-scale one—can establish its own metric structure. As Rothstein acutely observes, "In such cases we must distinguish two levels of hypermeter: a higher level, which is the level of the metric prototype; and a lower level, the level of the hypermeasures within the expansion. . . . Accordingly, we may speak of hypermeasures of higher or lower *structural order*."[35]

One might compare these different structural levels of hypermeter to differences between the key of a piece as a whole and the "key" of a passage following a modulation. No experienced listener expects a foreground "key" to persist; indeed, the tension it creates arises out of the necessity eventually to resolve it into the background tonic. Similarly, in our Mozart Quartet excerpt (Example 3.16), the two-measure hypermeasures within the expansion convey a different meaning from those of the prototype. Instead of marking stages in the forward movement of the tonal action, they "mark time" within a tonally static interpolation. In so doing they generate a very special kind of tension (for me, a comic tension) that dissolves only when forward motion resumes at the cadence.

Scarlatti, Sonata, K.78 (L.75), Minuet

Expansions can produce durational spans of any reasonable length, not just the groups of six, ten, or twelve measures that Schenker mentions. The lovely little Minuet that closes Domenico Scarlatti's Sonata, K.78, for example, falls into two eight-measure phrases, but even superficial listening reveals that these eight-measure units do not subdivide metrically in a normal way. Example 3.17 aligns the score (Example 3.17d) under three graphs. The topmost one (Example 3.17a) is arrhythmic; the middle two are rhythmicized graphs, but they are not in durational reduction. Examples 3.17b and 3.17c show that measures 1–2 are answered sequentially, starting in measure 3. The answer, however, does not reach a conclusion in measure 4. Instead, measure 4 expands into a three-measure unit (measures 4–6), delaying the expected conclusion until the end of measure 6. In other words, measures 1–2 form a prototype and measures 3–6 represent its varied reproduction, with measures 4–6 standing for a single measure expanded into three. Similarly, but in a slightly more compli-

EXAMPLE 3.17: D. Scarlatti, Sonata, K.78/L.75, Minuet, middleground and durational graphs

cated way, measures 11–14 (which correspond to measures 3–6) represent a two-measure model with a threefold expansion of the second measure. Underlying the eight-measure phrases of the foreground, therefore, are two six-measure units, the sixes divided into three twos.

   One of the most beautiful features of the Minuet is the rhythmic preparation that Scarlatti provides for the expansion of measures 4–6. One expects the passing tone g^2 at the end of measure 1 to move immediately to f^2 so that the third-progression a^2–g^2–f^2 would end at the downbeat of measure 2. Instead, an arpeggio figure delays the f^2 until the third beat of the measure. This slight delay motivates the much greater delay in measures 4–6 whereby the goal tone (now a^2) appears only at the third beat of the third measure. Note that the contents of measures 4–6 crystallize around an enlargement of the *Schleifer* figure of measure 1. The *Schleifer* shifts a^2, the main melodic note, from the first to the second beat of measure 1; this is the original impulse that generates both of the subsequent delays.

   I must leave to the interested reader the pleasant task of tracing the fantastic motivic references that enliven the foreground of this tiny masterpiece, but I shall devote a few words to the parallelisms that exist nearer the background. Example 3.17a shows a level only slightly later than the interruption that determines the two-part form of this piece. The two segments differ greatly in harmonic structure and, consequently, in the inner groupings of the top line; the melodic contours, however, are strikingly parallel. Each segment of melody contains five notes; each could fit quite easily into a duple meter, more or less as in Example 3.18. At the level shown in Example 3.17b, however, the sequential third-progressions make almost mandatory the division of each segment into *three* smaller units. It is at this level, therefore, that six-measure units arise, "which serve a diminution organically," to use Schenker's explanation.[36] At a still later level, of course, the six-measure spans are transformed into units of eight measures by the expansions discussed earlier.

Beethoven, Sonata, Op. 27, No. 1, Allegro molto vivace, measures 42–72

The Scarlatti Minuet shows that an expansion can occur together with an irregular (non-duple) meter that grows out of the tonal rhythm of a diminution; the two rhythmic devices, of course, are applied to different structural levels. Our next excerpt combines these two metrical irregularities with yet a third: the extended upbeat. This excerpt is the A♭-major Trio section of the Allegro molto vivace from the Beethoven Sonata whose C-minor section we analyzed in Example 3.1. (Following the Trio is a varied reprise of the C-minor section, creating a large ABA.) Example 3.19 shows the background progression and the first level of middleground of the A♭-major section; the tonal contents are quite simple, but they are sufficiently unusual to require a few brief comments. The top voice moves through a descending octave, $\hat{8}$–$\hat{1}$; the octave is subdivided, at the first middleground level, into a fourth and fifth ($\hat{8}$–$\hat{5}$–$\hat{1}$). In relation to the movement as a whole, the A♭ ($\hat{8}$) represents the upper neighbor of the C-minor section's $\hat{5}$. The extremely sparse harmonic structure and the virtually unprolonged bass line lend little support to the top voice and do not help it produce a strong sense of closure. The weak closure is a possibility here because the piece is not an independent one, but a part of something larger.

EXAMPLE 3.18: D. Scarlatti, Sonata, K.78/L.75, Minuet, underlying tonal and durational scheme

EXAMPLE 3.19: Beethoven, Sonata, Op. 27, No. 1 (*Sonata quasi una Fantasia*), Allegro molto vivace, measures 42–72, background and first level of middleground

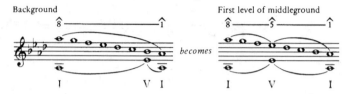

The division of the section into two big phrases could not be clearer, but the scansion of the two phrases can seem quite baffling at first. Particularly puzzling is the descending octave leap in the left-hand part of measure 66, which (together with the onset of the crescendo) seems to mark the beginning of an important span, but which remains out of phase with the repetition of the right hand's pattern in measure 64. This would suggest a rhythmic dissonance between the left hand and the right hand. Closer examination reveals that such is the case: the right hand plays a six-measure group (measures 58–63), which begins to repeat in measure 64; the left hand's change of register cuts across this division into sixes. Furthermore, the right hand's earlier entrance in measure 44 also initiates a six-measure span (measures 44–49).

We are now in a position to go more deeply into the metrics of this fascinating excerpt. Example 3.20 consists of a durational reduction in four levels. Levels a and b are the same tonally but represent different stages of rhythmic organization. Levels c and d are quite similar rhythmically as well as tonally; one might call level d a figuration of level c. The small number of levels reflects the fact that the background structure receives only a minimal contrapuntal elaboration. The analysis is best approached through level d. It shows, first of

EXAMPLE 3.20: Beethoven, Sonata. Op. 27, No. 1 (*Sonata quasi una Fantasia*), Allegro molto vivace, measures 42–72, durational reduction and tonal-rhythmic grouping

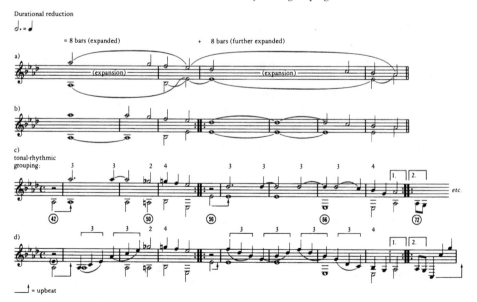

all, that measures 42–43 and 56–57 contain upbeat formations separate from the large met-rical spans. The first upbeat, though not part of the large metrical structure, influences that structure in two important ways: it sets up two-measure units as durational spans, and it completes an eight-measure (and, on a higher level, a sixteen-measure) unit at the end of the C-minor section, enhancing the downbeat character of measure 44.

I mentioned earlier in the essay that a span divided into six undifferentiated units could count as either three twos or two threes. The six-measure span of measures 44–49 offers a case in point, but a feeling for the organic connection of diminutions provides a solution. The arpeggio figure represents the enlarged transposition of measures 1–2, and the six mea-sures must therefore fall into two threes. Similarly, the six-measure spans starting in mea-sure 58 (measures 58–63 and 64–69) form two groups of three measures each; here melodic contours also support a scansion in threes. This means that the rhythmic dissonance—the conflict between the three-measure groupings of the right hand and the underlying duple meter—is quite sharp. The duple meter, it will be remembered, is announced by the two measures of upbeat; it continues in the harmonic rhythm of measures 50–55 and it explains the left-hand register change of measure 66.

The rhythmic dissonances come across more clearly in level c, which eliminates melodic figuration but retains the right hand's grouping in threes. Otherwise this level requires no further comment, and we can turn to levels a and b. A comparison of these two levels shows that I infer underlying eight-measure spans as the hypermeter of highest order in the ex-cerpt, and that I regard the twelve- and sixteen-measure units of the foreground as the prod-ucts of expansion. In both cases the expansion acts upon the initial harmony of the section and extends it enormously compared to the few other harmonies. In this excerpt, of course, no literal model precedes the first expansion; the prototype is accessible only through the inference of higher-level organization. Perhaps the expanded first phrase might be regarded as a sort of prototype that is further expanded in the second phrase. The further expansion makes possible the large-scale rhythmic dissonance (groups of six measures against groups of eight) that characterizes this section.

In this excerpt the tonal rhythm certainly does not determine the larger measure-groupings; the enormous expansion at the beginning of each phrase indicates the contrary. But, within the expansions, the inner groupings in threes reflect both the tonal rhythms and the motivic design; these inner groupings, therefore, "serve a diminution organically." Part of the difficulty of this excerpt results from the number of rhythmic manipulations that act upon rather meager tonal contents over a very short span of time. Since much of my rhythmic interpretation of this complexity results from the inference of higher-level organization, its validity remains ultimately unprovable though, I hope, demonstrable. I can only ask the reader to judge it on the basis of the whole piece in all of its significant aspects. In particular I would ask him to view both the three-measure groups and the underlying eight-measure units in the light of their origins in the C-minor section. (Incidentally, Tovey also infers two-measure upbeats and an eight-measure group starting in measure 38; but he does not mention the cross-rhythms nor does he infer metrical expansions of background prototypes.)[37]

I should like to give brief mention to two additional features of the Beethoven move-ment, though they do not relate to the topic of expansions. I read measure 72 at the *seconda volta* as a seventh measure reinterpreted as a first; in this way the three-measure upbeat of the reprise fits into a four-measure hypermeasure. And I should like to call the reader's attention to a characteristically Beethovenian treatment of surface rhythm. We have seen how dynamics and registral contrast in the C-minor section emphasized the second, metrically weak, *measures* of two-measure groups (pp. 9ff.). And in the Ab-major Trio section, the right hand's entrances emphasize the second, metrically weak, *beats* of 3/4 measures. In the reprise of the C-minor section, Beethoven writes out varied repeats with the slurred right hand syncopated against the staccato left; the syncopations stress the second, metrically weak, *halves* of the quarter-note beats.[38]

Mendelssohn, "Song without Words," Op. 102, No. 4

This beautiful piece is as complicated metrically as the Beethoven excerpt (Example 3.20) and far more complicated tonally. It is ruled by conflicts. The tonal conflicts arise because chromatically inflected notes tend to displace the diatonic scale degrees from which they originate; this process involves two note-pairs, Eb–E♮ and Ab–A♮. The sudden appearance of E♮ in measure 3 (displacing the previously established Eb) also signals the opening of a metric conflict: beat 3 seems to usurp the function of a downbeat.

The struggle for supremacy between beats 1 and 3 runs through the piece. Important points of articulation in the accompaniment always emphasize first beats (e.g., measures 1, 7, 12, 20, 29, 31, and 35), whereas the phrase beginnings of the melody emphasize third beats (measures 3, 8, 12, 14, 16, 22, etc.). These third-beat stresses set up a schema of metrical partitioning that, for much of the piece, is more strongly in evidence than the notated one. Yet it is the notated meter that governs the beginning of the piece in a way that creates reasonable suspicions about the legitimacy of the presumed downbeat at the third beat of measure 3. And the notated meter emerges very clearly both at the big final cadence (measures 29–31) and in the final phase of the coda (measures 35–40).

I shall attempt to deal with the metrical conflict in a durational reduction, but the tonal structure is sufficiently complex to require at least a middleground graph as well (Example 3.21). In presenting this graph I should like to call particular attention to the remarkable effect of the reprise—an aspect of composition in which Mendelssohn often demonstrates a truly astonishing imagination and virtuosity. The main issue in this piece is that the unusual and surprising beginning, with its striking entrance of the melody over the chromatic C7 chord, does not permit a literal recapitulation starting with a tonic. To maintain a sufficient degree of tonal (and psychological) tension, the chromatic chord must enter in a new and unpredictable way. That in itself poses no very great problem; the difficulty is to integrate this new path into the larger tonal progression of the piece.

Mendelssohn solves this problem by connecting the prolonged Bb of measures 16–18 with the Bb^7 chord of measure 23; note that measure 23 is an exact replica of measure 4 except for the crescendo-decrescendo signs, which occur only in measure 23. Their purpose is to emphasize the Bb^7 so that the performer can project its connection with the last stable event before it, the B♮ triad of measures 16–18. The extended $^6_5$ on E♮ of measures 19–22 represents the C$^7_{\sharp}$ of measure 3. Despite its long duration, it is not a harmony of high structural order; its tonal function is to lead to the F of measure 23, the unfolded upper fifth of the prolonged Bb chord. In another setting, so great an emphasis on a structurally subordinate element might be unconvincing; in this piece, however, the C$^7_{\sharp}$ takes a leading part in projecting the

EXAMPLE 3.21: Mendelssohn, *Songs without Words*, Op. 102, No. 4, middleground graph

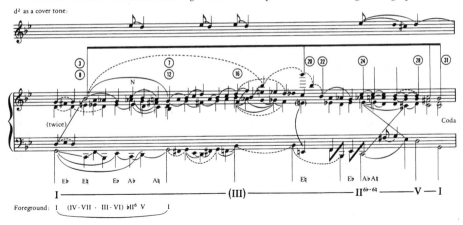

chromatic conflict between E♭ and E♮, and measures 19–22 contain the final climactic expression of E♮. Some such emphasis, therefore, is more than justifiable; it is a necessity.

I must mention a beautiful detail of the recapitulation, for it is a wonderful illustration of how the masters achieved a coherent foreground design. The descending arpeggio of measure 21 is decorated by seemingly insignificant chromatic lower neighbors that coalesce into a stepwise line, f♯¹–g¹–a¹–b♭¹ in measure 22. As Example 3.22 shows, this pseudo fourth (it is really the third g¹–b♭¹ decorated by a lower neighbor) transports to a new harmonic setting the exact pitches heard over tonic harmony in measures 1–3; its sequential repetition in measure 23 makes explicit a disguised parallelism in measures 1–4.

Example 3.23 analyzes the Mendelssohn piece by means of a durational reduction ($\mathbf{o} = \mathbf{\cdot}$) in four levels. The one nearest the foreground (level d) represents the metrical conflict by means of an additional staff, which shows notated third beats as downbeats. A perusal of levels a, b, and c reveals that important structural points, especially in the bass, fall on strong beats of the notated meter. And even level d, a slightly reduced foreground, shows the rival schemata moving out of and back into phase with one another. Although the apparent meter fills more time than the notated one, it is the notated meter that governs the beginning, the structural cadence, the end, and two important points of articulation: measures 7 and 20. As in the Schumann piece analyzed earlier, therefore, it is the notated meter that must be regarded as primary here.

The added staff above level d contains "premature" bar lines at measures 7, 12, 20, 27, and 35. In a sense these represent weak time points reinterpreted as strong, but these are reinterpretations of a highly unusual kind, for they result from the basic meter's overthrowing

EXAMPLE 3.22: Mendelssohn, *Songs without Words*, Op. 102, No. 4, measures 20–23 and 1–4

EXAMPLE 3.23: Mendelssohn, *Songs without Words*, Op. 102, No. 4, durational reduction

the rival meter that had usurped its authority. All of these reinterpretations connect, in one way or another, with the metrical expansions that form such a striking feature of the piece. The first expansion (measures 1–3) stretches the initial downbeat measure to a length of two and a half measures—long enough to establish the notated meter and to introduce E♭ as an important motivic element. The intrusive entrance of the C $^7_4$ chord in measure 3 disturbs both the established meter and the diatonic tonal pattern. In a kind of composed stretto, the second expansion (measures 7–8) forms a shortened repetition of the first; the rhythmic tightening continues after the second phrase, for there is no expansion at all at measure 12. Note how the shortening of the second expansion sustains the sense of surprise at the second entrance of the C $^7_4$. The third expansion (measures 20–22) has precisely the same length as the first, to which it corresponds, but the harmonic content is altogether different. The last expansion forms what one might call the coda of the coda (measures 35–40). I regard it as stretching the final downbeat of the piece into a complete four-measure group enlarged further by an added downbeat formation at the very end.

Perhaps the most interesting, and certainly the most challenging, of the piece's five expansions is the one that begins in the middle of measure 24 and continues through measure 30. The prototype for the expanded phrase is, of course, the very first phrase of the piece; through the expansion the reprise, which fills only one phrase, has a length commensurate

with that of the first section, whose contents occur twice. The added duration emphasizes the II[6] and V of the piece's final, structural cadence. Each of these harmonies occupies its own expansion. The II[6] fills four and a half measures compared to the half measure of its model (measure 5, second half). The V occupies two measures as against the one measure allotted to it in the opening phrase. A beautiful feature of the expanded II[6] is the chromaticized voice exchange that forms part of it and that powerfully enhances the effect of the structural cadence. It is during this cadence that the primary metrical schema receives its strongest and most sustained expression.

Conclusion

I began the first essay in this book by discussing the widespread belief that Schenker's writings reveal an almost complete neglect of rhythm. While agreeing that Schenker's work in the field of rhythm cannot compare in depth, scope, or comprehensiveness with his achievements in the areas of tonal structure and voice leading, I maintained that the charge of neglect is far from accurate, and that Schenker has much to teach us about rhythm. In concluding this final essay of this part of the book I should like to point out that almost every one of my analytic examples embodies ideas of Schenker's, either taken over directly or developed further by me. If the ideas elaborated in this article and the analyses that illustrate them reveal anything significant about musical rhythm and meter, they are testimony to the continuing creative force that emanates from the work of our greatest music theorist, Heinrich Schenker.

Notes

1. See Hugo Riemann, *Katechismus der Kompositionslehre* (Leipzig: Hesse, 1889), vol. 2, p. 17; Joel Lester, "Articulation of Tonal Structures as a Criterion for Analytic Choices," *Music Theory Spectrum* 1 (1979), p. 78; Heinrich Schenker, *Free Composition*, trans. and ed. Ernst Oster (New York: Longman, 1979), p. 122 and figure 141; Edward T. Cone, *Musical Form and Musical Performance* (New York: Norton, 1968), pp. 28–31; and Robert P. Morgan, "The Theory and Analysis of Tonal Rhythm," *Musical Quarterly* 64 (1978), pp. 446–47.

2. Mozart shifted the position of the bar lines in the otherwise completed duet "Bei Männem" from *The Magic Flute*; Schubert changed his mind twice about the position of the bar lines in the introduction and postlude of his song "Frühlingsglaube." See the new Mozart and Schubert editions (which include facsimile pages): W. A. Mozart, *Die Zauberflöte*, ed. Gernot Gruber and Alfred Orel, *Neue Ausgabe sämtlicher Werke*, series 2, vol. 19 (Kassel: Bärenreiter, 1970); and Franz Schubert, *Lieder*, ed. Walther Dürr, *Neue Ausgabe sämtlicher Werke*, series 4, vol. la (third version of "Fruhlingsglaube"; the first and second versions are given in vol. 1b) (Kassel: Bärenreiter, 1970).

3. The two articles reprinted as the first two chapters in this volume will be hereafter referred to as Rhythm I and Rhythm II.

4. See the very perceptive discussion in Oswald Jonas, *Introduction to the Theory of Heinrich Schenker: The Nature of the Musical Work of Art*, trans. and ed. John Rothgeb (New York: Longman, 1982), p. 10.

5. See Arthur Komar, *Theory of Suspensions: A Study of Metrical and Pitch Relation in Tonal Music* (Princeton: Princeton University Press, 1971), pp. 52–54; Maury Yeston, *The Stratification of Musical Rhythm* (New Haven: Yale University Press, 1976), pp. 65–67; and Fred Lerdahl and Ray Jackendoff, "On the Theory of Grouping and Meter," *Musical Quarterly* 67 (1981), pp. 486–89, and *A Generative Theory of Tonal Music* (Cambridge: MIT Press, 1983), chapter 2.

6. Rhythm II, pp. 210–15; this volume, pp. 62–65.

7. Lerdahl and Jackendoff, "On the Theory of Grouping and Meter," pp. 500–506, and *A Generative Theory of Tonal Music*, p. 17 and 30–35.

8. Rhythm II, pp. 215–22; this volume, pp. 65–70.

9. Donald Francis Tovey, *A Companion to Beethoven's Pianoforte Sonatas* (London: Associated Board, 1931), pp. 98–99.

10. Ludwig van Beethoven, *32 Sonatas for the Pianoforte*, ed. Artur Schnabel (New York: Simon and Schuster, 1935), vol. 1, p. 285.

11. Yeston, *The Stratification of Musical Rhythm*, p. 66.

12. The rhythmic compression of the rising fourth, d^2–g^2, articulates quarter-note spans as early as measure 2; Yeston surely exaggerates when he states that "measure 9 is the first clear representation of the meter signature," ibid., p. 85.

13. Schenker, *Free Composition*, p. 119.

14. Thrasybulos G. Georgiades, *Schubert: Musik und Lyrik* (Göttingen: Vandenhoeck and Ruprecht, 1967), p. 19, partially translated as "Lyric as Musical Structure: Schubert's *Wanderers Nachtlied*," trans. Marie Louise Göllner, in *Schubert: Critical and Analytical Studies*, ed. Walter Frisch (Lincoln: University of Nebraska Press, 1986), p. 87.

15. Heinrich Schenker, ed., *Die letzten fünf Sonaten von Beethoven, Sonate As-Dur Op. 110, Erläuterungsausgabe* (Vienna: Universal, 1914), p. 46 (introduction); rev. ed., ed. Oswald Jonas (Vienna: Universal, 1972), p. 51.

16. See Charles Seeger, "On Dissonant Counterpoint," *Modern Music 7* (1930), pp. 25–31; and Yeston, *The Stratification of Musical Rhythm*, pp. 78–79.

17. Edward E. Lowinsky, "On Mozart's Rhythm," in *The Creative World of Mozart*, ed. Paul Henry Lang (New York: Norton, 1963), p. 33.

18. Ibid., pp. 32–34.

19. The motto comes from a Mazurka by Clara Wieck, the fifth piece in her *Soirées musicales*, Op. 6. The citation is taken from the very beginning of the piece, where it is in the same metrical position as here, and where the downbeats are emphasized by accents.

20. Both the first and second editions (dating from 1837–38 and 1850–51, respectively) are given in Robert Schumann, *Werke*, ed. Clara Schumann (Leipzig: Breitkopf and Härtel, 1881–93), series 7, vol. 1, pp. 96–97 and 120–21. Most modern publications reprint only the second edition; both editions, however, may be found in Schumann, *Complete Works for Piano Solo* (New York: Kalmus, n.d.), vol. 1, pp. 105–6 and 132–33.

21. Schenker, *Free Composition*, pp. 124–26. Figures 149/3, 4, and 5 of *Free Composition* illustrate Schenker's extra downbeat measures.

22. See Rhythm II, especially pp. 214–15; this volume, pp. 63–65.

23. William Rothstein, "Rhythm and the Theory of Structural Levels," Ph.D. dissertation, Yale University, 1981, pp. 150–80. Rothstein's book *Phrase Rhythm in Tonal Music* (New York: Schirmer, 1989) has a good deal more about expansions. See especially Chapter 3, "Phrase Expansion," which relates Schenker's concept of earlier theorists, including Kirnberger, Koch, Reicha, and Riemann.

24. Schenker, *Free Composition*, p. 124. Schenker's term is *metrisches Vorbild*. See *Der freie Satz* (Vienna: Universal, 1935); 2d ed., rev. Oswald Jonas (Vienna: Universal, 1956), p. 192.

25. See Rhythm I, p. 285; this volume, pp. 19–20.

26. Schenker, *Free Composition*, p. 124.

27. Heinrich Schenker, "Mozart: Sinfonie G-Moll," *Das Meisterwerk in der Musik*, 3 vols. (Munich: Drei Masken Verlag, 1925, 1926, 1930, reissued as 3 vols. in 1 in slightly reduced facsimile, Hildesheim: Georg Olms; 1974), vol. 2, p. 146, trans. William Drabkin, in *The Masterwork in Music*, ed. William Drabkin, vol. 2 (Cambridge: Cambridge University Press, 1996), p. 87.

28. See Rhythm I, p. 285; this volume, pp. 19–20.

29. Schenker, "Mozart's Symphony in G Minor," pp. 68–69.

30. Heinrich Schenker, *Five Graphic Music Analyses*, new introduction by Felix Salzer (New York: Dover, 1969), pp. 36–37.

31. Schenker, *Free Composition*, figure 148/2.

32. Ibid., p. 124, footnote 4.

33. Rothstein, "Rhythm and the Theory of Structural Levels," p. 170.

34. Ibid., p. 171.

35. Ibid., p. 172.

36. Schenker, *Free Composition*, p. 124.

37. Tovey, *A Companion to Beethoven's Pianoforte Sonatas*, p. 99.

38. Compare this with the treatment of sforzandi in the Allegretto of Beethoven's Op. 14, No. 1, discussed in Rhythm II, pp. 220–22; this volume, pp. 69–70.

PART II

SCHENKERIAN THEORY

FOUR

Either/Or

I shall begin by citing a brief excerpt from that recent masterpiece, Italo Calvino's *Invisible Cities*. It is one of the passages in which Marco Polo converses with the Emperor Kublai Khan:

> Marco Polo describes a bridge, stone by stone.
>
> "But which is the stone that supports the bridge?" Kublai Khan asks.
>
> "The bridge is not supported by one stone or another," Marco answers, "but by the line of the arch that they form."
>
> Kublai Khan remains silent, reflecting. Then he adds: "Why do you speak to me of the stones? It is only the arch that matters to me."
>
> Polo answers: "Without stones there is no arch."[1]

Detail and Context

As a parable of the relation between detail and context in music, Calvino's little conversation could hardly be surpassed. It is of course a truism of Schenkerian analysis and, largely thanks to Schenker's work, a generally accepted idea these days that a compositional detail, like the stone in the arch, derives meaning from its context; the same note, chord, or melodic succession will "mean" different things in different surroundings. But it is also true that the larger shape manifests itself to the listener only after he has correctly understood certain crucial details, for unlike the curve of an arch, the underlying shape of a musical line is not always immediately evident to the person perceiving. The descending fourth shown in my Example 4.1, for instance, can be heard and recognized without any problem

Originally published in *Schenker Studies*, ed. Hedi Siegel (Cambridge: Cambridge University Press, 1990), pp. 165–79. An earlier version was read at the First International Schenker Symposium at the Mannes College of Music in April 1985.

EXAMPLE 4.1: A descending fourth: some possible interpretations

if all four notes occur in immediate succession. But if the fourth stretches over eight, or twenty, or sixty measures, as well it might, only through certain telling details will even the most skillful and experienced listener be able to hear that it forms the guiding idea of its context. And even after having perceived the fourth, the listener has obtained only a very incomplete and preliminary understanding, for as the example shows, even such a simple structure can mean many different things.

Everyone with a little experience in Schenker's approach learns that certain successions and combinations of notes inevitably create a forked path for the analyst, who must search for clues about which of two or more possible interpretations is the correct one, or about which of two or more "correct" ones is the truest artistically. With a bit more experience he may begin to be able to predict the direction of some of the forks, for an important but little discussed feature of the tonal system is the way that certain tonal configurations evoke specific clusters of possible interpretations. The descending fourth of Example 4.1 is one such configuration, and the example shows the likeliest interpretations; many other melodic figures make similar demands upon the analyst's judgment.

Harmonic Interpretation

It is probably in the sphere of harmony, however, that the most frequent and difficult problems arise, and it is mainly questions of harmonic interpretation that I shall discuss in this essay. A problematic character is inherent in the very nature of harmony, whose fundamental unit, the functional chord, or *Stufe*, exists not as a combination of particular sounds, but only as a kind of Platonic idea that can realize itself in many such combinations. There is no such "thing" as a I chord in C major, but only an idea that can find expression through the notes C, E, and G in any kind of simultaneous blending, through intervals created by two of these notes, through the note C alone, through such combinations as C–E♭–G, C–E–G–A, and C–E–G–B♭, through melodic lines of the most various shapes, through whole constellations of contrapuntal lines and chord successions controlled by the note C. As Schenker so beautifully expresses it in the Preface to his *Harmony*, "In contrast to the theory of counterpoint, the theory of harmony presents itself to me as a purely spiritual universe, a system of ideally moving forces born of Nature or of art."[2]

In this essay I shall discuss some of the ways context can illuminate detail and detail can clarify context with respect to harmonic interpretation and to questions of voice leading that impinge on harmony. I shall point out some of the kinds of clues to large structure that an examination of details can yield, though it is far from my intention to offer a "method for the reading of diminutions" or, God help us, a "theory of reduction." I strongly doubt that such methods or theories can be made to work, for I believe that the understanding of detail begins with an intuitive grasp of large structure, however imperfect or incomplete, a process that is ultimately resistant to rigorous formulation.

IV (II) or I?

Example 4.2a illustrates, in schematic form, a particularly frequent and sometimes trouble-some problem in harmonic analysis: is the governing chord of a given stretch of music a IV or a I? For this problem to arise, the IV (or perhaps II) must precede the I within the span in question, and a strong V must appear thereafter. In our abstract example, the "I" of the second measure can be heard either as a continuation of the initial (and obviously structural) tonic harmony or as a subordinate element connecting IV and V. As the little two-part pro-gressions of Examples 4.2b and 4.2c suggest, both of our harmonic interpretations rest on a foundation of logical and coherent voice leading. If we infer a IV, the e^2 of the melody is basically a passing seventh transformed into a consonance by the C chord under it. If we infer a I, the f^2 is a neighbor-note shifted to the downbeat, where it takes on the guise of a 4–3 suspension; here the F chord provides the consonant support. Which of the two read-ings is correct? The arid surface of our abstract example can provide decisive confirmation for neither interpretation; therefore one is as good or as bad as the other. This illustrates, incidentally, why the study of harmony must, to a large extent, involve itself with the analysis of compositions and with the writing of quasi-compositional exercises; to study the endless formulas in white notes that disfigure so many harmony texts is to learn almost nothing about the ways chords can be prolonged and, therefore, to learn too little about harmony.

How different is the picture that emerges from a study of the opening phrase of a Chopin Mazurka, quoted in Example 4.3. Here, too, we can question whether measures 5 and 6 con-tinue to express the prolonged tonic of measures 1–4 (Example 4.3a) or introduce IV as a new harmony (Example 4.3b), but unlike the abstract example, the Mazurka can give us reasons for our choice. On the basis of harmony and voice leading alone, we could hardly decide, for the setting is a spare and unpretentious one in which the beautiful melodic line receives a bare minimum of contrapuntal and harmonic support. The Mazurka, however, has a particularly refined and intricately worked out motivic design, which begins to un-fold in these opening measures. The basic figure of this design is the neighbor-note figure D♯–E–D♯ that I have sketched in above the music in Example 4.3a. Indeed it is largely this figure (an age-old "lament" motive) that carries out the "Mesto" character of the Mazurka.

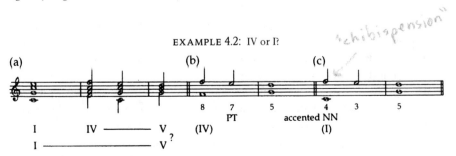

EXAMPLE 4.2: IV or I?

EXAMPLE 4.3: Chopin, Mazurka, Op. 33, No. 1

But to infer its presence requires that we hear a composed-out tonic in measures 2–6; reading a IV in measure 5, for instance, leads us to hear the d#² as a supported passing note rather than as the resolution of a neighbor-note and destroys the integrity of the figure, as can be seen in Example 4.3b. (A third reading, inferring a I in measure 5 and a IV in measure 6, is possible, and it would not affect the D#–E–D# figure in the soprano line. But the two measures are so clearly parallel that this reading seems rather capricious and arbitrary.)³

If we hear an overarching tonic harmony in measures 2–6 of our Chopin example, and, in my opinion, that is the only tenable interpretation, it is because of the motivic implications of the upper line and for that reason alone. The other factors that might influence our reading—phrase contour, rhythm, texture—would as easily (but no more easily) support our hearing a IV as governing the measures in question. That design often gives us a key to large-scale structure is hardly news; but the often crucial role of motivic details in specifying the governing harmony of a passage is, I think, not sufficiently acknowledged.

Such acknowledgment leads to another important insight. The possibility of interpreting our abstract example in two different, mutually exclusive, and equally valid ways might lead one to conclude that the same tonal configuration is just as ambiguous when it appears in a composition. And this conclusion, in turn, would lead one to believe that the three alternative analyses of Example 4.3, for instance, are equally good. But this belief would be erroneous. One of the three readings is truer to the Mazurka as a unique and individual work of art than are the other two, which can be considered valid only from a perspective that takes in general aspects of tonal structure but that excludes the specific features of the piece's design.

This is not to deny the possibility that ambiguity and multiple meanings might exist in tonal music; they certainly do exist. But their function, in my opinion, is more narrowly circumscribed than some analysts, perhaps misled by false analogies to language, seem to believe. It is just as much a part of the composer's art as it is of the sculptor's or painter's to be able to create clear and distinct shapes; the more clearly and vividly the listener perceives these shapes, the more fully and deeply will he live the life of the composition as he hears it.

Motivic factors are just as decisive in Example 4.4, the beginning of the slow movement of Haydn's Symphony No. 99. Here the fork in the road leads, on the one hand, to the inference of a prolonged II in measures 9–11 or, on the other, to interpreting the G chord of

EXAMPLE 4.4: Haydn, Symphony No. 99, second movement

measure 10 as a I that completes a tonic prolongation begun in measure 7. Only the first alternative deserves serious consideration. The way measure 11 repeats the beginning of measure 9, with its dotted turn and rising third, points to a connection in voice leading (see the brackets marked "x" in Example 4.4b). In addition, the rhythmic emphases and the inner articulations of the phrase—factors that were not decisive in the Chopin excerpt—support the inference of a prolonged II. Note, incidentally, that the melodic structure of measures 9–11 uses most of the same scale degrees—indeed almost the same notes—as measures 5–6 of the Mazurka (E–D–C–B here and D♯–E–D♯–C♯–B in the Chopin), but that contextual differences lead to interpretative ones.

This excerpt contains a wonderful motivic parallelism—subtler than any in Example 4.3 (though not subtler than some that occur later on in the Mazurka). The unstemmed notes on the staff above the graph in Example 4.4b show that the seemingly insignificant link of parallel thirds played by the bassoons at the turn of measures 6–7 reappears in fantastic enlargement in the violin melody of measures 9–12. This parallelism also suggests that II, not I, must govern measures 9 and 10, though in the absence of other supporting evidence so subtle and seemingly tenuous a connection would not determine the outcome. Apropos of its being tenuous I might mention that just this figure—a descending third and second combining into a fourth (or in this case a pseudo fourth)—serves as the primary agent of continuity in this movement, binding whole sections together (note that it already appears in measures 2–3).

Problems in Locating Boundaries

In this excerpt, more strikingly than in the Mazurka, the rival analyses differ significantly with regard to the boundaries that they establish between prolongational spans. In both, a I moves to a II⁶, but each establishes the frontier at a different point. Questions of boundary lines between prolonged chords arise all the time; their proper solution is a necessary step toward understanding the rhythmic shape of a passage—if you will, toward understanding its "harmonic rhythm" more fully than in the usual superficial way. In the Haydn excerpt, the boundaries are located with great precision, yet the effect is that of a continuous song, far removed from anything mosaic-like or segmented. Part of the reason lies in a kind of unity of color resulting from the very economical chordal vocabulary; there are G chords within prolongations of A minor, and A-minor chords within prolongations of G. The A chord of measure 8, for instance, should be heard as passing within a G-major harmony (G inflected to G♯ to lead to the A-minor prolongation of the next measure); it would spoil the rhythmic effect to hear the prolongation of II already beginning in measure 8. Even more significant than the pervasive use of G-major and A-minor sounds are the ever-present suspended sevenths and their derivatives, which culminate in the climactic suspended ninth of measure 15 (compare measure 15 with measure 2, out of which it grows).

The Apparent Tonic

The G chord in measure 10 of the Haydn example might be termed an "apparent tonic"— that is, a chord constructed like a tonic but without a tonic's function. It does not form the beginning or goal of a significant prolongational span, and it does not connect convincingly with another similar chord that does function as beginning or goal. Therefore it represents a relatively low-level event within the span of measures 9–11, whereas a true tonic is, in principle, the highest-level harmony within its span, ultimately generating all the others.[4] Deciding whether to read a chord as a true or only an apparent tonic is a very frequent analytic problem. Its solution is sometimes decisive for understanding the form of a piece.

Formal Divisions

Boundaries between prolongational spans—especially between those spans governed by structural harmonies—often coincide with points of formal articulation. In a sonata movement, the boundary between the interrupted V and the resumed structural I is also usually the boundary between the development and the recapitulation. Sometimes, however, the extension of a prolongational span bridges over the formal division. There are two beautiful instances of this in the Gavotte en Rondeaux from Bach's E-major Partita for Unaccompanied Violin; Example 4.5 shows one of them.

Example 4.5 quotes the end of the third couplet and the beginning of the fourth rondeau section; the couplet gravitates to and strongly cadences in F♯ minor (II), while the rondeau, of course, returns to E major.[5] One might be tempted to hear this return to E as occurring at the usual spot—the beginning of the reprise (measure 64, second half)—but this interpretation would be most unconvincing here. Since II lacks a direct harmonic relationship with I but has one with V, and since V appears prominently at the head of measure 66, it makes more sense, on harmonic grounds alone, to infer a connection II-V. Furthermore, that connection is composed out in the voice leading of the passage, whose "bass" passes by step from II through II⁶ to V. The reprise, then, begins with an apparent tonic—a passing chord between II and II⁶. Note how Bach, to achieve this stepwise bass, transforms the opening chord of the reprise from a $\frac{5}{3}$ to a $\frac{6}{3}$.

Because of its position in the form, the apparent tonic of this excerpt has an effect very different from that of the one in the Haydn movement. By unmistakably signaling a return to the rondeau, it simultaneously signals an imminent return to tonic harmony, though it does not embody that return. Here we have a true double meaning: the E chord does not function as a tonic, but, almost like some negative formulations in language, it asserts the existence of that which it is not. Furthermore, it acts upon the F♯ harmony that it prolongs in a most important way: it transforms it from the local tonic of measure 64 to the II on the way to the V of measure 66. Incidentally, one ought to reformulate the valuable notion of the "pivot chord" in the light of modulating passages like this one. In such passages one would find pivots on two levels. Here the "background pivot" is the prolonged F♯-minor chord itself, which changes in function from a local I to a II. But it is the E-major passing chord (the "foreground pivot") that effects this change in function.

EXAMPLE 4.5: J. S. Bach, Partita No. 3 for Unaccompanied Violin, Gavotte en Rondeaux

One might imagine that the presence of a formal division within a harmonic and voice-leading continuity would tend to break up that continuity, but here, I think, the opposite turns out to be true. The sense of harmonic arrival at the V of measure 66 and the sense of directed linear motion in the passage leading to that goal are, if anything, intensified by their play against the opposing force of sectional articulation.

Before leaving this example, I should like to mention one point of general significance. A fundamental difference exists between an apparent tonic, like the one that begins this reprise, and a chord of any other harmonic function consigned to a lower structural level than its position in the piece's form might at first seem to warrant. A dominant, say, at the double bar of a movement in a Bach suite can function as a relatively low-level divider rather than as part of the Fundamental Structure without necessarily ceasing to function as a dominant. But by definition a tonic is the highest-level harmony within any prolongation of which it forms a part; a demotion in rank necessarily strips it of its tonic insignia (but see note 4).

One Inclusive Structure or Two Successive Ones?

With our next example we come to a very different fork in the road (or perhaps a fork in a very different road). The choice here is between understanding the harmonic background of an extensive passage as comprising two large cadences or combining the two into a single, still more inclusive structure. As in the Bach Gavotte, the harmonic interpretation impinges upon our understanding of the piece's form, only here the problem involves the meaning of a whole section, not just a point of articulation. The piece in question is the Larghetto movement from Mozart's Piano Concerto in C Minor, and it is illustrated in the graphs of Example 4.6. The movement is composed as a rondo in five parts; its two episodes are in C minor and Ab major—VI and IV of the Eb-major tonality of the movement. The rondo theme itself has an ABA design, and a length of nineteen measures at its first appearance. The second return corresponds closely to the original statement, but the omission of a four-measure repeat reduces it to fifteen measures instead of nineteen. The first return, however, appears in drastically curtailed form, for it is represented by a mere four-measure phrase.

In his brief discussion of five-part rondo form in *Free Composition*, Schenker explains it as the combination of two three-part forms: ABA and ACA combine to form ABACA.[6] Schenker specifies that neither the variation nor the abbreviation of the A section in one or more of its later appearances effects a fundamental change in the rondo principle; abbreviation and variation, of course, both occur in this movement. According to Schenker, the B and C sections of a rondo have as their tonal basis the same elements as the middle sections of ternary forms: modal mixture, neighbor-notes, sevenths above the V chord, and so forth. In our Mozart movement, both episodes lead back to the rondo theme through retransitions composed around very strong dominant seventh chords; both times the seventh is in the soprano, forming an upper neighbor to the G of the movement's Fundamental Line. In the Ab section, the melodic Ab, seventh of the coming dominant, is prepared as a consonance. Example 4.6a, a middleground sketch of the entire movement, accords with Schenker's explanation of rondo form. Accordingly it shows two large cadences, I–VI–V–I and I–IV–V–I, before the structural I–V–I that supports the descent of the Fundamental Line in the third A section.

EXAMPLE 4.6: Mozart, Piano Concerto, K.491, second movement

(a) middleground sketch (measure numbers follow the upper voice)

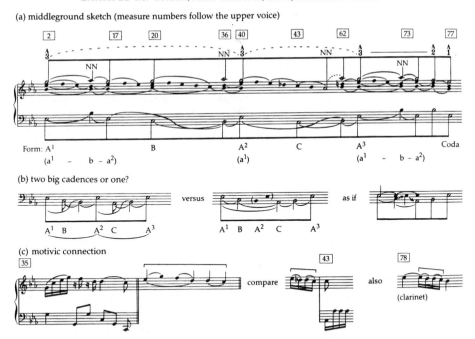

(b) two big cadences or one?

(c) motivic connection

This interpretation makes a good deal of sense, and it is certainly a defensible reading of the movement. Still, I find it less than completely satisfying, for I miss in it something that I hear in the music—a connection that is more than a casual, associative one between the C-minor and the A♭ episodes; like many commonsense explanations, this one fails to match the complexities of experience. Why must I hear the two episodes as closely connected? First of all, *pace* Schenker, the brevity of the second A section influences my hearing. Although the elaborate retransition effects a return to tonic harmony, that return seems to me to be too fleeting to match the weight of the first and third statements. Second, the orchestration—dominated in both episodes by the wind nonet—provides a strong coloristic link, a link reinforced by the piano, which both times provides a varied repeat of the wind parts. Third, the foreground keys, if heard as linked, fuse into a coherent progression: I (first A section) arpeggiating through VI (first episode) to IV (second episode), V⁷ (retransition), and I (third A section). Example 4.6b diagrams the two readings.

The second reading in Example 4.6b receives confirmation from a most beautiful and refined motivic link: the upbeat that introduces the A♭ section is a reminiscence—disguised but recognizable—of the melodic figure that closes the C-minor episode (Example 4.6c). Thus the second episode begins where the first one had left off, as though the brief intervening reprise had been a mere digression. Note that the coda begins with still another transformation of this same figure.

If the two episodes are linked (as I think they are), what, then, would be the harmonic meaning of the second A section? Surely it is no merely apparent tonic; the elaborate V⁷ that prepares it precludes any explanation of that kind. Indeed, when the reprise begins, one hears the E♭ major as a fully stable tonic that forms the goal of the large harmonic motion developed in the episode and retransition. But when it breaks off after only four measures, and when a new section begins that connects in tonal motion, orchestral color, and motivic design with the first episode, sensitive retrospective hearing will modify that initial impression of stability. This tonic return will be understood as a brief parenthetical statement that brings into momentary consciousness the tonal motion's point of departure just before it continues on to its next important goal.

As the third diagram in Example 4.6b points out, this incidental tonic return can be regarded as a special instance of the retained tone. The E♭ that begins the bass line is retained conceptually through the C-minor and A♭-major episodes, becoming the third and fifth of their respective "tonics." Not infrequently, middleground structures—linear progressions or arpeggiations—that compose out a prior verticality (as this E♭–C–A♭ composes out the fifth E♭–A♭) will be segmented in a way that allows the background structure to "peer through"; thus E♭–C–A♭ becomes E♭–C–(E♭)–A♭.

Both/And

If my reading of the Mozart movement is correct, it reveals a genuine double meaning: the large-scale bass motion traverses a descending arpeggio E♭–C–A♭; within the same time span, but less significantly, it also encompasses a return to E♭. That these two events can coexist without contradiction is due to the implicit presence of the E♭ throughout the arpeggiated motion. On the foreground, "polyphonic melodies" often reveal small-scale segmentations of a similar nature: the subject of Bach's Two-Part Invention in F Major embodies both a rising arpeggio and an initial note (f^1) that persists in returning.

Our final piece shows a double meaning of a different sort, one that involves a motivic association that persists in the face of a changed harmonic meaning. Everyone who has worked for a while with Schenker's approach will have run into bass lines that fill the gap from I up to V with both the third and fourth notes of the scale (and possibly with the second as well). Such lines pose an analytic problem: is the basic progression I–III (or I⁶)–V with the fourth scale degree passing between III and V, or is it rather I–IV (or II⁶)–V with scale degree 3 as the passing note? (If the line is completely stepwise, there is a third possibility as well: I–II–V–I, but it does not bear on the present discussion.) Example 4.7 shows the two possibilities.

Schenker addressed himself to this issue in *Free Composition*, in the section where he begins to show how the bass arpeggiation of the Fundamental Structure can be prolonged; indeed, my Example 4.7 is based on his Figure 14.[7] His explanation is most interesting. He begins by showing an arpeggiation 1–3–5, the most "natural" division of the rising fifth between tonic and dominant. He then indicates that the thirds formed by the arpeggio can be filled with

EXAMPLE 4.7: I–III/I⁶–V or I–IV/II⁶–V?

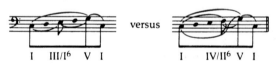

versus

I   III/I⁶   V   I   I   IV/II⁶   V   I

passing notes, producing a stepwise motion through the fifth; one or two of these stepwise notes will possibly fall away (basses tend to disjunct motion). And because of some emphasis built into the composition, one of the passing notes (scale degree 2 or 4) can become a focal point of sufficient importance to reduce scale degree 3 to a lower rank.[8] The type of emphasis that Schenker mentions is the one caused by the coincidence of the bass note in question with one of the notes of the Fundamental Line. Of course the same harmonic situation will often occur at lower levels where there is no question of supporting a note of the Fundamental Line; other kinds of emphasis (some of them related to the one Schenker cites) will then influence the analytic interpretation.

In Schubert's song "Auf dem Flusse," the broken chord E–G–B functions as a basic motive, linked both to the frozen river that forms the central image of the poem and to the protagonist's heart, whose icy crust and painfully seething interior are explicitly likened to the river. Rising figures that embody or reflect the motive permeate both the bass and the vocal line at middleground and foreground levels; changes in the motive follow the poem's imagery as it unfolds. The song is too long and too complex for me to discuss in its entirety here; in any case, many of its most interesting features do not bear directly on the topic of this essay.[9] Example 4.8a shows the basic motive, stated simultaneously in two forms: without elaboration in the bass and filled in with the briefest of passing notes in the upper voice. (At the beginning of the song, the vocal line is merely an embellished doubling of the bass. Not until measure 23 does an independent top line begin to develop.) And Example 4.8b quotes the postlude and sketches the way the motive dissolves into the final arpeggiated chord; the river becomes a mere blur on the horizon as the protagonist trudges on to new encounters.

With the change to major in measure 23 (Examples 4.8c and 4.8d), the arpeggio figure begins to undergo new transformations. The bass line of measure 23, E–G♯–A♯–B, remains close to the original form of the figure despite the upward register transfer of the first note. In particular the time frame—from downbeat to downbeat—remains the same. This one-measure statement, however, is nested within a larger bass motion whose contents, the linear progression E–F♯–G♯–A–A♯–B, stretch over the entire eight-measure phrase (see especially Example 4.8d). This structure traverses the same ground as the stepwise form of the basic motive (vocal part, measures 5–6), and it represents the biggest expansion and most significant transformation of the motive thus far in the song.

In the course of this expansion and transformation, one note of the line—the fourth scale degree (measures 28–29)—receives a double emphasis: it supports both the culminating note ($c^{\sharp 2}$) in a series of parallel tenths above the bass and $f^{\sharp 1}$, the note that connects most closely with the initial $g^{\sharp 1}$. The third scale degree, by contrast, recedes in importance; the harmonic structure of this phrase is surely I–II$^6_5$ rather than I–I^6–V. Here the emphasis on the active fourth scale degree mirrors the text, in which the narrator stops addressing the river and begins, however ineffectually, to act. The triadic arpeggiation 1–3–5, a Nature symbol, gives way to the dissonant passing tone that better expresses the world of human feeling and action. (In an almost uncanny way, Schenker's theoretical description of the prolonged bass line is embodied in the motivic design of this masterpiece.)

And yet this bass line, despite its changed harmonic meaning, grows out of the same higher-level structure as the 1–3–5 arpeggiation, and it must be regarded as a manifestation of the same underlying compositional idea. Unlike our earlier illustrations, where one and

EXAMPLE 4.8: Schubert, "Auf dem Flusse"

(a) measures 5–6, basic motive

(b) postlude

(c) measures 23–30, foreground
(upper 10ths)

(d) measures 23–30, middleground sketch
(upper 10ths)

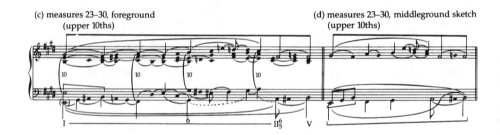

the same passage presented the listener with a choice between conflicting interpretations, here we encounter two distinct passages each with only one plausible interpretation. The difference in harmonic structure is far from negligible, but we can remain aware of it while also acknowledging the validity of a perspective from which the similarity in linear contour and over-all direction outweighs it. How important it is not to reify a theoretical construct like I–I⁶–V (remember Schenker's characterization of the theory of harmony as a "purely spiritual universe, a system of ideally moving forces"). Otherwise we run the risk of becoming imprisoned in our vocabularies and ways of thinking; without vigilance on our part, these can all too easily block our access to the music we wish to make our own.

Notes

1. Italo Calvino, *Invisible Cities*, trans. William Weaver (New York: Harcourt Brace, 1974), p. 82.

2. Heinrich Schenker, *Harmony*, ed. Oswald Jonas, trans. Elizabeth Mann Borgese (Chicago: University of Chicago Press, 1954), p. xxv.

3. But see Franz Eibner, "Chopins kontrapunktisches Denken," *Chopin-Jahrbuch* (Vienna: Notrig der Wissenschaftlichen Verbande Österreichs), pp. 106–97, especially figure 4c.

4. A seeming exception to this statement: interpolated or parenthetical passages and some instances of interruption-like segmentation may involve true tonics that belong to a lower level than

do one or more of the adjoining harmonies, but these tonics are displaced representatives of chords that are structural within a previous time span.

5. From a perspective that takes in the entire Gavotte, even the E major that is stabilized later in the return is not to be taken quite at face value, for large-scale tonal connections between the framing episodes take precedence over it. The issues are too complex for discussion here; I discuss the piece in some detail in a separate article, "The Gavotte en Rondeaux from J. S. Bach's Partita in E Major for Unaccompanied Violin," *Israel Studies in Musicology* 4 (1987), pp. 7–26.

6. Heinrich Schenker, *Free Composition*, trans. and ed. Ernst Oster (New York: Longman, 1979), p. 141.

7. Ibid., pp. 29–30 and figure 14.

8. I have discussed this issue in slightly more detail in "A Commentary on Schenker's *Free Composition*," *Journal of Music Theory* 25, no. 1 (1981), pp. 115–42, reprinted as Chapter 7 of this volume.

9. There is an incomplete middleground sketch in *Free Composition*, figure 40/2; the sketch reveals clearly the extent to which arpeggiated figures dominate the texture. Oswald Jonas, without mentioning the basic motive as such, discusses briefly some of its most fascinating transformations in his *Introduction to the Theory of Heinrich Schenker: The Nature of the Musical Work of Art*, trans. and ed. John Rothgeb (New York: Longman, 1982), p. 48. For a very different but interesting and thought-provoking approach to the song, see David Lewin, "Auf dem Flusse: Image and Background in a Schubert Song," in *19th-Century Music* 6, no. 1 (1982), pp. 47–59, reprinted in *Schubert: Critical and Analytical Studies*, ed. Walter Frisch (Lincoln: University of Nebraska Press, 1986), pp. 126–52.

Analysis by Key

Another Look at Modulation

Except for the point, the still point,
There would be no dance

(T. S. Eliot)

Until fairly recently, most musicians thought of Heinrich Schenker (if they thought of him at all) as the theorist who reduced whole pieces to three notes and denied that they modulated to different keys. Nowadays anyone familiar with music theory knows that Schenker did more than analyze the first movement of the *Eroica* as "Three Blind Mice" with a college education. But many still believe that he rejected outright the concept of key change, and indeed there is more justification for this misconception than for the other. Schenker was, to say the least, highly critical of the way the concept had been generally formulated and applied, and his own theory greatly reduces its scope. Near the beginning of *Free Composition*, for example, he writes as follows:

> But the most baneful error of conventional theory is its recourse to "*keys*" when, in its lack of acquaintance with background and middleground, it finds no other means of explanation. Often its helplessness is so great that it abandons even this most comfortable means of avoiding difficulties. Nothing is as indicative of the state of theory and analysis as this absurd abundance of "keys." The concept of the "key" as a higher unity in the foreground is completely foreign to theory: it is even capable of designating a single unprolonged chord as a key.[1]

Although Schenker thus acknowledged that keys might appear as "higher unities in the foreground," his own work—especially in its later phases—sheds little light on the compositional role of such higher unities; nor have later Schenkerians concerned themselves very much with this question. The time is perhaps ripe for theorists and other musicians to take another look at the notion of modulation and to see how far a greater

Originally published in *Music Analysis* 6, no. 3 (1987), pp. 289–318.

emphasis on key change can be incorporated into a monotonal approach like Schenker's. That hearing modulations belongs to our moment-by-moment experience of tonal music is so obvious as to need no comment. But a deep and intense hearing of music cannot be only from a moment-by-moment perspective, and existing conceptions of modulation have surely not done justice to the piece of music as a "com-position"—something put together to form a unity.

The Tonic as Center

To hear something in a key, we have to be aware of a tonic note, a pitch that functions as a center of orientation to which, directly or indirectly, we relate all the other pitches. The inference of a tonal center can result from several factors, singly or in combination. One factor, mentioned by a host of authors including Schenker, is the presence of a diminished fifth or tritone between $\hat{7}$ and $\hat{4}$, expressed either simultaneously (as in a V^7 chord) or in succession (as in a progression of IV or II to V).[2] This diminished fifth is indigenous to major and must be imported into minor to offset that mode's tendency to gravitate to its third scale step, a tendency produced by minor's own indigenous diminished fifth between $\hat{2}$ and $\hat{6}$. It is easy to hear how the diminished fifth clinches the key in measure 3 of the C-major Prelude from Bach's *Well-Tempered Clavier*, Book I (Example 5.1).

Of course our awareness of the tonic cannot come from a disembodied diminished fifth; we must hear it in a context that includes other pitches as well. In the Bach excerpt, all of the notes of the C-major scale appear by measure 3; in addition, measure 1 contains the tonic triad. Beginning with tonic harmony, though it is the norm, is by no means a prerequisite to our immediate feeling for the key. Chopin's Prelude, Op. 28, No. 18, sounds unmistakably in F minor at least from the end of measure 1, though a stable tonic chord does not appear until the very end of the piece. The dominant ninth, with its tritone Bb–E, locates F as the tonic pitch (although the only Fs in the citation are passing notes), and the emphasized Dbs suggest—even in the absence of Ab—that this F is going to be minor (Example 5.2). Tonal music's power to create a sense of future through the specificity of the expectations it can arouse has no parallel in any other kind of music of which I am aware; that its signals are perhaps as often contradicted as they are confirmed only serves to make musical time a more powerful symbolic representation of human temporal experience. And further, a piece that struggles to achieve its tonic presents a world of sound and feeling very different from one where the tonic is asserted as a given from the outset.

EXAMPLE 5.1: J. S. Bach, *Well-Tempered Clavier*, Book I, Prelude 1, measures 1–4

dim
5th

EXAMPLE 5.2: Chopin, Prelude, Op. 28, No. 18

The Tonic as Matrix

During the first nine or so measures of another Chopin Prelude, No. 24 in D minor, there is no diminished fifth C#-G to specify D as the tonic pitch. That the key of D minor is never in doubt during these measures results from the ever-present D-minor triad arpeggiated in both the left-hand ostinato and the melodic line; that the few non-harmonic notes all belong to the D-minor scale adds further confirmation. If we look a bit further—say up to measure 21—we shall see that the tonicized harmonies are the opening D minor, the F major of measure 15, and the A minor of measure 19, forming a huge expansion of the same arpeggio.

Despite its complex and unusual—perhaps unique—tonal plan, the Prelude sustains its key with a minimum of help from the diminished fifth on the leading note. Indeed, in seventy-seven measures of highly chromatic music, C# occurs only twice: before the reprise in measure 50 (introduced enharmonically as Db) and in the final cadential dominant, measure 64 (not counting a few rapid passing notes of no harmonic significance in measures 55–56). D minor is securely established as a key because the D-minor chord so clearly forms the matrix that generates the ostinato figure, the melodic line, and the large-scale harmonic structure of the Prelude's extended opening phase (measures 1–20).

Central to Schenker's work is the notion that the tonic triad, an image of the overtone series generated by the tonic note, functions as a matrix—the source of the Fundamental Structure that governs large-scale harmony (through the bass arpeggio) and melody (through the Fundamental Line) as well as the ultimate source of the middleground structures and foreground details that grow out of the Fundamental Structure. As matrix, the tonic triad has rhythmic properties: it defines the beginning and end of complete and self-contained harmonic and melodic progressions; it also provides the foundation for form and design, since motivic and thematic elements always connect (usually quite closely) to tonal structure. As Fred Lerdahl and Ray Jackendoff write, "the tonic is in some sense implicit in every moment of the piece."[3]

Obviously the tonic triad as matrix is a chord elaborately prolonged or composed out (*auskomponiert*); this applies to the main tonic of a piece (for Schenker the only true tonic) as well as for most temporary "tonics" produced by modulation. Every tonic conceived as a matrix is a prolonged chord, but not every prolonged chord is a tonic. The D-minor and G-major triads of Example 5.3 are not. Although D and G govern their prolonged harmonies, they have no special relation to the non-harmonic notes of the melodic lines, nor does either form the point of origin or expected goal of a self-contained tonal progression. D and

EXAMPLE 5.3: Prolongation within a C major *diatony*

$$
\begin{array}{cccc}
\text{C} & \text{D} & \text{G} & \text{C} \\
(\text{C: I} & \text{II} & \text{V} & \text{I }) \\
\end{array}
$$

G are centers of a sort, for they are harmonic roots or fundamentals, but they are centers in a much more limited sense than tonic notes, for they exercise no control over scalar functions, over the syntactic properties of subordinate chords, over form or design. Their governance is looser and far less elaborately hierarchical. In Schenker's terminology, the pitches of Example 5.3 are subject to the control of a C-major *diatony*. Thus although f^2 in measure 2 and b^1 in measure 3 are consonant with the roots of their chords, they project a dissonant character with respect to the C-major triad; and they eventually resolve into the third and root of that chord.

A Change or Center within a Prolonged Triad

The tonal center of a passage may change during the prolongation of a single harmony—a realignment, as it were, in the magnetic fields of the notes that form the musical atoms of the passage. Example 5.4 contains foreground and middleground reductions of the Presto section from the E-minor Prelude of the *Well-Tempered Clavier*, Book I. Tovey characterizes this passage as "first asserting the key of A minor (measures 23–26) . . . ; and thence proceeding for twelve steps . . . , till E minor is reestablished in measure 32. After this it quickly proceeds to a dominant pedal."[4]

Now it seems self-evident to me that the E-minor triad of measure 32, though containing the same pitches as the Prelude's tonic chord, does not function in a deep sense as a tonic—as a significant beginning or goal of motion. Instead it is a detail of motion, clearly on the way to the A-minor sixth at the head of the next measure, which continues the prolongation of IV begun in measure 23. The governing harmony of measures 23–33 is A minor (IV); within the prolonged IV, the E minor of measure 32 fulfills a contrapuntal function: it provides consonant support for the passing note b^1. At the same time, however, measures 30–32, with their prominent diminished fifth from A down to D♯, effectively cancel the tonic quality of the note A, so that the prolonged harmony changes its function; dropping its tonic guise, it stands revealed as the subdominant of E minor that, in a deeper sense, it has been all along. The two graphs of Example 5.4 attempt to depict these events.

As far as it goes, Tovey's description is correct—correct, that is, as long as we understand the "reestablished" E minor as an expected focal point or center, but not yet the boundary of a time span filled with the E-minor chord as a matrix. Indeed it is not even the boundary of a key, for it is difficult or impossible to specify just where in measures 30–32 the key of E minor begins to reappear (the boundaries of keys are often indistinct). Perhaps the greatest weakness of Tovey's interpretation is that its exclusive concentration on key succession seems

EXAMPLE 5.4: J. S. Bach, *Well-Tempered Clavier*, Book I, Prelude 10 (A) foreground reduction

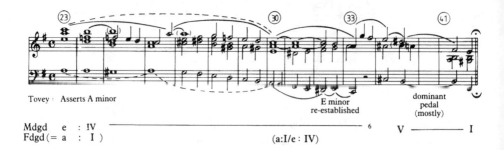

to have blocked access to the underlying IV–V–I progression and to an awareness of the vast difference in structural meaning between the E chord of measure 32 and a true tonic, say the final chord of the piece.

Changing the key of a prolonged harmony is a most important compositional resource, creating, as it were, a "pivot chord" of high structural order. Often, as in the Bach Prelude, an initially tonicized chord will begin to suggest a resolution to the main tonic before that resolution occurs (again projecting a sense of "future"). In many sonata-form movements in major, for example, the development continues to prolong the dominant that is tonicized in the second part of the exposition, but at the end of the prolongation (before the reca-pitulation) the prolonged dominant is heard as V in the tonic key. Sometimes, on the other hand, it is the first big tonic that prepares a change of key; it becomes transformed into a dissonant chord (perhaps an augmented sixth or diminished seventh) that functions as a chromaticized scale step in the new key—usually the key of the dominant (Example 5.5). Thus the boundaries of a prolonged harmony need not coincide with the often indistinct boundaries of a key area, nor need those of either coincide with those of a form section.

Schenker, by the way, was aware of the possibility of changing the sense of key within the prolongation of a single harmony; his graphs of the foreground and of later middle-ground levels often specify these key changes. An interesting and easily accessible example occurs in his analysis of the Largo from Bach's Third Sonata for Solo Violin. His Figure 1 shows the opening F-major tonic of the *Ursatz* transformed into a IV of C major; the latter "key," of course, represents a tonicized structural V. As the upper voice descends over V, the counterpointing of B♭ by G leads to a G-minor chord; since this chord is tonicized, Schenker shows a key change to G minor (still within a prolonged V of F). Before the pro-longation of V is concluded (indeed still within the prolongation of the dividing G-minor triad), the imminent return of a structural I is prepared, and Schenker shows a key change to F major. Thus the prolongation of a single harmony—V of F major—encompasses three keys, C major, G minor, and F major.[5]

Related to, though not quite the same as, key change within a prolonged harmony is the alternation of keys produced by a 5–6 or 6–5 interval succession. For instance, C major can alternate with A minor if the G belonging to the C-major tonic changes to an A (5–6) and if the A minor is tonicized. Similarly, A minor can give way to F major. If this kind of alternation stretches over much of the piece, the composer can leave in abeyance—at least for a while—the issue of which tonic is primary. Usually one presumes that the first tonic is

(B) middleground reduction

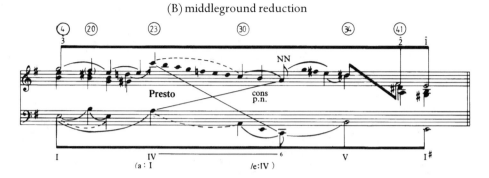

the main one, and often that presumption turns out to be correct; the second movement of Brahms's A-major Sonata for Violin and Piano is a good example. In Chopin's big dual-key pieces, on the other hand, the first tonic is always supplanted by its rival—think of the Fantasy, the Second Scherzo, the Second Ballade, etc. I am not going to address myself here to the question of whether any of these pieces has only one primary tonic; but I should like to suggest that the problem can't be explained away by asserting that for Chopin a relative major and minor form a single extended key. Since when does the notion of "key" involve two tonics of equal rank?[6] (In any case, this explanation founders on the F-major/A-minor Ballade, whose two keys are not relatives.)

Apparent Centers

In Example 5.2, the beginning of the Chopin F-minor Prelude, we saw a passage that implies F as center long before there is any tonic harmony. Of course the tonic appears eventually; the promise of the piece's beginning is kept. But although music mostly keeps its promises, it need not do so in the obvious way we might expect; like the Weird Sisters' prophecies in *Macbeth*, its messages sometimes admit of more than one interpretation. Measures 29–36 of the Scherzo movement of Schubert's Piano Sonata, D.845 (Example 5.6), have a pitch content very similar to that of Example 5.2. Following a firmly established C

EXAMPLE 5.5: Beethoven, Sonata, Op. 7, first movement

EXAMPLE 5.6: Schubert, Sonata, D.845, third movement

major (itself a tonicized III in the home key of A minor), the passage continues the C harmony, but in a way that makes it sound like a V in F minor. As the example shows, the expected F minor never materializes, for the chromatic pitches serve instead to prepare A♭ major.

Might we say that measures 29–36 of the Schubert excerpt are in F minor? Yes, I think, as long as we realize that they are "in" F minor in a more attenuated sense than the Chopin Prelude is. Hearing these measures as containing the V of F minor is part of our moment-by-moment experience of the piece, just as responding to a false clue is part of our moment-by-moment experience of reading a mystery novel. But in neither case is the experience grounded in the larger reality created by composer or author. The "tonic" is an expected center that is never confirmed; in no sense is its harmony a matrix for the pitch content of the passage. When we use the word "tonic" in analysis, we should do well to remember that it can represent quite different kinds of musical structure. We can quickly infer a tonic as center from signals given by other pitches; neither the tonic chord nor even the tonic note need be present. We can infer a tonic as matrix, however, only through the presence of at least two (and typically all three) of the tonic triad's constituent notes, and these notes must be spread out through time as the beginnings or goals of significant linear and harmonic structures.

"Keys" without tonics (like the "F minor" in the Schubert Scherzo) can enliven a musi-cal foreground precisely because they arouse specific expectations that they do not fulfill. (Passages of "roving harmony" which lack any distinct or abiding tonal focus create quite different, though equally valuable, effects.) In the second half of the eighteenth century, as Charles Rosen points out, cadences tonicizing VI occurred so frequently near the end of development sections as to become a cliché.[7] Rosen then shows how composers can avoid the cliché by withholding the expected goal: "One way of escaping the eternal cadence on vi preceding the return to I—or at least enlivening it—was by a cadence on V of vi, followed by a jump into the tonic and the main theme."[8]

One of Rosen's examples of this device is the Kyrie of Haydn's *Harmoniemesse*, a piece in sonata form; as he writes, "the cadence on vi (G minor) is neatly avoided."[9] But the G-minor harmony is not simply avoided as a cadential goal; it does not occur anywhere in the passage. As in the Schubert excerpt of Example 5.6, if this passage has a local tonic at all, it is an absentee tonic. Example 5.7 contains a voice-leading reduction of the development section, and shows that the putative V of G minor turns out to have a different function: it leads by downward arpeggiation from V to I in the progression V–(III♯)–I. This event resonates with important motivic implications that I cannot go into here, but the quotation following the graphs shows how the chromatic melodic line of the entire development section is prefigured in the section's opening phrase.

Like Tovey's account of the Bach Prelude, Rosen's analysis is correct but insufficient. His pointing out the non-fulfillment of an expectation is perfectly valid, but he does not go on to explain what in fact does happen. Non-events have their importance, but partly, at least, in the light of the outcome that their expectation masks. And none of the great composers—least of all Haydn, with his unparalleled powers of invention—makes compositional choices just to avoid stereotypes; indeed, they are often more willing than lesser musicians to use clichés if the context is appropriate.

Part of the difference between Rosen's approach and mine probably results from the differing perspectives of a historian dealing with common stylistic features of a large number of pieces and a theorist examining fewer pieces in greater detail. If I encounter a number of

EXAMPLE 5.7: Haydn, *Harmoniemesse*, Kyrie, development

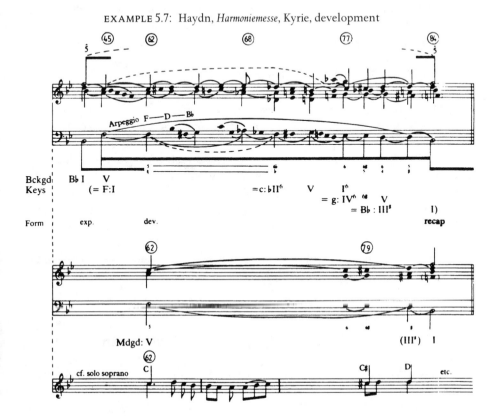

development sections that tonicize VI or suggest that they are going to do so, my interest is captured by the specific tonal structures that the composer creates: with Beethoven, for example, the root of VI might be an upper neighbor to V (Op. 10, No. 2, I), a passing note between the root and third of V (Op. 7, I), even part of an arpeggiation from I down to IV (Op. 79, 1).[10] For me these functional differences are of paramount importance, but that does not invalidate the notion that the common key area forms a stylistic link among these pieces. Sancho Panza and Jeeves are very different characters, but they belong to a common literary tradition.

Interestingly enough, the specific structure found in the Haydn Kyrie also forms a stylistic link among many late Classical development sections, though of course not as many as the tonicization, confirmed or unfulfilled, of VI. In a recent article, David Beach has shown that many of Mozart's developments show a downward arpeggiation from V to I through III; others use III as part of a descending motion within a prolonged V.[11] A sharing of the perspectives of historian and theorist will, I hope, lead to an increased awareness of specific voice-leading techniques (together with more general features like key or "key" succession) as elements of style.

Tonicizations Contradicted by Voice-Leading Continuity

In the Haydn Kyrie, the III♯ of a V–III♯–I arpeggio suggested the key of G minor even in the absence of a G-minor chord. But what if there had been such a chord? The literature abounds with cases where a chord functions locally as a V and, at the same time, has a different and more significant long-range function. The A-major chord that ends the development of Beethoven's "Spring" Sonata, for instance, follows a rather prominent D-minor triad and is surely heard, at least initially, as its dominant. But the magical effect of the recapitulation depends on the motion down a third from A major to the home tonic F, on the concomitant chromatic adjustment of C♯ to C, and on the way the melodic line that grows out of the A major prepares the return of the tonic theme. And the way Beethoven composes this long-drawn-out A chord more and more obliterates our (or at least my) sense that it is going to resolve, in fact, to D. Imagine how the piece would sound if the A really did move to D, and the D to F! The structural bass progression of this development, then, is V–(III♯)–I—exactly the same as in the Haydn Kyrie (Example 5.8). That there is a key succession D minor–F major is undeniable, but here the dominant of the D-minor key has a higher syntactic value than its tonic. It helps to remember that the elements of linear structure in music are pitches, not keys. To say that the note A (or D) moves to F is to employ a useful metaphor; to say that the key of D (or A) moves to the key of F is not. A key is a network of relationships that stretches through all of musical "space" and that can hardly be said to "move."

Monotonality; Key Succession as Large-Scale Chord Progression

The Beethoven and Haydn illustrations, where the governing linear and chordal pitch structure differs from the succession of keys, call into question a frequent analytic assumption—

EXAMPLE 5.8: Beethoven, Sonata for Piano and Violin, Op. 24, first movement, development

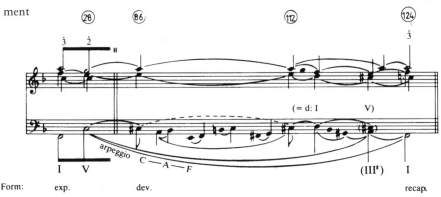

that key successions are simply chord progressions writ large. This is by no means a recent notion: in the earliest stages of modern harmonic analysis, theorists attempted to relate secondary keys—at least those most frequently employed—to the whole piece rather than regarding them as separate and self-contained entities. Schenker praises C. P. E. Bach for conceiving of "keys" as prolonged *Stufen*, drawing this inference from Bach's referring to the goals of modulation as scale degrees in the main key ("fifth with major third, sixth with minor third," and so on).[12] But Bach was by no means the only eighteenth-century theorist to define in this way the relation between primary and secondary keys. Both Rameau[13] and Kirnberger do so; and Kirnberger[14] even uses Roman numerals to indicate the scale degrees in the main key on which the new "tonics" fall.

The most beautiful formulation of this idea that I know stems from Brahms, though the precise wording comes from his pupil, Gustav Jenner. In discussing his lessons in song composition, Jenner writes:

> The position and form of the cadences is closely bound up with the path of modulation. Here Brahms demanded the utmost restraint and consistency. In the disposition of even a very long song with extended and self-contained episodes, the main point was to express fully the primary key and to reveal its control over secondary keys through clear relationships. *In this way, so to speak, the sum of all the keys employed in a piece appeared like an image of the primary key in a state of activity.*[15] [italics mine]

For me, at least, Jenner's simile conveys more truth than much technical description along similar lines, largely because it suggests a *difference* between the intensity of a primary key activated by modulation and the lesser intensity of a key not so activated. Compare, for example, this citation from the fifth edition of *Grove's Dictionary of Music and Musicians*: "The same rules apply to key progressions which apply to any harmonic progression. . . . Those progressions to or from the tonic which are in themselves complete and satisfactory within the key find an equally satisfactory counterpart in the wider sphere of modulation."[16] The idea is plausible because it is well expressed and partly true. But only partly. The article's main example of modulation in Baroque music is a chart of the key scheme of the Allemande from the Fourth French Suite. The analysis shows (correctly, I think) that the main modulations are from E♭ to B♭ to C minor to E♭. But is VI–I a "complete and satisfactory" return to a tonic within the key? Hardly. Nor is the picture any better when we consult the many transient and hinted-at keys shown in the chart, for taking them into account yields a return to I from II.[17]

The problem with this partly valid approach is its failure to give due weight to linear, contrapuntal structure. The tonicized C minor in the Bach Allemande is indeed part of the return to I: as Example 5.9 shows, it moves within V from B♭ to D, and the D goes on to the tonic E♭. The return to I, then, is not from VI (C minor), but from a prolonged V that encompasses the tonicization of VI. The area governed by V changes its key focus several times: first from B♭ major to C minor, then through several tonicized chords (A♭ major and F minor) that belong both to C minor and to E♭ major, and, before the final cadence, to E♭; the core of these occurrences is a rising linear progression B♭ (tonicized)–C (tonicized)–D–E♭.

Because the key areas of the Allemande function within a contrapuntal web of great (but typically Bachian) complexity, we cannot begin to understand them without coming to terms with the voice-leading structure of the piece. In Example 5.9, I have tried to illuminate the parts of this structure relevant to the subject of this essay; I suggest that the graphs be read at first in the order presented, from background to foreground. Much of the difficulty posed by the piece results from the many transfers in register and from part to part (e.g., bass to soprano). One structure disguised by such transfers is the rising fourth-progression from B♭ to E♭. Starting with level b, the example shows that this large-scale linear progression forms an enlargement of a motivic element fundamental to the Allemande and indeed the entire Suite. The list of keys (eleven in ten measures of music!) comes from the *Grove* article, whose author has underlined the important, structural keys and has placed the transient ones in parentheses. Note the curious place where a structural return to E♭ is read; as in Tovey's account of the E-minor Prelude, this comes from analyzing by key without considering voice leading and chord prolongation.

Schenker's early writings about modulation also sometimes overlook linear factors, but he does not make the mistake of equating all key successions with chord progressions. In his *Harmony*, he distinguishes among three categories of chromatic elaboration: tonicization, where there is no sense of departure from the tonic key; illusory keys (*Scheintonarten*), where the diatony, or diatonic framework (*Diatonie*), recedes into the background but still exerts a controlling influence; and true modulations, which do not return to their point of origin, and which remain independent of any overarching diatony.[18]

Schenker's illusory keys behave more or less as the *Grove* article indicates: they can be regarded as expansions (and sometimes as chromatic equivalents) of diatonic scale steps. He cites the C-major passage in the exposition of the first movement of Beethoven's Piano Sonata, Op. 7 (measures 81–89), and shows—very convincingly, I think—that the V–I of C major represents an expanded and chromatically elaborated VI–II progression in the locally governing key of B♭ major.[19]

Schenker's main example of real modulation is the development section of the same movement, about which he says, "The keys are real keys, and their sequence is: C minor, A♭ major, F minor, G minor, A minor, D minor. It would be illicit to do violence to this situation by explaining all these keys or part of them as consequences of the B♭-major diatony which concluded the first part of the movement."[20] Six real keys in a not very long develop-

EXAMPLE 5.9: J. S. Bach, French Suite No. 4, Allemande

* Keys from *Grove*, 5th Edn, Vol.5, p.810

ment section! And Schenker was the one who was to complain about the "absurd abundance of keys" in conventional analysis. But the keys are really there, at least on the surface, and it required a fundamental change in the way we think about music—a change that Schenker himself was to bring about—before musicians could convincingly relate the key changes in such passages to a larger tonal context.[21]

What Schenker was eventually to discover was that key successions might very well result from linear activity within a harmony (or a progression of harmonies), and that a governing diatonic structure, ultimately derived from the tonic triad, could unify even such heterogeneous elements. Example 5.10 is a middleground sketch of this development section. Rather amazingly, its tonal core has a good deal in common with that of the Bach Allemande shown in the previous example (compare Examples 5.9a and 5.9b with Example 5.10a). In neither piece is that core accessible to casual listening. In the Bach, it is embedded in a complex tissue of voice leading; in the Beethoven, it is obscured in simpler fashion by the unexpected and dramatic contrasts of key.

Evidently Schenker did not realize that the first four of his "keys"—C minor, A♭ major, F minor, and G minor—make a group. Indeed, all of them are diatonic elements of C minor, and though they do not form a clear progression in the key of C minor, they do lead into a chord—the augmented sixth of measure 162—that is derived by chromaticized voice-exchange from the C-minor triad (Examples 5.10b and 5.10c). (The appearance of G minor rather than major in measure 159 tends to weaken the impression of C minor as a key, especially since the G minor itself becomes the upper third of the augmented sixth. Of course a different continuation to the G-minor area might have effected a reevaluation of the entire passage and affirmed in retrospect the inference of a C-minor diatony.)

With the D chord of measure 163, we have arrived (a bit prematurely) just one step away from our goal, E♭. Nothing would be easier than to transform the D harmony into a dominant $^6_5$ of E♭, more or less as actually happens at the end of the development. But the music, as though unable to see the path directly before it, stumbles and gets lost. Instead of reaching E♭, the bass rises through its enharmonic equivalent, D♯, to E. (The movement has displayed a kind of fatal weakness for E—witness the C-major episode in the exposition, as well as other passages.) The A minor that ensues is seemingly at the furthest remove tonally from the home key of E♭, but it represents in fact a step in the journey back. Inflected to become a dominant chord, it leads to D minor, and this time the D is transformed into a leading note and takes us home. Thus the "keys" that begin and end the development—C minor and D minor—crystallize around notes of a linear progression leading up from V to I. The other "keys" serve either to extend the C-minor chord (not key) at the beginning of the development or to lead into the D minor at the end, saving the situation after a "false move" had seemingly lost the thread of tonal continuity. This interpretation conforms to the disposition of the development in two phases, measures 137–68, with C as the main bass note, and measures 169–88, centering on D. (The sense of starting again in measure 169 speaks against inferring a connection from the D-major chord of measure 165 to the D minor of measures 181ff.)

Unquestionably the tonal daring of this development, which ventures on keys so remote from the main tonic, is one of the factors that differentiates it from other pieces that contain similar voice-leading structures—the Bach Allemande, for example. Schenker's graphing technique does not emphasize visually such differences, and to a casual reader, graphs

EXAMPLE 5.10: Beethoven, Sonata, Op. 7, first movement, development

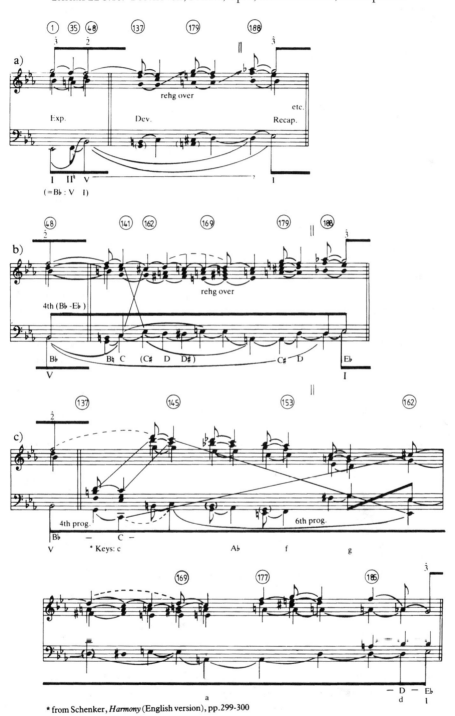

* from Schenker, *Harmony* (English version), pp. 299-300

of the Allemande and of the development might look pretty much the same. But anyone reading the Beethoven graph correctly—with ears as well as eyes—will *hear* the difference that the excursion to A minor makes. And of course the analyst could easily refer to the key plan in a text accompanying the graph, or label some of the keys in graphs of the later levels, as Schenker often does. Critics of Schenker sometimes wonder at his seeming unconcern for such striking features of the music he analyses. True enough, he often does not call attention to them, but they are usually features that are right on the surface and much easier to hear than the middleground structures that weld them into a unity.

Key Relationships

In a very general way the evolution of musical style in the eighteenth and nineteenth centuries includes as an obvious feature a greater and greater use of large-scale (modulatory) chromaticism, much as far earlier centuries saw a growth in the use of local chromaticism, from a simple choice between Bb and B to the extravagances of Gesualdo. Musicians tend to characterize the modulatory style of a piece or period by means of a spatial metaphor: modulations are "close" or "distant." Few of us would deny, I think, that the Bach Allemande modulates only to closely related keys, whereas the modulatory path of the Beethoven development encompasses far more remote relationships; the pieces are not stylistically atypical in this regard. The "distance" between successive keys also influences our time sense, for a key creates a feeling of a more or less extended "now"—a "specious present," to use that unattractive expression—and key relationships have a lot to do with the ways these "nows" flow one into the other or isolate themselves.

Theorists from Kirnberger to Schoenberg have attempted to establish a taxonomy of key relationships without, as far as I can see, agreeing among themselves or with the practice of the great composers. We can decide, perhaps, on a few general principles: a scarcity of common harmonic and melodic elements places two keys into a remote relation (unless mitigated by mode mixture), the immediate succession of two tonics sounds disconnected when these tonics are a major second apart, and so on. But to combine such criteria into an elaborate system is pointless. Trying to understand from an abstract schema how the modulations work in a piece is rather like trying to understand the power structure of a large corporation from the official charts of who reports to whom, without taking into account the possibility that the president's secretary (who doubles as his mistress) might be a more powerful person than any of the vice-presidents.

I can think of two pieces in C minor that contain prominent tonicizations of E minor; they are the first movement of Beethoven's Op. 13 and the C-minor chorus ("Denn es wird die Posaune schallen") from No. 6 of Brahms's *German Requiem*. In the Beethoven, the E minor at the beginning of the development (measure 137) represents a chromatic passing note from a firmly established Eb major (III) to an F-minor chord that moves through F# to the dominant, G. In no way is this "key" the direct outgrowth of the movement's C-minor tonic, although it does connect two elements (Eb and F) that are projected from a governing C-minor diatony. The Brahms, on the other hand, uses the E minor (measure 88) as an expanded III borrowed from the tonic major. It occurs within a I–♮III–V–I progression and is far more startling than the E minor of the Beethoven precisely because of its abrupt confrontation with the prevailing C-minor environment, because it occurs at the beginning of the chorus, and because it usurps the place of an important diatonic harmony (III). Aside from the obvious fact that both passages are E-minor episodes within C-minor pieces, I see no reason to adopt an approach (like Schoenberg's Theory of Regions) that would regard them as equivalent. That theory is interesting and is superior to much previous thought about modulation. But it breaks down, in my opinion, because it tries to systematize the most diverse tonal materials and procedures according to a rigid schema of purely harmonic functions, and because it fails to take into account the contrapuntal structures that create the diversity; how much do we really learn about these E-minor episodes from assigning them both to Class 4 (Indirect and Remote) of the Regions?[22]

"Illusory Keys of the Foreground"

When Schenker writes about modulation in *Free Composition*, he uses a stock phrase, "illusory keys of the foreground" (*Scheintonarten des Vordergrundes*). In some ways the term is an unfortunate one, but tracing its implications can yield valuable insights into Schenker's thinking and can perhaps lead to a clearer conception of modulation in general. First of all, *Tonart* in German often means local key, as distinct from *Tonalität*, a global concept in which tonal events, including local keys, relate to the center of a whole piece or large section. English usage also distinguishes "key" from "tonality," but perhaps not as consistently. As we have seen, Schenker was using the term "Scheintonart" as far back as his *Harmony*, where he defined it as an expanded harmony subordinate to a framing diatonic structure, but intensified through its transformation into a seeming "key." This transformation is effected through chromaticism, rather as in Schoenberg's Theory of Regions. At the time of *Harmony*, Schenker's conception of "diatony," though very broad, did not necessarily encompass whole pieces: in the first movement of Beethoven's Op. 7, for instance, the Eb diatony of the beginning would give way to a Bb diatony later in the exposition; the development, lacking any overarching diatonic framework, would contain real modulations to self-contained keys.

Schenker's later writings often retain his earlier terminology, whose meaning shifts with the evolution of his thought; making life easier for his readers by explaining these shifts is not his way. Thus his final formulation in *Free Composition* includes the notions of diatony, tonality, and illusory key. Now, however, the terms "diatony" and "tonality" apply to whole pieces. The conjunctly ordered pitches of the major and minor scales, functioning in relation to the tonic center (rather than as a mere "collection" as in some other conceptions of diatonicism), form the materials of diatony; this notion is most clearly exemplified in the pitch contents of the Fundamental Line, with its motion directed to the tonic note as goal. It is essentially the practice of counterpoint, based on a clear distinction between consonance (octave, fifth, third) and passing dissonance that organizes the line around a center rather than leaving it a mere succession of pitches.[23] This diatonic structure, no longer conceived as localized, abides implicitly throughout the piece, even where the music is most chromatic or moves into the most distant keys, rather like the pantheists' God, who indwells in every aspect and phase of Nature.[24]

The term "tonality" is applied to the enriched tonal contents of the foreground, unified, like the simple elements of diatony, through their relation to the tonic; these contents may include both local chromaticism and modulation to illusory keys.[25] If diatony permeates the whole piece, then the "real modulations" that Schenker discusses in *Harmony*—changes of key that cannot be subsumed under a controlling diatonic structure—must be non-existent. All of the keys of the piece, therefore, turn out to be like the *Scheintonarten*, or illusory keys, of the earlier theory; and preserving the terms shows how much of Schenker's later theory was already implicit in his earlier.

But if all keys (other than the unfolded tonic of the underlying diatony) are illusory, why bother with the adjective at all? It seems less useful than in *Harmony*, where only some of the keys in a piece are conceived as illusory. In addition to preserving his own earlier terminology, Schenker probably wanted to emphasize the monotonality of his later theory, which holds that in a deep sense each piece can have only one "real" tonic. The notion that a piece can be a unified structure in one main key and at the same time traverse several other secondary keys is very hard to express in terminology that does not seem self-contradictory. Schoenberg has a point when he criticizes Schenker's term "tonicization"; after all, he says, each key (*Tonart*) has only one tonic. Yet Schoenberg does more or less the same thing when he uses Roman numerals to analyze music in non-tonic regions. What does "I" in the Subdominant Region mean, if not a local tonic?[26]

Schenker's referring to "illusory keys" gives him a way out of this terminological difficulty, but it is perhaps the quick and safe rather than the scenic route. By lumping all "keys" together into a single category, Schenker necessarily treats the subject of modulation in a far less differentiated way than in *Harmony*, which distinguishes between tonicizations, illusory keys, and real modulations. Furthermore, by locating all "keys" at the foreground ("illusory keys of the foreground," keys as "higher unities in the foreground," etc.), Schenker minimizes possibly valid distinctions between large-scale, structural modulations and smaller, local ones.

Surely the dominant key in the second half of a sonata exposition, say the B♭ major in Beethoven's Op. 7, has a different structural meaning from the transient "keys" of the development; and that difference is obscured rather than illuminated by calling them all "illusory keys of the foreground." The B♭ major of the exposition is the matrix within which a highly ramified structure develops: a subordinate diatony in the form of an upper-voice fifth-progression descending from $\hat{2}$ (supported by a full harmonic cadence), and even an illusory key dependent upon a framing B♭ major—the C-major passage discussed in *Harmony*. Despite some obvious shortcomings, Schenker's earlier theory gave a clearer picture of this aspect of harmonic structure than *Free Composition* does. I do not see on what basis the later Schenker locates structural keys (like the dominant area in a sonata exposition) in the foreground, when he assigns the fifth-progression from $\hat{2}$ to the very first level of middleground and acknowledges that this upper line, together with its cadential bass, forms an *Ursatz*-like structure transferred to a later level.[27]

When is a "key" a key? This question has no definite answer, and the wildly varying approaches of different analysts to the same piece indicate just how slippery the concept of key is. In a not uninteresting article about the Andante con moto from Beethoven's G-major Concerto, Klaus Körner reads a modulation to A minor in the first solo passage, and he derives consequences from that "modulation" (measures 7–8), which consists of one applied $\frac{6}{5}$ chord and one A-minor triad.[28] Writing about the same movement with greater insight into its harmonic structure, Charles Rosen states that it hardly ever gets away from the tonic and that, except for one brief modulation to D major, it is conceived as an expanded E-minor chord.[29]

Using Schenker's theory of levels (but not his consigning all "keys" to the foreground), one can at least begin to see the distance from the background at which the impression of a new, temporary diatony begins to emerge. Surely those "keys" that prolong extensively a note of the Fundamental Line (like the composing-out of $\hat{2}$ over V in a sonata exposition), those that compose out a structural neighbor-note (frequent in ABA and rondo forms), and those that emerge during a stretch of the *Urlinie* (notably $\hat{5}$–$\hat{4}$–$\hat{3}$ over III in minor) represent important shaping elements; indeed, when the composing-out process leads to an *Ursatz*-like progression in the subordinate "key," the modulation can help bring about a relatively self-contained formal section. In all such cases, I think, one is perfectly justified in speaking of structural modulations and in viewing the key sense as arising at a level considerably prior to the foreground. In my view Schenker weakens his treatment of form by his unwillingness to regard any key change as more than an epiphenomenon.

Between these large structural key changes and the fleeting tonicizations that some authors call modulations, there is a vast range of possibilities. That range does not lend itself to exact demarcations, so that it is impossible to prove, for example, that the first solo in the second movement of the Beethoven Fourth Concerto does *not* contain a modulation to A minor. Still, one can feel (and I certainly do) that reading new keys at such places is destructive of good analysis in that it isolates details and blurs significant differences. Schenker is certainly right in criticizing analyses that contain an "absurd abundance of keys," impossible though it is to determine just where an abundance begins to be absurd.

Between brief tonicizations and large-scale, generously ramified "keys," one might distinguish a few important categories. There are "keys," for example, with full harmonic cadences, but without melodic closure. There are others that have an initial "tonic" but that end with a dividing dominant harmony. There are still others that lead through what Schenker calls an "auxiliary cadence" to a closing tonic; often these lack an opening tonic.

Among the most curious cases are those "keys" whose tonics never arrive, as in the Schubert excerpt of Example 5.6; these, if any, are "illusory keys of the foreground." Sometimes, however, such "keys" can play quite a significant role in the design of a piece. In the first movement of Mendelssohn's String Quartet in E Minor (Op. 44, No. 2), the second part of the exposition is in a G major (III) that follows fourteen measures (!) of what seems to be a prolonged V of B minor, so that the initial impression is V–VI in that key. Related deceptive cadences occur at two significant junctures later on in the movement, before the recapitulation and in the coda; these, however, are followed eventually by the appearance of the tonic initially expected (both times the main E-minor tonic of the movement), producing a very special sense of large-scale resolution.[30]

A Sample Analysis

Cherubino's Arietta "Voi che sapete," from Act II of *Le Nozze di Figaro*, provides an appropriate final example for this study. The second section of its ABA design contrasts very little in rhythm and texture with the simple first section and its modified da capo; the representation in the orchestra of Susanna's accompanying guitar requires a certain uniformity. Tonally, however, the two sections could hardly differ more, for the second, after a straightforward beginning in the dominant key, moves suddenly into areas whose connection to each other and to the B♭ diatony of the whole is difficult to understand.

The problem centers on measures 37–52, which contain a fully tonicized A♭ major (measures 37–44) including a cadential bass and melodic closure on A♭. Following the phrase in A♭ is a modulatory part that culminates in a G-minor cadence (measure 52); the relation of this G minor to what precedes and follows it is far from obvious. The problematic nature of this passage did not escape the notice of Schoenberg, who discusses the aria briefly in Chapter 9 of *Structural Functions*. Schoenberg reads the A♭ as ♭MD (dominant of the flat mediant) and points to Beethoven's use of the same region in the opening themes of his Piano Sonatas, Op. 31, No. 1 and Op. 53. Because the region is so uncharacteristic of Mozart, and because the return to the tonic is so long and roundabout, Schoenberg ventures the astonishing hypothesis that the aria is a subtle *Musical Joke*: Cherubino, the author of the poem, is also the composer, and with this extravagant modulation, Mozart is hinting at his professional incompetence. The region to which Schoenberg assigns the A♭ major—the flat mediant's dominant—is also, he explains, the subdominant of the subdominant.[31] Siegmund Levarie, who also analyses "Voi che sapete," opts for the latter function in a reading based on the system of Hugo Riemann.[32]

In my view the A♭ major is neither V of ♭III nor IV of IV. In any case, the function of a key area can only be understood in relation to context and not on the basis of some abstract schema. As a step toward understanding this passage, let us look at its broadest tonal context, which is blessedly clear. Example 5.11 shows the first middleground level; the analysis derives the aria's three-part form from interruption, with the B section a prolongation of the dividing V. Schenker's well-known analysis of the second song from *Dichterliebe* shows a similar relation between interrupted structure and ABA form, only in "Voi che sapete" the V of the B section takes on a seventh to prepare the tonic harmony of the reprise.[33]

It is in the B section that Mozart sets most of the poem—twenty-four of its thirty-two lines. He composes them as three groups of eight lines each, and he individualizes each of the groups through a specific feature of its musical setting. The first group (measures 21–36) establishes the dominant key quite securely, but avoids closure in that each of its eight-

EXAMPLE 5.11: Mozart, *Le Nozze di Figaro*, Act II, "Voi che sapete," first middleground level

measure phrases cadences on the dominant, C. The second group (measures 37–52) embarks upon a modulatory adventure; its two eight-measure groups end with perfect cadences, the first in A♭ and the second in G minor. In between is another full V–I progression, this time in C minor (measures 48–49), but its cadential effect is weakened by rhythm: the C-minor goal falls at the beginning of a four-measure unit and becomes a subdominant in the approaching cadence in G minor. The intense third group (measures 53–61), gradually rising to a climax and quickly falling away, is the shortest; the ostensibly innocent sexuality of the poem is given rather explicit musical expression (Cherubino surely knew rather more than he was letting on). In this group, the lines of text (two of which have heretofore occupied four measures) are set in a kind of stretto and fill two, two, two, and three measures. From the perspective of tonal structure, the first group stabilizes the dominant key area, the second is modulatory and developmental, and the third is a retransition that evokes the tonic key long before the reprise brings back a structural tonic harmony.

Examples 5.12, 5.13, and 5.14 attempt to show how this sequence of events relates to the aria's larger tonal structure; each deals with a single phase of the B section's tonal plan. Example 5.15 will combine these views into a comprehensive middleground sketch of the section. As Example 5.12 indicates, the appearance of A♭ major is not quite unprepared, for it follows the brief mixture with F minor that colors the cadence of measures 35–36 (and paints the words "ch'ora è martir"). In my view, the succession of "tonics" F major/minor (measures 21–36), A♭ major (measures 37–44), and C minor (measure 49) arpeggiates the F triad in its minor form; if I am right, Schoenberg had things exactly backwards when he called A♭ the dominant of the flat mediant. Where is the D♭ major to which this A♭ relates as a V? It would be far preferable to call A♭ the flat mediant of the dominant, for the key area does in fact crystallize around the lowered third of a broken F chord. The A♭, however, is not a scale step in the *key* of F, for the impression of F as tonic begins to disappear at measure 36.[34] It is the *chord* of F minor, and not the key, that provides the basis for this strain, rather like a sonata development where dominant harmony continues to direct the musical motion after the dominant key has finished for good. To think of the A♭ major as IV of IV (Levarie's explanation) also seems wrong to me: E♭ as a tonic occurs nowhere in the Arietta. (In my experience, IV of IV, though common enough as a chord, is seldom to be encountered as a key except in very fleeting tonicizations.)

EXAMPLE 5.12: Mozart, *Le Nozze di Figaro*, Act II, "Voi che sapete," measures 35–49

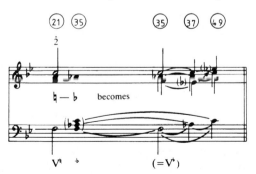

EXAMPLE 5.13: Mozart, *Le Nozze di Figaro*, Act II, "Voi che sapete," measures 35–52

Example 5.13 shows how the prolonged F chord of Example 5.12 is continued. If we think of the large bass motion F–(A♭)–C as an unfolded fifth, the D that follows the C would represent a sixth. That D, in turn, leads to the G minor by the motion of a descending fifth. To sum up, the bass line that spans the first two of this section's three inner groupings constitutes the *unfolding* or horizontalization of the contrapuntal progression 5–6–5 (F–C, F–D, G–D).

After the G-minor cadence, the vocal line moves to its climax on e♭², intensified by a doubling at the higher octave in the flute (measures 58–59). There is an apparent discrepancy between the melody and the harmony here. The melody note has a higher syntactic value than the brief C-minor chord that supports it; e♭² prepares the seventh over the prolonged V shown in Example 5.11, whereas the C minor has no such large-scale function. This syntactic value is reflected in the sonic emphasis Mozart accords the e♭² as the event that caps an extended phase of increasing intensity. Functioning within a larger context (from measure 52), the climactic e♭² relates obliquely to the last high-level bass note, the G of measure 52; the reappearance of G in measure 58 helps to clarify this connection. Since the vocal line in these measures unfolds a fourth b♭¹–e♭², the passage as a whole projects an E♭ sixth chord (G in bass, B♭ and E♭ in soprano). Understood this way, measures 52–58 continue the earlier 5–6–5 alternation with another sixth, G–E♭, an interval of the middleground not literally present on the surface but clearly implied by context (Example 5.14). In measure 60, the G transfers from the bass into an upper part (oboe doubled by the violins), where it continues up to A and then on to B♭ in the reprise. The linear structure that governs the plan of modulation is thus a rising fourth-progression related to those found in the Bach Allemande and Beethoven Sonata discussed earlier (Examples 5.9 and 5.10). In addition to the obvious differences in key succession, the Mozart also differs in that the bass adds the root of V below the rising linear progression to allow a strong harmonic resolution into the reprise.

Example 5.15 presents three middleground views of the B section. From it we can see how a repeated detail—the use of the enharmonic note-pair C♯/D♭—forms a common element that persists through the many changes in tonal orientation; a foreground graph (or a glance at the score) would show more instances.[35] One insufficiently acknowledged aspect of modulation is the way a composition's tonal plan might allow for the untransposed repetition of characteristic pitch configurations (like the C♯–D and D♭–C here) through changes of key.[36] From level c we can also begin to view the relation between tonal structure and text-setting. The rather Schubertian move to A♭, for example, with its sudden jump down a third and

EXAMPLE 5.14: Mozart, *Le Nozze di Figaro*, Act II, "Voi che sapete," measures 52–62

unexpected chromatic inflection, occurs just as Cherubino describes how he feels now cold, a moment later hot, and then cold again. Quoting the A section's cadential tag in the remote key of A♭ gives a false air of stability to this precarious harmonic region and seems to fix Cherubino in his predicament. And the long preparation for C minor, which arrives only to lose itself in the coming G-minor cadence, paints his seeking an unknown good, far from where he is.[37]

More remarkable than any of these beautiful details is the relation between the Arietta as a whole and the dramatic situation. Levarie, who has many valuable things to say about the text-setting, suggests that the poem with its fourteen lines hints at that courtliest poetic genre, the sonnet; of course he is quick to add that neither da Ponte's rhyme scheme nor Mozart's ABA design really supports this inference.[38] I am not convinced that the poem adds up to a sonnet in any significant way, but the context of Levarie's idea—that the aria expresses a tension between an "abandonment to free fancy" and the "decorum" of the social setting—seems right. The aria's configuration as a whole—a wildly modulatory middle section contained within the frame of two rather placid sections in the tonic—is emblematic of its singer, whose adolescent turbulence makes him a compulsive flirt and gets him into one scrape after another, but never causes him to lose his suavity and charm. The song, like the singer, reflects the elegant but disordered society that forms the opera's milieu; like a tiny window strategically placed, this little aria opens out on some of the most important dramatic issues of the opera.

My derivation of the aria's complex tonality from an underlying B♭ diatony illustrates the difference between Schenker's approach and other monotonal theories, notably Schoenberg's. Schenker's notion of *Auskomponierung* allows him to find meaningful larger contexts for chords (including tonicized chords) that are not under the control of an immediately perceptible local tonic. He can do this because he recognizes counterpoint as a shaping force in composition, a force that can give rise to successions of chords and, indeed, to "keys." Giving counterpoint its due also allows Schenker to recognize the vastly different roles that the same "region" can play in different contexts: e.g., ♭VII in what is essentially a tonic prolongation at the beginning of Beethoven's Op. 53 and the A♭ major as part of an unfolded V in "Voi che sapete."

I hope that I have shown convincingly that Mozart's return to B♭ is not the intentionally (though subtly) botched process that Schoenberg seems to have thought it was. That return is not really from A♭, as Schoenberg suggests; the A♭ is part of a larger F harmony (V) which sheds its tonic stability without ceasing to direct the progression of chords and "keys."

EXAMPLE 5.15: Mozart, *Le Nozze di Figaro*, Act II, "Voi che sapete," middleground graph

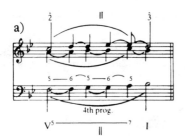

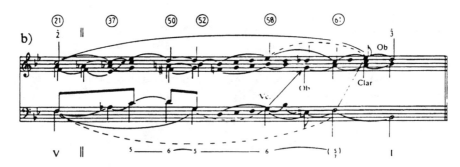

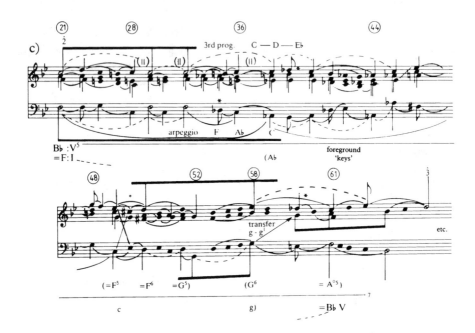

EXAMPLE 5.16: A possible middleground structure

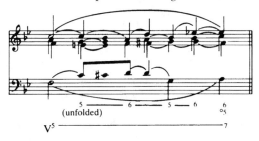

The prolongation of V goes through three phases: tonicizing F (measures 21–36), unfolding it in minor form (whence the A♭) before leading it to G (measures 37–52), and bringing the G up to A counterpointed below by the return to an F that is now unequivocally a dominant (measures 53–61).

Schenker's approach can lead to an understanding of how the seemingly unrelated "keys" of the aria's B section form an integrated whole; in this regard it is much more successful, I think, even than Schoenberg's Theory of Regions, to say nothing of analytic methods that simply produce a string of keys. At the same time one must remember that the integrative powers of the arpeggiated F chord and of the linear progression F–G–A–B♭ assert themselves against a strong centrifugal counterforce that sets up quasi-independent key centers at later levels. To concentrate on background continuity to the exclusion of foreground disruptions is to produce a skewed picture of a piece or passage. Example 5.16 shows a possible middleground structure very similar to the B section of "Voi che sapete" but with almost none of its richly chromatic elaboration. Despite the underlying similarity, how different it is!

A reasonably comprehensive and faithful analysis, then, will balance moment-by-moment and global perspectives by showing the connections among foreground tonicizations, large modulations belonging to the middleground, and inclusive background structure. This procedure will be in no way contradictory to the spirit of Schenker's approach, even though it may give more attention to the fluctuations of the foreground than he did, especially in his later writings. Good analysts should be able with little difficulty to assimilate to their interpretations an acknowledgment of the expressive and form-making potential of key change. The problems of coherence and continuity that Schenker was the first to solve—often indeed the first to pose—will, I think, continue to be far more intractable.

Notes

1. Heinrich Schenker, *Free Composition*, trans. and ed. Ernst Oster (New York: Longman, 1979), p. 9. There seems to be a misprint in the English edition: the word "foreground" near the end of the first sentence should read "background," as in my citation.

2. Heinrich Schenker, *Harmonielehre* (Vienna: Universal, 1906), pp. 162–73, issued in abridged English translation as *Harmony*, ed. Oswald Jonas, trans. Elizabeth Mann Borgese (Chicago: University of Chicago, 1954), pp. 126–29.

3. Fred Lerdahl and Ray Jackendoff, *A Generative Theory of Tonal Music* (Cambridge: MIT Press, 1983), p. 295.

4. J. S. Bach, *Forty-eight Preludes and Fugues*, book 1, ed. Donald Francis Tovey (London: Associated Board, 1924), p. 85.

5. Heinrich Schenker, "Joh. S. Bach: Sechs Sonaten für Violine; Sonata III, Largo," in *Das Meisterwerk in der Musik*, 3 vols. (Munich: Drei Masken, 1925, 1926, 1930, reissued as 3 vols. in 1 slightly reduced facsimile, Hildesheim: Georg Olms, 1974), vol. 1, p. 61, trans. John Rothgeb in *The Masterwork in Music*, ed. William Drabkin, vol. 1 (Cambridge: Cambridge University Press, 1994), pp. 32–33. Rothgeb's translation had appeared earlier in *Music Forum* 4 (1976), pp. 142–43.

6. This is an idea that seems to be gaining currency. See Charles Rosen, *Sonata Forms* (New York: Norton, 1980), pp. 295–96; and Jeffrey Kallberg, "Chopin's Last Style," *Journal of the American Musicological Society* 38 (1985), p. 274. In an excellent recent article David Lewin has argued cogently about the dubious value of "solving" theoretical problems by inventing new terms or slanting existing ones to make the problems disappear; see "Music Theory, Phenomenology, and Modes of Perception," *Music Perception* 3 (1986), pp. 327–92.

7. Rosen, *Sonata Forms*, p. 251.

8. Ibid., p. 255.

9. Ibid., p. 258.

10. This interpretation of Op. 79 is Ernst Oster's. See his note on sonata form in Schenker, *Free Composition*, p. 139. In Op. 79, the expanded VI is expressed as a major chord (E major) and it appears at the beginning of the development.

11. David Beach, "A Recurring Pattern in Mozart's Music," *Journal of Music Theory* 27, no. 1 (1983), pp. 1–29.

12. Heinrich Schenker, "Die Kunst der Improvisation," in *Das Meisterwerk*, vol. 1, p. 15, translated as "The Art of Improvisation," trans. Richard Kramer, in *The Masterwork*, vol. 1, p. 4. For Schenker, Bach's formulation was in keeping with his own conception of keys as prolonged "scale steps of tonality" (*Tonarten als Stufen der Tonalität*), a conception revealed in many of the graphs of *Das Meisterwerk*. The Bach citation is from Carl Philipp Emmanuel Bach, *Essay on the True Art of Playing Keyboard Instruments*, trans. and ed. William J. Mitchell (New York: Norton, 1949), pp. 440–45.

13. Jean-Philippe Rameau, *Treatise on Harmony*, trans. Philip Gossett (New York: Dover, 1971), pp. 267–69, in the original edition, *Traité de l'harmonie réduite a ses principes naturels* (Paris: Ballard, 1722), reprinted in facsimile as vol. 1 of Jean-Philippe Rameau, *Complete Theoretical Writings*, ed. Erwin R. Jacobi (American Institute of Musicology, 1967), pp. 248–51.

14. Johann Philipp Kirnberger, *The Art of Strict Musical Counterpoint*, trans. David Beach and Jürgen Thym (New Haven: Yale University Press, 1982), pp. 121–37; the table with Roman numerals is on p. 124. This publication includes vol. 1 and part 1 of vol. 2 of Kirnberger's *Die Kunst des reinen Satzes in der Musik*, 2 vols. (Berlin and Königsberg, 1776–79, photographic facsimile bound in one volume, Hildesheim: Georg Olms, 1968), pp. 103–20. The table with Roman numerals is on p. 106.

15. Gustav Jenner, Johannes Brahms als Mensch, Lehrer und Künstler: Studien und Erlebnisse (Marburg in Hessen: Elwert, 1905), p. 38.

16. H. K. Andrews, "Modulation," in *Grove's Dictionary of Music and Musicians*, 5th ed., ed. Eric Blom (London: Macmillan, 1954), vol. 5, p. 807.

17. Ibid., p. 810.

18. Schenker, *Harmonielehre*, pp. 396–99; *Harmony*, pp. 299–300. The English version translates *Diatonie* as "diatonic system" and *Scheintonarten* as "simulated keys"; the divergent translations in my text conform to Oster's terminology in *Free Composition*.

19. Schenker, *Harmonielehre*, pp. 391–94; *Harmony*, pp. 295–98.

20. Schenker, *Harmonielehre*, p. 397; *Harmony*, pp. 299–300.

21. Tovey reads exactly the same key succession; see his *A Companion to Beethoven's Pianoforte Sonatas* (London: Associated Board, 1931), pp. 36–37.

22. See Arnold Schoenberg, *Structural Functions of Harmony*, rev. ed. (New York: Norton, 1969), pp. 20, 68, and 75. Incidentally, Schoenberg regards diatonic II in major (which he calls Dorian) as belonging to the same class of regions as these E-minor passages in C minor and as more distant from

the tonic than, say, ♭III in major. But are not both E-minor passages far less normal than the tonicization of II in Beethoven's First Symphony, I, measures 19–23, or any of the numerous arrivals on II after the double bar in Bach's suite movements (e.g., Fourth French Suite, Sarabande, measures 13–16)? Schoenberg's classification of the distances from the tonic of the various regions sometimes seems counterintuitive and not in accordance with historical evidence, but I doubt that any other systematic account of "distance" would be much of an improvement.

23. Schenker, *Free Composition*, pp. 11–12. Of course the octave line would yield the most complete literal expression of an underlying diatonic structure, but the whole structure can be inferred from the lines starting on $\hat{5}$ or $\hat{3}$.

24. The "Erläuterungen" that Schenker published in the last two issues of *Der Tonwille* and in the first two volumes of *Das Meisterwerk* illustrate the notion of diatony in connection with a not yet definitive explanation of the *Urlinie*. See Figure 3, which shows an ascending Fundamental Line through the octave, organized into three "tone-spaces": $\hat{1}$–$\hat{3}$, $\hat{3}$–$\hat{5}$, $\hat{5}$–$\hat{8}$. A glance at this diagram will help to elucidate Schenker's comments in *Free Composition*. See "Erläuterungen," *Der Tonwille*, vol. 4. no. 2/3 (Vienna: A. Guttmann Verlag, 1924), p. 49.

25. In a valuable recent article, Matthew Brown has shown that Schenker's conception of tonality is fully chromatic, and that chromatic elements begin to appear at relatively high middleground levels; see "The Diatonic and the Chromatic in Schenker's Theory ol Harmonic Relations," *Journal of Music Theory* 30, no. 1 (1986), pp. 1–33.

26. Arnold Schoenberg, *Harmonielehre*, 4th ed. (Vienna: Universal, 1922), pp. 213–14. Schenker, of course, made it quite clear that his tonicized harmonies were not real tonics.

27. Schenker, *Free Composition*, p. 134. When Schenker states that the prolongation of $\hat{2}$ over V in an exposition "will naturally involve chromatics," he means that it will become an "illusory key."

28. Klaus Körner, "Formen musikalischer Aussage im zweiten Satz des G-Dur-Klavierkonzertes von Beethoven," *Beethoven-Jahrbuch*, ed. Hans Schmidt and Martin Staehlin (Bonn: Beethovenhaus), vol. 9 (1973/77), p. 208.

29. Charles Rosen, *The Classical Style* (New York: Viking, 1971), p. 392.

30. The literature contains even more unusual examples of key treatment; one of them, Variation 21 from Brahms's *Variations on a Theme of Handel*, forms the subject of a particularly fascinating discussion by Schenker in *Der Tonwille*, vol.4, nos. 2–3 (1924), pp. 25–26. This variation is in G minor and is the only one to depart from the B♭ tonality of the piece as a whole. Embedded in the texture, however, is what amounts to a quotation of the Theme's upper line. Every one of the main notes is present in the variation, most of them occurring as grace-notes. The remarkable thing is that this "quotation" maintains exactly the pitches of the B♭ Theme; they are not transposed into their G-minor equivalents. Schenker reads the variation in the key of G minor, but he shows the notes of the Fundamental Line in the B♭ major from which they originate; as he says, the variation "oscillates between two worlds."

31. Schoenberg, *Structural Functions of Harmony*, p. 69. Schoenberg's actual words are these: "The difficulty of finding a second illustration of this kind, coupled with some other circumstances (for instance, the long roundabout return of the tonic), suggests the following hypothesis: the page, Cherubino, accompanies himself [not so!] and is also the author of the poem. Has he not also composed the music? Did not Mozart by such extravagant features hint at Cherubino's professional imperfections?" Apropos of the difficulty of finding other instances of this "region," the Andantino of Mozart's Piano Concerto, K.449, a movement in B♭ major, contains a large-scale prolongation of A♭ major (measures 52–59); the home tonic does not reappear until measure 80. The finale of the same concerto (in E♭ major) has a brief but striking passage in D♭ minor (measures 258–61). And measures 59–65 of the F-major song "Abendempfindung" tonicize E♭ major. Do these features also hint at "professional imperfections"?

32. Siegmund Levarie, *Mozart's Le Nozze di Figaro* (Chicago: University of Chicago, 1952, reprinted in facsimile, New York: Da Capo, 1977), p. 82.

33. Schenker, *Free Composition*, figure 22b.

34. A more neutral designation of the A♭ region, for example as subtonic (or ♭VII), would have been far better. This reading would be perfectly compatible with Schoenberg's approach; he infers a minor subtonic (F minor within G major) in his analysis of the development section from the first movement of Haydn's Symphony No. 94. See Schoenberg, *Structural Functions of Harmony*, pp. 147–49.

35. Levarie's analysis of the aria contains perceptive comments about the connections between local chromaticism and modulatory plan, including an emphasis on the importance of the enharmonic pair C♯/D♭. See especially Levarie, *Figaro*, pp. 83–85.

36. See my article "Beethoven's Sketches for the First Movement of His Piano Sonata, Op. 14, No. 1: A Study in Design," *Journal of Music Theory* 26, no. 1 (1982), pp. 1–21.

37. Because they do not relate to the treatment of modulation, I shall not discuss the many madrigalisms, for example on "diletto," "martir," etc.

38. Levarie, *Figaro*, p. 81. James Webster has pointed out that in fact there are thirty-two lines in the poem as printed in the original libretto, not fourteen. The lines are in *quinario* meter (five syllables per line), and the first stanza of four lines is repeated at the end of the printed poem, just as it is in the aria. See his article "The Analysis of Mozart's Arias," in *Mozart Studies*, ed. Cliff Eisen (Oxford: Oxford University Press, 1991), pp. 133–35.

The Triad as
Place and Action

Any triad that is composed out has both a kinetic and a static aspect; when we hear it, we experience changes occurring within a relatively stable field. The changes comprise the successions of pitches and pitch combinations that we hear as melodic lines, counterpoint, and harmony, all deployed within intervals belonging to the composed-out chord. The stable field comprises the pitch content of that chord, projected from its root, extended in time, and intuited by the listener out of the complex of sounds that constitute the piece. This fluctuating pitch content can lead to an impression of stability because of the felt persistence of the chordal root throughout the time span the chord occupies—also, perhaps, from the theoretical possibility that the root might go on persisting indefinitely or even forever, a possibility that some minimalist composers have unfortunately come close to concretizing. But even in the music of pre-postmodern tonality, a prolonged tonic chord, projected from the tonic note as root, will normally abide through the ever-changing tonal content of a whole piece.

Obviously, the melodic, contrapuntal, and harmonic successions that make up the kinetic aspect differ considerably from piece to piece, whereas the stable tonal field consists of the notes of a tonic triad and hence would seem always to be the same, except for the major or minor quality of the triad. And at the most remote level of structure, it is indeed always more or less the same. But by "tonal field" I refer to a complex of horizontalized triadic intervals: the tonal space of the *Urlinie* together with all the additional triadic spaces opened up by the middleground and foreground, including those of the bass. The way this expanded field becomes manifest through the prolongational levels—the emphasis that accrues to the various chordal sounds, the temporal order in which these sounds appear, the pacing

Originally published in *Music Theory Spectrum* 17, no. 2 (1995), pp. 149–69. An earlier version was read at the annual conference of the Music Theory Society of New York State at Queens College in October 1993.

of their succession, the sounds' registers and their direction relative to each other, the amount of friction between lines and framing chord—all of these and other factors reflect back on the underlying triad so that the field of one piece is different from that of another. Sometimes, especially in short pieces, the tonal fields can be almost as particularized as the melodic lines, voice leading, and harmony, so that the prolonged triad takes on a specific local color; we can think of it as analogous to a place or milieu within which actions— melodic, contrapuntal, and harmonic—occur. To a large extent the tonal actions over time are what create the local color. The actions, of course, will constantly modify the milieu, hut a core of perceived stability will abide through these changes.

Chopin, Prelude in E Minor

The Opening Tonic

Consider Chopin's E-minor Prelude, Op. 28, No. 4. An immediately striking feature is the absence of any root-position tonic triad until the very end. Most pieces, of course, begin in a condition of harmonic stability with the tonic note in the bass, and even those that begin on I⁶, like the Chopin, usually get to a stable tonic early on. To be sure, Chopin's descending bass line reaches the tonic note in measure 4, but the E supports a seventh chord, not a triad, and the continuation of the E in measure 5 is marked in the left hand by a chromaticized 7–6 resolution into a C-major sound that clashes with the right hand's A. The bass E, therefore, is in no sense a goal; in fact, it exists in a setting far more unstable than the opening G. As I have written elsewhere, the 7–6 on E forms part of a chain of 7–6 suspensions in the left-hand part, elaborating a progression in parallel $^6_3$ chords, and itself the basis of further rhythmic and tonal elaboration.[1]

The Descending Bass

If we hear the opening chord as representing a structural tonic, then we feel the lack of a stabilizing root underneath it, a feeling that imbues the lowest voice with a strong tendency to descend in the direction of the missing E. The opening G is, one might say, a tone belonging to a middle voice thrust into the role of a bass and pulled in the direction of the appropriate bass sound. Thus the part of the tonal field that lies below the G is gravitationally charged, as it were, and becomes a presence in the piece even before we hear any of it. When the E of measure 4 turns out to be a transitional element rather than a goal, the bass must perforce continue its descent to the next available resting point, the B that marks the midpoint of the Prelude, the goal dominant of its first long phrase (measures 10–12). Since the Prelude, like a number of the Op. 28 pieces, has the form of a large period, the second phrase constitutes a varied and intensified consequent, closing the structure with a resolution to a final tonic. Here, too, as in the antecedent, the bass line traverses a descent from G to B before finally arriving at the E. In keeping with the bass's downward drive, the cadential V–I is a descending fifth, not an ascending fourth, and the octave doubling makes it a veritable descent into the depths.

The action of the Prelude's bass line, then, occurs within a tonic deprived of initial support; the bass is drawn downward until it comes to rest at the end. Thus the framing triadic notes take on the contour shown in Example 6.1a; the prolonged tonic triad is formed along a steeply descending slope. A bass line could hardly traverse a registral field much larger than this one; and, more significantly, the time frame is the biggest possible, coextensive with the piece, making this descent a particularly drastic response to the restlessness of the Prelude's first sound. Example 6.1b quotes the opening phrase of a Schumann piece whose bass line has a contour very much like that of the Chopin, and there are similarities in the upper parts as well. But the Schumann reaches a stable tonic after four measures rather than twenty-five, and there is no bass doubling at the cadence to open up the lowest possible register of the piano. The profound difference in affect results, no doubt, from many factors in combination, but one of them is surely the immense scope of Chopin's descending bass and the dark color this bass lends to the prolonged tonic harmony.

Descending Upper Voices

In the Prelude, the descending impulse is not confined to the bass. As Example 6.2 illustrates, the dissonant suspensions—especially the prominent sevenths—intensify the downward motion of the left hand's upper voices as they follow the descent of the bass. It comes perhaps as no surprise (at least to readers of this volume) that the Prelude's Fundamental Line descends, but the almost exclusively downward direction of the melodic diminutions is quite out of the ordinary. Only the initial upbeat, its recomposition in measure 12, and the climactic stretto passage of measures 16–17 show significant upward movement. In addition, the B–C–B figure of the right-hand part, taken up as C–B by the left hand's upper voice (measures 5–8) and bass (measures 9–12), has the typically intense downward drive of $\hat{6}$–$\hat{5}$ in minor. And, finally, the resolution of the big melodic line, both in the antecedent and in the consequent, is transferred down an octave into an inner voice. Thus the descending fifth of the Fundamental Line is transformed at the foreground into a twelfth, further darkening the sound of a melodic line that mostly lies in the low end of the soprano range.

Stylistic and Generic Factors; Programmatic Implications

The $\hat{5}$–$\hat{6}$–$\hat{5}$ and $\hat{6}$–$\hat{5}$ neighbor-note figures in minor have a long association with the affect of grief (inherited from Phrygian compositions of the Renaissance); and minor-mode basses descending chromatically to $\hat{5}$ (also embodying Phrygian characteristics) have been lament figures since the seventeenth century. Semitonal intensity combined with downward motion seems an appropriate musical analogue to actions and feelings associated with loss, sadness, and death. These stylistic features could hardly be given greater prominence than in this Chopin Prelude, and they occur in a setting of intense pathos—note the almost monotone melodic line broken by the outburst at the stretto passage and subsiding at the end. The pathos is heightened by a generic factor: the cantabile right hand and accompanimental (but very polyphonic) left hand make the Prelude an instrumental song and cause it to address us in the first person singular of a stylized singing voice; this, I believe, would legitimize our inferring an emotional character from the tone of that voice.

For many reasons, I find it difficult to contemplate this song for the keyboard without attributing to it a programmatic character—I hear it as a vision of death, perhaps the imagination of one's own death. I would go so far as to suggest that even the very moment of

EXAMPLE 6.1: (A) Chopin, Prelude, Op. 28, No. 4, bass contour

(B) Schumann, Albumblatt No. 5 from *Bunte Blätter*, Op. 99, measures 1–4

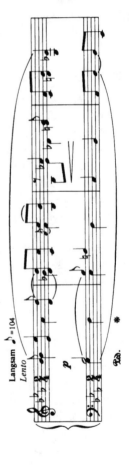

death is evoked in measure 23 in the rest with fermata before the final cadence. The ambiguous harmony immediately before the great silence—is the bass B♭? A♯?—would be a fitting symbol of the unknowable. Needless to say, I don't require anybody—not even my students—to believe in this program, but I find that many people do seem to have an emotional reaction to the piece that would be compatible with its being strongly tinged with grief, mourning, and the thought of death. That reaction is certainly due in part to associations with the Prelude's motivic design and to other stylistic aspects, for these relate to countless explicitly death-oriented pieces—funeral marches, threnodies, operatic death scenes, and the like. But the Prelude's overpowering pathos also inheres in the way it reveals its tonal field, in its governing tonic at first cast adrift without anchor and then pulled further and further down until it finally hits bottom.

Mendelssohn, "Song without Words" in G Major, Op. 62, No. 1
The Opening Tonic

Mendelssohn's "Song without Words" Op. 62, No. 1, is not so obviously extreme a piece as the Chopin Prelude, but it, too, builds up its tonal field in a most individual fashion. Although the root-position opening tonic is not suppressed as it is in the Chopin, it occurs in a very special way. In its first appearance, it follows one and a half measures of a preparatory inverted dominant only to vanish after half a measure. It reappears only twice more: at measure 6 in the modulating consequent phrase that completes the first A section, and again at measure 24 just after the beginning of the reprise. Both times, as at the beginning, the tonic has the briefest duration compatible with the harmonic rhythm of the piece, where almost no harmony lasts less than half a measure (there are only two quarter-note chords, one of which is passing, and they do not appear until measure 30). Example 6.3, a not very detailed middleground graph, shows how sparingly the tonic triad is used.[2]

Thus, although the opening tonic of the fundamental structure is composed out through twenty-six and a half measures, the root-position triad itself remains backstage throughout most of its prolongation, making only three fleeting appearances for a combined total of one and a half measures. Each time that this elusive triad appears, it forms the resolution of a dominant $^6_5$, one and a half measures long, dwarfing the duration of the tonic. The tonic's brevity is not its only rhythmic peculiarity, for it is the initial focus of a metrical conflict. In characteristically Mendelssohnian fashion, the piece begins in mid-measure, but with a sonic emphasis (see the accent sign) that makes it sound like a downbeat.[3] The sforzando that appears in the middle of measure 2 would tend to confirm the metrical pattern that the opening seems to initiate, except that the tonic resolution just before it and the cadential dominant of measure 4 create first-beat accents that call into question this pattern of midmeasure downbeats.[4] The tonal field becomes charged thereby with unusually strong kinetic impulses. No sooner does the music touch ground with the G-major chord than it bounces back into the air, the tonic's tentative downbeat quality contradicted by the very next rhythmic event. In Example 6.4, I have recomposed the beginning of the piece in order to remove much of the metrical conflict; notice how this changes the character of tonic harmony.

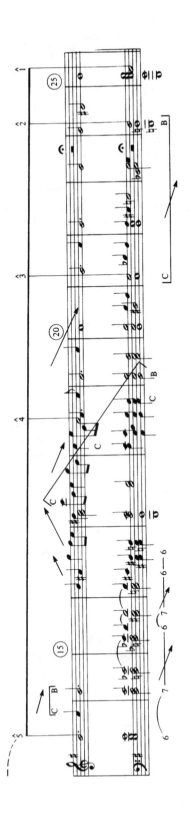

EXAMPLE 6.2: Chopin, Prelude, Op. 28, No. 4, downward motion

EXAMPLE 6.3: Mendelssohn, *Songs without Words*, Op. 61, No. 1, middleground graph

EXAMPLE 6.4: Mendelssohn, *Songs without Words*, Op. 62, No. 1, beginning rewritten

Bass Line and Harmony

If Chopin's initial I⁶ creates an effect of centripetal motion, pulled toward the root position, Mendelssohn's tonic creates an almost opposite effect, resolving its preparatory dominant and then acting as a springboard for movement away from the center. In contrast to the Chopin, the larger direction of its bass line does not seem to be determined from the outset; the shape of the opening phrase, however, strongly suggests a predominantly rising contour for the bass line as a whole. The bass's very first move is an ascent from the leading tone to the tonic, and the entire four-measure phrase expresses a rising motion from I to V. Since the phrase would seem to constitute the antecedent half of a parallel period, we have every right to expect a consequent that would close off the first part of the piece, perhaps somewhat like Example 6.5, another of my attempts at recomposition. Had Mendelssohn composed such a consequent, he would have given the initial big tonic prolongation just the sort of rhythmic grounding whose absence is such a distinctive feature of the piece.

Instead, Mendelssohn writes a modulating consequent that leads to a cadence in III, B minor. Thus the first big move of the bass line, spanning the whole first section of the piece, is from G up to B (as shown in Example 6.3). The middle section continues this bass ascent, culminating on a C that supports a subdominant transposition of the opening two measures. This tonicized C major would normally go on to a dominant whose bass note, D, would form the strongest possible goal for a rising motion that began on the tonic as well as the usual point of articulation before a reprise. Well, Mendelssohn does move to a dominant, but it is to the inverted dominant on F♯ rather than a root-position chord on D, and the F♯ is held back until the reprise begins. Thus the bass line through the beginning of the reprise becomes a large-scale unfolding: G–B–C–F♯ rather than the more usual rising fifth G–B–C–D. This middleground unfolding is as beautiful as it is unusual, but the absence of D as goal and linear climax gives the bass line a somewhat unfulfilled quality. This is because the large-scale motion of the bass has not yet succeeded in projecting the horizontalized fifth G–D at which the line seems to have been aiming.

D as a long-range goal of the bass line, withheld through most of the piece, finally arrives in the reprise. Only the first four measures of this section recapitulate the opening; the remainder encompasses a powerful drive to the long-delayed D and the resolution of that D to the G-major tonic. The motion to V occurs in two phrases in a kind of antecedent/consequent relation. The antecedent stops short on a deceptive cadence; the consequent takes up and completes the motion in order finally to resolve it in a powerful authentic cadence. Example 6.3 shows that a unified linear impulse underlies the reprise despite the

EXAMPLE 6.5: Mendelssohn, *Songs without Words*, Op. 62, No. 1, consequent phrase rewritten

semicadence in measure 26 and the deceptive cadence in measure 30: a motion from G (supporting I) to B (supporting I⁶) to C (supporting IV) to D (V) and G (I). Note that this bass line traverses the same ground as the A and B sections, with their motion from G to B to C, but this time the bass ascent finally reaches a culminating D, supporting a cadential V sufficiently impressive in itself and made all the more impressive by the broad linear ascent leading to it—a tonal arch that spans virtually the entire piece.

As mentioned above, the antecedent phrase of measures 1–4 remained unresolved, for its consequent initiated a move out of the tonic key rather than an authentic cadence in it like the one I invented as Example 6.5. In a sense, the whole rest of the piece becomes that missing consequent, now vastly expanded and occurring in seemingly self-contained stages: from G to B, from B to C, and finally from G again through B and C to D and G. Example 6.6 shows how the initial bass motion points out a path through the piece's tonal field, a path that the rest of the piece will traverse. The pitches that most clearly define the tonal field here (indicated by asterisks in Example 6.6) are the G and B of the first section, the C of the middle section, and the D and G of the reprise. Note the stepwise ascent of the culminating pitches: B, C, and D. Two of these pitches—the bass C of measures 18–20 and the goal D of measures 33–34—do not really connect with each other structurally, for each belongs to a different linear entity: the C is part of the big unfolding of the first and middle sections, and the D is the goal of an upward arpeggiation from the tonic of the reprise (and, at a higher level, from the opening tonic). Nonetheless, the C and D have strong associative links—based on pitch proximity, harmonic expectation, and analogous climactic position—that transcend the structural disjunction. When we infer what I call a tonal field, we do so by contemplating the governing tonic in the light of middleground and foreground events. In so doing, we may well have reason to bridge over divisions between prolongational entities and structural levels, since all such entities and all levels are present, or at least implicit, in the foreground.

The Upper Voice

Although D is a very prominent note in the upper voice, especially at the beginning and end of the piece, it is not part of the Fundamental Line. It is, however, an important presence in the piece, and is largely responsible for a characteristic feature of its sound—an unusual preponderance of diminutions that lie above, rather than below, the Fundamental Line, and that remain disconnected from a resolution into the tonic note.[5] If this piece were a painted landscape, it would be by a Dutch master, with a lot of sky showing above a rather low horizon. The D is involved in some particularly ingenious melodic parallelisms,

EXAMPLE 6.6: Mendelssohn, *Songs without Words*, Op. 62, No. 1, initial bass motion and its consequences

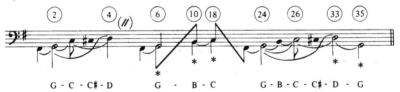

G - C - C♯ - D   G - B - C   G - B - C - C♯ - D - G

as Example 6.7 shows. Both the neighbor-note E and the superposed high G are invariable elements of these parallelisms, but these invariable elements appear in such different rhythmic and harmonic settings that each occurrence seems a fresh event.

Expressive Implications

Both in its structure and its texture, the *Lied* is characterized by lightness and fluidity; at the same time, it projects tensions early on whose resolution requires the completion of virtually the entire piece. In its kinetic aspect, it emphasizes tonal flux and rhythmic instability to a remarkable extent, delaying to the last possible moment any goal that might bring more than the most temporary completion and resolution. Now any piece of tonal music, with its upbeats and downbeats, its dissonances resolving into consonances, its rising and falling linear progressions, its directed harmonic motions, can be felt to express (or at least suggest) tension and release, inhalation and exhalation, striving and attainment, desire and fulfillment. The expression of these qualities in the Mendelssohn, therefore, does not distinguish it from a thousand other pieces. What is special, however, is the constantly shifting ground within the tonic prolongation and the extent to which tension and striving overshadow release and satisfaction, at least until the piece reaches the big final cadence. To me, the *Lied*'s unremitting tonal and rhythmic fluctuations suggest ever renewed and mutable desire, on the one hand, and incomplete and transitory fulfillment, on the other. The ubiquitous sighing figure of two slurred notes adds to the mood of longing and desire—again, as in the Chopin, the expressive character of a human voice simulated in an instrumental song. Note how the longing is, as it were, built into the prolonged tonic triad, whose bass line rises through the whole piece until the arrival on the dominant provides a goal and permits a definitive resolution.

It may seem strange to associate nineteenth-century Germany's sunniest composer with its gloomiest philosopher, but the piece does put me in mind of some of Schopenhauer's writings on music, in one way even more than the *Tristan* Prelude, which is often rightly felt to reflect them. Schopenhauer hears the tensions and releases of music as mirroring the strivings and satisfactions of the Will, though purged of the suffering which an active Will inevitably creates for a person. In normal life, the satisfaction of desire "is always like the alms thrown to a beggar, which reprieves him today so that his misery may be prolonged till tomorrow."[6] Only in art, and especially in music, for Schopenhauer, do these partial and fleeting satisfactions eventually lead to genuine fulfillment. The *Tristan* Prelude conveys the longing without the fulfillment—the Will, as it acts in life, turned into music. The Mendelssohn conforms more closely to Schopenhauer's view of the Will as embodied in music, for the partial resolutions lead, step by step, to fulfillment in the splendid final cadence.

Beethoven, the "Storm" Movement from the Sixth Symphony

Descriptive Aspects

When I wrote, near the beginning of this essay, that one might sometimes think of a prolonged triad as analogous to a place or milieu, I meant just that: "analogous to," not "descriptive of." But occasionally music can be written in such a way as really to permit the

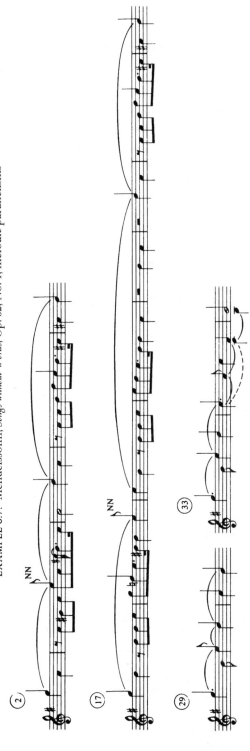

EXAMPLE 6.7: Mendelssohn, *Songs without Words*, Op. 62, No. 1, melodic parallelisms

suggestion of a place in the natural world. As far as I know, however, such cases are restricted to music with a text or descriptive title, music as part of a drama, or music with an explicit and convincing program; for instance, the fourth movement, "Gewitter, Sturm," from Beethoven's Sixth Symphony. Among the many remarkable aspects of this remarkable movement is the way the stormy world it depicts penetrates below the descriptive details of the foreground into the underlying triadic substance.

Even in its purely descriptive aspects, the movement is a masterly achievement, with wonderfully evocative musical symbols for thunder, lightning, wind, and rain. I have indicated these in Example 6.8, which is a kind of road map of the movement, pointing out characteristic surface motives with their programmatic implications as well as some important details of dynamics and orchestration and a preliminary orientation to the linear/harmonic structure. Most of the programmatic tags are mine, but a few are supported by the sketches, where Beethoven writes "Donner," "Bliz" [sic], and "Regen" next to figures that resemble, more or less, those in the completed work.[7] Of special importance is the first-violin figure of measure 5, although its programmatic meaning is difficult to specify, for it is not the imitation of a natural sound or movement like those of thunder, lightning, or rain. For reasons I shall go into later, I label it "dark cloud," but with a question mark. For the most part, Example 6.8 is self-explanatory, and we can proceed to a discussion of the movement's form and tonal structure.

Relation to Preceding and Following Movements

The movement is not self-contained. It breaks into the third movement's peasant dance and continues directly into the shepherd's song of the fifth movement. As the careted numbers above the top voice in Example 6.8 show, the big melodic line is a rising third-progression $\hat{1}$–$\hat{2}$–$\hat{3}$, connecting the last Fundamental-Line tone of the third movement with the initial Fundamental-Line tone of the Finale. In other words, the upper line forms an *Anstieg* or initial ascent, rather than a descending fundamental line. The structural anomaly points up the very special character of this piece, for such a rising line would normally arch over a movement's opening phrase rather than the movement as a whole.

Tonal Structure and Form

We are now in a position to take a closer look at the complex and unusual tonal structure. Example 6.9 is a voice-leading graph of the movement; to make the discussion easier to follow, I have divided the graph into seven sections, indicated by numbers between the staves. The movement begins (No. 1) with a rumble of distant thunder, produced by a low tremolo Db in the celli and basses. This pitch forms the bass of a VI in F minor, so the juncture between movements represents a deceptive cadence. As is often the case, the VI initiates a chromatic passing motion that links the dominant seventh at the end of the dance with the F-minor tonic that finally resolves it in measure 21. The rising motion, intensified toward the end by a crescendo, forms the perfect musical equivalent of the storm's building up.

The fortissimo F-minor tutti (No. 2) signals the thunderstorm's arrival in full force. The timpani enter for the first time in the symphony; the thunder is now close at hand. If ever there was a good instantiation of Edward Cone's notion of a structural downbeat following

EXAMPLE 6.8: Beethoven, Symphony No. 6, fourth movement, programmatic aspects

EXAMPLE 6.8 (*continued*)

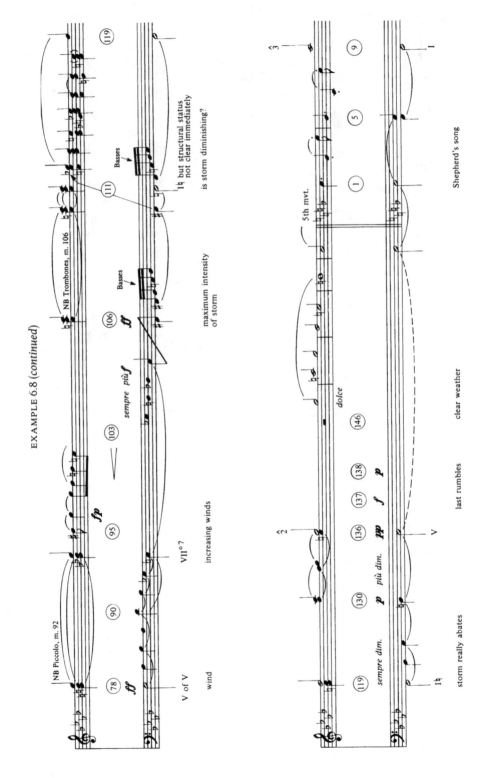

EXAMPLE 6.9: Beethoven, Symphony No. 6, fourth movement, graph

EXAMPLE 6.9 (continued)

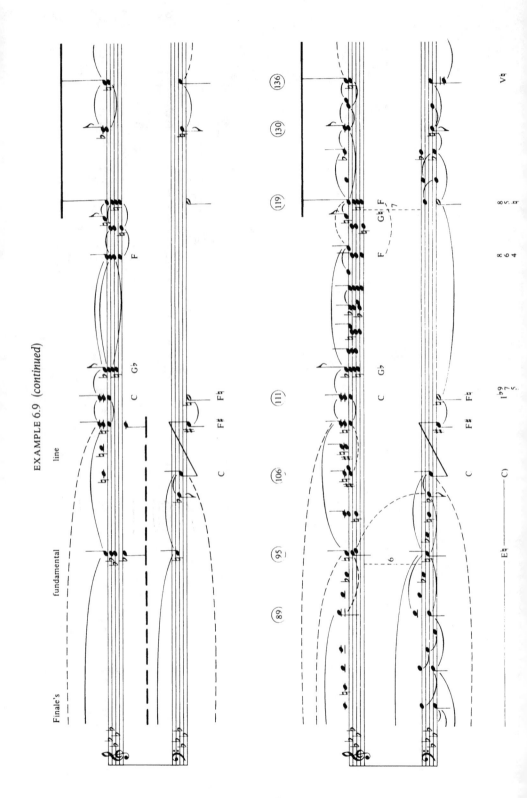

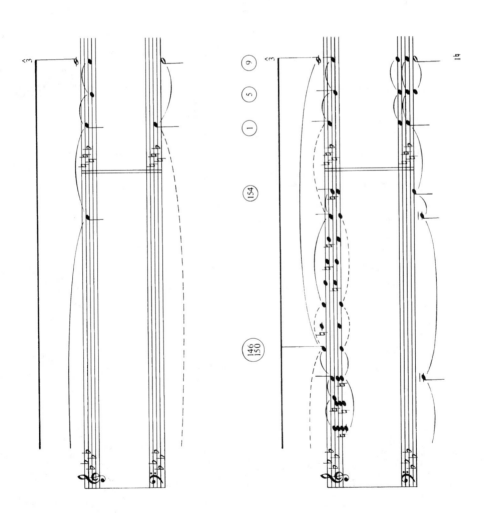

an extended upbeat, this is it.[8] The downbeat represents the true tonal beginning of the movement, with the extended upbeat of the first twenty measures functioning as a transition from the third movement. Motivically, however, these measures do belong with what follows, for they present or at least prefigure the most important elements of the movement's design. Note the bass part of measures 21–32. Beethoven suggests the roar of thunder by a rapid four-note figure, F–G–Ab–Bb, whose last note remains unresolved. But against this impressionistic rumbling, the celli play a five-note figure which resolves the Bb to C. The unresolved dissonance of the basses becomes a unique kind of ornament—remotely related to the acciaccatura of Domenico Scarlatti and his contemporaries—a dark sonic color, which stains the harmony without obliterating it.

The F-minor tonic chord of measure 21 persists for four measures, but never returns during the subsequent course of the music. Although the greater part of the movement composes out tonic harmony, it mostly does so by means of an extended dominant prolongation, after which the tonic returns as a major chord. This extremely sparing use of the tonic triad is perhaps the one feature that links the movement to the other two pieces discussed in this essay.

The arrival on the dominant marks a new phase of the movement's tonal structure (No. 3), a phase characterized by unexpected and sometimes bewildering harmonic shifts, often intensified by sharp contrasts in dynamics and orchestration. The main outlines, however, are clear enough: the C-major dominant changes to C minor in measures 49–55. What follows (No. 4) is a motion to G (measures 78–80) in falling fifths: A major (measure 56), D major becoming F# diminished seventh (measures 64–71), G. The A-major chord that initiates this motion is tonally far removed from its C-minor environment, and the D major does not proceed immediately to the goal G, but moves through a detour of Bb minor. Thus, the moment-by-moment experience of this passage is fraught with uncertainty despite the clear harmonic direction of the underlying progression.

The detour to Bb minor (measures 70–74) calls for special mention, for it echoes quite closely a similar move made not long before, in measures 51–53. The move is unusual enough to make its repetition both striking and significant. Each time, the V^7 of Bb minor is preceded by a diminished seventh chord on F#, whose bass is inflected down to F♮. The first time, the Bb minor turns out to be a neighbor-note chord to the locally governing C minor. We should probably expect a similar outcome the second time, for the seventh chord on G of measures 76–77 would normally proceed to C, but instead the G itself becomes the main harmony at the beginning of the next passage. Retrospectively, therefore, the Bb minor is best understood in relation to the G, not the C; it would function as its startlingly chromaticized upper third.

The next phase of the bass (No. 5) is a motion of a sixth from G to E♮, subdivided by the notes of a diminished seventh chord: G–Bb–Db–E; the E, another major turning point, arrives in measure 95 (No. 6). It supports a diminished seventh chord, VII^7 of F minor. We can group this diminished seventh together with the C chords of measures 35, 49, and 55, and with the G chord of measure 78, as a continuation of the prolonged dominant. Thus the large contour of the bass is formed by an arpeggio, C–G–E♮, which we might well expect to culminate on C as the root of V, especially since the approach to the movement's biggest climax in measures 93–96 occurs over a chromatic descending bass that seems to be aimed at a V or perhaps a $^6_4$; note the augmented sixth on Db in measure 106. Of course such an arrival would be a fairly normal conclusion for the extended dominant prolongation. Well, C arrives in the bass, but the upper parts suppress the expected V, substituting an F♯ diminished seventh. The surprise is rhythmic as well as harmonic: the C appears prematurely on beat 3, rather than on the following downbeat. Immediately thereafter, on beat 4, the big climax arrives, on the same diminished seventh, but now with F♯ in the bass. In Example 6.10, I attempt to explain the rather baffling harmony of this passage, starting with a normal V–I progression (Example 6.10a), inserting an anticipatory ⁶₄ over V (Example 6.10b),[9] adding some of the specific features of the prolonged V (Example 6.10c), and finally (Example 6.10d) adding the chromatic alterations that produce the climactic diminished seventh.

The diminished seventh continues for four more measures, but in measure 111, the bass F♯ is inflected downward to become F♮. This F, which goes on as a bass pedal for nine measures, constitutes, in fact, a return to the movement's structural tonic. When it first appears, however, it supports a dissonant formation, a minor ninth chord, whose ninth, G♭, contin-

EXAMPLE 6.10: Beethoven, Symphony No. 6, fourth movement, approach to climax

ues the F♯ sound of the diminished seventh. As the pedal persists, we become increasingly convinced of the importance of the F, but at first we cannot be sure that it represents a true tonic arrival rather than, say, a V of IV. Only with the F major of measure 119 (No. 7) is its status evident beyond a doubt: clear harmony and clear weather. From that point on, the music moves fairly directly to the dominant that underlies the transition to the Finale.

I believe that it is no accident that the overwhelming climax of measure 106 occurs at a diminished seventh chord on F♯. Recall that this very diminished seventh has occurred twice before, in measures 51 and 68. In both earlier passages, the F♯ moved down to F♮, exactly as it does in measures 106–11. Furthermore, in all three passages, the F♯ comes from a C, either directly, as in measures 51 and 106, or indirectly, as in measure 68, where the C-minor chord is the starting point of the harmonic progression that includes the diminished seventh. Example 6.11 draws together these three related passages. Now an F♯ that descends to F has a lot in common with a G♭, and the first of these F♯s really functions as a G♭. We can determine this because the seventh chord on F to which it resolves moves to a chord of B♭ minor (Example 6. 11a). The F♯ in measure 68 (Example 6.11b) is more complicated, for its foreground and background meanings differ: its immediate (foreground) resolution is also to B♭ minor, but this occurs as a temporary halt in a larger motion to G major, so basically (in the background) the F♯ really is an F♯.

The climactic passage is the most problematic of all (Example 6.11c). As Example 6.10 shows, the diminished seventh on C (third beat) appears where a ♮⁶₄ might well be expected. In relation to that expectation, the F♯ is really what it seems to be: an alteration of F. In relation to its resolution, however, it behaves like a G♭, and the upper-voice C–G♭–F that follows is, as it were, a clarification of the earlier bass progression. And yet an irreducible residue of "F♯-ness" remains in the climactic diminished seventh, allowing us, in retrospect, to understand it as representing tonic harmony.

Example 6.11d indicates that all of these moves from C to F♯ or G♭ and then to F derive from a prominent motive heard at the opening of the movement: the first-violin figure of measure 5. On Example 6.8, I labeled it "dark cloud" but with a question mark. Its register might plausibly suggest something high up, possibly in the sky, but one might also think of it as a kind of mental cloud—the countryfolk's first inkling that a storm is brewing. And indeed one need not adopt a specifically programmatic interpretation at all. The important thing is to realize that the figure is a kind of portent, a small sign that something big—and in this case bad—is about to happen. For this innocent-seeming figure is the seed from which the shattering climax of the movement grows. The two bass progressions of C–F♯–F♮ keep the motive in our ears and effect a connection between the little cloud, if that is what it is, and the full-blown tempest. They also embody the unpredictability of the storm, for we cannot be sure, at least at first, whether the chromatic sound is F♯ or G♭. In this connection, note the piccolo part of measures 93–95, whose G♭ becomes an F♯ to rise to G. The enharmonic change is not notated, but the first-violin part of measure 95 repeats the figure with an F♯ notation. This piccolo part, by the way, gives us the highest pitches in the entire symphony, so the F♯/G♭ ambiguity is as prominent as can be.

The climactic F♯ diminished seventh and the melodic diminished fifth C–F♯ form a particularly appropriate symbol—almost a musical icon—for the destructive power of a violent storm. The tonic pitch is altered and distorted just when a cadential resolution is in progress, and the distortion shakes the tonal world to its foundations. Only when the F♯

EXAMPLE 6.11: Beethoven, Symphony No. 6, fourth movement, C–F#–(G♭)–F

turns silently into a G♭ and leads down to F do we begin to regain our bearings in the tonal milieu. For a moment, the storm was so severe that we failed to recognize our home, even though we were standing right in front of it. That the storm will now start to abate is, I think, foretold by the very violin figure (in measure 5) that I read as a portent of its fury and destructiveness. Just as the G♭ in that figure resolves to an F, so does the F♯ of the big diminished seventh. The storm-buffeted landscape that Beethoven evokes slowly returns to normal together with its musical analogue, the deformed tonic triad. Example 6.8 shows that the bass part at the climax still contains the unresolved dissonance I mentioned earlier (measure 106), but when the F♯ resolves to F♮, the figure changes to a triadic arpeggiation containing a normal (i.e., resolved) passing tone.

The foreground features of this passage are as remarkable as the disguised motivic connection and unusual tonal organization that underlie it. There is, for example, a kind of harmonic collision between the diminished seventh chord and the expected dominant or $^6_4$ chord whose place the diminished seventh usurps. In addition, there is a concomitant rhythmic collision, the diminished seventh invading the anticipated time span of the previous augmented sixth chord. And finally, there is the trombone entrance, which completes the orchestration almost at the very end of the movement. The movement as a whole is an outstanding example of the "sublime" in music, and the trombones, with their aura of supernatural awe, join in the climax for more than the decibels they provide. It is significant that the trombones remain during the Finale, whereas the timpani drop out. The drums might suggest a return to thunder and bad weather, but the religious connotations provided by the trombones are entirely appropriate to the last movement, which Beethoven composes as a kind of hymn.[10]

On 9 December 1910, Gustav Mahler conducted the New York Philharmonic on tour in Buffalo, New York, having visited Niagara Falls with his wife Alma earlier that day. After the evening's concert, Alma writes in her memoirs, Mahler returned to the hotel in high spirits: "'I have realized today,' he said, 'that articulate art is greater than inarticulate nature.' He had been conducting the Pastoral symphony and had found it more tremendous than all the Niagara Falls."[11] Well, perhaps if he had been able to conduct the waters of Niagara, he might have found them as "tremendous" as the symphony, but they still would not have been "articulate art." If any part of the symphony gives the impression of "inarticulate nature," it is the storm movement. And if any part of that movement gives such an impression, it is the big climax, which provides a visceral impact perhaps unprecedented in the symphonic literature. But at the same time, this climax forms the culminating moment in a fascinating web of motivic associations; and these associations impinge upon the tonal structure in a totally original manner: one of the characteristic pitches threatens to undermine the tonic triad itself. The sonic impact, the motivic design, and the threatened but ultimately preserved structure all form iconic symbols that project the descriptive, programmatic aspects of the movement. Could any composer but Beethoven have combined physical excitement and visionary musical thought in so compelling a way?

Notes

1. Carl Schachter, "Schenker's Counterpoint," *Musical Times* 129, no. 1748 (1988), pp. 528–29. I discuss other aspects of the Prelude in "Chopin's Prelude, Opus 28, No. 4: Autograph Sources and

Interpretation," in *Chopin Studies 2*, ed. John Rink and Jim Samson (Cambridge: Cambridge University Press, 1994), pp. 161–82.

2. There is an excellent analysis of the Mendelssohn in Allen Cadwallader's essay "Form and Tonal Process: The Design of Different Structural Levels," in *Trends in Schenkerian Research,* ed. Allen Cadwallader (New York: Schirmer, 1990), pp. 5–10. The reader may wish to compare Cadwallader's more detailed graphs with my Example 6.3.

3. In his book *Phrase Rhythm in Tonal Music* (New York: Schirmer, 1989), pp. 199–213, William Rothstein has an extensive and most informative discussion of conflicting downbeats in Mendelssohn's *Songs without Words.*

4. In his unpublished paper "Strange Dimensions: Regularity and Irregularity in Deep Levels of Rhythmic Reduction," Frank Samarotto uses the evocative term "shadow meter" to refer to patterns of accent and non-accent that are at variance with those of the basic meter, but that are strong and consistent enough to create a rival metrical schema (paper read on March 29, 1992, at the Second International Schenker Symposium, held at the Mannes College of Music). At the beginning of the Mendelssohn piece, it is very difficult to determine which of the rival meters is substance and which is shadow. As is usually the case with Mendelssohn, however, the notated meter eventually wins out.

5. Cadwallader, in "Form and Tonal Process," shows that the D is involved in three fundamental motivic elements: a line from B to D, one back from D to B, and a D–E–D neighbor-note figure.

6. Arthur Schopenhauer, *The World as Will and Representation,* trans. E. F. J. Payne (New York: Dover, 1969), vol. 1, p. 196.

7. See Gustav Nottebohm, *Zweite Beethoveniana: nachgelassene Aufsätze* (Leipzig: C. F. Peters, 1887), p. 370; and Dagmar Weise, ed., *Ein Skizzenbuch zur Pastoralsymphonie Op. 68 und zu den Trios Op. 70, 1 und 2* (Bonn: Beethovenhaus, 1961), vol. 2, pp. 60, 67, and 81. I have been able to study only the published sketches, which are by no means all that exist.

8. Edward T. Cone, *Musical Form and Musical Performance* (New York: Norton, 1968), pp. 24–26.

9. This $^6_4$ usage, not uncommon in the later Beethoven and in Brahms, represents a kind of conflation of dominant and tonic harmonies. The $^6_4$ enters as if it were a cadential embellishment of V, but the V is elided, so the $^6_4$ is transformed into an anticipation of the coming tonic. For a particularly beautiful example of this usage, see Beethoven's Piano Sonata, Op. 110, third movement, measures 114–16.

10. See F. E. Kirby, "Beethoven's Pastoral Symphony as a *Sinfonia caracteristica,"* *Musical Quarterly* 56 (1970), pp. 618–19.

11. Alma Mahler, *Gustav Mahler: Memories and Letters,* ed. Donald Mitchell, trans. Basil Creighton, 3d ed., rev. and enlarged Knud Martner and Donald Mitchell (Seattle: University of Washington Press, 1975), pp. 183–84.

A Commentary on Schenker's
Free Composition

General Features

The Translation

Heinrich Schenker's *Der freie Satz* is surely one of the most important books on music in the entire Western tradition; it is also one of the most difficult. *Free Composition* is the late Ernst Oster's magnificent English translation of this work, amplified by extremely helpful annotations, most of them by Oster himself, but some by Oswald Jonas, who edited the second German edition, and by John Rothgeb, who checked the translation after Oster's untimely death. Splendidly produced by Longman, Inc., with the financial assistance of the American Musicological Society, this publication will be of inestimable value to the many musicians and scholars interested in Schenker's ideas, most of whom are English-speaking; it will make possible a continuing discussion of these ideas over the coming years. *Free Composition* at once deserves and requires such a discussion on the part of the musical community. It deserves it because of the importance and scope of the ideas it contains; it requires it because some of these ideas are conveyed in language of an almost Delphic compression and obscurity.

I should like to mention at the outset that Ernst Oster was my colleague and close friend and that I was marginally involved in the publication of *Free Composition*. I contributed the brief biography of Oster that appears at the end of the book, and I was consulted about some doubtful points in the translation. Normally I would not review a publication to which I was an interested party, but in this case I felt that my doing so would not be wrong; the book has been available in German for almost half a century, and its importance is generally acknowledged. It is my hope that my partisanship—that is, my long involvement with Schenker's work—might make me able to shed light on parts of the book that some readers would otherwise find obscure. What I should like to accomplish with this review is to

Originally published in the *Journal of Music Theory* 25, no. 1 (1981), pp. 115–42.

provide an orientation to a few of Schenker's ideas for readers who know something about his approach, but who have little direct experience with his writings.

I can't imagine that we shall ever have a better translation of Schenker than this one. Indeed, I suspect that German readers who are fluent in English will consult *Free Composition*, partly for its excellent notes but also because, as Allen Forte remarks in his introduction, the English version is often clearer than the original. This clarity is the result not only of careful and painstaking translation but also of brilliant interpretation by someone with an unsurpassed understanding of Schenker's musical ideas and writing style. Of course any translation—even one that renders faithfully a clear and simple original—must also be an interpretation. But the interpretative task that confronted Oster is of a magnitude that few English-speaking readers could be aware of, unless they, too, had attempted to struggle with the original. Therefore, although I do not intend to discuss the translation in much detail, I should like to cite one brief but problematic passage.

In § 16, headed "The fifth in nature and art," Schenker writes, "Die Natur freilich kennt nur die eine Quint, kein anderes Intervall neben ihr." Oster's translation reads as follows: "Nature, of course, knows only the fifth *that appears in the overtone series*, and no other *kind of fifth*" (my italics). A more literal translation, however, would read more or less like the following: "Nature, of course, knows only the one fifth, and no other interval." It seems to me that Oster's English makes more sense than Schenker's German, but perhaps it makes slightly more than Schenker intended. One of Oster's interpretative alterations (the first italicized passage) is certainly correct. "Die eine Quint" must mean the fifth of the overtone series, though this meaning would hardly be self-evident to every reader of the original. His second departure from literalness, however, may be open to question (the second italicized passage). It probably reflects the fact that Schenker's "kein anderes Intervall" stands in contradiction to the notion, expressed throughout *Free Composition* (and in earlier writings), that the octave and third, as well as the fifth, are given by Nature. Oster's interpretation may therefore be correct, but we can never be sure; Schenker contradicts himself at times, and he might have done so here. This passage occurs in the course of a discussion of the bass arpeggiation (which uses only the fifth); the context lends some plausibility to the more literal translation, as does the sentence preceding this one, which states (not quite accurately) that the earliest polyphony restricted itself to fifths. Excellent as it is, then, Oster's translation does not (and could not) solve every problem posed by the original; there are passages in *Der freie Satz* whose meaning will always be open to question.

Schenker's Achievement

In some of his earlier theoretical writings—especially in the two volumes of *Kontrapunkt*—Schenker had disclosed an astonishing capacity both for the precise formulation of music-theoretical principles and for their systematic presentation. Judging from the format and from some of the language of *Free Composition*, one gets the impression that he strove for an even greater degree of precision and rigor in the later work. I don't think that the attempt was completely successful; viewed purely as a "theoretical" work, *Der freie Satz* falls short of *Kontrapunkt* in comprehensiveness, consistency, and elegance. Nonetheless, it represents a greater achievement than *Kontrapunkt*, for its subject matter is so elusive, complex, various, and resistant to systematic presentation that one must marvel at what Schenker accomplished. The principles of tonal structure that he demonstrates illuminate the masterpieces of an entire musical repertory; he shows the validity of these principles in analyses that are immeasurably superior to any produced before him. No other music theorist has achieved anything even remotely comparable.

The Three Parts

Free Composition falls into three main parts in accordance with the well-known categories of structural level: background, middleground, and foreground. In Part I, "The Background," Schenker describes the forms of the Fundamental Structure; in Part II, "The Middleground," he describes the first prolongational level; in Part III, "The Foreground," he describes the contents of the second and subsequent levels. On the whole this format works very well, but at one point the frame does not quite fit the picture, for the arrangement seems to locate the boundary between middleground and foreground at the second level of prolongation—a level that, in most pieces, is still quite close to the background.

I am certain that Schenker did not mean to suggest that the foreground begins in principle at the second level; both his graphic analyses and his explanations reveal that he located the foreground at or near the musical surface (see Figure 22b of *Free Composition*). I don't know why Schenker includes all of the levels beyond the first in Part III, but I believe that it is because these levels (as he describes them) can contain prolongational events characteristic of the foreground as well as those "transferred" from the background and the first level of middleground. In any case, it is impossible to specify generally the level at which the foreground begins, for it will vary from piece to piece. Schenker is inconsistent in his use of the term "foreground." Sometimes he applies it to the absolute "surface" of a piece, sometimes to a slightly deeper level.[1] His best formulations reconcile these slight discrepancies by pointing to the possibility that the foreground might contain more than a single level.[2] It seems to me that little is gained by efforts to demarcate the more detailed levels of the middleground from the less detailed ones of the foreground.

Structural Levels

In his Introduction (p. xix), Allen Forte refers to Schenker's notion of structural levels as "the major concept that governed his approach to the study of tonal music." The concept is indeed a remarkable one; it has had an extraordinary influence on the evolution of music theory since Schenker, and (as has often been noted) it anticipates recent developments in linguistics and other non-musical fields. But Schenker's conception of "level" differs considerably from that of many later thinkers, whether in music or in other disciplines. Anyone looking at Schenker's graphic analyses will soon notice that the events on a given level are not all of the same rank; the subordination of some events to others often appears very clearly in Schenker's notation. The events, therefore, are not all "on the same level," at least in the usual sense. (It is perhaps worth mentioning that *Schicht,* Schenker's term, means "layer" rather than "level" and thus does not imply an equality of status as strongly as the English term.) The differentiation of rank within a single level begins with the Fundamental Structure. In the line $\hat{3}$–$\hat{2}$–$\hat{1}$, for example, the $\hat{2}$ functions as a passing tone and is obviously dependent on the chordal tones that frame it. Just these three notes would give us two "levels" without considering the bass arpeggiation and without reckoning in the tonic triad and even the tonic note as one or more prior "levels."

Schenker's middleground levels, like the Fundamental Structure, show a combination of principal and subordinate elements. Of course the events carried over from a prior level will necessarily have higher rank than the "new" ones, but even among the latter, Schenker mixes together primary and dependent pitches. Thus a linear progression—say one that descends a fifth from the $\hat{2}$ of the Fundamental Line—may appear "all at once" at the first middleground level rather than in stages (the arpeggiated fifth first and the stepwise connection only later). As a result, Schenker's levels tend to depict coherent tonal structures—complete linear progressions, arpeggiations, couplings, unfoldings, etc.—rather than the fragmentary "reductions" of some later analysts. The advantage of coherence that accrues to Schenker's method more than compensates for any loss of rigor, especially since one can usually reconstruct without much trouble the stages omitted from his presentation of a given prolongation. The fact that fewer levels are required is also an advantage when one is dealing with long and complicated works.

The Composing-Out Process

One could argue that *Auskomponierung* (compositional elaboration or, not quite in English, "composing-out"), rather than structural levels, is the central concept in Schenker's thought. In any case, the idea of levels cannot be separated from this process, for they mainly arise out of its most important components—the horizontalization and, often, the stepwise filling-in of a chord or chordal interval. Whereas the notion of levels can be applied to many fields, *Auskomponierung* is uniquely a property of music and, more specifically, of contrapuntal music (horizontalization obviously presupposes a prior verticality). Any "levels" that might exist in monophonic music would have a very different meaning than those Schenker deals with, for they would not come about through the process of horizontalization.

"Nature" and "Art"

The composing-out process and the levels it gives rise to represent a hard-won synthesis of the sometimes conflicting demands of "nature" (as manifested in the internal structure of the single musical sound) and "art." Nature, for Schenker, means limitless development and transformation; art means selection, abbreviation, and resolution. Nature provides the overtone series; art selects the triad and compresses its "naturally" wide range to fit the human voice. The overtone series is a simultaneity; the art of music is based on succession in time and must arpeggiate the triad. Nature knows no end; art employs the dissonant passing tone to create the need to resolve and the consequent possibility of goal-oriented motion.

Schenker bases very little of his theory on the overtone series, but that little is of great importance. From it he derives the major triad and the triadic consonances: the octave, fifth, and major third. In the overtone series he sees a pattern in nature for musical composition; a piece of music is, among other things, a symbolic re-creation, an image, of the relationships that exist in a single musical sound. Of course one can reformulate Schenker's theory so that the overtone series does not figure in it at all; one would have to do little more than substitute "triad" for "overtone series." Most of the theory would remain intact, but something important—even essential—would be lost: the connection between the simplest musical element, the single tone, and the masterpieces of the great composers in all their complexity. I would urge readers not to dismiss what Schenker has to say about the overtone series before giving it careful thought.

Linear Progressions

It is in the linear progressions that a synthesis between "nature" and "art," between chord and line, is most completely achieved. The intervals that the progressions traverse are the triadic consonances and their inversions: octave, fifth, third, fourth, and sixth. (Schenker's seventh-progressions are, in my opinion, only apparent linear progressions or, at best, borderline cases.) The beginning and the goal of the progression form a "natural" interval. Between these points, however, stretches a stepwise line whose unfolding inevitably produces one or more dissonances against the prevailing harmony. The dissonances, of course, must resolve, and they must do so in the direction of the goal tone, for the goal is determined by the larger context. (The Fundamental Line—the "first" linear progression—obviously has no larger context; but none is needed, for the goal, the tonic note, is the primary focal point of the entire structure.) It is thus not only the stepwise line but also the need to resolve dissonances that draws together the beginning and goal tones of a linear progression and makes it a more cohesive structure than an arpeggio, whose motion is intensified by no such constraint.

   Schenker regards linear progressions as the *sine qua non* of music as an art. Their coherence epitomizes his view of musical coherence in general. It is not a coherence that results from uniformity but one that is based on the interaction between contrasting elements—in the linear progressions, between the chordal interval and the stepwise connecting notes, between consonance and dissonance, between motion and goal, between "nature" and "art." I believe that it is mainly to preserve the coherence of the linear progressions (that is, to preserve their tension and their kinetic character) that Schenker tends to combine at a single level elements of obviously different rank.

The Number of Levels

One of the confusing aspects of *Free Composition* is that it sometimes appears to be more rigorous than it really is. For instance, Schenker maintains that the number of levels for any given piece could be ascertained precisely, though the number would vary from piece to piece. He goes on to add that his previously published works frequently reveal the exact number of levels of the compositions discussed (p. 26, §48). I wish that he had specified which of his analyses do, in fact, show the exact number of levels. I would venture a guess that none of them do, for it seems to me that Schenker's tendency to treat each level as a synthesis of background and foreground events (using these terms in a relative rather than an absolute sense) precludes any such precision. If I am right, then Schenker's levels are something other than the rigorously logical constructs that he seems to have thought they were.

   To cite a case in point, the *Five Graphic Music Analyses* show the levels with remarkable clarity and provide as detailed a picture of the tonal structure of the pieces as any analyses by Schenker (or, probably, anyone else). Yet it would be easy to construct additional levels that lie between some of those that Schenker shows. And in fact, *Free Composition* contains just such a "missing" level on the very first page of musical examples. Figure 7b is a middleground graph of the Chopin Etude, Op. 10, No. 8, one of the pieces analyzed in *Five Graphic Music Analyses*; it shows a level that is intermediate between the second and third middleground levels of the earlier publication. Adding this missing level to *Five Graphic Music Analyses* would in no way improve the reading found there, for as I indicated above, one can easily supply the intermediate levels that are missing for any of the prolongational entities of one of Schenker's analyses. And for some short pieces—perhaps even one as long as the Chopin Etude—one might be able to construct a "complete" set of levels for the entire piece.

But for longer pieces it might be difficult or even impossible to delineate the levels much more rigorously than Schenker himself does. In a given piece, a prolongation of $\hat{5}$ might go through nine stages and one of $\hat{2}$ (perhaps several pages further on) through eleven. How would one correlate the nine levels with the eleven? I think that any correlation must be at least partly arbitrary; yet one could not construct a "complete" set of levels for the whole piece without one. And even if one could do it in a plausible way, I wonder whether the result would be worth the effort. I doubt that this is an avenue for approaching the really important issues of a composition, and I doubt that one could assimilate the correlation to one's hearing of the piece.

I am not advocating careless or willful interpretations, and I do not underestimate the importance of presenting the levels clearly and logically. But using Schenker's approach, one *can* show the relation of complete prolongations to each other and to the whole piece; this, it seems to me, is of paramount importance. Might not the levels *within* some of these prolongational events develop independently of one another? There are good reasons why Schenker sometimes explains a complex passage by means of an ancillary series of graphs, separate from those for the whole piece.

The Coherence of the Levels

Much more important than determining the number of levels is perceiving and understanding how they hang together. Schenker lays special stress on what he calls the *Fühlungnahme* (rapport or contact) among the levels. By this he means that the prolongations are not mere embellishments which might take any form as long as they are syntactically correct, but that a unifying impulse informs the entire complex of levels. Whether the Fundamental Line begins on $\hat{3}$, $\hat{5}$, or $\hat{8}$ is related to how the later levels are to develop (p. 14, §14). And the diminutional patterns of the foreground are articulated in some sort of correspondence with significant events at deeper levels. Ultimately the connections among tonal structure, form, and design depend upon this coherence of the levels.

Schenker often writes about the levels as if they were animated by kinetic impulses that travel from one level to another; thus the foreground contains the "goals" to which the earlier levels lead (p. 68, §183). It is unfortunate that Schenker did not explain exactly what he meant by this metaphor. He was obviously not referring to the important goals of tonal motion, for they already occur at earlier levels. Of course the finely differentiated details of the foreground represent "goals" of a kind, for they can be thought of as the final result of the process of transformation and elaboration that leads from the background through the middleground to the foreground.

Schenker probably meant something of the kind, but he may also have had another, less obvious, idea in mind. Although each level, starting with the background, represents a synthesis of chord and line, of consonance and dissonance, of "nature" and "art," the syntheses are not without their conflicts and contradictions. The disjunct bass of the Fundamental Structure, for example, conflicts with the linear, contrapuntal tendency of "art" music and motivates the contrapuntally prolonged basses of the first middleground level. The unsupported dissonances in the Fundamental Lines from $\hat{5}$ and $\hat{8}$ contradict the composing-out process, which requires consonance; the contradiction often leads to a transformation of the dissonance into a consonance at a later level. A bass that counterpoints upper-voice dissonances may create parallel fifths or octaves and may thus constrain later levels to correct the voice leading. In short, an imbalance at one level might help to determine the course of the next and, in that sense, lead to a "goal"—the restoration of equilibrium. It is perhaps worth pointing out that Schenker begins his first chapter with a quotation from Hegel.

The Chronology of the Levels

Schenker rightly insists that the levels convey no specific information about the chronology of composition but that they show logical relationships between simple and complex tonal successions (p. 18, §29). He adds that the levels are not to be read only from background to foreground but also from foreground to background. Yet in discussing the levels he constantly uses language ("anterior levels," "later levels," "goals") that suggests a temporal succession. If this succession exists neither in the process of composition nor in the sequence of events in the piece itself, just where is it? Of course one can dismiss the question by deciding that Schenker's words are not to be taken literally, but one would lose something by doing this. The temporal sequence, it seems to me, occurs in the process of apprehending the relationships between simple and complex tone-successions. As Schenker writes (p. 6), "a relationship actually is to be 'traversed' in thought—but this must involve actual time." And although the "traversal" can start with either background or foreground, the direction from background to foreground is unquestionably the primary one—hence "first level," "later levels," etc. The necessity of "traversing" the levels in time, incidentally, is a reason why one cannot base Schenker's approach on "perception"—especially if one's idea of perception is a single hearing by a person of average musical gifts. (This is not to deny the indispensable perceptual component of Schenker's approach, which he rightly insists upon so vehemently.)

The Background

Collateral Reading

In his Preface, Ernst Oster wisely suggests that readers of *Free Composition* delay studying Part I ("The Background") until they have finished reading most of Part III ("The Foreground"). Oster's reason—that an understanding of the opening part requires knowing a good deal about Schenker's entire theoretical system—is completely valid. Reading Part III will not supply all of the necessary information, but it will at least introduce the reader to Schenker's way of approaching music. In addition, I would urge readers to consult the chapter dealing with "The Natural Tonal System" in *Harmony* (pp. 3–44 of the English edition) for both its similarities and its dissimilarities to Schenker's later formulations. In *Harmony*, for example, Schenker emphasizes the connection between motivic repetition and the formation of tonal systems. This connection surely foreshadows his later idea of "rapport" between foreground and background. Yet the idea of levels is not more than hinted at in *Harmony*, and motivic repetitions are conceived much more narrowly than in Schenker's later writings. Readers who know German will also find it helpful to consult a short essay from *Tonwille*, "Gesetze der Tonkunst," presumably an excerpt from a preliminary version of *Der freie Satz*.[3] In this essay Schenker gives a particularly clear account of what he means by "nature" and "art."

The Fundamental Structure

Part I of *Free Composition* amply repays the careful and repeated readings that are necessary if one is to understand it. It is perhaps the most remarkable segment of the book (I am thinking particularly of Chapters 2 and 3) and is certainly one of the outstanding examples of theoretical thought in the entire literature. What is astonishing about it is the wealth of implications that Schenker can derive from the simplest tonal relationships. Much of the basis of his approach is to be discovered here; in addition (and another way of saying much the same thing) fundamental properties of the tonal system are revealed. Schenker is able to show the generating power of the tonic triad with respect to melody (conceived in the broadest possible way), counterpoint, harmony, and form.

In §26, Schenker states that a Fundamental Structure, simple as it is, can form the content of a foreground; such a foreground would mainly consist of simple figurations (rather than genuine prolongations) of the background. This statement, whose import is not explained, accompanies the two analytic graphs of Figure 7, which, confusingly, do not seem to illustrate it at all, for they show fairly elaborate middleground prolongations rather than the figurations of which Schenker speaks. Oster discusses this contradiction in a masterly footnote that includes some brilliantly revealing comments about the two pieces that Schenker cites; he indicates that Schenker probably meant to show a connection between the Fundamental Structures of these pieces and the foreground content of their opening measures.

Oster's footnote contains wonderful analytic insights and constitutes a miniature introduction to Schenker's approach. Nevertheless, I think that he may not have been correct in his interpretation of what Schenker meant here; I believe that Schenker really intended to say that the foreground of an entire piece (and not just of its opening measures) might consist mainly in a figuration of the Fundamental Structure. It is true that the illustrations seem to contradict, rather than to confirm, the point he is making; but pieces exist that do illustrate it—for example, sets of variations with fairly simple themes (like the second movement of Beethoven's Op. 57, shown in Figure 40/8 of *Free Composition*).

The point seems to be an important one to Schenker. He repeats it in §252 (p. 97) without at all suggesting that he is referring only to the opening measures of a piece. I think that there is a good reason for his attaching importance to this idea. If a figurated Fundamental Structure can be a foreground, then the Fundamental Structure must provide those tonal elements that are necessary to produce a coherent piece of music. Examples of this possibility, therefore, would provide a particularly strong confirmation for the basis of Schenker's theory.

Underlying Assumptions

Schenker frequently emphasizes the simplicity of the Fundamental Structure; certainly, compared to even the least complicated foreground, the Fundamental Structure is indeed simple. But compared to the triad from which it originates, the Fundamental Structure is a rather complicated construct, for it depends on a number of prior assumptions about tonal organization in music. Among these are the following:

1. A significant connection exists between the triad as a simultaneity and as an arpeggio, complete or incomplete.
2. The triadic intervals (octave, fifth, and third) are consonant and can function as beginnings and goals of motion.
3. The interval of the fifth defines triadic roots and tonic notes.
4. The tonic note is the final goal of tonal progression.
5. Upper-voice tonal progression is basically conjunct, bass motion disjunct (in keeping with the traditionally sparse diminution of the bass part—see Zarlino and others).
6. Dissonances arise melodically and must resolve melodically—that is, by step.

I don't think that many musicians would disagree with these assumptions, whether or not they agree with the conclusions that Schenker draws from them.

$\hat{3}$, $\hat{5}$, and $\hat{8}$

The lower voice of the Fundamental Structure always appears in the same way, as an arpeggiation from I up to V and back down to I. The upper voice, however, can take one of three possible forms: it can begin on $\hat{3}$, $\hat{5}$, or $\hat{8}$. In all three cases it will descend to $\hat{1}$, and $\hat{2}$ will coincide with the bass's V. Of the three possibilities, the one beginning on $\hat{3}$ is the simplest and least problematic. Each note of the upper voice is supported as a consonance by the bass; as a consonance it can form the starting point for prolongation at any subsequent level.

Schenker described the line from $\hat{5}$ as a more problematic tonal structure and analytic construct. The tonal problem centers on $\hat{4}$, which passes as a dissonance (fourth) over I in the bass and which, therefore, cannot be composed out at the next level. The analytic problem results from the fact that three notes—$\hat{5}$, $\hat{4}$, and $\hat{3}$—occur above I, forming an "unsupported stretch." The analyst must keep in mind the possibility that the Fundamental Line might begin on $\hat{3}$ and that the line from $\hat{5}$ to $\hat{3}$ might be a prolongation belonging to a later level. Some recent theorists, going much further than Schenker, conclude that a Fundamental Line from $\hat{5}$ is an impossibility or at least a great rarity. Peter Westergaard, for example, calls attention to the fact that $\hat{4}$ produces a dissonance when it occurs above any note of the tonic triad and infers that it is "presumably for this reason that 5–4–3–2–1 lines are so rare in the underlying structures of tonal music."[4]

I read once about a Chinese emperor who was shown a giraffe, brought from Africa by explorers. "What is this beast?" he exclaimed, horrified. "It ought not to exist!" One can be pretty sure that giraffes did not become plentiful in the zoological gardens of China, at least during that emperor's reign. Similarly if one assumes that lines from $\hat{5}$ ought not to exist, one will probably seldom, if ever, encounter them. But without such an assumption one will find that they are anything but rare, though perhaps not as common as lines that descend from $\hat{3}$. For many pieces a reading from $\hat{5}$ makes more sense than any other interpretation, for it accounts best for the articulative elements of the middleground and foreground. The first movements of Mozart's A-minor Sonata and of the *Appassionata* are particularly well-known examples of such pieces.

The consonant support of each note of the Fundamental Line is not an overriding issue for Schenker, though it is one that he takes into account in his interpretations of the middleground. Schenker conceives of the Fundamental Structure as a kind of second-species counterpoint with dissonant passing tones, rather than as a first-species counterpoint restricted to consonances. Or to put it another way, Schenker's Fundamental Structure is not primarily a succession of vertical intervals, but rather two horizontal lines in counterpoint, with vertical consonances at the beginning and end. The conjunct upper voice fills in the "tone-space" created by horizontalizing an interval of the tonic triad. All of the notes between the first and the last are passing; some are dissonant and some consonant. The $\hat{2}$ is conceptually *dissonant* in relation to the horizontalized triad even though it receives the consonant support of the bass. At subsequent levels, the notes of the Fundamental Line will possibly evolve in different ways. Some may be richly elaborated, others less richly, still others not at all. Yet each is an essential element in the structure, because each makes possible the stepwise progression from the beginning to the goal, and thus makes possible the synthesis of chord and line.

I believe that Schenker was right in asserting the possibility of $\hat{5}$-lines while, at the same time, calling attention to their problematic features. The very problems have their positive implications, for problems at one level can provide direction and goals for subsequent ones. Thus the dissonant $\hat{4}$ might evoke a IV or II for support and in that way add harmonic content and sharpen tonal definition. Or the unsupported stretch $\hat{5}$–$\hat{4}$–$\hat{3}$ might lead to a tonicization of III in minor and integrate into the unfolded tonic of the background structure the potentially disruptive tendency of minor to gravitate to III. In some ways structural progressions with $\hat{5}$-lines lead more readily to the expansion of tonal content than do the less problematic ones with $\hat{3}$-lines.

Fundamental Lines that descend from $\hat{8}$ are another matter. Anyone going through Schenker's published analyses can see very quickly that octave lines occur less often in the later publications than in the earlier ones. In at least one case, Schenker went back to a piece that he had already analyzed and substituted a $\hat{3}$-line for the earlier $\hat{8}$-line, as we can see by comparing the graphs of Beethoven's Op. 10, No. 2, I, in Volume 2 of *Meisterwerk* and in *Free Composition*.[5] The tendency to read fewer octave lines undoubtedly goes together with an increasingly clear understanding of background relationships; the "Fundamental Lines" of the earlier writings often include elements that Schenker would have assigned to the middle ground at a later stage in his work. Among these elements might be the first three or five notes of some of the octave lines.

In *Free Composition* Schenker describes the lines from $\hat{8}$ as still more problematic than those from $\hat{5}$; there are now two unharmonized dissonances ($\hat{7}$ as well as $\hat{4}$) and a much longer unsupported stretch ($\hat{8}$–$\hat{3}$). In addition there are difficulties with octave lines that Schenker does not mention. In major, $\hat{7}$'s tendency to ascend to $\hat{8}$ produces a counterforce to the descending Fundamental Line that does not exist with lines from $\hat{3}$ or $\hat{5}$. And the unsupported stretch is so long that even the expanded basses of the first middleground level do little to modify its effect, as we can see from Schenker's Figure 18. Only the presence of more than one bass arpeggiation creates a somewhat more balanced outer-voice structure (Figures 19b and 20/4).

To the best of my knowledge only four out of the almost three hundred pieces and movements cited in *Free Composition* are read from $\hat{8}$; of course Schenker may also have read $\hat{8}$-lines in a few of the pieces from which only excerpts are cited. The four pieces are the Allemande and Courante from Bach's Sixth French Suite, Brahms's song "Wie bist du, meine Königin," and the Trio from the Menuetto movement of Mozart's Piano Sonata, K.331. Of the four, the Mozart seems to me to be the most convincing example of an octave line. What might at first appear to be a doubtful feature of Schenker's analysis—the very different readings of similar material in measures 1–6 and 37–42—actually tends to confirm it, for the sections are not identical, and their differences point to an emphasis on D the first time and on A the second. In evaluating this reading one should bear in mind the fact that *three* bass arpeggiations support the octave progression. And most significantly, the piece is a Trio rather than a self-contained movement; the D of the upper voice gets a special importance from its connection with the C♯ of the Menuetto's Fundamental Line.

The analysis of the Brahms song is worthy of careful consideration, for it is one of the few examples in *Free Composition* where Schenker comments on the relation between text and music; his remarks, although brief, are very sensitive and revealing. Schenker's depiction of the $\hat{8}$-line is partly convincing, but the part that (to me at least) is not convincing seems very doubtful indeed. Schenker reads an unsupported stretch of four notes—$\hat{5}$–$\hat{4}$–$\hat{3}$–$\hat{2}$—over V, and the stretch is as lacking of support in the foreground as it is in the background. And to make it worse, the $\hat{4}$, $\hat{3}$, and $\hat{2}$ all appear in one measure (19) as three eighth notes in the piano part. I believe that a better reading of the song might be possible, but it would involve both a different interpretation of the harmonic structure and the disappearance of Schenker's octave line.

The apparent simplicity of the Bach suite movements could not be more deceptive; the pieces are densely contrapuntal and very hard to grasp. I believe that Schenker had worked out detailed analyses of the entire Suite, possibly with a view toward eventual publication in a new series of *Urlinie-Tafeln*. Ernst Oster, who had these papers in his possession (together with much of the rest of Schenker's *Nachlass*), once mentioned to me that Schenker had encountered great difficulties with these pieces and that the analyses had gone through many different versions. I hope that the complete analyses will be published someday; it would be most instructive to test the octave lines, as shown in *Free Composition*, against Schenker's interpretation of the voice leading in all of its detail. The graphs printed in *Free Composition* are too sketchy to convince me either that the octave lines are valid or that they are not, though I am inclined to think that they are not.

Even though $\hat{8}$-lines do not figure prominently among the analyses in *Free Composition*, Schenker was obviously unwilling to give them up. Indeed, the amount of space devoted to them in the earlier chapters is altogether out of proportion to the space they occupy in the later part of the book, where most of the examples from the literature are cited. Schenker was undoubtedly convinced that octave lines fulfill the basic premises of his system and that they occur in the works of the masters. Of course if they don't occur, one would have to reformulate some of the premises, and Schenker's four examples do not seem to me to make out a very good case for octave lines. Still, I would like to keep an open mind about them. For one thing, they do exist at later levels as the top-voice structures of whole sections, including relatively independent sections like the Mozart Trio. It does not seem out of the question that they might occur in at least a few truly self-contained pieces. I know one piece (but only one so far) where I believe that the best reading is from $\hat{8}$. The piece is the A-minor Prelude from Book I of the *Well-Tempered Clavier*, and I was put on to it by Oster, who told me in passing that it was one piece where he was convinced that an octave line existed. I don't know his reading, but I have worked out one for myself and have found that the $\hat{8}$-line accounts best for both the large-scale voice leading and the motivic design. It is a difficult piece and one that I could not possibly discuss adequately here, but I might mention that the basic plan appears to be rather like Figure 18/2 of *Free Composition*.

The Middleground

The First Level

Part II of *Free Composition* deals with the prolongational techniques of the first level beyond the background; these techniques fall into four main categories:

1. Prolongations of the bass including space-filling motions between I and the V above it and the appearance of two bass arpeggios under a Fundamental Line.
2. Divisions of the Fundamental Structure. Schenker discusses two possibilities: interruption in the case of lines from $\hat{3}$ and $\hat{5}$, and the division of $\hat{8}$-lines into $\hat{8}$–$\hat{5}$, $\hat{5}$–$\hat{1}$.
3. Expansions and modifications of the Fundamental Line through modal mixture, the use of $\flat\hat{2}$, upper neighbor notes, substitution (e.g., of $\hat{7}$ for $\hat{2}$), linear progressions, and arpeggiations.
4. The panoply of voice-leading categories that Schenker devised to account for connections between voices and for manipulations of register, among these such well-known techniques as *Übergreifen, Untergreifen, Ausfaltung,* and *Koppelung* (translated here as "reaching-over," "motion from the inner voice," "unfolding," and "coupling").

It is important to remember that all of this material can also appear at later levels; none of it is restricted to the first. In one piece, for example, the use of interruption will divide the Fundamental Structure so as to create two large form segments; the interruption, consequently, will belong to the first prolongational level. In another piece, interruption will occur within a single parallel period that forms part of a larger section; the interruption will belong to a later level. Schenker does not offer any criteria for assigning the proper level to these prolongations. The omission is probably justified by the difficulty or even impossibility of discussing this issue in a general way—the relationships between levels will vary from piece to piece.

In other ways, however, Schenker's organization of this material is open to legitimate criticism. For one thing, some of the prolongations tend to relate much more directly to background structure than others. Contrapuntal prolongations of the bass, interruption, "structural" neighbor-notes, and large-scale initial ascents frequently help to articulate the form and define the tonality of whole pieces, whereas substitution, reaching-over, and many other prolongations usually shape parts rather than the whole. Therefore, Schenker seems really to be discussing "levels close to the background" rather than the "first level" specified by his chapter heading. Actually, the order in which the material appears corresponds roughly to its "distance" from the background and thus helps to offset the misleading impression produced by the heading and by some of Schenker's explanations.

A related problem is the material that Schenker excludes from the first level and discusses only in Part III. Had he restricted himself to such techniques as interruption or the filled-in ascending bass arpeggio, the exclusions would make perfect sense. But given what is included, there seems to be little justification for not including more. Thus the inversion of the bass arpeggio into a descending progression (e.g., I–VI–IV) certainly belongs in principle to a later level than the ascending arpeggio I–III–V. And a bass motion down from I to V (perhaps I–VI–V or I–IV⁶–V) is further from the background than a rising motion that might lead through II or IV. However, I–VI–IV or I–VI–V seems to me to be at least as close to the background as the I–VI–I that Schenker includes in the first level in connection with a neighbor-note to $\hat{5}$ (p. 42, §108).

The material of Part II, then, is not presented quite as systematically as it might at first appear to be. I rather doubt that it can ever be systematized in the way that the simpler materials and procedures of strict counterpoint can, but I think that Schenker's presentation could possibly be improved upon by someone with sufficient knowledge and willingness to work. Despite its shortcomings, Part II remains an indispensable resource for anyone who wants to understand music. Schenker's totally new and highly important conception of the relation of form to tonal structure is based, to a considerable extent, on procedures first discussed in Part II.

Contrapuntally Prolonged Basses

The first middleground technique that Schenker describes is that of filling-in the space between the initial I and the V of the bass arpeggiation. The way he shows this process (in Figure 14) is most interesting. The first stage is a complete arpeggiation through the third; passing tones then compose out the arpeggio creating a conjunct line from I to V. This procedure would seem to suggest that the motion from I to V is necessarily subdivided at the III or I⁶ produced by the arpeggiated bass, but this is not at all what Schenker intends. He states that II or IV (of the stepwise bass) might receive an emphasis from a tone of the Fundamental Line that coincides with one of them. In that case the III would recede in importance and assume a passing function—another instance of the mutual adjustment of chord, consonance, and "nature" on the one hand and line, dissonance, and "art" on the other.

And indeed, except in minor, the path to V leads far more characteristically through IV or II than through III or I⁶. Each in a different way, IV and II introduce the possibility of a subsidiary fifth relationship into the progression from tonic to dominant and thus add to the harmonic content of the piece. In addition, the stepwise motion from I to II and from IV to V adds an intensely linear quality to the bass part. It is important to note that Schenker uses his characteristics interlocking slurs (I-IV–V or I-II–V) only for progressions involving IV and II, not for those arpeggiating through III or I⁶. In this way he conveys the far more intense motion to V produced by II or IV.

Schenker believed that a bass part, in principle, could not receive the extensive diminutional elaboration characteristic of the uppermost part; basses tend to move in slower values and with more disjunct motion. Consequently a fully developed passing motion from I to V is not always possible; skips—perhaps from I to IV or II to V—are sometimes unavoidable. Still, even the partial filling-in of the fifth from I to V reveals the activity of the linear-melodic principle, whose tendency to move by step must sometimes adjust to and compromise with the kind of progression appropriate to a bass. It seems to me that Part II of *Free Composition* contains the best solution we have to a problem that has vexed theorists since Rameau: what is the basis of the progression from IV to V? The basis is contrapuntal; that is why it eluded Rameau and his followers. IV moves to V as the result of a space-filling motion that composes out the leap of a fifth from I to V.

One shortcoming of the section on contrapuntally prolonged basses is Schenker's restricting his illustrations to progressions in major. This restriction creates no difficulties in Part I, for differences of mode have no bearing on the Fundamental Structure except, perhaps, for octave lines, which seem slightly less problematic in minor. But at the first middleground level, the differences already take on considerable significance. In particular the use of III in minor requires comment. If III already appears under $\hat{5}$, the stretch $\hat{5}$–$\hat{4}$–$\hat{3}$ can unfold over the sustained III. At a later level the $\hat{5}$–$\hat{4}$–$\hat{3}$ can receive the support of a cadence tonicizing III, in which case the melodic line will assume the guise of $\hat{3}$–$\hat{2}$–$\hat{1}$ in the mediant "key." This possibility is unique to minor; the emphasis it gives to III is such that a IV or II[6] that follows will necessarily have the function of a passing chord rather than a goal. This creates significant implications for form, especially sonata form in minor. Later in the book Schenker shows such middleground progressions (Figures 154/2 and 154/3), but he does not do so at this point, nor does he refer to the later illustrations.

I should like to make one more observation about the contrapuntally prolonged basses. As Figure 16 shows, the introduction of II or IV provides consonant support for $\hat{4}$ in a $\hat{5}$-line, thus reducing the unsupported stretch. At the same time, however, this procedure transforms $\hat{3}$ into either an unsupported dissonant passing tone (over IV or II) or the sixth of a $\frac{6}{4}$ formation above V. In either case $\hat{3}$ becomes a more active tone than in the Fundamental Structure. Sometimes, but by no means always, a later level will provide consonant support for the passing $\hat{3}$, usually in the form of an apparent "I" interpolated between IV (or II) and V. Even then, the conceptually dissonant character of the $\hat{3}$ is evident to any listener who takes in the larger context. To provide at once consonant support for $\hat{4}$ and stability for $\hat{3}$ requires the use of two bass arpeggiations, as shown in Figure 19.

Interruption

Schenker's discussion of this most important technique is reasonably clear, and it is made still clearer by some excellent footnotes provided by Jonas, Oster, and Rothgeb. Schenker obviously regarded the discovery of interruption as one of his greatest achievements, it is perhaps the most important component of his conception of form. I don't intend to write about interruption here, but I do wish to comment on one of its frequent by-products: the upward transfer of the seventh of V^{8-7}. Such a transfer can occur in connection with an interrupted $\hat{3}$-line; it tends to bridge over the structural division by leading into the second branch of the interrupted progression. (Schenker regards the transferred seventh as subordinate to the $\hat{2}$, yet he includes it in his discussion of the first level—a striking instance of his mixing together at one level elements of obviously different rank.)

One aspect of Schenker's discussion has far-reaching implications. In Figure 23b he shows both the octave and the seventh of V^{8-7} transferred up; his notation reveals that he regards the seventh, rather than the octave, as the main tone. This interruption reflects the fact that the seventh, which creates the effect of a neighbor-note, forms a much closer connection with the Fundamental Line than does the octave. For this reason the *dissonance* is the background element (in a relative sense) and the consonance is the embellishment. This is often true of V^{8-7} in other situations as well; although the seventh is essentially a passing tone, it is not always subordinate to the *particular* octave that precedes it, for that octave may have merely an immediate preparatory function rather than any long-range one. Measure 95 of the last movement of Beethoven's Sixth Symphony gives a particularly clear illustration of this possibility, as do the many cases where composers of the eighteenth century write V^{8-7} with the octave as an appoggiatura and the seventh in large notation. At other times, however, the octave may be the main note, as in the opening measures of Chopin's Impromptu, Op. 36, where motivic considerations would hardly permit any other interpretation.

What this means is that one can never hope to arrive at a correct view of the background by simply making a "reduction" of the foreground, for example, by eliminating dissonances, chromatics, or non-tonic notes. Without some sense of the background, one can't begin to understand the foreground; it might be precisely those dissonant or chromatic elements a reduction would eliminate that form the "background" of a passage. But if one needs to understand the background to make sense of the foreground, one also needs to understand the foreground to make sense of the background—a seemingly hopeless impasse. Actually, it's a heuristic problem that confronts people all the time and in areas far removed from musical analysis: one can grasp neither the part without the whole nor the whole without the part. But one copes, somehow. One looks up words in the dictionary to find out how to spell them, but if one can't spell them at all, one can't look them up; a dictionary won't be of much help to someone who thinks "cat" might be spelled "hqz" or "bbbbb." In analyzing music one begins in somewhat the same way as in looking up words—with hypotheses about the shape of the whole or about some of the parts. Only there is no dictionary to tell the analyst whether his guesses are right or wrong.

Expansions and Transformations of the Fundamental Line

I'm not going to write about Schenker's discussion of mixture or $\flat\hat{2}$, but his treatment of neighbor-notes at the first level requires some comment. At this level he limits the possibilities to upper neighbors of the $\hat{3}$ or $\hat{5}$ as initial tones of the Fundamental Lines. Furthermore, the neighbor must return to a consonance, as in strict counterpoint. Although he does not mention it here, Schenker evidently excludes the sixth of a cadential $^6_4$ on the grounds that it is not a true consonance but represents instead a rhythmically displaced dissonant passing tone (Figure 76/1 and Schenker's comment on p. 71, §196). This exclusion marks a change from as late a publication as *Five Graphic Music Analyses*, where one of the pieces—the Bach chorale—is analyzed with just such a "resolution" into a $^6_4$ at the first prolongational level.

Curiously enough, the chorale does not even contain the $^6_4$ that Schenker shows; the neighbor-note is followed by a passing seventh over IV. Schenker seems to suggest that this seventh stands for a $^6_4$ over V—more or less the opposite of the much more convincing explanation in *Free Composition*, p. 71. It would seem from this uncharacteristically strained analysis that Schenker had problems in formulating this part of his theory. Even in *Free Composition*, the treatment of the neighbor-note is not completely satisfactory, at least not to me. Schenker excludes from the first level incomplete neighbors, that is, neighbors that do not really resolve but that might return to a passing dissonance (Figure 76, first progression). But in so doing he must also exclude some of the important IV or II chords that would normally appear at this level. In a piece with a $\hat{3}$-line, IV $^5_3$ must and II can support an upper neighbor; the progression to V excludes a resolution of the neighbor. Of course one might argue, with some justification, that a IV under an incomplete neighbor belongs to a later level than one under a note of the Fundamental Line. Yet Schenker includes in his first level elements (like the I–VI–I progression cited earlier) that would seem still further away from the background.

Linear Progressions and Upper-Voice Arpeggiations

In these sections Schenker discusses descending linear progressions that compose out a tone of the Fundamental Line, ascending linear progressions that culminate in the first tone of the Fundamental Line (initial ascents), and finally rising arpeggiations that lead, like initial ascents, to the first tone of the Fundamental Line. Schenker's careful distinction between rising and falling lines is worthy of attention, for it characterizes his entire approach to voice leading from the Fundamental Structure (with its rising bass and falling top line) through middleground prolongations like those he is discussing here to the tiniest diminutions of the foreground. That melodic figures are not uniformly invertible—that some tend to rise and others to fall—is an important part of contrapuntal tradition, stretching back through the *Manieren* of the Baroque and the norms of Palestrinian counterpoint to the *trecento* and perhaps even further.[6] Schenker shows that this distinction is, in a way, still preserved in the masterpieces of the late eighteenth and nineteenth centuries; in so doing he demonstrates this repertory's continuity with earlier compositional (and his own continuity with earlier theoretical) tradition.

Schenker describes four kinds of descending linear progression: fifths from $\hat{5}$ and $\hat{2}$ and thirds from $\hat{3}$ and $\hat{2}$. The first three possibilities mimic Fundamental Lines from $\hat{5}$ and $\hat{3}$ ($\hat{2}$ simulating $\hat{5}$ in the dominant "key") and transfer into the middleground these elements of the background. (The basses to these linear progressions may also simulate the background arpeggiation; this permits the transference to the middleground of the forms of the Fundamental Structure from $\hat{3}$ and $\hat{5}$.) Because they replicate, on a smaller scale, the structures of whole pieces, these linear progressions frequently produce large-scale (and relatively self-contained) form segments in the foreground. The third-progression from $\hat{2}$, on the other hand, does not constitute a simulated Fundamental Line, and it is less often form-making than the other progressions. Its special feature is that it provides an opportunity to introduce the leading tone into the upper voice in a prominent way—as the goal tone of a linear progression.

Schenker does not discuss the possibility of composing-out $\hat{5}$ by means of a third-progression. This seems a less likely possibility than the four he describes, since this third-progression neither replicates the Fundamental Line nor adds a significant new element to the upper voice. Still, the particular necessities of a piece might give rise to such a third-progression, as in a familiar but very complex example—the E-minor Prelude of Chopin.

The initial ascent (rising linear progression) and the upper-voice arpeggiation are related prolongations, since both produce a composing-out of the Fundamental Structure's first vertical interval. Most significantly, Schenker refers to the unprolonged statement of this interval as a chordal "anticipation" or "abbreviation"—an abbreviation because the simultaneity ("nature") is not transformed into line ("art"). (See p. 13, §12, and p. 46, §122.) This formulation shows how much Schenker regarded music as fundamentally linear; the widespread idea that for Schenker music is basically harmonic is, at best, an oversimplification. In a way, Schenker eats his cake and has it, for he also calls the initial ascent a "retardation" or "delay" (p. 46, §124). The contradiction is easily resolved. From the perspective of "nature" the initial ascent effects a delay in the entrance of $\hat{3}$ or $\hat{5}$; from the perspective of "art" the unprolonged opening interval compresses into a simultaneity what "ought" to he a melodic entity.

More than any of the other means of *Auskomponierung*, the initial ascent and the rising upper-voice arpeggiation create a counterforce to the descending Fundamental Line. It is probably for this reason that they often occur over very wide spans—over stretches of time equal to or even greater than those filled by the Fundamental Line. Schenker presents some magnificent examples of large-scale arpeggiation, but except for the Haydn "Emperor Hymn," his illustrations of the initial ascent do not reveal the possible scope of this technique. Readers who want supplementary material might look at Schubert's "Wanderers Nachtlied," D.768, and (more difficult) the G-major Prelude from Book I of the *Well-Tempered Clavier*.

Voice-Leading Prolongations

The prolongational techniques that Schenker describes in Sections 8 through 15 of Part II, Chapter 2, are fairly well-known and require little comment here. Since these techniques often characterize events near the musical surface, Schenker began to describe them at an early stage of his investigations of the Urlinie. He certainly refined his formulations in later writings—especially in *Free Composition*—but the basic ideas remained pretty much the same. That he had already discovered many of these techniques, most of them completely new to music theory, during the *Tonwille* period shows the incredible scope of his musical vision and intellectual powers. Later Schenkerians have organized the material slightly differently and have attempted to clarify some of Schenker's ideas, but without adding any really new concepts. One such attempt at clarification occurs in this publication. Oster has provided an extremely helpful note about Übergreifen (reaching-over)—perhaps the most elusive and hard to understand of these techniques.

Schenker takes great pains to show how the various prolongations differ from each other—what it is, for example, that distinguishes an unfolding from an arpeggiation or a coupling. There are good reasons for making these distinctions: a student of the approach needs to learn how to recognize the prolongations and to tell them apart. Still, Schenker draws the distinctions so sharply that an inexperienced reader may not be able to see that some of the techniques overlap others. "Reaching-over," for example, is an outgrowth of the polyphonic technique of voice crossing though, to be sure, it does not require a texture of obbligato voices. "Upward register transfer" consists in placing a note into a higher octave. The two techniques are by no means the same—reaching-over does not depend on octave equivalency, and upward transfer can exist within a single voice part. Still, there is an area of overlapping in that the upward transfer of an inner-voice tone might place it above the previously highest voice, thus "reaching-over" the top voice. Schenker's Figure 23b shows a register transfer, but it could serve as a model for his reading of Chopin's Etude, Op. 10, No. 8, measure 14, which he labels "Übergreifen" (reaching-over) in *Five Graphic Music Analyses*.

The Foreground

The Later Levels

Part III divides into five chapters that deal with: (1) the elements of strict counterpoint in "free" composition; (2) the structural levels beyond the first one; (3) specific foreground events, that is, those that do not occur at the background or the first level; (4) meter and rhythm; and (5) form. This part is by far the longest of the three, a fact Allen Forte takes note of in his Introduction, where he cites the amount of space devoted to the foreground as evidence against the widespread view that Schenker was concerned only with large structure. Forte's point is valid even if one takes into account Schenker's including in Part III *all* of the prolongational levels beyond the first. What is more, the sections that deal with surface events, with diminution, reveal an artistic vision that no other writer on music has ever shown. Of course Schenker's explanations of the sequence of events on the surface owe much of their lucidity to his clairvoyant perception of events below the surface; the foreground becomes clear only where there is also an understanding of the deeper levels.

Schenker's belief that the process of prolongation is partly one of differentiation is reflected in the varied materials dealt with in the five chapters. Chapters 4 and 5, in particular, read less like a continuation of the first three chapters than like essays on rhythm and form viewed in the light of the voice-leading principles presented in Parts I and II.

The Concepts of Strict Counterpoint

Schenker believed that the materials and procedures of strict counterpoint are always implicit in compositional foregrounds, even in those that seem most at variance with the "rules" of counterpoint. Moreover, these same materials sometimes appear quite literally on the musical surface. Part III, Chapter 1, attempts to show the relation of strict to free counterpoint; its organization more or less parallels that of Volume 1 of *Kontrapunkt*. The chapter is anything but a comprehensive treatment of this vast subject which would require an entire book. Fortunately, excellent supplementary material is available both in Schenker's own writings and in those of his followers.[7]

The one aspect of this subject that I should like to discuss briefly is the composing-out of the dissonant passing tone, in particular, the passing seventh. Schenker maintained that a dissonant passing tone (for example, 4 as a seventh over V) could not be composed out unless it is first transformed into a consonance. This position has occasioned a good deal of misunderstanding, probably because Schenker's explanations are inadequate and confusing. He was certainly not trying to say that seventh chords cannot persist for a long time or that prolonging techniques—arpeggiations, linear progressions, unfoldings, voice-exchanges, and others—cannot occur within, say, a V^7. Indeed, his analyses frequently show just such extensions and manipulations of seventh chords, Figure 100/2b of *Free Composition* being a particularly striking example.

So much for what Schenker was *not* trying to say; what he *was* trying to say is less easy to determine. Part of the problem is that he begins (§177) by stating that a seventh cannot be composed out unless it is transformed into a consonance; almost immediately afterwards he cites two examples (Figures 62/3 and 62/4) in which an untransformed seventh is, in fact, composed out; his comments nowhere touch on this blatant contradiction. Fortunately, Oster has provided a highly important footnote (p. 64) with what is surely the correct explanation of Schenker's view. Briefly, the interval of the seventh cannot be horizontalized with its upper note conceptually retained (as the initial note of a descending linear progression, for example), since the notion of the retained tone presupposes a vertical relationship contrary to the passing function of the seventh. Oster goes on to point out the circumstances in which a seventh can appear linearly without contradicting its passing function. The one point that I would add to his explanation is that Schenker was not discussing simple foreground figurations of seventh chords; he distinguished between such figurations and genuine prolongations that open up new structural levels.

Oster's footnote also sheds light on the two anomalous examples. Both are development sections by Beethoven, and both really prolong the seventh as a retained tone, thus treating it as an essentially vertical interval rather than as the by-product of melodic motion. Oster cites an unpublished note of Schenker's that shows him to have been fully aware of the contradiction between at least one of these examples and his theory. For Schenker, it would seem, Beethoven went beyond the borders of tonality in these two developments; the prolonged dissonance treatment would reveal a non-tonal tendency in these two pieces which, in all other respects, are completely tonal. Schenker did not approve of the prolonged dissonance; he called it a "harmonic sin." Still, Schenker's analyses show the prolonged sevenths very clearly—evidence against the view that he contorted his readings to provide confirmation for his theories. Of course one wishes that he had addressed himself in print to the contradiction revealed here, but in view of how much he managed to say, it is no wonder that he left some important things unsaid. I am not sure that the last chapter has been written about the prolonged seventh—especially, perhaps, about prolongations of V^7—but Schenker's position seems on the whole to be tenable. From my own work I would judge that seventh-progressions like the two by Beethoven are highly exceptional.

The Later Structural Levels

Part III, Chapter 2, goes over the same ground as the second chapter of Part II, but from the perspective of levels beyond the first. The most important, and by far the most difficult, section is the one on linear progressions (Section 6). Its importance lies partly in the precision with which it explains contrapuntal organization in free composition—specifically the counterpoint produced by two or more simultaneous linear progressions. Schenker maintained that one of these progressions is necessarily the "leading progression" and that the other (or others) is subordinate to it. The leading progression would be the one more directly connected with deeper levels; harmonic factors—agreement or disagreement with the governing chord—are often decisive in determining such a connection. Thus in the opening nineteen measures of the C-major Prelude of Book I of the *Well-Tempered Clavier*, both the upper voice and the bass contain octave-progressions. Here the bass progression leads because the subdivision at g in measure 11 agrees with the tonic harmony, whereas the soprano's b^1 does not (p. 80, comments on Figure 95e, Ex. 3).

That there is *always* a leading progression might be open to question. In a counterpoint between scale degrees $\hat{3}$–$\hat{2}$–$\hat{1}$ and scale degrees $\hat{5}$–$\hat{4}$–$\hat{3}$, where both lines compose out tonic harmony, each might be a plausible candidate for leading progression, though context will sometimes suggest one or the other. Even if it is not universally applicable, the concept of leading progression is highly productive, for it enables one to get a clear idea of connections among the levels and of relationships between chord and line. Schenker used the idea to account for some troublesome instances of apparent harmonic ambiguity and of dissonance treatment. These problems often arise when a series of parallel thirds, sixths, or tenths (contrapuntally favorable progressions) produces an emphasized note that contradicts the prevailing harmony and, often, causes a dissonance not easily explained by the categories of strict counterpoint.

Example 7.1 shows the beginning of a little piece by Schumann. The soprano of measure 1 contains a brief unfolding, e^2–c^2–e^2, whose thirds are further composed out by miniature linear progressions at almost the latest foreground level. The bass follows the upper-voice line at the tenth below, thus: c^1–a–c^1. The a, unlike the soprano's corner notes, disagrees with the prolonged tonic and, in addition, forms a seventh against the sustained g^1 of the middle voice. How does one account for this dissonance? The fact that the g^1 is a pedal point does not really explain the dissonance as it might were there a change of harmony at the third quarter of measure 1 (e.g., a IV in the progression I–IV–V–I over a pedal point). One cannot call the dissonant a an accented neighbor decorating b (which, in turn, decorates c^1), for such an interpretation would fly in the face of the soprano's tonic prolongation, of the metric structure, and of the motivic thirds—three factors that are interrelated here.

Schenker never published an analysis of this piece, but his solution would probably be to maintain that the soprano line leads here in that it alone elaborates tonic harmony and thus connects with deeper levels. To be sure, c^1, the main note of the bass, represents the I of the Fundamental Structure, but the rest of the bass line results solely from counterpointing the upper voice at the tenth below. This lower line, then, would belong to a later level than the soprano and would relate only to the soprano rather than to the prolonged tonic. For

EXAMPLE 7.1: Schumann, *Album for the Young*, Op. 63, No. 3, "Trällerliedchen"

Schenker, incidentally, a line that accompanies another at the third, sixth, or tenth is not a "doubling."[8] It is an obbligato part, but one whose special feature is that is does not participate directly in the composing-out of the governing chord, but forms instead a contrapuntal relation with another line that does so participate.

The dissonance, then, results from a conflict between two processes that go on simultaneously: the composing-out of tonic harmony and the contrapuntal motion in tenths. There is no doubt that the tonic prolongation is the stronger of the two; that is why the seventh creates no real ambiguity. The situation would be quite different in strict counterpoint, where each vertical sonority stands for itself alone and each dissonance must relate directly to an immediately neighboring consonance (neighboring in pitch and in temporal succession). In a species exercise (say two third species against a cantus firmus in the middle) the dissonance would be inexplicable; the lower-voice a would contradict the g^1 of the cantus firmus. But in composition, unlike strict counterpoint, vertical sonorities can form part of larger, more comprehensive structures; the composing-out of chords and harmonic relationships between chords provide just the larger organizing principles that are lacking in a species exercise. Both in *Harmony* and in the two volumes of *Kontrapunkt*, Schenker draws analogies between the *Stufen* (literally "scale steps," harmonic degrees conceived abstractly) of composition and the notes of the cantus firmus in strict counterpoint. The analogies are highly meaningful, but Schenker makes it clear that the functions are by no means identical. One difference is that the definiteness with which the *Stufen* can be expressed, together with their tendency to control a succession of sounds, permits a less restricted use of dissonance in free composition, where, indeed, the dissonant clashes can have a positive value (*Harmony*, English edition, pp. 159–60).

In the hands of a bad composer, lines in parallel thirds, sixths, and tenths can produce intolerable tonal ambiguities and cacophonous dissonances. This is especially true if, as sometimes happens, two linear progressions occur at once, each counterpointed in parallel motion. Mozart made use of this possibility in a wonderfully dreadful passage in the *Musical Joke* (IV, measures 108–43). Good composers (when not writing jokes) forestall such dangers by effecting compromises between the opposing tendencies of the contrapuntal setting and the prolonged harmony. Most often, it is the contrapuntal setting that must yield by moving to another interval at particularly sensitive points. A "non-harmonic" interval at an important point of closure, for example, would be a virtual impossibility. If a line G–F–E–D–C, for instance, were counterpointed at the tenth below, the A that would occur under the last note would threaten any sense of closure; a composer, therefore, would probably substitute a C, unless there were compelling reasons to avoid closure. Schenker draws attention to these compromises in Figures 95 and 97 and in his comments on pp. 79–81.

Conclusion

In the course of a single essay, it would be impossible to discuss more than a small part of the incredible wealth of ideas contained in *Free Composition*. In making my selection I decided not to go into the last three chapters. Part III, Chapter 3, is, on the whole, the most easily accessible of all, and while Chapters 4 and 5 have their difficulties, each deals with so specialized a topic that it would almost require the format of a separate essay to discuss each of them. The serious student of Schenker needs to know more of his work than *Free Composition*, though it is certainly the single most important work that he wrote. How fortunate it is that Longman, Inc., who produced *Free Composition* so beautifully, is planning an entire series of Schenker in English. The realization of this plan would bring enormous benefits to the musical community of the United States (and, possibly, to those of other English-speaking countries). This publication of *Free Composition*, then, is not only a highly important event in its own right but also a momentous first step.

Notes

1. On p. 26, §49, Schenker states that his most detailed graphs (*Urlinie-Tafeln*) represent the "penultimate prolongational level, after which follows the foreground." But in *Five Graphic Music Analyses* (new introduction by Felix Salzer [New York: Dover, 1969], pp. 56–61), the final, most detailed graph of the Chopin C-minor Etude is labeled "Vordergrund" (foreground).

2. See p. 96, first paragraph of §252.

3. Heinrich Schenker, *Der Tonwille*, no. 2 (1922), p. 3.

4. Peter Westergaard, *An Introduction to Tonal Theory* (New York: Norton, 1975), p. 426, footnote.

5. Heinrich Schenker, *Das Meisterwerk in der Musik*, vol. 2 (Munich: Drei Masken Verlag, 1926), appendix IV to p. 49, translated as *The Masterwork in Music*, ed. William Drabkin, vol. 2 (Cambridge: Cambridge University Press, 1996), pp. 26–27, and *Free Composition*, trans. and ed. Ernst Oster (New York: Longman, 1979), figure 101/4.

6. This tendency is very clearly evident in the music of Landini. See my article "Landini's Treatment of Consonance and Dissonance," *Music Forum* 2 (1970), pp. 130–86, especially pp. 170–76.

7. In Schenker's writings, see especially the section "Die dissonanz ist immer ein Durchgang, niemals ein Zusammenklang," in *Meisterwerk*, vol. 2, pp. 24–40, translated as "The Dissonant Interval Is Always a Passing Event, Never a Composite Sound," in "Further Considerations of the Urlinie: II," trans. John Rothgeb, in *The Masterwork in Music*, vol. 2, pp. 9–19. Also see Felix Salzer and Carl Schachter, *Counterpoint in Composition: The Study of Voice Leading* (New York: McGraw-Hill, 1969), chapters 6, 7, and 9; John Rothgeb, "Strict Counterpoint and Tonal Theory," *Journal of Music Theory* 19, no. 2 (1975), pp. 26–84; and Oswald Jonas, *Introduction to the Theory of Heinrich Schenker: The Nature of the Musical Work of Art*, trans. and ed. John Rothgeb (New York: Longman, 1982), pp. 52–61.

8. As is suggested by Joel Lester in "Articulation of Tonal Structures as a Criterion for Analytic Choices," *Music Theory Spectrum* 1 (1979), p. 76.

PART III

WORDS AND MUSIC

EIGHT

Motive and Text in
Four Schubert Songs

Music set to words can reflect them in many different ways. Perhaps the most fascinating and greatest settings are those where the tonal and rhythmic structure, the form, and the motivic design embody equivalents for salient features of the text: grammar and syntax, rhyme schemes and other patterns of sound, imagery, and so forth. Structural connections between words and music occur frequently in the art-song repertory—above all, in the songs of Schubert. Yet they seem to have attracted less attention, at least in the published literature, than prosody, tone painting, and affect.[1] In this essay I shall concentrate on one type of connection—that between the imagery of the poem and the motivic design of the music. The examples come from four Schubert songs: (1) "Der Jüngling an der Quelle" (D.300); (2) "Dass sie hier gewesen," Op. 59, No. 2 (D.775); (3) "Der Tod und das Mädchen," Op. 7, No. 3 (D.531); and (4) "Nacht und Träume," Op. 43, No. 2 (D.827).

"Der Jüngling an der Quelle"

Our simplest example comes from the coda of this early song.[2] The poem is by the Swiss writer Johann von Salis-Seewis; since I am going to discuss only one detail, I shall not quote the whole text, but only the last two lines. The words are those of a boy, unhappy in love, who tries to forget his coy friend in the beauties of nature. But they bring renewed desire rather than consolation; the poplar leaves and the brook seem to sigh her name, Luise. The final lines, as Schubert set them,[3] go as follows:

ach, und Blätter und Bach	ah, and leaves and brook
seufzen: Luise! dir nach	sigh, "Luise!" for you.

Originally published in *Aspects of Schenkerian Theory*, ed. David Beach (New Haven: Yale University Press, 1983), pp. 61–76.

The song is pervaded by a typically murmuring accompaniment pattern, which imitates the sound of the leaves and brook. Example 8.1, which quotes the beginning of the introduction, illustrates. Note that the right-hand part centers on the broken third $c\sharp^2$–e^2.

The introductory material returns in measures 23–26 to become the main part of the coda. Rather unusually, this coda is not a simple postlude for the piano; the singer joins in, repeating the name Luise (Example 8.2). His exclamations are set to the very pitches—$c\sharp^2$ and e^2—that have pervaded the accompaniment. There is even a return to the $c\sharp^2$, which recalls the oscillating piano figuration (see the brackets in Example 8.2). Like the boy in the poem, the listener hears an indistinct pattern transformed into a clear one; the sounds of nature become the girl's name, and the murmuring accompaniment becomes a melodic figure of definite shape. Schubert creates his musical image out of a structural connection between accompaniment and melody: Both center on the prominent pitches $c\sharp^2$ and e^2. This connection is underlined during the last three measures, in which the piano continues alone with only $c\sharp^2$–e^2 in the right-hand part; the murmuring dies away into a final block chord, which, rather unusually, has the fifth, e^2, on top.

Artless as it is, the musical image that Schubert creates in "Der Jüngling an der Quelle" has points of similarity with some of his subtler and more complex settings of words. As a consequence, the passage is a good introductory example of his practice. The following features deserve mention:

1. The transformation of the accompaniment into a melodic idea has nothing to do with "tone painting," although the accompaniment itself, of course, is intended to summon up the sound of leaves and water. Nor does it convey a "mood," although few listeners, I suspect, would complain that Schubert had failed to match the emotional tone of the words.

2. By associating accompaniment and vocal line Schubert creates a musical analogy to the sequence of ideas in the poem; the accompaniment is to the melodic figure derived from it as the indistinct sounds of nature are to the specific name that they evoke. Without the words, any extramusical association would disappear, but the connection between accompaniment and melody would remain perfectly comprehensible as a musical relationship. This is typical of Schubert's method, which sustains a remarkable equilibrium between sensitivity to the text and compositional integrity.

EXAMPLE 8.1: Schubert, "Der Jüngling an der Quelle," measures 1–3

EXAMPLE 8.2: Schubert, "Der Jüngling an der Quelle," measures 23–29

Yet it would probably be going too far to maintain that "Der Jüngling an der Quelle," played as an instrumental piece, would sound completely natural. This is because the pervasive $c^{\#2}$–e^2 is too neutral a figure and is treated with too little emphasis to justify its very conspicuous transformation into a melodic idea at the end of the piece. It is the words, which begin by invoking the murmuring spring and whispering poplars, that draw the listener's attention to the accompaniment and thus supply the necessary emphasis.

3. In creating his musical image Schubert reaches a far higher level of artistry than Salis-Seewis, for the poem, charming as it is, merely asserts that the leaves and brook sigh the girl's name. Of course the name itself—"Luise"—sounds more like whispering leaves and water than, say, "Katinka" would. But this is the easiest kind of onomatopoetic effect, with little inner connection to the poem as a whole. In Schubert's song, on the other hand, the musical image *is*, in symbolic form, what the words talk about; it grows out of the earlier part of the song with wonderful naturalness.

"Dass sie hier gewesen"

This song is set to a beautiful poem by Rückert. Schubert probably wrote it in 1823, it was published in 1826.[4] I am going to discuss the first stanza, composed to the following text:

Dass der Ostwind Düfte	That the east wind
Hauchet in die Lüfte,	Breathes fragrance into the air,
Dadurch tut er kund	In that way he makes it known
Dass du hier gewesen.	That you have been here.

The musical style of "Dass sie hier gewesen" could hardly be more different from that of "Der Jüngling an der Quelle." The tonal ambiguity of the opening measures is such that a listener hearing them without knowing where they come from could easily date them from the 1890s rather than the 1820s.[5] No tonic triad appears until measure 14; indeed, the listener receives not even a clue that the piece is in C major for six measures at a very slow tempo (Example 8.3). The very first sound is doubtful. It turns out to be a diminished seventh chord with an appoggiatura, f^3, in the top voice, but for a measure or so the listener might hear the chord as G–B♭–D♭–F rather than the G–B♭–C♯–E sonority that in fact it is. After we have our bearings about the diminished seventh, we remain in the dark as to the function of the D-minor chord to which it resolves; a listener might easily take it for a tonic. The attraction of C as center begins to be felt only in measures 7–8 and is not evident beyond a doubt until the authentic cadence of measures 13–14. Comparing Schubert's music with the words, we can see how marvelously it embodies the semantic and syntactic structure of this involuted sentence, whose import becomes clear only with the key predicate clause—"that you have been here"—the clause to which Schubert sets the clinching authentic cadence of measures 13–14.[6]

Although the motivic design of this passage is not as strikingly original as the tonal organization, it, too, connects with the words in a most wonderful way. The piano's opening statement contains a four-note figure in an extremely high register: f^3–e^3–d^3–$c\sharp^3$. The four notes belong together, for they project into the melodic line the prevailing diminished seventh chord, of which the e^3 and $c\sharp^3$ are members . But the very slow pace and the strong subdivision into twos make it easier to hear two groups of two notes each than a coherent

EXAMPLE 8.3: Schubert, "Das sie hier gewesen," measures 1–16

EXAMPLE 8.4: Schubert, "Das sie hier gewesen," motivic design

four-note figure. As Example 8.4 shows, the vocal line uses the four-note figure as a motive, quoting it directly (measures 3–4) and elaborating on it (measures 5–8 and 9–12). When the tonally definitive cadence of measures 13–14 arrives, the character of the melodic line begins to change: the pace quickens; there are no chromatics and no dissonant leaps. Yet for all the contrast, there is a connecting thread: the melodic line over the V⁷ of measure 12 is our four-note figure—at a new pitch level, in a different harmonic context, in quicker time values, but nonetheless the same figure. Even the distribution of non-chord and chord tones remains the same. In its new form the motive no longer divides into two times two notes; the coherence of the four-note group has become manifest.

Let us now compare the central image of the poem and the motivic aspects of its setting. A perfume in the air signifies that the beloved has been here. The perfume—a melodic idea barely perceptible as such, floating in an improbably high register within a tonal context of the utmost ambiguity. The person—the same melodic idea but now with distinct outlines, a definite rhythmic shape, the greatest possible clarity of tonal direction. Certainly many compositional elements contribute to this astonishing example of text-setting: rhythm, texture, register, and tonal organization, as well as motivic design. But only the motivic aspect conveys the *connection* between perfume and person, conveys the notion that, in a sense, the two—sign and signified—are one.

"Der Tod und das Mädchen"

The song was written in February 1817 and was published in 1821. The text, a poem by Matthias Claudius, is as follows:

Das Mädchen
Vorüber, ach vorüber
Geh, wilder Knochenmann!
Ich bin noch jung! Geh, Lieber,
Und rühre mich nicht an!

Der Tod
Gib deine Hand, du schön und zart Gebild!

Bin Freund und komme nicht zu strafen.
Sei gutes Muts! Ich bin nicht wild!
Sollst sanft in meinen Armen schlafen!

The Maiden
Go past, ah, go past,
Wild skeleton!
I am still young! Go, dear,
And do not touch me!

Death
Give me your hand, you beautiful and
  tender creature!
I am a friend and do not come to punish.
Be of good courage! I am not wild!
You shall sleep softly in my arms!

The poem is a dialogue, and Schubert, altogether appropriately, composes the song as a dramatic scene.[7] The piano introduction clearly represents a vision of Death; the Maiden's outcry is an agitated recitative; Death's reply is set to a recomposition of the introductory material. In a piece as short as "Der Tod und das Mädchen" marked contrasts between sections can prove disruptive. That Schubert creates a continuous musical discourse despite the changes in tempo, rhythm, and texture is partly due to the presence throughout most of the song of a basic motive, which serves as a link between the contrasting sections. The first statement of the motive occurs at the very beginning of the introduction in the next-to-highest part. The motive is a double-neighbor figure decorating a: a–bb–g–a (Example 8.5). Note that this figure is the main melodic event at the beginning of the song, for the uppermost part, prefiguring the monotone character of Death's speech, simply repeats a single pitch.

The motive's first transformation occurs with the Maiden's first word, "Vorüber." The three syllables are set to three notes—a^1–bb^1–a^1—a compression of the opening figure, with g omitted. In a sense this transformation is implicit in the first statement of the motive (measures 1–2), where the bb is much more prominent than the g on account of its higher pitch and stronger metrical position. As Example 8.6 shows, the first half of the Maiden's speech is permeated by the neighbor-note figure. After the first "Vorüber" an expansion of it stretches over four measures (9–12) of the middle voice. And with the despairing cry "Ich bin noch jung!" of measures 12–14 the figure breaks out into the open, transposed up a fourth.

In the second half of the Maiden's speech (measures 15–21) the motive does not appear. But it pervades the accompaniment to Death's reply, as can be seen in Example 8.7. The figure resumes its original four-note form, but is altered by rhythmic enlargement (measures 22–25, 25–29, etc.), voice-exchange (measures 26–27 and 34–36), and the chromatic transformations Bb/Bb and Gb/Gb (measures 34–36, 37, and 40). In addition the phrase in Bb (measures 30–33) most probably contains a statement of the motive, transposed up a fourth and with the two neighbors in reverse order. The similarity of the accompaniment at "Ich bin nicht wild" to the Maiden's "Ich bin noch jung" certainly seems to reflect the parallelism in the text.

The motivic design of Der Tod und das Mädchen" parallels the emotional progress of the poem in a remarkable way. The basic motive itself—the double-neighbor figure—is a most appropriate one for a song about death. Its most prominent tones—A–Bb–A—form a musical idiom that has had an age-old association with ideas of death, grief, and lamentation. The musical basis of this association is surely the descending half-step ($\hat{6}$–$\hat{5}$ in minor) with its goal-directed and downward motion, its semitonal intensity, and the "sighing" quality it can so easily assume. Note that the three-note figure with its descending half-step

EXAMPLE 8.5: Schubert, "Der Tod und das Mädchen," measures 1–2

EXAMPLE 8.6: Schubert, "Der Tod und das Mädchen," motivic expansion

occurs literally only when the Maiden speaks; Death's reply softens the B♭–A with the inter-polated G and the very slow melodic pace. As Death continues to speak the motive under-goes subtle tonal changes. With his promise of sleep (measures 33–34), the B♭ changes to B♮; the despairing half-step descent is heard no more. At the same time the G changes to G♯. Owing to this upward inflection a half-step still remains in the double-neighbor figure, and with it melodic tension and goal-oriented progression. But now it is a rising half-step (G♯–A), signifying hope rather than despair.[8] With the d of measure 37, the Maiden surely dies. (This low tonic is far more expressive than the alternative higher one; any singer who can reach it should certainly choose it.) At the Maiden's death, the double-neighbor figure appears in its original rhythmic shape for the first time since the introduction. It decorates a major tonic chord, and both neighbor-notes lie a whole step from the main note. In this final statement there is no half-step, no strongly goal-oriented progression; the music, like the Maiden, is at peace.

EXAMPLE 8.7: Schubert, "Der Tod und das Mädchen," motivic design in Death's reply

"Nacht und Träume"

Universally regarded as one of Schubert's greatest songs, "Nacht und Träume" appeared in print in 1825, but was written much earlier, probably in 1822 or 1823.[9] The author of the poem was Matthäus von Collin, a friend of Schubert's, some of whose songs were first performed at Collin's home. According to the *Neue Ausgabe sämtlicher Werke*, Schubert possibly had the poem in manuscript, for the text of the song differs considerably from the published version of the poem.[10] The text, as Schubert set it, appears below.

Heil'ge Nacht, du sinkest nieder;	Holy night, you descend;
Nieder wallen auch die Träume,	Dreams, too, float down,
Wie dein Mondlicht durch die Räume,	Like your moonlight through space,
Durch der Menschen stille Brust.	Through people's quiet breasts.
Die belauschen sie mit Lust,	They listen in with pleasure,
Rufen, wenn der Tag erwacht:	And call out when day awakens:
Kehre wieder, holde Nacht!	Come back, lovely night!
Holde Träume, kehret wieder!	Lovely dreams, come back!

Like "Der Tod und das Mädchen," "Nacht und Träume" contains a tonal pattern that permeates the song and that helps to connect music and text. Here, however, the design is much less obvious than in the earlier song. The basic tonal pattern does not take on the form of a concrete melodic figure with a definite rhythmic shape, as does the double-neighbor figure at the beginning and end of "Der Tod und das Mädchen." It is therefore not a pattern that would become evident through a conventional motivic analysis.[11] And it does not occur only at the foreground, but penetrates deep into the underlying tonal structure. Therefore the motivic design becomes accessible only if we take into account the song's large-scale linear and harmonic organization.

A good place to begin is with the G-major passage of measures 15–19. The passage is extraordinarily beautiful and is obviously of central significance to the song—"central" in an almost literal way, for the passage begins at the midpoint of the poem and, more or less, of the music. Its importance is underscored by the striking chromatic chord progression B major–G major of measures 14–15, by the long silence in the vocal part, and by the very slow pace of the chord progressions—six measures (14–19) of just one chord per measure.

What is the function of the prolonged G-major chord? At first one would probably think of it as ♭VI (♮VI)—the submediant triad borrowed from B minor. As a descriptive label, ♭VI would not be wrong, but it would not give us much insight into the behavior of this G-major chord. That the behavior is most unusual can be seen from Example 8.8. The progressions

EXAMPLE 8.8: Schubert, "Nacht und Träume," G-major chord in measures 15–19 shown at a and b are typical for ♭VI. At a the bass moves down in thirds (bass arpeggio) to the II$^6_5$ borrowed from the minor. At b the bass is sustained, and an augmented sixth is added above it. In both progressions, ♭6̂ eventually descends to 5̂, either in the bass or in an upper part. This is what one would expect a chromatically *lowered* sound to do. How different is the progression shown at c, a reduction of measures 14–21 of "Nacht und Träume." "♭VI" does not occur within a connected bass line, either arpeggiated or scalar, for its lowest tone moves up an augmented second (measure 20). Nor does ♭6̂ resolve to 5̂, either in the bass or in an upper part. In the bass, the augmented second leaves the G♮ hanging. In the "tenor" the g♮ is sustained into a diminished seventh chord (measure 20), then transformed enharmonically to f×, which *ascends* (measure 21) to g♯.

A glance at the score will show that a melodic progression F♯–F×–G♯ occurs in measures 2–3 of the introduction; the F× functions as a chromatic passing tone. In measure 4 the reverse progression, G♯–G♮–F♯, answers the chromatic ascent; here the G♮ is a chromatic passing tone. In its rising form (F♯–F×–G♯) the chromatic progression recurs twice before the G-major passage (in measures 7–8 and 9–10). It appears again immediately after the G-major passage as a consequence of the fact that measures 21–27 form an almost unaltered repetition of 8–14. And the postlude contains two G♮s, which obviously refer back to the F×s and G♮s heard earlier on. F×/G♮ appears far more often than any other chromatically altered sound—so often, in fact, and so characteristically that it must be regarded as a motivic element. In Example 8.9, a voice-leading graph of the entire song, asterisks point out the various statements of F×/G♮.

The interpretation of the piece shown in Example 8.9 hinges on the idea that the section in G major derives from the earlier passages containing F× or G♮. This idea is corroborated by the fact that the section is followed immediately by the restatement of one of these passages. And a careful study of the voice-leading context provides further substantiation. As Example 8.9 shows, the prolonged G chord of measures 15–19 contains a middle-voice G♮ that comes from F♯ (measure 14) and that changes to F× before moving up to G♯ in measure 21. This melodic progression is the fantastic enlargement of the motivic F♯–F×–G♯ that occurs three times earlier in the song, as well as once in inversion (see the brackets on the lower stave of Example 8.9). In this enlargement, the F×, a chromatic passing tone, becomes transformed enharmonically; as part of a locally consonant triad it is stabilized and extended in time so that its passing function is disguised. Now we can begin to understand why ♭VI behaves so differently here from the typical usages shown at a and b in Example 8.8: it is because the guiding idea of the passage is the rising middle-voice progression F♯–F×–G♯. The G♮ of the middle voice represents the foreground transformation of an underlying F×; that is why it moves up. And the G♮ of the bass does not function linearly—hence its lack of connection with the material that follows. Its purpose is to produce a root-position major triad—the most stable of all chords—and thus to provide support and emphasis for the G♮ (F×) of the middle voice.

By combining in a single sonority two different and contrasting orders of musical reality, Schubert gives this song a great central image; the song embodies a musical symbol of dreams. The G-major section crystallizes around a most transitory musical event—a chromatic passing tone. Yet, while we are immersed in it, it assumes the guise of that most solid tonal structure, the major triad. Only at "wenn der Tag erwacht" does its insubstantiality become manifest; it vanishes, never to return except as an indistinct memory in the G♮s of

EXAMPLE 8.9: Schubert, "Nacht und Träume," middleground graph

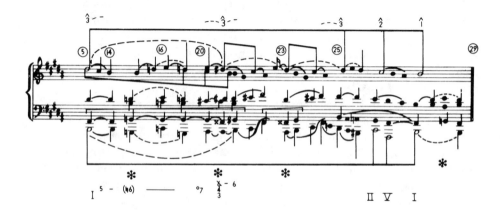

the coda. In "Nacht und Träume," it seems to me, Schubert approaches the limits of what music composed to a text can achieve.

Quite apart from its fantastic relation to the text, the G-major passage is most remarkable, for the principles of tonal combination and succession that govern it are applied in a very special, perhaps unique, manner. Since its complex voice leading cannot be demonstrated adequately in a single graph of the whole piece, I should like to close this essay by presenting a contrapuntal explanation of the passage (Example 8.10). The graph proceeds from background to foreground and contains five levels:

a. The basis of the passage is the connection of the prolonged B-major tonic of measures 1–14 to the G♯-minor $^6_3$ of measure 21. The inner-voice progression f♯–g♯ forms the intervals of a fifth and sixth (5–6) above the sustained tonic in the bass.

b. The motivic f♯–f✗–g♯ arises in the tenor, caused by the chromatic passing tone f✗. The f✗ is incorporated into a diminished seventh chord that leads to the G♯-minor $^6_3$. Note that the upper voice splits into two parts, one decorating d♯² with its upper neighbor e², the other descending through c♯² to an inner-voice b¹.

c. Another chromatic passing tone, d♮², appears in the uppermost voice.

EXAMPLE 8.10: Schubert, "Nacht und Träume," contrapuntal explanation of the G-major passage, measures 14–15

d. The f✗ of the tenor is anticipated so that it coincides with the soprano's d♮². Thus the two chromatic passing tones occur simultaneously, their coincidence producing a "chord" enharmonically equivalent to a G-major $^6_3$ (B–f✗–d♮²).

e. The apparent G-major chord is stabilized. The f✗ changes enharmonically to g♮ in order to produce a triadic structure. And G♮ is added in the bass, thus making a root-position sonority.

Notes

1. A notable exception occurs in Appendix A of Oswald Jonas, *Introduction to the Theory of Heinrich Schenker: The Nature of the Musical Work of Art*, trans. and ed. John Rothgeb (New York: Longman, 1982), pp. 149–61. Jonas was the first to discuss in a systematic way the implications of Schenker's ideas for the analysis of music composed to a text; his treatment of the subject contains many remarkable insights. A splendid study of a Brahms song is to be found in Edward Laufer, "Brahms: 'Wie Melodien zieht es mir,' Op. 105/1," *Journal of Music Theory* 15, nos. 1–2 (1971), pp. 34–57, reprinted in *Readings in Schenker Analysis and Other Approaches*, ed. Maury Yeston (New Haven: Yale University Press, 1977), pp. 254–72. In my opinion, the most profound insights into the relation of music and words—especially in Schubert songs—were achieved by the late Ernst Oster. It is a great misfortune that he published none of his work in this area.

2. The date of composition is unknown; according to the revised Deutsch catalog, it was probably written in 1816 or 1817. See Otto Erich Deutsch, *Franz Schubert: Thematisches Verzeichnis seiner Werke in chronologischer Folge*, rev. Werner Aderhold, Walther Dürr, Arnold Feil, and Christa Landon (Kassel: Bärenreiter, 1978), pp. 183–84.

3. Schubert made a slight change in the words either inadvertently or to produce a rhyming couplet at the end (the original is unrhymed). Salis had written "mir zu" (to me) and not "dir nach" (for you). But either way, the leaves and brook speak her name.

4. Deutsch, *Franz Schubert*, p. 466.

5. Richard Capell finds the opening similar to Wolf's "Herr, was trägt der Boden"—a similarity that seems rather external to me. See Richard Capell, *Schubert's Songs* (London: Ernest Benn, 1928), p. 200.

6. Both Capell (ibid., p. 200) and Tovey have commented perceptively on the relation of the music's tonal structure to the syntax of the poem. See Donald Francis Tovey, *Essays and Lectures on Music* (London: Oxford University Press, 1949), p. 132.

7. Professor Christoph Wolff, in a highly interesting lecture at the International Schubert Congress (Detroit, November 1978), pointed out the operatic character of this song and suggested possible antecedents in the oracle scenes of Gluck's *Alceste* and Mozart's *Idomeneo* and in the two statue scenes of *Don Giovanni*.

8. I would certainly not maintain that every rising half-step in music denotes hope and every falling one despair. But in connection with a text that deals with death, upward and downward motion can easily take on extramusical significance, especially if the composer draws attention to it by varying previously heard material.

9. Deutsch, *Franz Schubert*, pp. 522–23.

10. Franz Schubert, *Neue Ausgabe sämtlicher Werke*, series 4, vol. 2, part b, ed. Walther Dürr (Kassel: Bärenreiter, 1975), p. 323.

11. A detailed analysis of *Nacht und Träume* appears in Diether de la Motte, *Musikalische Analyse (mit kritischen Anmerkungen von Carl Dahlhaus)*, 2 vols. (Kassel: Bärenreiter, 1968), vol. 1, pp. 61–71. There is no mention of the basic motive.

NINE

The Adventures of an F♯

Tonal Narration and Exhortation in
Donna Anna's First-Act
Recitative and Aria

In a well-known letter to his father, Mozart discussed how he went about writing an opera, in this case *The Abduction from the Seraglio*. Osmin's uncontrollable rage, for instance, was to be expressed by a sudden and unexpected change in key and time. Just after the apparent end of his F-major aria, following a bit of dialogue with Pedrillo, Osmin launches into the aria's A-minor pendant, composed in a new meter and tempo and with new orchestration *alla Turca*. Mozart pointed out that he avoided the most closely related key, D minor, as inappropriate to Osmin's violent outburst, but emphasized that he would not choose a remote key either, for Music, he said, must remain Music and must please the hearer even in the most frightful situations.[1]

It is significant that Mozart regarded the F-major and A-minor music as parts of a single aria, despite the changes of key, time, and instrumentation, and the brief dialogue in between. Most modern analysts would infer two separate pieces, and with regard to tonal structure they would be right. But the two pieces form a dramatic unit: they are phases in the unfolding of a single situation. Mozart's calling them one aria might seem to support the currently fashionable rejection of musical unity as an analytic presumption, especially in the criticism of opera. Until we remember, that is, that Mozart did insist upon moving to a related key, so the notion of unity, or at least one of its aspects, the relatedness of parts, informed his description after all. Mozart writes nothing about other sources of musical continuity between the aria's two sections. But a link between the two key areas certainly exists: it is constituted by the pitches F and E, the only contrasting sounds in the two tonic triads. These sounds form a two-note motive that occurs prominently in both parts, as we can see in Example 9.1.[2]

Originally published in *Theory and Practice* 16 (1991), pp. 5–20. An earlier version was read at the Second International Schenker Symposium at the Mannes College of Music in March 1992.

When writing *Don Giovanni*, Mozart confronted a libretto that contained far more "frightful situations" than anything in *Seraglio*, and the music for its violent and tragic episodes is correspondingly closer to the edge. His words to Leopold, however, can still serve as a useful point of departure for the exploration of even as extreme a piece as the accompanied recitative that precedes Donna Anna's Act I aria (see Example 9.2). The recitative, like many others, is tonally open both at the beginning and at the end. Thus it begins *in medias res* with the B♭ major of the preceding music, and after two transitional measures breaks into C minor, its real starting point. It then traverses several subordinate keys before closing into the aria's D major, a goal pretty remote from the recitative's C minor.

As the example shows, the recitative takes its tonal point of departure from the two preceding pieces: the quartet "Non ti fidar" and Don Giovanni's brief secco recitative. His effusive farewells in this recitative unmistakably bring to Anna's mind the voice and manner of the disguised assailant who had entered her rooms, tried to rape her, and killed her father. Donna Anna's accompanied recitative begins still in B♭ with only the low strings playing— horrified recognition taking shape in the depths of her mind before bursting into consciousness in the full orchestra's C-minor outburst two measures later. She proclaims Giovanni's guilt to Don Ottavio, who is incredulous and asks for an explanation. Her narrative begins in G minor and, after prolonging that harmony, modulates to A minor, tacitly setting up a preparatory dominant for the D-major aria.

With Example 9.3 we begin a more detailed study of the recitative; the numbers under the graph identify the various subdivisions of its tonal structure and form. In No. 1 we see the two measures of transition and the first main section (measures 1–16). That the transitional measures continue the key of Giovanni's farewell speech suggests to me that they also represent the time frame of that speech; therefore Anna's realization can be understood as taking place while Giovanni is speaking. (If these measures had begun, say, with a preparatory dominant of C minor, such an impression could hardly have arisen.)[3] At the arrival on C, her horror is embodied in a powerful musical symbol: the main melodic line begins with a startling dissonance, F♯ (♯4) as an upward-resolving appoggiatura. Although the resolution to G takes place immediately, the force of this tritone is by no means spent, for the F♯– G becomes a middleground motive that permeates the recitative's first half and even helps to direct its modulatory plan. Note in particular the chromaticized voice-exchange (measures 10–14) that brings the F♯ into the bass line, where it leads into the cadential dominant. Unlike any of the later key areas of the recitative, this C minor is composed with both a full cadential closure and a large-scale linear descent in the upper voice. This solid foundation in the middleground supports a powerful foreground presence, especially in the orchestral textures, which have an almost symphonic fullness. The tonal continuity of the passage is provided by the orchestra more than by the singers, whose broken-off interjections punctuate the otherwise continuous orchestral discourse—the opposite of the usual figure/ ground relationship in a recitative.

The next segment of the recitative is a brief secco passage; in it Anna assures an incredulous Ottavio that she is not mistaken, and he asks her to recount her story. As Example 9.3 indicates (see No. 2), this passage modulates from C minor to its dominant key, G minor, the bass line consisting only of the notes F♯ and G; our primary motive becomes a structural element. The beginning of Anna's narrative (No. 3) resumes orchestral accompaniment, but with only the strings and continuo playing. Here the locally governing G chord

EXAMPLE 9.1: Mozart, *The Abduction from the Seraglio*, Osmin's Act I aria, F–E motive

EXAMPLE 9.2: Mozart, *Don Giovanni*, Act I, Nos. 9–10, key plan and dramatic situations

No. 9: quartet.
Elvira warns
Anna about
Giovanni.

Secco recit:
Giovanni
offers Anna
his help-
then goes off.

No. 10: Accompanied
recit. Anna
recognizes Giovanni as
her father's killer.

Anna's
narrative

Aria: Anna
urges Ottavio
to avenge her
father's death.

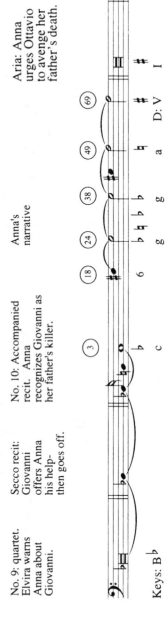

Keys: B♭

223

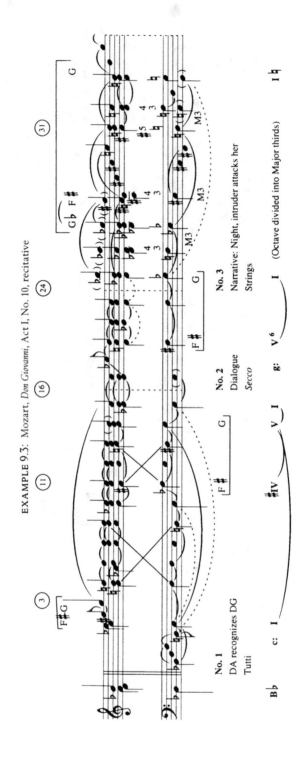

EXAMPLE 9.3: Mozart, *Don Giovanni*, Act I, No. 10, recitative

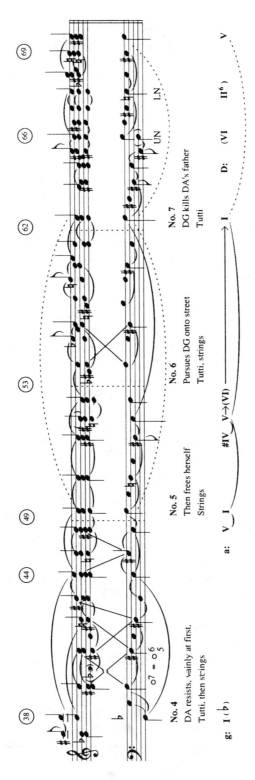

225

is extended by a chain of descending major thirds through an octave: G minor, E♭ minor, B minor, G major changing to minor. Surely this is one of the earliest examples in the literature of chord progression by the equal subdivision of the octave. As the graph indicates, the triadic roots are connected by applied dominants: the bass line thus produced harbors a whole-tone scale, whose even-numbered notes support the $\frac{4}{3}$ position of the applied dominant chords.

Less striking than the implicit whole-tone line but more significant for the compositional design is a disguised reference to the F♯–G motive. When the E♭-minor chord arrives, the uppermost note in the orchestra is the first violins' G♭ (measure 29), a note which holds for three measures before it mutates to F♯ over the V of B minor. The F♯, in turn, continues for seven measures more, making the G♭/F♯ the most persistent orchestral sound in the entire passage; the resolution to G occurs in measure 35.[4] The enharmonic transformation of the motivic F♯ into G♭ is perhaps an iconographic symbol of Don Giovanni's disguised identity, and the whole passage is a remarkable portrayal of Anna's confusion and disorientation. Note that she begins her narration in the second measure of the passage, over the E♭-minor triad. Thus the passage is well under way as she begins to sing, beautifully fitting her words, "Era già alquanto avanzata la notte." The E♭ minor, replacing an expected major chord, gives a peculiarly dark musical color to the fateful night whose events she recounts.

G major, the end point of the descending major thirds, is the place in her narration where she describes Giovanni's grabbing hold of her. She then tells how she cried in vain for help, and the full orchestra takes up her cry with a quotation of the recitative's C-minor motive, but now in G minor. That brings us to No. 4, which shows a modulation from this G minor to A minor. The key change symbolizes a turning point in Anna's struggle with Giovanni. G minor represents an offshoot of C minor, the key associated with Giovanni's attempted rape. As long as G is the center of tonal orientation, Giovanni has the upper hand. A minor, by contrast, belongs rather to the domain of D, the key of Anna's aria, and the A tonic arrives as she describes her success in freeing herself from his embrace. In depicting this "terrible situation," Mozart did not blanch at juxtaposing these two remotely related keys, despite his earlier words to his father. The hinge of the modulation is the tacitly reinterpreted diminished seventh of measure 40, whose D♯ is first heard as an E♭ belonging to G minor, but then resolves to E, eventually as dominant of A. At a deeper level the V of A minor represents the addition of a harmonic root to G♯, which forms a chromatic connection between the two local tonics, G and A.

At the arrival on A minor (No. 5, measure 49), she describes her wrenching herself free. The strings close off this seemingly successful phase of her narrative with a cadence, but a deceptive one on F. Thus Mozart depicts her success as somehow incomplete; and in fact she is not content merely to escape but immediately takes the offensive. The full stop on A occurs only when she has chased Giovanni out of the house and onto the street. But after she describes her escape from Giovanni's clutches and over the F chord of the deceptive cadence, Ottavio exclaims, "Ohimè, respiro." I cannot help feeling that he is relieved at least partly because he will not be marrying "damaged goods." That much I am willing to read into the libretto, but I do not share E. T. A. Hoffman's notion that Giovanni actually had had his way with Anna. Nothing in the libretto supports this idea, as far as I can see. If there is any possible justification for it *in the music*, however, it would be the irony one might infer from an inconclusive cadence at just this juncture of the drama.

For the third time in the recitative, the full orchestra enters with a version of the open-ing C-minor outburst (No. 6, measure 54). The ensuing tutti passage is transitional, adding to the bass E and F of the deceptive cadence an ascending line through F♯ and G♯ that fills in the V–I progression in A minor. The harmonic closure corresponds to the end of this im-portant phase of her story: her driving Giovanni out of her house. The next and last phase—the arrival and death of her father—is necessarily brief, for she witnessed only its very be-ginning and its aftermath. As the graph (No. 7) shows, the prolongation of A is effected by neighbor-note chords that mostly belong to D major, so that when A returns at the very end of the recitative, it is unmistakably a V of D.

We are now in a position to take a somewhat longer view of the recitative (Example 9.4). Since C minor is the first and the most fully developed key area in the recitative and since it forms a stepwise link between B♭ and D, I regard B♭–C–D as the guiding bass pro-gression (Example 9.4a). The G minor and A minor can be understood harmonically as minor dominants of the C and D (and the A actually becomes a major chord). From a contrapuntal perspective, these "dominants" function as unfolded upper fifths of the C and D, and the A forms a sixth above C that leads from one fifth to the other. Thus the key sequence C minor, G minor, A minor, D major represents a huge enlargement of a 5–6–5 contrapuntal progression unfolded in the bass line. And as Example 9.4 shows, even the transition from B♭ to C hints at another 5–6–5, for the B♮ of measure 2 would nor-mally support a $\frac{6}{3}$ or $\frac{6}{5}$ chord.

EXAMPLE 9.4: Recitative as unfolded 5–6–5 progression

The bass unfolding has a dramatic as well as a musical purpose: it allows Mozart to compose on two tonal planes, one representing present, the other past, dramatic time. The primary bass line, B♭–C–D models three phases of an evolving present. B♭ is the time before Anna recognizes Giovanni as her assailant and her father's killer; C minor is her recognition; D is her trying to bend the future to her will through Ottavio. The secondary component of the unfolded bass, G–A, models past time in the manner of a flashback; only Ottavio's interjections bring us back to the present, but they are hardly what is essential here. Curiously, the G minor could evoke something like a memory in real-time for listeners who know the opera very well. In the first scene, Anna leaves the stage as her father enters, and the music at this juncture has just turned to G minor. In fact, the father's first words to Giovanni are sung over F♯–G in the bass, the same notes that lead into her narrative. It is as if she is returning to the very place she had left in the earlier scene.

The large-scale motion of the upper voice does not show a bifurcation like the bass, but it, too, might suggest a dipping into a deeper region of consciousness. The descending 5̂-line of the C-minor part represents a motion into the inner voice. As Example 9.4b shows, this is followed by a gradual ascent effected by a series of melodic progressions, each one reaching over the one before and gradually building a tension that is released only with the closure of the line on the aria's F♯. That closure occurs, of course, at the same time the bass arrives on its D, returning us to present dramatic time with the completion of the big 5–6–5 progression.

EXAMPLE 9.5: (A) Contrapuntal structure

(B) conflicting hypermeters

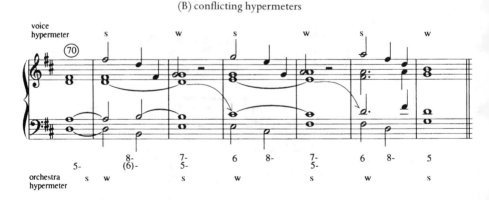

Curiously enough, and perhaps not coincidentally, the aria begins with a sequential fore-ground progression that continues a 5–6–5 ascent, as if the vast intervallic structure deep underneath the recitative's modulatory plan rises to the surface and becomes an immedi-ately perceptible element of the aria's design (Example 9.5a). Now, of course, the 5–6 ex-changes occur as vertical rather than as horizontally unfolded intervals, and the ascending sequence remains in one key.

In "Or sai," the 5–6 progression has an unusual rhythmic shape (Example 9.5b). Each 5–6 pair is deployed within a two-measure hypermeasure, and the cello and bass line clearly defines the fifths as accented, for only their bass notes appear on downbeats (measures 70, 72, 74, and 76). The accentual pattern is, of course, usual for a 5–6 series, conforming as it does to the fourth species of Fuxian counterpoint. But the singer's first downbeat contains a powerful accent on a high note, starting a pattern that repeats at two-measure intervals. These accents occur in the orchestra's weak measures, setting up a conflicting pattern of two-measure hypermeter. This makes the singer swim against the tide, as it were, of the surging and turbulent accompaniment, and suggests an enormous force of will controlling powerful emotions; note that the orchestra's pattern gives way to the singer's at the begin-ning of the next phrase. In the course of composing "Or sai," Mozart revised the vocal line so that these high notes, representing tenths above the rising bass, would fall on down-beats, and this revision sharpens the metrical conflict between singer and accompaniment (Example 9.6).[5]

Mozart's revision eliminated a foreground motivic connection of considerable beauty. In his original conception, the rising sixths that are so prominent a melodic feature of both the vocal line and the orchestra (in measures 76–77 and 79–80 and many parallel places) were prepared by the vocal line's beginning gesture; in the revised version, the connection disap-pears. This loss is more than offset, however, not only by the intensified conflict between metrical schemata but also by the projection of a deeper-level design element. I refer spe-cifically to our F♯–G idea, which surfaces again in a completely new context and with re-versed tonal functions—G is now dependent on F♯. Example 9.7, a middleground graph of the aria, points out the salient instances of this compositional idea.

Of course it would be difficult to compose a piece in D major that refrained from juxta-posing F♯ and G, but the rhetorical emphasis these pitches receive in the aria goes far be-yond the necessities imposed by the tonal system. That emphasis begins together with the vocal line, whose first two prominent notes are F♯ and G.[6] It continues in the large melodic connection linking all three phrases of the aria's A section. F♯ in the first phrase (measure 70) moves to its upper neighbor G in the second phrase (measure 77), which in turn resolves to F♯ at the beginning of the third phrase (measure 80). In this third phrase F♯ and G take on the illusory appearance of a self-contained two-note figure, as in the recitative. This is be-cause the resolution of G to F♯ occurs across parts, transferred from voice to orchestral bass and back to voice. The last G (measure 82) also resolves into the bass, allowing the vocal line

EXAMPLE 9.6: "Or sai," original form of melody

Or   sai   chi   l'o-   no-   re   ra-   pi-   re   a me   vol-   ge   chi   fu   il   tra-   di-

EXAMPLE 9.7: Middleground graph of the aria

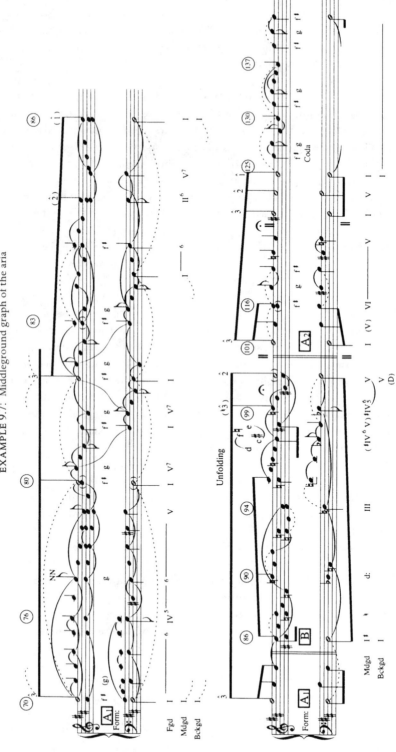

to "reach over" F♯ and achieve high A as a climax note. The high note, overcoming the downward pull to F♯, perhaps embodies Anna's resolute efforts to persuade a still resistant Ottavio to take up her quest for retribution. It is especially in this third phrase with its apparent F♯–G figures that the associative connection to the recitative becomes clear. The boldness of this connection takes one's breath away. Unlike Osmin's aria, whose F-E motive emphasizes the relatedness of the two key areas, this composite piece uses as its link an initially disturbing sound, foreign to the recitative's first key but integral to the key of the aria.[7] Thus the invariant pitches bring out the distance between the keys. The aria assimilates the strident, dissonant F♯ of the recitative into a consonant structure; it looks forward to a resumption of normal life after Don Giovanni's disruptions of the moral order will have been avenged. In the aria, the G becomes associated with C♯, and the resultant diminished fifth becomes an important new element, enhancing the attractive power of F♯ supported by D as a consonant goal (Example 9.8).

The aria as a whole is a modified da capo piece, whose symmetrical and closed form opens up at two places: the fermata at the end of the B section and the expanded big cadence and coda that end the second A section. The contrast between the two main sections allows Mozart to reveal Anna's contrasting feelings: her "giusto furor" at Giovanni's crimes and her grief over the loss of her father. In general, the A sections express her anger, and the B section, with its turn to the tonic minor, expresses her sorrow. But the inner form of each main section shows a similar alternation of expression, with the predominant affect of the section giving way to the other emotion. The A section's second phrase, set to the words "che il padre mi tolse," is the most moving of these mood changes, for its softer melodic contour and quieter orchestration come right in the middle of a syntactic unit (between a noun and its modifying relative clause). This makes Anna's feelings of outrage and grief appear to occur simultaneously rather than in mere succession.

The F♯–G motive is absent from the B section—almost inevitably so, because the turn toward D minor reduces opportunities for introducing F♯ in any very prominent way. The background of the big melodic line is a movement from $\hat{3}$ through ♮$\hat{3}$ to $\hat{2}$ as goal of an interrupted structural progression. This line, however, is delayed almost to the end of the section by means of a large-scale unfolding: D–C♯, F♮–E. It is D–C♯, the lower component of the unfolded melodic line that forms the structural core of most of the section. The goal note (the $\hat{2}$ of the interrupted Urlinie) is suppressed in the foreground in favor of a downward arpeggiation to the inner-voice region at the fermata (measure 99). This is very reminiscent of the melodic contour at the end of the recitative, a resemblance heightened by the recitative-like rhythms of both the vocal line and the orchestra. Thus the da capo enters with much the same kind of preparation as did the corresponding material at the beginning of the aria.

Except for a bit of rhythmic foreshortening at the beginning, and some slight changes of orchestration, the return to the opening material follows the same course it did originally. But just where we would expect a final resolution to the tonic (measure 116), Mozart surprises us with a deceptive cadence. The brief turn to B minor gives Mozart an opportunity to bring in his F♯–G idea, and he does so with a vengeance, as it were. The B-minor context gives it a much more intense and agitated character than in D major, a character further promoted by Mozart's dynamics: fortes on the G neighbor-notes and pianos on the F♯s, creating the impression that the figure is now G–F♯ answering F♯–G.

EXAMPLE 9.8: "Or sai," diminished fifth

Even here, however, Mozart is not yet done. He goes on into a long coda, where both the vocal part and the orchestra use the F♯–G and G–F♯ figures very prominently. Particularly moving is the writing at the very end. The orchestra ends with a long G resolving to F♯. In a sense these last two melody notes form the delayed answer to the urgent and demanding F♯–G at the beginning of the recitative. But the musical and dramatic resolution is not yet complete. After the great energy and forte dynamics of the preceding music, the subito piano and the failure of the melody to return to 1̂ subvert the sense of closure, and they propel the listener to the next episodes, where Don Giovanni is seen to be very much alive and flourishing.

Appendix

Translation of *Don Giovanni*: Act I, No. 10

Recitative:

DONNA ANNA: Don Ottavio! I am dead!

DON OTTAVIO: What's wrong?

DA: For pity's sake, help me!

DO: Dearest, have courage!

DA: O Gods, O Gods! That man is the murderer of my father!

DO: What are you saying?

DA: Don't doubt it any longer; the last words that evil man uttered, the whole way he spoke, reminded me of that villain in my rooms who—

DO: Heavens! can it be that under the sacred mantle of friendship—but what happened? Tell me about this strange event.

DA: The night was already somewhat advanced when, unfortunately alone in my rooms, I saw a man enter, wrapped up in a cloak. At first I thought it was you, but then I saw how deceived I was.

DO: (*agitated*): Heavens! continue!

DA: He approaches me silently and wants to embrace me; I try to free myself. And he holds me tighter. I shout! Nobody comes; with one hand he tries to muffle my voice, and with the other he holds me so tight that I think I'm lost.

DO: Traitor! and then?

DA: Finally the pain, the horror of the attempted outrage increase my strength so that by dint of wriggling, twisting, and bending, I free myself,

DO: Oh! I can breathe.

DA: Then I cry out more loudly, call for help. The criminal runs away; boldly I follow him onto the street to stop him; and I become the assailant of my assailant. My father comes running, demands to know who he is, and the villain, who is stronger than the poor old man, completes his misdeeds by killing him.

Aria:

> [*A section*] Now you know who tried to steal my honor, who the traitor was that robbed me of my father. I demand vengeance of you, your heart demands it.

> [*B section*] Remember the wound in that poor breast, think of the ground covered with blood if the ardor of your righteous anger should abate!

> [*Da capo*] Now you know who tried to steal my honor, who the traitor was that robbed me of my father. I demand vengeance of you, your heart demands it. [*At deceptive cadence, measure 116*] Remember the wound; think of the blood. [*Then, measure 119 to end*] I demand vengeance of you, your heart demands it.

Notes

1. Letter of 26 September 1781. See Wilhelm A. Bauer, Otto Erich Deutsch, and Joseph Heinz Eibl, eds., *Mozart: Briefe und Aufzeichnungen*, vol. 3: *Gesamtausgabe* (Kassel: Bärenreiter, 1962–75), pp. 161–64. Mozart's words are: "Die Musick, auch in der schaudervollsten lage, das Ohr niemalen beleidigen, sondern auch dabei vergnügen muß folglich allzeit Musick bleiben Muß." The letter is quoted in translation and with interesting commentary in Alfred Einstein, *Mozart: His Character, His Work* (New York: Oxford University Press, 1945), pp. 384–86.

2. By a curious coincidence, an even better-known F-major/A-minor piece—Chopin's Second Ballade—links its two keys by means of the same two pitches. I believe, however, that the Chopin, unlike the Mozart aria, is best understood as the composing-out of a single background tonic in A minor.

3. A similarly non-naturalistic representation of time—succession standing for simultaneity— occurs in some of Shakespeare's dialogues, for instance, in the exchange between Kent and Lear after Cordelia is disinherited. In a realistic dialogue, Lear would hardly give Kent time to finish his speeches before interrupting with his furious outbursts.

4. The famous cycle of major thirds in the first movement development of the *Appassionata* also projects a fundamental motivic idea: the neighbor-note figure E♭/D♯–E♮–E♭ represents E♭–F♭–E♭— the transposition into the mediant of the $\hat{5}$–$\hat{6}$–$\hat{5}$ whose primary form is, of course, C–D♭–C.

5. A recent and highly important article by James Webster, "The Analysis of Mozart's Arias," in *Mozart Studies*, ed. Cliff Eisen (Oxford: Oxford University Press, 1991), pp. 101–99, presents a multifaceted approach to these works, including a great deal of information about the rhythmic aspect of text–music relationships, especially in the operas with Italian texts (pp. 133–37). Webster maintains that the prosodic structure of the verse line normally translates into a two-measure musical unit (he calls it a phrase). There are two main accents, of which the second is, in principle, the stronger. If one applied this idea to "Or sai," one would read the primary accent not on "sai" (the first downbeat) but on the "no" of "l'onore" (the second downbeat). And consequently one would acknowledge no rhythmic conflict between singer and orchestra. To my ear, such a conception of the aria would rob it of much of its dramatic power. In general, I think that Webster derives his accentual schemes too exclusively from the text and overlooks the diversity of musical accentuations; many aspects of the music can contribute accentual patterns of various sorts, often in conflict with each other. Especially at the beginning of an aria, what I call "tonal rhythm"—the rhythmic aspect of tonal combination and succession—can produce important structural accents on the tonic harmony that falls on the first downbeat of the vocal part. Webster's first example is "Voi che sapete" from Act II of *Le Nozze di Figaro*. According to his explanation, the "pe" of "sapete" gets the primary stress. But that syllable falls on a passing tone within an initial ascent, supported by V$^6_5$ neighbor-note chord between two tonics. Furthermore, the pronoun "Voi" is placed in apposition to "Donne" a few measures later on, and the text becomes intelligible only if that connection is projected. For me, therefore, the primary accent in these two measures should fall on the singer's first downbeat, "Voi."

6. The motivic implication is, I think, a reason not to sing an appoggiatura on the first of the repeated Gs of "l'onore."

7. An exclusively reductive approach to the analysis of this work would result in the elimination of the recitative's F♯ perhaps as the very first step in the analysis, thereby blocking access to the primary compositional idea that connects recitative and aria. On the other hand, hypothesizing background and middleground structures as a point of departure would not lead any more readily to a recognition of this idea, which does not conform to any such structures. What is needed at the outset is a close reading of the foreground as it unfolds, event by event, and an ear that can take in associations between events—an ear like that of an intelligent and sensitive performer. An understanding of background and middleground will, it is hoped, eventually take shape from this reading of the foreground, and that understanding will, in turn, clarify the foreground. In this later process, of course, both reduction and the inference of underlying structures (e.g., the big 5–6 unfolding in the recitative's bass) will play a part.

PART IV

ANALYTICAL MONOGRAPHS

xerox for class

Bach's Fugue in B♭ Major,
Well-Tempered Clavier,
Book I, No. 21

In principle the analysis of a fugue should present no problems essentially different from those encountered in other types of music. Fugal procedures, after all, grow out of the contrapuntal and harmonic elements fundamental to tonality. And two fugues by the same composer may well differ by at least as much as two rondos, two sonata movements, or two nocturnes.

Unfortunately, what we might expect in principle does not always coincide with what we find. As it happens, the analysis of fugues involves difficulties which, if not fundamentally new, are often unusually intractable. There are, I think, several reasons for this. The first and most important is that masterpieces of fugue tend to be dense, tightly knit webs of voice leading which concentrate into relatively short musical spans a fantastic number of contrapuntal, harmonic, and motivic relationships.

Furthermore, in the fugue (and in other genres based upon imitation), important thematic elements constantly shift from voice to voice; this can make it difficult to determine the controlling outer-voice structure. A solution to this latter problem is often blocked if we hear the various elements of fugal design—subject, countersubject, episodes, etc.—as entities separable from the fugue as a whole. All too often a conventional theoretical training in fugue tends to bring about this unproductive approach to hearing. A study of the enormous literature on fugue will show how infrequently the fugal theorists have been able to reassemble into some kind of connected whole the *disjecta membra* produced by their analyses.[1]

Preliminaries

Fugue 21 (*Well-Tempered Clavier*, Book I) is in three "voices," each with a range of about two octaves (soprano, c^1–c^3; alto, e♮–f^2; bass. E♭–f^1). It fills forty-eight measures and is in through-

Originally published in *Music Forum* 3 (1973), pp. 239–67.

composed form. The subject begins on the fifth step of the scale; the answer, therefore, is tonal. There are two countersubjects; both, especially the second, often undergo minor changes owing to contrapuntal, harmonic, or instrumental exigencies. Only two episodes occur (measures 19–22 and 30–35); the second contains a free contrapuntal inversion of the first. The accompanying chart (see Example 10.1) shows at a glance the clear and simple design. Note that the subject and answer enter alternately and in pairs throughout the piece, and that these entrances shift from voice to voice with complete regularity.

Linear–Harmonic Contents

One might well begin such a study with an analysis of detail and end it with a comprehensive view of the whole piece. Two considerations led me to follow a different course. First, the linear-harmonic contents of the Fugue do not reflect the simplicity of its formal design. The reader, I think, will find it easier to follow the section-by-section analysis of detail if he can relate it to a larger framework. My second reason was my wish to counteract the prevalent (though usually unstated) assumption that a fugue is pieced together out of its parts and that these parts are independent entities, intelligible when separated from each other and from the work as a whole. For these reasons I shall begin with a discussion of background and of the more remote levels of middleground. I shall then proceed to a section-by-section analysis of the foreground. This essay will conclude with a more detailed middleground graph which, I hope, will help the reader to unify the distant and the immediate perspectives.

EXAMPLE 10.1: Chart of the overall design

	⑤		⑩		⑮	
top voice	S	CS 1	CS 2	A
middle voice		A	CS 1	CS 2
bass			S	CS 1

(Exposition)

	⑳		㉕		㉚
from bars 3, 4 S	from S, bar 3	CS 1	CS 2	from S, bar 1
from CS 1	(rests)	S	CS 1	(filling voice)
from CS 2	from S, bar 1	CS 2	A (modified)	from S, bar 3

(Extension)   (Episode 1)   (Middle Group of Entrances)   (Episode 2)

	㉟		㊵		㊺
from S, bar 3	from CS 1	S	CS 1	from CS 2
from S,	from S, bars 1, 2 CS 1	A	from S, bar 3
bar 1	from CS 2 CS 2	CS 2	from CS 1

(Incomplete Entrance)   (Closing Group of Entrances)   (Final Cadence)

The subject drives so surely to d^2 (measures 4 and 5), and the d^2 functions so clearly as the beginning of the Fugue's large-scale melodic progressions, that the Fundamental Structure seems hardly open to question. It consists of a melodic line falling a third from d^2 through c^2 to $b♭^1$, this line supported by a harmonic progression I–V–I. Example 10.2a shows the first level of prolongation and, although still very abstract, begins to indicate the Fugue's individual profile. Of particular importance is the neighboring tone $e♭^2$ supported by subdominant harmony; strictly speaking, this is an incomplete neighbor, as the d^2 following it functions as a passing tone. Note that the indicated register of the top voice is the one in which it actually unfolds in the piece.

In Example 10.2b, the middle-voice tone, $b♭^1$, of the preceding graph becomes activated and forms part of the melodic line; the vertical third and fourth become unfolded into the horizontal dimension. Note the bass arpeggio $b♭–g–e♭$, which subdivides into two thirds the progression from I to IV. The melodic passing tone, d^2, is now shown as part of a cadential $^6_4$ over the V.

EXAMPLE 10.2: Middleground graphs

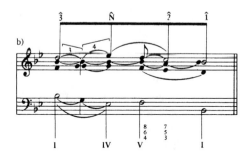

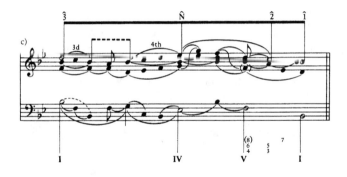

Example 10.2c adds considerably more detail; this graph should be the primary source of orientation for the detailed analyses to follow. Note that the unfolded third and fourth of the preceding graph have become stepwise linear progressions. The third is supported by a harmonic elaboration of the tonic; the bass motion supporting the fourth gives rise to the C-minor coloration of measures 26–35. This graph, although more detailed than the preceding ones, is still highly synoptic; in particular, events which occur over a span of several measures are here compressed into a single chord (the very first tonic chord, for example). At this stage, obviously, the measure numbers can function only as a rough guide to the contents of the graph as they relate to the piece. Nevertheless, the graph offers a basis for understanding the inner articulations of the through-composed form.

The Fugue falls into three connected segments; the beginning of each new one overlaps the ending of the preceding one. The first segment (measures 1–19) contains the exposition plus a two-measure extension. Structurally it is governed by the descending third of the top voice supported by a prolonged tonic and a transition to G minor effected by the initial third of the bass's descending arpeggio. The second segment (measures 19–37) contains the first episode, the middle group of entrances, the second episode, and the "false," incomplete entrance of measures 35–36. This segment is unified by the linear progression of an ascending fourth in the top voice, supported by a bass motion of a third leading from G minor to E♭ major (conclusion of arpeggio). The final segment (measures 37–48) includes the closing group of entrances and final cadence. This segment contains the structural denouement of the Fugue; the top voice descends from the neighboring e♭² to c² and b♭¹, and the harmony progresses from IV to the final V and I.

Foreground

First Segment (Measures 1–19)

Example 10.3 contains a detailed graph and a somewhat reduced one of the first nineteen measures. I would suggest that the reader first consult the reduction (Example 10.3b), which provides an easier orientation. The bass plan and the harmonic scheme are not difficult to follow. The first entrance expresses tonic harmony; there is no bass, of course, but B♭ is clearly implied. The second entrance (answer) begins on the tonic and moves to the dominant (measures 8–9). The third entrance picks up the dominant and moves to the tonic (measures 12–13). The added soprano entrance (answer) moves again to the F chord; this F functions more importantly as a transition to the coming G minor than as a harmonic elaboration of the tonic. The motion is effected through a chromatic passing tone, f♯.

Example 10.4 is intended to help clarify the direction of the top voice from the beginning to measure 13. It shows the beautifully simple and ingenious manner in which the culminating tones of the subject and two countersubjects join together to form a coherent melodic progression. The subject drives clearly and purposefully to d², the first tone of the Fugue's fundamental melodic line. The d² moves to c² at the end of the first countersubject and through that tone to the b♭¹ that ends the second countersubject. Note that Bach has composed his subject and countersubjects so that they form both triple counterpoint when combined vertically and a large-scale melodic progression when heard one after the other.

EXAMPLE 10.3: Detailed graph of the first segment (measures 1–19)

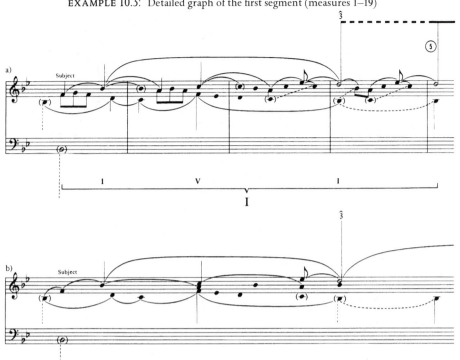

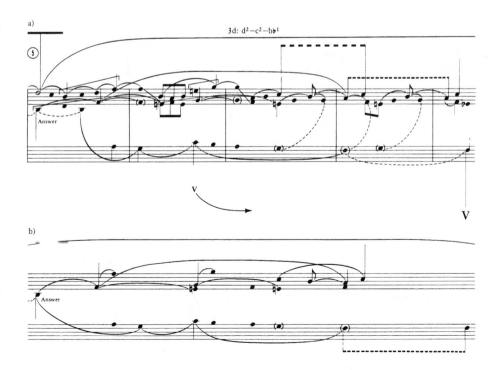

a)

4th: b♭¹, bars 12–13, to c², bars 29–30, to d²,

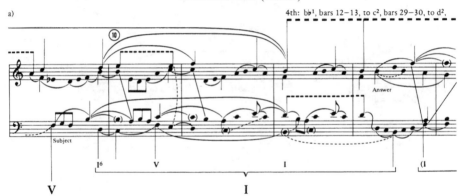

b)

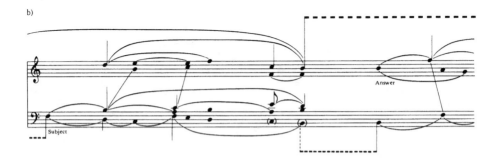

a)

bar 36, to e♭², bar 37

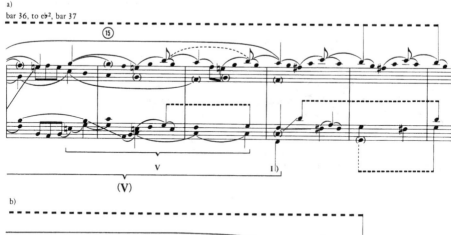

b)

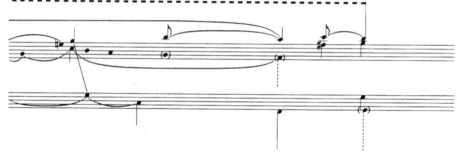

EXAMPLE 10.4: Top voice in measures 1–13

The top voice of measures 13–19 is easier to follow and should be clear from Example 10.3 without additional graphs or lengthy discussion. The main point to observe is that the b♭¹ of measures 12–13 is prolonged but not in its original register; instead, an upward-moving transfer of register (b♭¹–b♭²) takes place, the arrival at b♭² coinciding with the appearance of the G-minor chord.

Subject   We can now proceed to an examination of the subject and of other elements of the Fugue's design. I would suggest that the reader relate these discussions of detail to the larger framework provided by Example 10.3; as we go on, Example 10.3a will probably become clearer and easier to follow.

The subject is a rather complex melodic line; however, its fundamental idea shines clearly through the elaborate detail. This idea is a melodic progression rising a third from b♭¹ through c² to its goal, d² (Example 10.5a).[2] In Example 10.5b we see this essential motion abstracted from the subject; this example adds the clearly implied harmonic support b♭–f¹–b♭ (the f¹ is not implied but actually occurs as the seventh tone of measure 2).

Example 10.5c begins to show the development of this nucleus into the complete subject. Of particular importance is the incomplete neighbor, e♭², whose appearance enables the goal tone to fall upon a first rather than a third beat. Comparing Example 10.5c with Example 10.2a reveals an interesting symmetrical relationship between the melodic outline of the subject and the top-voice structure of the Fugue as a whole. An incomplete neighbor on e♭² figures prominently as an embellishment of both the ascending subject and the descending Fundamental Line. In the subject it leads into the goal tone; in the large structure it follows the initial tone.

Example 10.5c contains two other features requiring comment. In the lower "voice" the fifth f¹–b♭ appears filled in by a stepwise passing motion. In addition the b♭¹ and c² are followed by brief descending progressions which produce a counterforce to the upward urge of the subject's Fundamental Line. As a result the line rises in three overlapping segments (through *Übergreifstechnik* or reaching-over) rather than in a single, unbroken curve.

As so often happens in Bach's polyphonically conceived melodic lines, our subject strongly hints at suspensions. These are shown in Example 10.5d by the sevenths that begin measures 2 and 3. The implied suspensions are significant for the performer; once aware of them he will play the opening sixteenths of measures 2 and 3 as the continuation of the preceding tones, not as new beginnings. As we shall see, the first countersubject will bring into actuality these hinted-at suspensions.

Example 10.5e concentrates on important melodic diminutions and on rhythmic features. Observe how the neighboring figure of measure 1 is carried through into measure 2—a relationship disguised in the subject by the sixteenth-note figuration. The notes in

EXAMPLE 10.5: Analysis of the subject

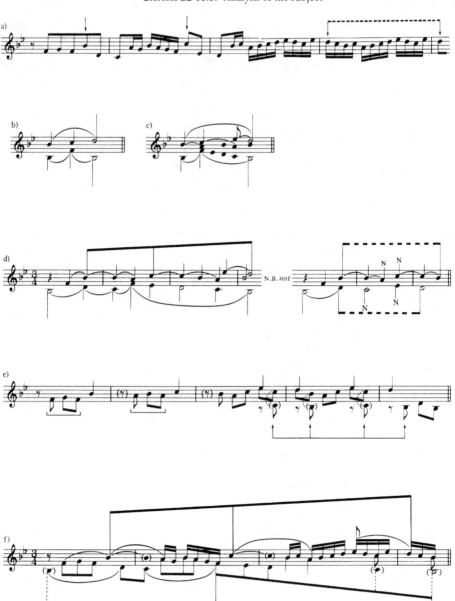

parentheses (c¹ and b♭) represent the conclusion of the subject's lower "voice" as shown in Examples 10.5c and 10.5d. In the subject, this lower "voice" is broken off and is completed in its proper register only at the beginning of the next entrance (measure 5). However, the sixteenth-note figuration conceals the missing tones in a higher register. The placement of these tones serves to prepare for the rhythmic position of the first tone of the answer (see arrows).

Example 10.5f shows the completed subject minus the repetition in measure 4, which will be discussed below. Only one point requires some comment. The sixteenth notes of measure 3 are the inversion of those of measure 2. This was pointed out by Tovey, whose brief but instructive remarks about this Fugue stress the importance of melodic inversion in its design.[3] A most unusual feature of the subject is the repetition in measure 4 of the contents of measure 3. Although measure 4 brings in no new material, the repetition does make important contributions to the Fugue's design. In the first place, it creates a rhythmic balance between measures 1–2 and 3–4. In addition the repeated measure adds to the beauty of the voice leading at the next entrance. A most important feature of the second entrance is its delayed statement of b♭, the tone that completes the subject's lower "line." Now the first beat of measure 4 contains an obligatory b♭^{1} as part of the resolution of the diminished fifth a^1–e♭^{2} of measure 3. If the subject were shorter by a measure (in other words, if measure 3 were left out), the two b♭s would come in at almost the same time, to the advantage of neither one. By means of the repetition, Bach first has us hear the resolution a^1–b♭^{1} of measure 4. Once this has taken place, we can direct our attention to the b♭ of measure 5, whose effect is further enhanced by the measure's delay. In both countersubjects Bach has the fourth measure repeat the third; by thus emphasizing the repetition, Bach makes of it one of the salient elements of the Fugue's foreground design.

Answer   As Example 10.6a indicates, Bach answers tonally both the first and the third tones of the subject; the second tone, however, is answered at the fifth (here, of course, the lower fourth). These changes in the answer produce an emphatic statement of tonic harmony in measure 5 (note the voice-exchange) that functions both as a goal for the contents of measures 1–4 and as the point of departure for the coming progression to F major (V). The second entrance, unlike the first, is not grounded in a single prolonged harmony; it consists instead of a transition from I to a tonicized V. The beginning of the answer contrasts with the subject contrapuntally as well as harmonically. The first tone does not belong to the middle but rather to the lowest "voice" of the horizontalized B♭ chord. As such it begins the lower part of the answer's implied polyphony. As before, the line and the harmonic movement are fulfilled only at the beginning of the next entrance (bass, measure 9). Example 10.6b gives a detailed picture of the answer.

EXAMPLE 10.6: Analysis of the answer

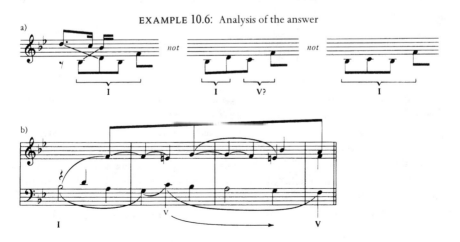

Later Entrances   The modulatory quality of the second entrance will characterize most of the later entrances of the subject as well as the answer. Only the E♭ entrance of measure 37 expresses a single sonority. If the reader will refer to Example 10.3, he will see that the bass entrance of measure 9 bears a very different meaning from the opening statement of measures 1–4. The first tone now functions as the root of the F chord and, consequently, as the harmonic goal of the preceding four measures. Although the prolongation of the B♭ chord begins on the third beat of measure 9, the chord is stabilized only at the end of the subject (measures 12–13).

Countersubjects   There is no audible break between the subject and the first counter-subject; the simplest and best interpretation is to regard the last note of one as the first of the other. In later entrances Bach often adjusts the beginning of this countersubject to fit the prevailing harmonic and contrapuntal conditions.

In contrast to textbook prejudices in favor of "independent" voice leading, Bach makes the first two measures of this countersubject markedly dependent upon the subject or answer (see brackets, Example 10.3). The most prominent features of these measures (at the second entrance, measures 6–7) are the suspended sevenths, which transform into audible reality the hinted-at suspensions of the subject. The graceful interplay of the two voices with the suspensions and their resolutions tossed from one to the other creates a beautifully light and transparent texture. As Example 10.3a shows, the second suspension (soprano, measure 7) is resolved only at the lower octave and in the alto voice.

The latter half of the countersubject reinforces the answer by moving in parallel thirds with it for part of its course. The repeated tones of measures 7–8, however, constitute a new and important element. They emphasize the tone c^2, here the fifth of the F chord, and in a broader context the second step of B♭ over a prolonged dominant. If the reader will refer back to Example 10.4, he will recall that the c^2 forms part of the governing melodic progression of the Fugue's exposition.

In its first statement (measures 9ff.), the second countersubject begins with a stepwise motion filling in an embellishing third above a prolonged d^2. In subsequent entrances, the corresponding measures often vary both in meaning and in melodic content. The last two measures recur without change; the line parallels the sixteenth notes of the subject. In so doing it sounds, here two octaves higher, the "missing" c and B♭ at the end of the subject (see tones in parentheses, Example 10.5e).

Second Segment (Measures 19–37)

This middle segment is the longest of the three and, in some ways, the most difficult to understand. As I mentioned earlier, the governing idea is a stepwise ascent in the top voice from bb^1 to eb^2, the structural neighbor-note (see Example 10.2). This melodic progression is supported by a bass motion leading from submediant to subdominant (as the end of the bass arpeggio). Example 10.7a attempts to give the reader a better orientation by showing the turning points through which the melodic progression becomes manifest. The reduction of Example 10.7b indicates that each melodic step is embellished by its upper third, thus: bb^1–d^2, c^2–eb^2, d^2–f^2, eb^2. The general course of the bass line is clear. The tone c arrives only in measure 35, but it belongs to the entire C-minor section (measures 29–35). The primary

EXAMPLE 10.7: Overview of the second segment (measures 19–37)

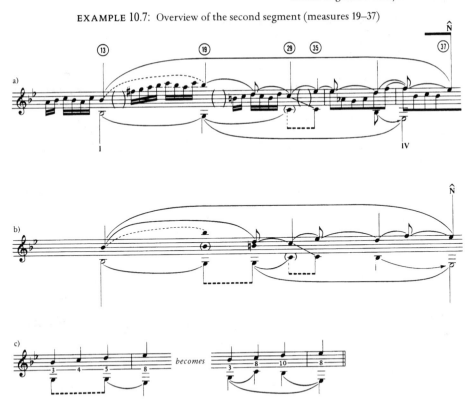

function of this C minor is contrapuntal, to provide support for the otherwise dissonant passing tone, c² (Example 10.7c).

First Episode (Measurers 19–22)

Example 10.8, which includes the first episode and the middle group of entrances, forms the continuation of Example 10.3. Smaller graphs of detail will be added as needed.

The materials of this episode derive completely from the subject, the top voice from measures 3–4 and the bass from a free melodic inversion of measure 1 (see Example 10.9). The harmonic function of this episode is not the usual one of leading to a new key area. G minor has already arrived in measures 18–19; however, it has not been stabilized by a root-position dominant. The episode leads to just such a dominant and therefore serves to stabilize the G minor. This is an episode within a single prolonged sonority, leading from the fluid, unstable tonic (really only a potential tonic) of measures 18–19 to the explicit dominant of measure 22 and making possible the stable, confirmed tonic of measures 25–26. The voice leading of the episode, as is so frequent with Bach, crystallizes around a suspension series, here harmonically elaborated by means of descending fifths (see Examples 10.8a and 10.8b).

Middle Group of Entrances (Measures 22–30)

The G-minor entrance of measure 22, like that in B♭ (measure 9), begins over a dominant, which progresses to a tonic that becomes firmly grounded only in measures 25–26. The bass entrance of measure 26 begins with the

EXAMPLE 10.8: Detailed graph of the second segment (measures 19–37)

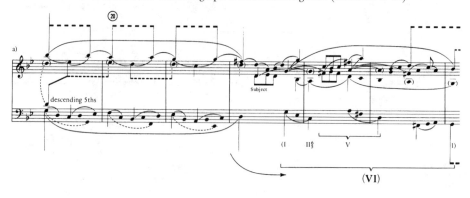

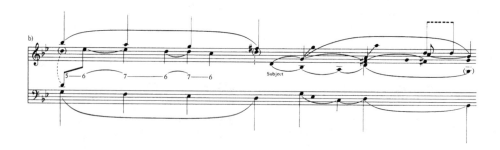

rising third characteristic of the answer; one would expect, therefore, that the entrance would continue as in Example 10.10a and would lead to D minor. Instead Bach leads to C minor by lowering the melody a whole step from the fourth tone on (Example 10.10b). This change is necessary, creating as it does the possibility for the ascending melodic fourth which governs this middle segment of the Fugue, and permitting a logical progression to the culminating E♭ entrance of measure 37.

The larger melodic shape and the basic voice-leading progressions of this section become clear only when considered in relation to what has gone on before. As Example 10.11 indicates, measures 13–19 contain the octave transfer b♭¹–b♭² over a retained middle-voice d¹. In measures 19–25 the top and middle voices exchange their tones:

The d² then proceeds to c² in measures 29–30. Example 10.11a shows these events in some detail; Examples 10.11b and 10.11c offer progressive reductions and eliminate the octave transfer to point up the larger patterns of voice leading.

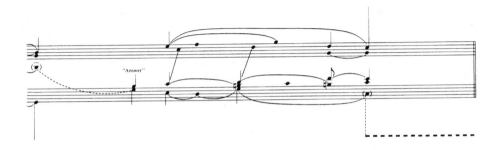

Second Episode and Incomplete Entrance (Measures 30–37)

The second episode falls into two parts (measures 30–32 and 33–34); the second part is based upon a contrapuntal inversion of the first. As it happens, the first of this episode is itself a free inversion of Episode 1; the bass of measures 30–32 echoes the soprano of measures 19–21 while the soprano of 30–32 resembles, but in modified form, the bass of 19–21 (see Example 10.12). More important than the change of melodic pattern is the changed significance of the voice leading. Instead of the descending fifths of measures 19–21, we now find a stepwise series of $^6_3$ chords, all but the first preceded by lower neighbors. In contrast to the first episode, the third eighth note of each measure is now a neighbor rather than a chordal tone (see Example 10.13).

In measures 33–34, the sixteenth notes, previously in the bass, move to the soprano; the left hand part takes over the eighth notes, distributing them between two voices, as is shown in Example 10.14. The contrapuntal inversion of measures 33–34 coincides with an important harmonic shift. In measures 30–33 the melodic lines have moved down the G-minor scale, thus suggesting a return to G minor as a key area. However, the G-minor $^6_3$ of measure 33 is not stabilized. Instead the b♭ (bass) is inflected to a b♮ (middle voice, measure 34) leading to C minor. The G-minor chord, therefore, functions as a minor dominant within the progression I–V♭–♮–I of C minor (measures 30–35).

EXAMPLE 10.9: First episode (measures 19–22)

Example 10.15 gives a detailed picture of the whole episode. As mentioned above, the second episode, like the first one, moves within a single key area (here C minor). The structural meaning of this episode is the following. With one exception, all entrances of the subject or answer have ended in (or have been immediately followed by) a local tonic chord in root position. The one exception has been the entrance of measure 27, which has not concluded with a C-minor triad in root position. The episode provides the missing c in the bass, but only after a delay which generates a considerable tension, a tension only dissipated by the triumphant E♭ entrance of measure 37.

The arrival of c in measure 35 coincides with what would seem to be a C-minor entrance in the alto. However, only the first measure really corresponds to a statement of the answer; the second measure is changed in order to point the way to E♭ major (see Example 10.16). As Example 10.15 shows, Bach leads from the C-minor chord to the V of E♭ through an F-minor seventh; this chord provides a smooth harmonic transition and breaks up parallel fifths as well. The reader will perhaps have noticed that the harmonic path of this middle segment of the Fugue traverses a series of falling fifths (G, measures 19–26; C, measures 26–35; F and B♭, measure 36; E♭, measure 37). This progression in fifths does not form the path of motion from the G minor to the E♭ chord; it results, rather, from the harmonic elaboration of the progression given in Example 10.2c.

Final Segment (Measures 37–48)

This last part of the Fugue poses three interpretive problems for the analyst: the melodic analysis of the E♭ entrance (measures 37–41); the structural meaning of the return to B♭ in measures 44–45; the leading of the upper voices over the cadential dominant. The reader should consult Example 10.17 in connection with the discussion below.

EXAMPLE 10.10: Bass entrance of measure 26

EXAMPLE 10.11: Melodic shape and voice leading in measures 13–30

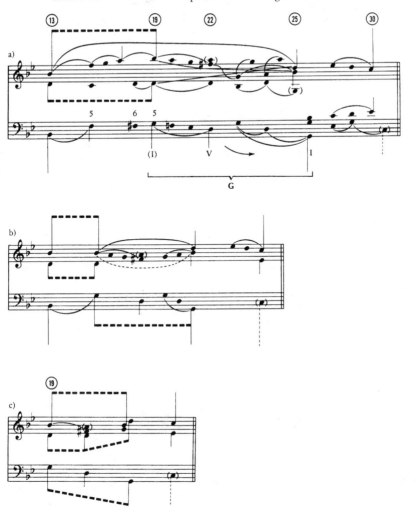

The E♭ statement of the subject (measures 37–41) is in itself no different from previous entrances. However, its relation to immediate and distant environments requires us to give it a different interpretation. Whereas other entrances lead up to their main melodic tones in the third and fourth measures, this one states its principal tone, e♭², near the beginning (measure 37), the subsequent ascent to g² must be heard as an embellishment above the main tone. My reasons for this reading are the following. Over the long span, the e♭² forms the stepwise continuation of d², the top-voice tone of the initial prolonged tonic; the g² of measures 40–41 enters into no such far-reaching connections. The immediate context also points up the importance of e♭². Unlike any previous entrance, this one is non-modulatory and begins on a chord of tonic color preceded by its dominant. As a result, the first important melodic tone is grounded in a stable harmony. In addition the melodic tones d² and f² of

EXAMPLE 10.12: Episode 2 as free inversion of Episode 1

EXAMPLE 10.13: Voice leading in Episode 2

EXAMPLE 10.14: Contrapuntal inversion in measures 33–34

EXAMPLE 10.15: Detailed graph of Episode 2

from b♭, bar 13

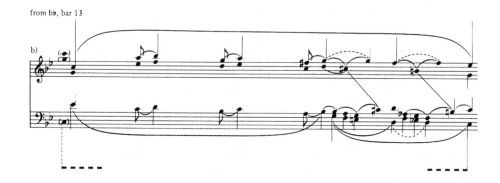

measure 36 converge upon the e♭². Both harmonic and melodic forces make the beginning of this entrance sound like an arrival and not a point of departure.

The entrance of the answer (measures 41–45) moves from E♭ major to the B♭ chord of measures 44–45; the B♭ triad is preceded by a root-position dominant that arises out of a change in the second countersubject. Despite this harmonic emphasis, the B♭ chord is insufficiently stabilized to constitute a tonic of structural significance connected with the prolonged B♭ harmony of the exposition. Instead I read it as the upper fifth of the subdominant effecting a transition to the cadential dominant of measures 45–48, and awakening our expectation of the final tonic that is to appear in measure 48. I believe that if Bach had heard a structural return to the tonic in measures 44–45, he would have redistributed the entrances among the voices so that d² would appear in the soprano; this would have reinforced the connection with the opening tonic. (Of course such a redistribution would have a profound impact on the structure and design of the Fugue; it would have become a different piece.) As it is, the top voice of measures 44–45 is, so to speak, up in the air, continuing the embellishing g² of the previous entrance with f²; only over the final dominant will the top voice take up and conclude its Fundamental Line. (The registral association of the tones F and G occurs in the top voice and bass throughout the Fugue: f²–g–f², measures 5–11, top voice;

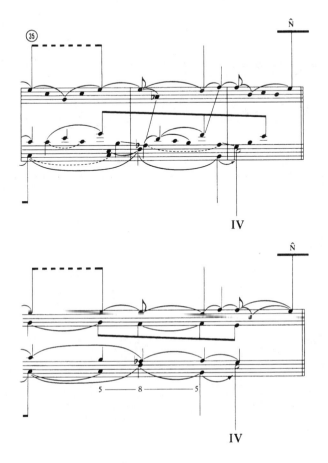

EXAMPLE 10.16: Shift to Eb-major in measures 35–37

F–G, measures 17–25, bass; g²–f², measures 40–45, top voice. The connection with the opening of the subject is evident.)

In measure 45, the contrapuntal inversion of the outer voices creates a chord succession $\frac{7\ 6}{5\ 4}$ over a decorated dominant pedal in the bass. As Example 10.17 indicates, the $\frac{6}{4}$ and not the seventh chord is the leading element here. The interchange between the outer parts transforms the Bb $\frac{5}{3}$ of measures 44–45 to a cadential $\frac{6}{4}$ but one with the "wrong" tone, bb², in the soprano. A further interchange, this time between the top and the middle voice, brings

EXAMPLE 10.17: Detailed graph of the final segment (measures 37–48)

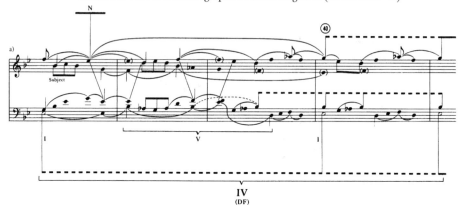

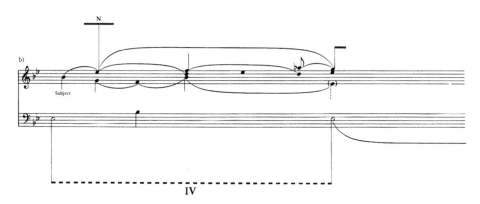

in d² (measure 47) as the delayed continuation of e♭² (measure 37) leading to the final melodic descent through c² to b♭². It is this last interchange that justifies the amusing "extra" repetition of the bass figure in measure 47.

Conclusion

Example 10.18 is a middleground graph important to the understanding of the whole Fugue. The reader who has gone through this essay will, I am sure, be able to understand it without any further comment.

    In concluding this study I would like to devote a few words to the relationship between fugal analysis and the traditional study of fugue. Many would agree, I think, that a regime of academic fugal theory would for the most part hinder rather than help us in undertaking an analysis such as the one I have presented in this essay. At one time or another we have all learned (and some of us still teach our students) to construct Frankensteinian fugues, robbing one graveyard for the subject, another for the countersubject, a third for the episodes. Such exercises have a value, of course. But too many textbooks (and teachers

mention in wrap up. Concur w/ Schachter

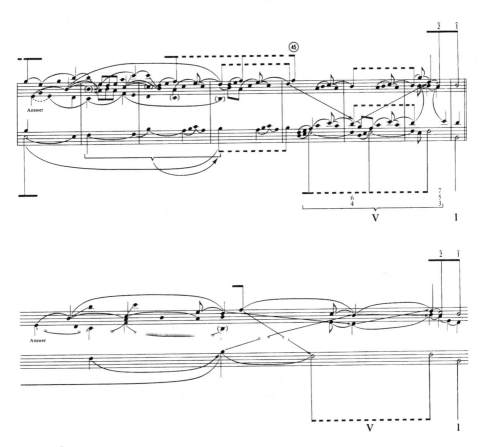

EXAMPLE 10.18: Middleground graph

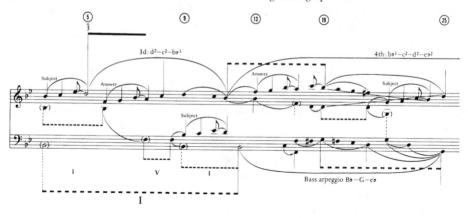

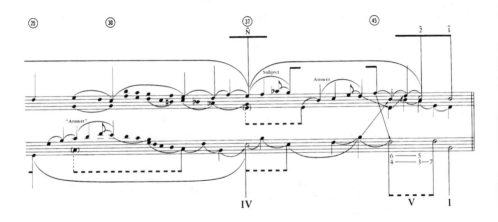

as well, I would suspect) display their timid little monsters—or, worse yet, the blueprints for assembling them—as if they were touchstones by which we might evaluate the "deviations" of a Bach or Handel.

In teaching, to be sure, it is best to confront the student with one new problem at a time. One can hardly avoid, therefore, presenting separately the different elements of fugal design: subject, answer, countersubject, episodes, etc. The mistake—and it is an avoidable one—is to transfer this approach to the analysis of fugal masterpieces; a pedagogical help in teaching the student to write fugues becomes a stumbling block to the understanding of fugues by the great composers.

I believe therefore that any course of study in fugue should include as an integral part of the approach the analysis of complete fugues in a manner that goes beyond the identification of elements and proceeds to an understanding of their function within the whole. Of course the kind of analysis that I have attempted here makes greater demands upon student (and teacher) than conventional description does. However, many who would be unable at first to undertake such an analysis themselves would, with proper guidance, be able to hear, understand, and respond to many important features of the composition. I would maintain that if a student could not follow, for example, the course of the soprano voice in measures 1–13 of our Fugue, he ought not to be writing fugues at all. On the other hand, the student who learns to attain a comprehensive view of such compositions—dense with meaning and rich in detail—will have strengthened his musical instincts in a way hardly to be achieved by other means.

Notes

1. To be sure, the published literature on the fugue, although largely a desert, contains a number of oases. The classical treatises quoted and discussed in Alfred Mann, *The Study of Fugue* (New Brunswick: Rutgers University Press, 1958), present much valuable information. The writings of Donald Francis Tovey, though restricted to the musical foreground, can be remarkably insightful. And Heinrich Schenker left us an indispensable essay, "Das Organische der Fuge," *Das Meisterwerk in der Musik* (Munich: Drei Masken Verlag, 1926), vol. 2, pp. 57–95; translated as "The Organic Nature of Fugue," trans. Hedi Siegel, in *The Masterwork in Music*, ed. William Drabkin, vol. 2 (Cambridge: Cambridge University Press, 1996), pp. 31–54. Schenker's essay contains an exhaustive analysis of the Fugue in C Minor, *Well-Tempered Clavier*, Book I; although the analysis as such is not, in my opinion, completely convincing, it nonetheless remains immeasurably superior to any other fugal analysis known to me.

2. Hugo Riemann maintained that the subject continues through the third note of measure 5. See his *Katechismus der Fugen-Komposition*, part I, 2d ed. (Leipzig: Max Hesses Verlag, 1906), p. 144. This is certainly incorrect.

3. See J. S. Bach, *Forty-eight Preludes and Fugues*, book 1, ed. Donald Francis Tovey (London: Associated Board, 1924), pp. 158–59.

ELEVEN

Chopin's Fantasy, Op. 49

The Two-Key Scheme

"If a well-written composition can be compared with a noble architectural edifice in which symmetry must predominate, then a fantasy well done is akin to a beautiful English garden, seemingly irregular, but full of surprising variety, and executed rationally, meaningfully, and according to plan."[1] Carl Czerny, who wrote this passage around 1836, was using the word "fantasy" to mean an improvised, as distinct from a composed, piece. His remarks, however, apply equally well to the written-out fantasies of J. S. and C. P. E. Bach, Mozart, and Beethoven, for as the name suggests, these are pieces designed to sound like improvisations, abounding in evaded cadences, abrupt modulations, and unexpected juxtapositions, and tending strongly to emphasize flux and surprise at the expense of stability and order.

Few genres of tonal composition offer the musical analyst so many difficulties as does the fantasy; most of these difficulties relate to issues of unity and continuity, for the disruptions at the surface can make it hard to discern any guiding idea or underlying plan. Such is the case with the piece that forms the subject of this chapter, Chopin's great Fantasy, Op. 49. Written some five years after Czerny's words, it represents one of the last manifestations of a remarkable musical tradition; probably the decline in public improvisation spelled the end of the composed fantasy as a viable genre, except in debased and popularized forms like the medley of national airs and the operatic potpourri.

This Fantasy has a complex and highly original tonal structure, one feature of which it shares with a fair number of Chopin's larger works. Like the Second Ballade, the Second Scherzo, and the Bolero, to name some of the others, our Fantasy begins and ends in different keys. Such a departure from the norms of tonal composition always poses certain ques-

Originally published in *Chopin Studies*, ed. Jim Samson (Cambridge: Cambridge University Press, 1988), pp. 221–53.

tions for anyone trying to understand a piece in which it occurs. These are: (1) Is the piece tonally unified? Can one understand it in relation to a single governing tonal center, or does it flesh out a progression from an initial center to a closing one of equal status? (2) If there is a single primary tonic, which one is it? (3) How does the composer establish its primacy? and (4) What is the artistic purpose of the two-key scheme; how does it influence the piece's larger shape, its details, and its expressive character?[2]

With respect to the Fantasy, I have always felt that the answers to the first two questions were clear: there is a governing tonal center, and it is Ab major, the closing key, rather than F minor, the opening one. The fact that the piece is almost universally known as the "Fantasy in F Minor" is, I think, beside the point. Pieces that change their main (or seemingly main) tonic are usually known by the first "key"; this is for easy identification and does not represent an analytical judgment. Many musicians (among them Czerny) refer to Beethoven's Op. 77 as the "Fantasy in G Minor," although the initial G minor lasts for about three measures.[3] It is my impression, by the way, that most musicians who have thought about the Chopin Fantasy's tonal scheme agree with me in hearing Ab as the primary center.[4]

In this essay I shall try to support my judgment about the Fantasy's tonal structure by pointing out the strategies that tend to establish Ab as main tonic (the third of the questions listed above). I shall also attempt to examine the compositional implications of the two-key scheme (the last of my four questions). In doing so, I shall make use of the analytical approach of Heinrich Schenker, who regarded Chopin as one of the greatest composers, and whose work has done so much to illuminate his genius.

The Form: An Overview

In one important way Chopin's Op. 49 differs from the description by Czerny quoted at the beginning of this essay, and interestingly enough, it differs in the direction of regularity, for symmetry, created by the transposed repetition of large sections, predominates far more than in any of the great eighteenth-century fantasies that I know. Example 11.1, a chart of the form, shows the extent of this repetition. After an introductory slow march in two strains comes a passage in the arpeggiated texture that might well begin a keyboard fantasy (compare Mozart's Fantasy in D Minor). Here, however, it forms a transition from the march to a chain of linked phrases; most of the phrases are eight measures long, and most of them change the previous texture, rhythm, melody, or harmonic focus in some noticeable way. I call this chain a "cycle," for it recurs twice, the first time broken off and the second time complete. Consulting Example 11.1 together with the score will show that measures 155–79 (the incomplete cycle) contain the same material as measures 68–92 and that measures 235–315 are a slightly varied transposition of measures 68–148; this is more large-scale repetition than would be usual in a sonata-form movement, let alone a fantasy. That it is artistically possible here is due, first of all, to the richly varied thematic design, whose many elements are indicated in a rather simple-minded way by lower-case letters above the horizontal line in Example 11.1. And more important, the three cycles are phases of one continuous process; each return—even in exact transposition—brings with it a new function and a new meaning.

EXAMPLE 11.1: Chart of the form

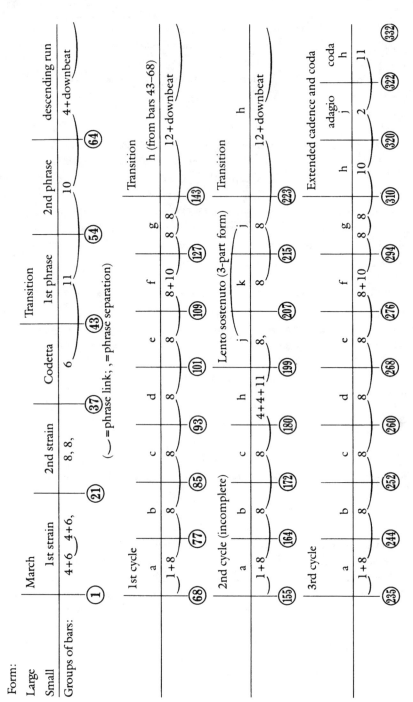

The Tonal Structure: An Overview

The uncharacteristically symmetrical form relates closely to the Fantasy's tonal structure, about which I can now begin to make some preliminary observations. (The following brief discussion is based upon Example 11.1, which should be consulted together with the score.) The opening march clearly centers on F. The mode, basically minor, changes to major for the second of its two strains; the codetta hints at the return to minor that coincides with the beginning of the arpeggiated transitional passage.

At the beginning of the first cycle, we still hear F as tonic, but the ensuing tonal instability weakens its pull without at first establishing a new center of comparable strength. Gradually, however, E♭ major emerges as just such a center, and before the cycle ends, we are solidly in E♭. Of course the transposition of this process that occurs during the third cycle leads us to A♭, our closing center. The A♭ receives the additional emphasis of the extended cadence and coda, which provide the structural resolution of a melodic $\hat{3}$–$\hat{2}$–$\hat{1}$ over I–V–I. And owing to the repetitive, cyclical design, the ear can easily connect the final A♭ with the previous E♭ and infer a large-scale progression of dominant to tonic.

The second, incomplete, cycle and the Lento sostenuto section that follows it remain, I believe, in the domain of the E♭ harmony. I hope to substantiate this belief when I discuss these sections in detail; here I shall simply point to the emphasized tonal areas—E♭ major and minor, G♭ major, and B major (=C♭)—and suggest that their combined presence is certainly compatible with the assumption of an underlying E♭ center that mixes major and minor modes.

Now the succession F minor, E♭ major, A♭ major makes a logical progression toward A♭ as a goal; it makes no such progression in F minor. Therefore, the possibility that F represents the governing tonic of the Fantasy can, I think, be ruled out. And the march's closure occurs much too soon and is much too weak to bear comparison with the powerful final cadence, which forms the resolution not just of one section but of the whole Fantasy. This makes most unlikely the notion that F and A♭ enjoy equal status.

Of course only a comprehensive view of the Fantasy—one that relates detail to the large structure—can provide a fuller answer to the question of tonal unity. I hope to provide such a view in a section-by-section discussion. And since one needs some feeling for the whole in order to make any sense of the parts, I should like to present first a picture of the Fantasy's large-scale tonal structure, encompassing the background and the earlier levels of the middleground (Example 11.2). The reader can regard this picture, in its several stages, as a hypothetical construct to be tested against the discussion of detail that follows.

Example 11.2a shows the Fantasy's background structure together with what I would regard as the first level of middleground. (In its harmonic aspect and in the contour of the bass line, the example corresponds to none of Schenker's models of the first middleground level—a fact that points to the uniqueness of the Fantasy's tonal plan.) The bass line divides into two phases, indicated in the graph by ascending and descending stems. The first phase consists of what Schenker calls an "auxiliary cadence"—a progression that leads via V to I, but that lacks a structural I at the beginning. Here, of course, the F-minor

EXAMPLE 11.2: Tonal plan

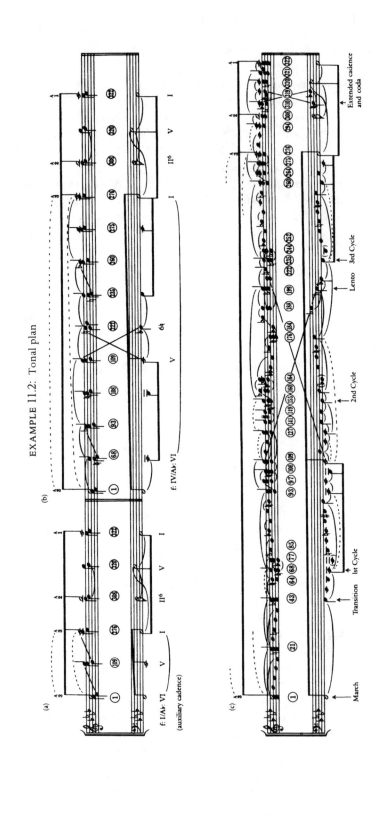

chord replaces the missing opening tonic; from the perspective of the whole piece, the F minor represents VI of A♭ (or, expressed in contrapuntal terms, the V's upper neighbor). At the beginning, however, and for a long time thereafter, the F minor seems to function as the Fantasy's tonic, as is indicated in the graph.

Auxiliary cadences often shape individual thematic elements in tonal compositions—the opening idea in the first movement of Beethoven's Piano Sonata, Op. 31, No. 3, for example. Very occasionally, as Schenker has pointed out, the harmonic framework of a whole piece (Brahms's Intermezzo, Op. 118, No. 1, is an instance) will consist of an auxiliary cadence.[5] The Fantasy represents an intermediate case: most of the piece is taken up with the auxiliary cadence, but the structural closure at the end includes a complete background progression: $\hat{3}$–$\hat{2}$–$\hat{1}$ over I–V–I.

The upper voice of Example 11.2a is much less unusual than the bass. $\hat{3}$, the first note of the Fundamental Line, is already present over the F-minor triad; a registral coupling, c^2–c^3, shifts the $\hat{3}$ from its original position into the Fantasy's obligatory register (*obligate Lage*), in which the resolution to $\hat{1}$ takes place. The coupling is achieved by means of two upward register transfers, indicated in the graph by diagonal lines.

In any graph as distant from the foreground of the piece as this one, measure numbers can serve only as a rough guide, for notes that occur together in the graph will often shift away from each other at later levels. The F at the beginning of the bass line, for instance, occurs in measure 1, but the c^2 of the upper voice enters only in measure 3. Using the measure numbers as an approximate guide, we can see that the auxiliary cadence spans almost the whole piece. The F-minor chord governs the march and the transition; the E♭ chord appears in the course of the first cycle (see measure 109) and continues in force through the second cycle and the Lento sostenuto episode; A♭, the true tonic, arrives definitively in measure 276. The structural V coincides with the adagio, sostenuto of measure 320; the I follows in 322, but a♭², the goal of the Fundamental Line ($\hat{1}$), is delayed until the very last measure.

The most striking aspect of the next level (Example 11.2b) is the filling-out of the bass: two smaller auxiliary cadences replicate the main one and serve as prefixes to the V and I. The subordinate cadences shape the harmonic direction of the first and third cycles; of particular importance is the shift to minor within the prolonged C chord of the first cycle (measure 93). This change is one of the most decisive tonal events in the Fantasy, for it marks the turn away from F minor and toward A♭.

The augmented sixth chord that precedes the beginning of the third cycle relates to the preceding E♭ chord through the technique of *chromaticized voice-exchange*; the crossed diagonal lines express the chromatic relationships that connect notes belonging to different parts.

Example 11.2c adds enough detail to show the essential tonal contents of each of the Fantasy's developmental phases (or form sections, although the latter term suggests clearer sectional articulations than in fact exist). The reader should consult this graph together with the still more detailed graphs of the individual "sections" that follow, much like a visitor to London or Paris who, in using the wonderful published guides to those cities, first finds the street he seeks on a detailed map of its neighborhood and then looks at the synoptic map of the whole city to find out where he is going in relation to where he is.

The March (Measures 1–43)

Although the opening march is cast in the role of an introduction, it has little of the normal character of one. In no way an open-ended section obviously directed toward coming events (compare, by way of contrast, the introduction to the Polonaise-Fantasy), the march is outwardly the most stable part of the piece. Though some of the phrases are linked together with Chopin's usual finesse, each one contains a strong closing cadence; each of the two strains leads the melodic line to a closure on î; and there is even a codetta to round off the section.

And yet the march sounds not at all like a self-contained whole. Chopin's refined art can create an impression of completeness and, at the same time, subtly undermine this very impression. In the march, Chopin accomplishes this feat, first of all, through his treatment of register and dynamics. The repeated unison motto explores the lowest reaches of the keyboard in a way that prepares the listener for a work of vast scope. And the fortissimo outburst that momentarily shatters a dynamic level of almost unrelieved piano similarly tells us that the march must be merely a prologue to the main action.

Even more important than dynamics and register is the treatment of tonal structure, shown in Example 11.3, a foreground graph of the first strain. The fortissimo of measure 19, for example, underlines a harmonic tension that chafes at the confines of the march's closed form. And that tension, prophetically, is directed toward Ab major. The second phrase's cadence in Ab (measures 7–10)—in itself a perfectly normal prolongation of III in minor— is extended by two measures, creating far more emphasis than is needed for purely local harmonic purposes. The drive toward Ab resumes in the fourth phrase with greater urgency (hence the crescendo to fortissimo), but the promise of Ab is not yet to be fulfilled; the unexpected and irregular resolution of a seeming cadential $^6_4$ (measure 19) turns the motion back to F minor. Yet this urge toward Ab, frustrated for the moment, is the opening phase of a process that will ultimately topple the ostensibly unassailable F minor of the march.

The struggle between F minor and Ab major—a struggle carried out in the domain of tonal structure—is perforce reflected in the Fantasy's motivic design, for in tonal music the motive is never separable from the linear and harmonic forces that operate in the background. Chopin's instinct for the motive—his ability to connect contrasting ideas through what Schenker calls "hidden repetitions," his related ability to connect large structure with detail through the enlargement of basic melodic figures—is one of the most striking aspects of his compositional genius.[6] It is given full play in the Fantasy.

Example 11.4 shows, in schematic form, the tonal matrix within which much of the motivic life of the Fantasy develops. It consists of nothing more than the tonic triads of F minor and Ab major, the beginning and closing "keys." As with any pair of diatonically related triads with roots a third apart, two notes above the bass—here Ab and C—are held in common, while the remaining one is constrained to move: F moves to Eb.

How does the Fantasy's motivic design concretize the abstract pitch relationships shown in Example 11.4? By placing emphasis on the motion of F to Eb, by doing so in both F-minor and Ab-major contexts, and by incorporating the note-pair F–Eb into melodic figures of significantly similar contour. This process begins with the Fantasy's first idea—the unison

EXAMPLE 11.3: March, first strain

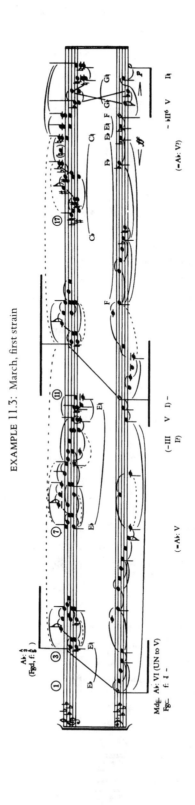

EXAMPLE 11.4: "Matrix"

motto of measures 1–2 (Example 11.5). The passage spans a descending fourth, F–C, expressed as the stepwise linear progression F–E♭–D♭–C. The even pacing of this linear progression (two notes per measure) and the repetitive, sequential character of the melodic diminutions would normally tend to divide the passage's flow symmetrically into whole-measure segments. But the staccato sign given to the first note (and to neither of its sequential analogues) disturbs this symmetry, dividing the four-note linear progression into one note plus three (F/E♭ D♭ C). This is because the ear separates slightly the detached F from the sustained E♭, D♭, and C, and it groups the latter notes together. Thus if performed as Chopin wrote it, the opening motto projects an emphasized E♭—potentially an element of the A♭ triad—between the principal notes, F and C. Unfortunately, many pianists and some editors slur the first two notes and, by changing this tiny detail, weaken the coherence of the whole piece. (Emerson's remark that foolish consistency is the hobgoblin of little minds certainly applies to those musicians who prefer a machine-like uniformity to the inspired diversity found here.)

Chopin's staccato has another far-reaching consequence: it reveals an important motive. Without it, the motto would be dominated completely by the descending fourth, F–C, an interval outlined by the first two notes, repeated sequentially, and filled in by step to form the structural outline of the whole motto. The descending fourth, in both its disjunct and its conjunct forms, is one of the leading elements in the design of the Fantasy; the symbol "x" in the analytic illustrations will point out its significant occurrences. Important as it is, the fourth is slightly obscured in its initial presentation, for the staccato articulation makes it possible to hear another figure (marked "y") starting with the second note. In later statements of the motto (measures 5, 11, and 15), figure "y" is further emphasized by changes in register. As the Fantasy goes on, this figure—subordinate at first—takes on more and more importance until it finally assumes as important a role as the descending fourth.

The connection of the motto (measures 1–2) with the full chordal setting (measures 3–4) involves an indirect chromatic adjustment: the E♭ of measure 1 must give way to E♮ over dominant harmony (the E♮ is implicitly present over the C of measure 2 even before it becomes an actual sound). This chromatic relationship—here more hinted at than expressed overtly—becomes a decisive factor in the later unfolding of the Fantasy; the process begins in measure 10, and continues in measures 18–19, where E♮ and F♭, its enharmonic equiva-

EXAMPLE 11.5: Motives "x" and "y"

lent, are the principal tonal agents of the march's climactic event: the frustrated move to-ward A♭ major and subsequent resolution in F minor.

Of course the Fantasy, like just about any of Chopin's major works, will explore many different chromatic paths. It is a characteristic of tonal chromaticism, however, that a single altered note (often in association with its enharmonic transformation) will tend to func-tion as the primary chromatic element of a given piece. In the Fantasy, that role is inevitably assigned to E♮ and F♭, because of their connection to E♭ and F, the diatonic pitches whose relationship helps to express the two-key scheme. Two additional chromatic sounds—B♮/C♭ and F♯/G♭—are to assume special importance as the Fantasy unfolds; significantly, both receive some prominence in the march (measures 16–18, 19–20, 25, and 27). The occurrence of important chromatic pitches is indicated in Example 11.3 and many later graphs.

Example 11.6 continues Example 11.3 with a graph of the F-major strain, which emerges as if on the spur of the moment out of the unexpected major tonic of measure 20. Not count-ing the cadential flourish or the six-measure codetta, it consists of only a single repeated eight-measure phrase, and functions primarily as a pendant to the strain in minor. Although it lacks the sense of tonal conflict that characterizes the first strain, it manifests a compen-sating density of contrapuntal and harmonic texture, so much so that graphs on two levels are required to give an adequate picture of its structure. The more reduced graph (Example 11.6a) gives the better preliminary orientation; note in particular that the D♭ chord of mea-sures 25–27 becomes an augmented sixth chord that connects (through a chromaticized voice-exchange) with the B♭ chord of measure 24. Thus the triads on B♭ and D♭ and the augmented sixth chord combine to express a prolonged subdominant harmony—a proce-dure very characteristic of Chopin.[7]

Note that the descending fourth F-C is expressed chromatically in the "alto." In terms of strict voice leading, the chromatic line transfers into the bass and culminates in the D♭–C of measure 27; doublings of these notes also complete the motive in its original register. This reminder of the doleful opening motto falls like a shadow across the brightness of the F major (in addition the very low octave C of measure 22 connects in register with the oc-tave F of measure 20 and also serves to recall the motto).

Unlike the march's two principal strains, both of which break off cleanly with well-articulated cadences, the codetta merges into the next section. The neighbor-notes b♭ and d♭¹ of the last $^6_4$ chord (measure 42) are taken up into the figuration of the following arpeg-gio passage; their resolution is completed only with the F-minor chord of measure 44. And the low octave Fs of measures 41–42 dissolve into the broken octaves that initiate the first arpeggio. In Example 11.6b, measures 36–38, note the indication of motive "x" in registral expansion; the allusion is made possible by the descending register transfers of the right-hand part, which prepare the low register in which the arpeggios begin.

The Transition (Measures 43–68)

It was the late Oswald Jonas who first explained, more than fifty years ago, that the guid-ing idea of this wonderful passage is the descending fourth, F–E♭–D♭–C, of the opening motto.[8] I have incorporated Jonas's idea into Example 11.7, a voice-leading graph of the sec-tion and a continuation of Example 11.6. In addition to forming the bass line of the passage

EXAMPLE 11.6: March, second strain

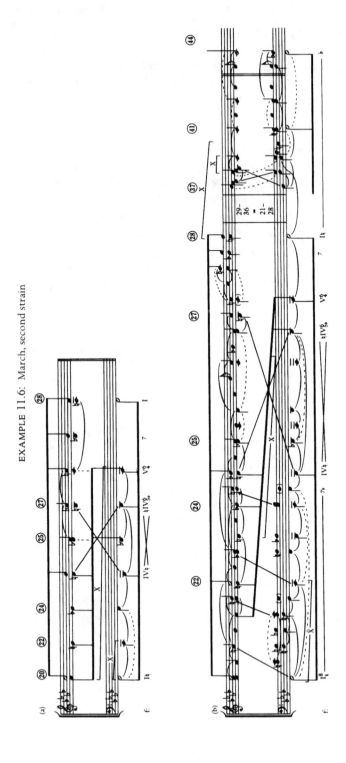

EXAMPLE 11.7: Transition

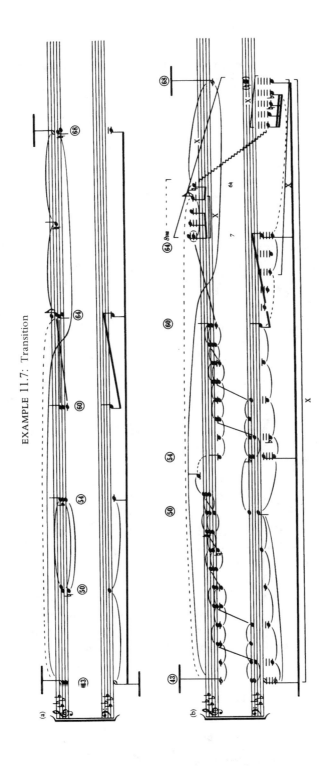

271

(Jonas's point), the motto appears, in a huge registral expansion, in the colossal descending run of the right hand (measures 64–68) that leads from the keyboard's highest F to its lowest C. Within the run, the first four notes and its octave transpositions form a diminution of the motto; the last of the four notes, C, represents a suspended seventh that resolves to C♭. (Locally the suspension's preparation forms part of the subsidiary F-minor chord that immediately precedes the run; in a deeper sense, the suspended C carries over from the structural F-minor chord that begins the whole passage. The more reduced graph makes the large-scale connections clear.)

The orthography here is confusing but characteristic: the C♭ really functions as a B♯, producing an augmented sixth above the bass's D♭, and resolving into the C-major chord that begins the next section. There is, I think, a significant association between this C♭ (=B♯) and the uses of C♭/B♯, also members of augmented sixth chords, in the march (measures 18, 27, and 35); the sonority of the augmented sixth and the rising semitone of its resolution mark many of the critical junctures in the Fantasy's development, and take on a motivic meaning. (Here and elsewhere in this essay, I have changed Chopin's spelling to clarify the sense of the passage.)

The large-scale descent of the bass is elaborated in a most unusual manner: through motion in consecutive rising thirds. Thus the move from F down to E♭ (the first step in the descending fourth) is accomplished through the bass (and root) succession F–A♭–C–E♭–G–B♭—an eleventh (F–B♭) subdivided into five consecutive thirds; the B♭ then becomes a preparatory dominant to the E♭ that follows. It is surely no coincidence that the first of these rising thirds—F–A♭—expresses the urge toward A♭ major that has already manifested itself in the first strain of the march, and that will determine the tonal direction of the whole work. And, as we shall see, transpositions of this primary rising third will play an important role in the Fantasy's middleground structure, so the interval itself becomes a design element.

As Example 11.8 shows, the motion in rising thirds is associated with the presence of figure "y." The first statement of the figure here is at the same pitch level—C–F–E♭—as its very first occurrence at the opening of the march. Note that the F is suspended over the A♭ chord, resolving on the third triplet eighth note of measure 45; as the bass moves up by thirds, equivalent suspensions appear over each new step. Chopin's autograph reveals an elaborately careful and lucid notation of the suspensions; his notation was ignored, or at any rate not reproduced, by most editors, starting with the French first edition (the Henle edition has it right). How characteristic it is of Chopin to dissolve a kind of imitative counterpoint, fraught with motivic significance, into what might seem to be a merely pianistic transitional passage. As the tempo accelerates, the triplet eighth notes project more and more clearly not only the melodic shape of figure "y," but also an approximation of its original rhythmic contour and duration. Eventually a partially new idea—a complete neighbor-note figure

EXAMPLE 11.8: Motive "y"

in dotted rhythm—grows out of figure "y"; appearing first in measures 50–52, it will recur each of the many times an arpeggiated passage based on this one appears.

The three double octaves that punctuate the arpeggios in measures 52–53 will become another important articulative element in the Fantasy's design, recurring in measures 153–54, 197–98, and 233–34. They can be traced back—indirectly, but, I believe, unquestionably—to the octave sonority of the opening motto. The connecting links are better expressed in musical notes than in words (Example 11.9).

The First Cycle (Measures 68–155)

The contra C at the head of measure 68 is at once the last note of the transition and the first note of the first cycle.[9] This sort of overlap, which we observed first at the beginning of the transition, characterizes all the phrase connections within the cycle. Although several phrases end with V–I progressions, all of these are so arranged that the V comes at the end of one eight-measure group and the I at the beginning of the next one (e.g., measures 100–101, 108–9, and 126–27). Thus even apart from the striking deceptive cadences and other unexpected chord successions at phrase junctures, the cycle is singularly free of "normal" phrases—that is, tonal–durational units in which the tonal goal falls within the time span of the durational unit.

And since most of the rest of the Fantasy is given over to restatements (partial or complete) of the cycle, the overlapping of phrases and of large sections pervades almost the entire piece. Indeed, in the almost three hundred measures from the beginning of the march's codetta to the end of the Fantasy, there is only one phrase (measures 199–206) that cadences without an overlap—and its cadence lacks a conclusive melodic line. Avoiding strong cadences and closed form sections is a traditional trait of the fantasy as a genre; overlapping phrases to create continuity is a hallmark of Chopin's style; but surely this piece represents an extreme instance of these tendencies (perhaps *the* extreme instance) both in the tradition of the genre and in its composer's output.

In its thematic contents as well as its overlapped phrase structure, the cycle seems to have neither a definite beginning nor a definite ending. The first unit, an agitato passage in syncopated rhythm (measure 68), composes out a chord of dominant, not tonic, function; in addition, it has the character of a bridge passage, not a stable theme. And the unit that one would expect to close the cycle—a quick march (measure 127)—debouches through a deceptive cadence (measure 143) into an arpeggiated passage clearly derived from the one in measures 43–68; like that earlier passage, it leads into the agitato syncopations, and the cycle, again without a stable beginning, resumes.

EXAMPLE 11.9: Octave sonority

The many sudden and surprising changes of tonal focus make the larger harmonic structure of the cycle very hard to grasp. In my view, a first step toward understanding this structure is realizing that the splendid A♭-major cantilena of measures 77–84 does not constitute an arrival at the structural tonic of the Fantasy's tonal background. The episode enters without harmonic preparation and closes without achieving a harmonic resolution; in no way are its eight inconclusive measures—striking and beautiful though they are—sufficient to replace the powerful F minor that has dominated the piece so far. Like the moves toward A♭ in the march and transition, this one is rather a vision of the Promised Land than an arrival in it; this time, however, the vision is on the way to becoming a reality.

Example 11.10 forms a continuation of Example 11.7, and shows on two levels the linear-harmonic contents of the cycle. In the less detailed graph (Example 11.10a), we can see that the origin of the A♭ chord is contrapuntal rather than harmonic. It results from an interval-progression 5–6 above C accompanied by the chromatic inflection E♮–E♭ (again note the use of E♮ as primary chromatic); the addition of the root A♭ in the bass produces the stable $\frac{5}{3}$ position of the A♭ triad.

Example 11.10 indicates that the A♭ passage occurs within a broad and eventful prolongation of a C triad that changes its quality from major to minor and its local harmonic function from dominant to temporary tonic. It is in the bass line that the coherence of this C prolongation is most readily apparent; the ascent from D to G of measures 85–92 continues from the earlier C (measures 68–76) almost as if the passage in A♭ had never taken place. A fall to C balances the earlier stepwise ascent and stabilizes the C minor with a dominant to tonic resolution (measures 92–93). Note, by the way, how the accompaniment figure of measures 93–94 resumes the pattern of measures 68–73; this textural association underscores the connection between the C minor and the earlier C major.

With respect to the logical motion of the bass, the A♭ episode is a kind of digression or parenthetical interpolation. But its appearance marks a critical point in the struggle of A♭ to assert itself as the governing tonic of the Fantasy. The passage follows a pedal on C (measures 73–76) that proclaims itself a preparatory dominant to some kind of big statement in F minor. That statement, of course, is never made. Thus the A♭ theme, though not yet the expression of a stable underlying tonic, does represent the negation of what has seemed, up until now, to be such a tonic. At no further point in the cycle will F function as a strong center of tonal gravity; the weakening of F minor leaves the field open for other forces to emerge. How fitting, in a fantasy, that it is this visionary episode that transforms our sense of tonal realities![10]

The prolonged C triad of measures 68–93 has undergone two transformations: from major to minor quality and from dominant to tonic function. It will soon experience a third change, for its term as tonic is very brief; it must yield to the E♭ major that is about to emerge as an important new center. Indeed, from the perspective of tonal structure, the main purpose of measures 93–142 is to introduce the E♭ and to stabilize it so that it takes on a weight commensurate with that of the opening F minor. Chopin's manner of accomplishing these tasks is highly unusual, yet highly suitable for a fantasy—that genre where the unusual almost becomes the norm.

A superficial reading of the Fantasy might lead one to infer a structural arrival on I of E♭ in measure 97; a prolongation of E♭ would underlie the rest of the cycle. Yet the E♭ of measure 97 hardly sounds like a point of arrival at all, let alone one that initiates the prolonga-

EXAMPLE 11.10: First cycle

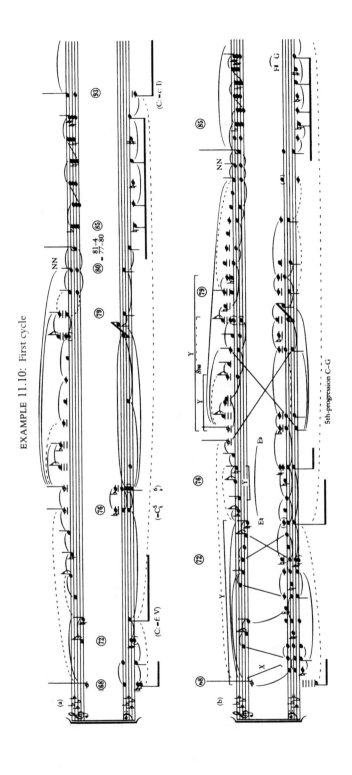

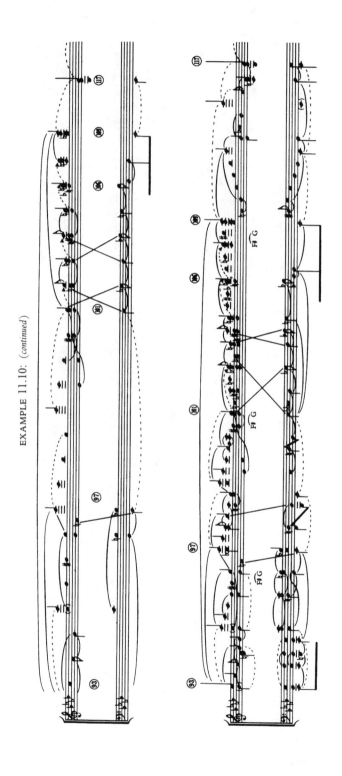

EXAMPLE 11.10: (*continued*)

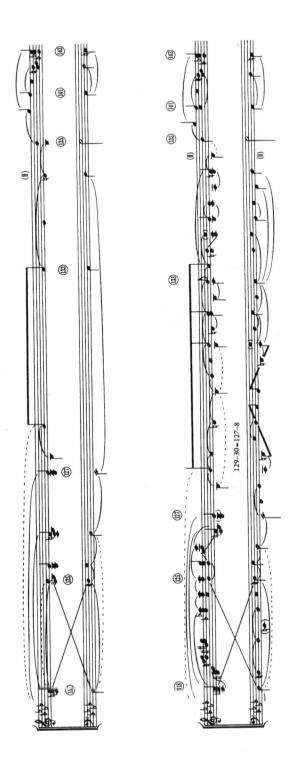

tion of a structural harmony. In the first place, it enters without any harmonic preparation. In the second place, it brings with it no change in design: the upper voice merely repeats a third higher the melodic line of measures 93–96. Now the E♭ that recurs at measure
100 does follow a dominant, and does introduce a new left-hand figure. But the V is brief,
the new left-hand figure accompanies a melodic line that continues the motive heard just
before, and most important, the entire phrase is still clearly on the way to something more
stable.

That "something" is, of course, the big E♭ chord of measure 109, which undoubtedly does
sound like a point of arrival, and the most important one so far in the piece. That this is so
is mainly due to the preparatory V pedal of measures 106–8, whose insistence is emphasized
both by the crescendo and by the contrast between the repeated B♭ octaves and the very active
bass line of the immediately preceding measures. As I hear it, the bass line of the cycle has as
its deep structural core a motion from C through B♭ to E♭: that is, from the prolonged C of
measures 68–95 to the B♭ pedal of 106–8 to the E♭ that continues from measure 109 to the
end of the cycle and, as we shall see, beyond. This bass structure forms the first of the subordinate auxiliary cadences shown in Examples 11.2b and 11.2c.

The E♭ triad of measure 97, then, would function rather as the upper third of the previous C minor than as a harmony of deeper structural significance. (In this connection, compare Schenker's reading of Mozart's Symphony No. 40, first movement, measure 28, where
he does not interpret the B♭ chord as structurally connected with the coming prolongation of B♭.)[11] Here the vehement E♭ of measure 97 enters as if to overthrow the C minor—
an ingemination, in the region of the dominant, of the Fantasy's F-minor/A♭-major conflict. (And in the last cycle, the conflict will be replicated at its primary pitch level: F/A♭ instead
of C/E♭.) An E♭ major stabilized by a preparatory V, like the one of measure 109, would
not convey a sense of conflict, hence the "premature" and, I think, non-structural E♭ of
measure 97.

From the perspective of larger tonal structure, the next phase of the cycle contains a
cadence in E♭ ($\hat{3}$–$\hat{2}$–$\hat{1}$ over I–V–I, measures 109–27) made more emphatic by the rhythmic
expansion that delays the arrival on the final I. The expansion takes the form of a passage
interpolated within the prolonged V of measures 116–26. Note that the first move of the
passage is to a $^6_5$ chord on B♮ (measure 119)—a chord whose contrapuntal meaning emerges
clearly enough from Example 11.10b. The graph, however, does not tell the whole story,
for the association of the chord with C minor is unmistakable; thus the struggle between C
minor and E♭ (F minor and A♭ in the third cycle) flares up briefly just before the latter key
celebrates its triumph.

As always in the Fantasy, the goal tonic of the cadence overlaps the beginning of the next
unit—a march-like parallel period composed almost in strict antecedent-consequent relation. I say "almost" because of the overlap that binds the goal V of the antecedent to the
opening I of the consequent (measure 135) and because of the startling deceptive cadence
that, in denying the expected resolution on E♭, prevents the cycle from closing and propels
the piece into a transitional passage based on the one of measures 43–68.

The function of the dissonant chord (measure 143) that creates the "deception" is not
immediately clear. Indeed, only when we approach the second cycle shall we see that it results from the chromatic inflection of the II⁶ that arrived in measure 141. (In graphing the
deceptive cadence, I have once again attempted to clarify the meaning of the passage by using

enharmonic equivalents of some of Chopin's notes. I shall have recourse to this procedure in some later illustrations as well.)

The larger melodic contours are clearer and less problematic than the bass line and large-scale harmonic organization. In studying Example 11.10, note the frequent use of voice-leading devices—upward register transfer and reaching-over—that carry the upper line into higher regions. This upward tendency characterizes the leading of the upper voice through-out the Fantasy. In this connection, the first two phrases of the march and the arpeggios of the transition are emblematic; the rising thirds that we encountered there are mirrored in the cycle, but spread out over huge spans of time.

The ascending impulse of the Fantasy's upper line relates both to the two-key scheme by rising third and to figure "y," whose rising fourth and falling second also produce a third between the first and last notes. Example 11.11 traces this figure in its various incarnations from the opening of the piece through the Ab episode. Particularly impressive is the con-trast between the agitato C–F–E♮ of measures 73–75 and the songful C–F–E♭ that begins the Ab theme. Unlike the "y" figure, which takes on a prominent role especially in the first half of the cycle, the "x" figure of the falling fourth is much less in evidence than earlier on in the Fantasy. Two important episodes, however—the agitato passage (measures 68ff.) and the closing quick march (measures 127ff.)—begin with leaps of a descending fourth, and its influence can perhaps also be traced in the octave bass of the march and the upper line of the Ab episode (especially measures 78–81).

After the Ab episode, the cycle is strongly colored by the chromatic pitch F♯, which leads to G, usually as the culminating event of a rising line. Example 11.10b shows the significant instances; note especially the bass of measures 85–92 and the upper line of measures 106–9. The very Chopinesque chromatic sequence that begins in measure 101 is clear in its general orientation but far from easy to understand in its details. The problems are both notational (Chopin's typical enharmonic spellings) and compositional (the use of *rhythmic shifts* to cre-ate pseudo chords out of passing notes). In Example 11.10b I have tried to disentangle the voice leading of measures 101–2; the sequential repetitions would follow the same principles.

The Second Cycle and the Lento Sostenuto (Measures 155–235)

The dying away of the incomplete second cycle, the surprising advent of a fragmentary "slow movement" in triple time, the almost brutally abrupt resumption of alla breve meter and quick tempo in the transition to the third cycle—all of these produce the highest concen-tration of surface contrast in the Fantasy. Yet underlying this kaleidoscopic surface is the elaboration of a single prolonged harmony whose unifying power fuses the contrasting passages into one large formal component. The prolonged harmony is the dominant, E♭ major, that governs the end of the first cycle; somewhat like the development of a sonata

EXAMPLE 11.11: Motive "y"

movement, this composite section moves within a previously established structural harmony, transforming it from a local tonic into a dissonant chord requiring resolution.

But the tonal path taken here differs from any found in a normal sonata development, for the two-key scheme of the Fantasy does not permit a resolution to the primary tonic, A♭, at the beginning of the third cycle. It is therefore to the F-major chord that begins the next cycle that this prolonged dominant must find its way. Chopin's solution to the compositional problem posed here is shown in Example 11.12; he alters chromatically the E♭ harmony so that it becomes the augmented sixth chord G♭–B♭–D♭–E♮; the augmented sixth, in turn, resolves into the F chord (Example 11.12a). (Note that each of the three cycles is introduced by an augmented sixth.) As I mentioned in connection with Example 11.2, a chromaticized voice-exchange effects the connection of the diatonic E♭ harmony and its altered derivative; voice-exchanges are frequent occurrences in the Fantasy, both on a huge scale like this one and as surface events, as in measures 101–2, which express almost the same tonal contents within a two-measure span.

The Lento sostenuto passage in B major (a notation of convenience for C♭) leads directly into the augmented sixth; Chopin utilizes the enharmonic equivalence of dominant seventh and "German" augmented sixth by transforming the unresolved V⁷ that ends (or rather fails to end) the Lento (measure 222) into the German sixth (measures 227–34) that prepares the third cycle. (As so often with Chopin, the notation does not reflect this change in function.)

Example 11.12b reveals the voice-leading origin of the B♮ (C♭) major in a 5–6 motion combined with the downward inflection of a major third, G♮, into the minor third, G♭. The addition of a root in the bass and the introduction of a preparatory dominant stabilize the C♭ triad so that it can serve as the basis of a relatively self-contained passage.

Much of the dramatic intensity of this part of the Fantasy grows out of its chromaticism, and the chromaticism here hinges on the various functions of the single sound F♯/G♭, as can be seen in Example 11.12d. We have seen how the first cycle gives prominence to rising chromatic lines that culminate in F♯–G. As Example 11.12d points out, the arrival of the second cycle is marked by the same chromatic succession (the F♯ notated as G♭, measures 149–55—again note the augmented sixth). How beautifully does Chopin stabilize this sound in its G♭ incarnation when he turns to E♭ minor and G♭ major in the passage that serves as a kind of codetta to the cycle (measures 184–98). The stabilized G♭ (written as F♯) continues throughout the Lento episode, but its stability turns out to be deceptive—the still point at the center of a storm—when the sound is incorporated into the dissonant augmented sixth that hurls it down to F. (Compare the three G♭ octaves in measures 197–98 and 233–34.)

The second cycle is not an exact transposition of the equivalent portion of the first; harmonic necessities impel substantive changes in two passages (see measures 158 and 172/180). These necessities involve the prolongation of the E♭ chord that was mentioned above. As Example 11.12d indicates, the harmonic path leads from the opening G major (measure 155) to B♭ major (measure 160) and E♭ major (measure 176). The episode in G♭ (measure 164) is interpolated between the B♭ and the rising sequence that continues it. Like the equivalent passage in A♭ of the first cycle, it does not form part of the harmonic framework; but, again like the earlier passage, it foretells important future developments—the turn toward G♭ as a preparation for the B (C♭) episode and the directing of the larger structure of the section toward the augmented sixth on G♭.

EXAMPLE 11.12: From first cycle to third

The movement from the end of the first cycle through the transition into the second cycle is composed with extraordinary subtlety into a sequence of events rich with multiple meanings (Example 11.13). To begin with, the dissonant chord that interrupts the expected cadence (measure 143) could resolve either as a $\frac{4}{2}$ to F♭ major or (as a diminished third chord) to B♭; the latter is by far the likelier possibility. Of course the chord does neither; through chromatic inflection, it is transformed into the augmented sixth on A♭ that moves to the G of measure 155. And yet when B♭ arrives in measure 160, it fulfills the seemingly broken promise of the earlier passage; even the diminished seventh on A that introduces B♭ serves as a reminder of the earlier sonority. (The asterisks under the A's in Example 11.13 convey this association.)

And the G chord that begins the new cycle (measure 155) also carries a double meaning; eventually it turns out to function as an altered III of E♭, but at first it sounds like the V of C minor. The hint of C minor at the outset of this cycle looks back to the C-minor/E♭-major conflict of the preceding one. And finally, the strong tendency toward G♭ transposes to a new pitch level the movement by rising third that permeates the entire Fantasy.

After it achieves a harmonic closure on E♭ (measures 176ff.), the cycle moves on to a variant of the arpeggio passage that, this time, seems to die away in the manner of a codetta rather than moving forward (measures 180–98). However, the G♭ harmony on which it dies away does not form a natural goal, and it enters quite without the kind of preparation that might stabilize it, at least temporarily. In retrospect, therefore, the G♭ is understood as a preparatory dominant for the B (C♭) of the Lento sostenuto.

Except for the sixteen-foot doublings of the bass line, the Lento episode is written almost entirely within the range of the human voice and in a texture close to that of four-part choral music. With its simple ABA form (3 x 8 measures) and meditative, hymn-like character, it presents the greatest imaginable contrast with the tempestuous passages of the preceding cycles. And yet it is as intense as any part of the Fantasy. That this is so results from two factors: the relation of the episode to its larger context and its highly chromatic tonal fabric. A glance back at Example 11.12b will remind us that the B-major harmony that governs the Lento originates out of the combination of G♭, a chromatic passing note, and C♭, a chromatically inflected upper neighbor; elements of tension and flux freeze for a few moments into the semblance of a stable structure. The two generating notes (written enharmonically as F♯ and B) are, of course, two of the three main chromatic elements of the Fantasy, as discussed previously; E♮, the third element is a prominent feature of the melodic line (measures 202, 205, etc.).

The eight-measure phrase that begins the Lento is not very chromatic, but the B section (measures 207–14) manifests the complex chromaticism of Chopin's late style in all its power and beauty. Example 11.14, which gives a comprehensive picture of the Lento and the brief transitional passage that follows it, does not have enough levels to explain this chromatic passage; I have therefore added a graph of part of the B section (Example 11.15). As I understand it, much of the chromaticism results from the introduction of the sound G♭/F♯; in particular, the succession G♮–F♯ mirrors the G–G♭ that helps to connect the end of the first cycle to the beginning of the third one (again consult Example 11.12). How moving is the effect of the F𝄪 and G♮ that Chopin adds to the reprise in measures 216 and 220 as an echo of the B section.

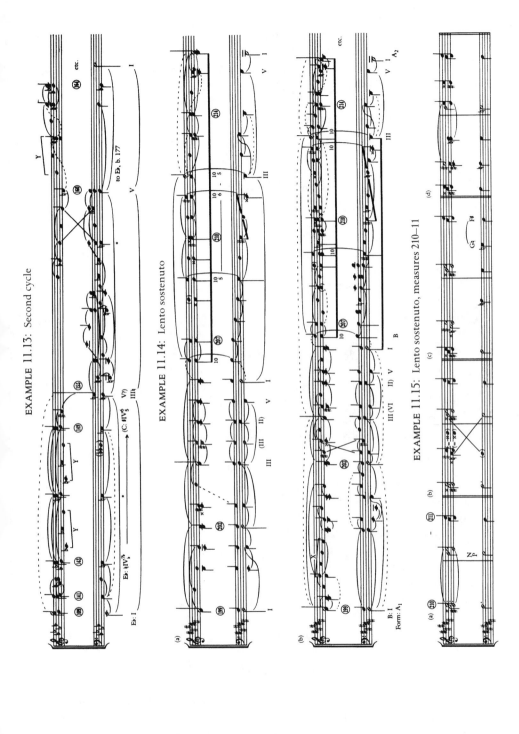

EXAMPLE 11.13: Second cycle

EXAMPLE 11.14: Lento sostenuto

EXAMPLE 11.15: Lento sostenuto, measures 210–11

Another essential key to understanding the chromatic passage is the notion of rhythmic displacement (or shift) already cited in connection with Example 11.10b. This technique creates simultaneities out of notes that lack an inherent harmonic connection, producing chordal successions that are harmonically nonfunctional, obedient to a purely contrapuntal logic. I am thinking particularly of the last two beats of measure 210 and the first two of measure 211; note, however, that the larger framework within which these sonorities move makes perfect harmonic sense.

The Third Cycle, Extended Cadence, and Coda (Measures 235–332)

Although the third cycle is an almost literal transposition of the first, it is in no way a mere copy. Its different position within tonal space and musical time gives it an altogether different function and meaning and even changes the local effect of some of its component parts. The C-major harmony within which the first cycle begins, for example, is strongly rooted in the key of F minor, which it seems to continue. The corresponding F-major chord that opens the third cycle does not follow a previously established B♭ minor; instead it follows the foreground key of B major (C♭)—as drastically unrelated a sonority as one could hope to find. (To be sure, the beginning of the cycle suggests the key of B♭ minor, but the key never becomes more than a suggestion, for the B♭-minor triad occurs only in passing.) Whereas the first cycle forms a direct connection between the F minor of the march and E♭ major, the third cycle connects directly only with its goal—A♭ major—and not with the events immediately preceding it.

The lack of a strong focal point at the beginning of the cycle makes the magnetic attraction of the A♭ major all the more overwhelming; in a good performance, its arrival in measure 276 becomes a veritable epiphany. That this is so is also due to the long and careful preparation that Chopin provides for this arrival: the moves toward A♭ in the march, transition, and first cycle, and the return to a prolonged F chord in the third cycle, which makes the cycle replicate on a smaller scale the structure of the whole piece.

Even a casual comparison of the two complete cycles will reveal many differences of detail; these involve changes in pitch content, dynamics, articulation, and voicing. Although no single change alters the musical substance very much, their combination produces an intensity that reflects the climactic position of the third cycle in the Fantasy's form, the last curve, as it were, in an ascending spiral that culminates in the arrival on the A♭ tonic. Precisely for reasons of form I believe that pianists and editors should observe all textual differences. This includes avoiding the alteration of the bass notes in measures 112 and 116 (of the first cycle) to make them conform to the A♭ version (measures 279 and 283). Chopin may perhaps have written octaves on E♭ in the earlier passage, as some have suggested, only because he was writing for a piano that did not extend down to subcontra B♭, but we still ought to play what he wrote and not some conjectural "improvement." And there is something to be said for saving the admittedly more effective later version for the triumphant tonic statement at the close. Similarly the piano dynamic that Chopin requires for the quick march that begins in measure 127 must be strictly observed despite—or indeed because of—the sempre forte in the corresponding passage at the end.

Example 11.16 depicts the final part of the Fantasy—the deceptive cadence of measures 308–10, the resumption of motion toward harmonic closure in a passage that incorporates the transition and a quotation of the Lento sostenuto's opening measures into the work's structural cadence, and the brief coda, based on measures 188–98. (For reasons of space I have omitted detailed voice-leading graphs of the third cycle; anyone who wanted to could construct his own, using Examples 11.2c and 11.10 as models.) Unlike the corresponding deceptive chord at the end of the first cycle, the one in measure 310 leads fairly directly into the dominant harmony that forms its goal; in so doing it expresses the Fantasy's primary chromatic element, Fb, and makes good the promise of the opening march's frustrated moves toward Ab. A comparison of measures 319–20 with measures 18–19 and of the descending chromatic run of measures 316–18 with the one in measures 64–68 will begin to show how many threads are tied together in this climatic passage.

In a piece whose main tonic arrives only after a long struggle and whose large formal components, almost without exception, fail to achieve closure, a quick and facile final cadence would be disastrously out of place. The deceptive progression that extends the final cadence, therefore, is a compositional necessity. Its effect is far more powerful than that of its analogue at the end of the first cycle, or any of the other deceptive cadences in the Fantasy. This is so precisely because the progression it interrupts is perceived by any experienced listener to be a motion toward final closure.

That closure represents the resolution both of immediate tonal tensions and, indirectly, of all the processes whose lack of resolution has kept the Fantasy in a constant state of flux almost without parallel in the literature. The closing V and I, therefore, must enter like characters in a drama; no simple cadential formula would suffice here. But a dramatic gesture without musical content would prove even more inadequate—I need not cite as evidence any of the countless programmatic pieces whose musical emptiness turns their dramatic discourse to bombast. Chopin's solution to this compositional problem is as fulfilling musically as it is dramatically; it includes the final transformations of the Fantasy's two main motives. As Example 11.16 shows, the upper line moves into the Allegro assai of the coda with the notes f^2–eb^2–db^1–c^1—the descending fourth of the opening motto with pitches untransposed but now expressing Ab major as clearly as it once did F minor. (The g^2 just before the f^2 is an accented neighbor or appoggiatura; this is one of the few configurations in tonal music where a neighbor-note is embellished by its own neighbor.) And the rising arpeggios that follow carry figure "y" into the highest possible register, dwelling for a moment on the crucial notes F and Eb before disappearing into the blue. The Fb of the penultimate chord seals the victory of Eb and of the Ab harmony to which it belongs—no trace of F♮ remains!

In reviewing a Chopin biography, Bernard Shaw disputed the ridiculous notion that any piece not in sonata form must be program music. He wrote, "Now a Chopin ballade is clearly no more program music than the slow movement of Mozart's symphony in Eb is."[12] The statement holds true, needless to say, for the Fantasy as well. This does not rule out the possibility that extramusical ideas might have played a part in the creative process that led to the Fantasy, the Ballades (Mickiewicz's poems), or, for that matter, the Mozart slow movement; once achieved, however, the works stand on their own, sustained by their extraordinary musical values.

Among the musical values of all of these works is their narrative quality; but the narration is a musical one, carried out by tonal structure, texture, form, and motivic design. To

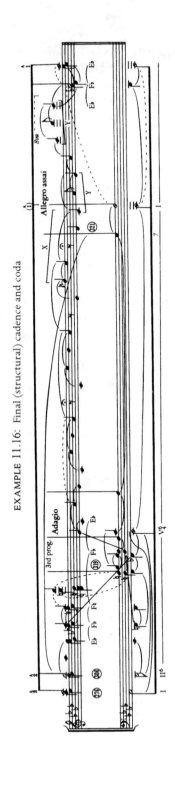

EXAMPLE 11.16: Final (structural) cadence and coda

my way of thinking there would be nothing wrong in imagining a program to make more vivid one's image of the musical narration so long as one did not take it too seriously or begin to believe that the piece was "about" one's concoction. For the Fantasy, in particular, it would at first seem easy enough to construct a fairly convincing, though inevitably trite, program— probably something along the lines of *Les Préludes* or *Tod und Verklärung*. After all, Chopin himself calls the opening section a "march," and it is clearly a march of solemn—even funereal—character. The subsequent course of the piece—the struggle between the two keys, the victory of A♭, the celebration of that victory in a march-like episode of triumphal character—is almost impossible to describe except in metaphors that come close to suggesting a program.

But the Fantasy mocks any attempt to force its musical narrative—fraught though it is with human feeling—into a story of victory over death or tragedy and triumph. For in the end there is neither tragedy nor triumph, but only the unfathomable magic of a dream. The deceptive cadence interrupts the victory celebration like the Red Death at the Masque, but the interruption does not lead to the sort of violent conclusion to which Chopin was so often drawn.[13] (And a violent conclusion would hardly fit the Fantasy's "optimistic" move from F minor to A♭ major.) What follows instead is the urgent appeal of the Adagio sostenuto, an appeal to which the final tonic yields no definite answer, for the piece ends like a dream, its elements dissolving into nothingness just when we think we have finally grasped their meaning.

Notes

1. Carl Czerny, *A Systematic Introduction to Improvisation on the Pianoforte*, Op. 200, trans. and ed. Alice Mitchell (New York: Longman, 1983), p. 2.

2. See Felix Salzer, "Tonality in Medieval Polyphony," *Music Forum* 1 (1967), pp. 65–67. See also Harald Krebs, "Alternatives to Monotonality," *Journal of Music Theory* 25, no. 1 (1986), pp. 1–16; and L. Poundie Burstein, "The Non-Tonic Opening in Classical and Romantic Music," Ph.D. dissertation, City University of New York, 1988.

3. Czerny, *A Systematic Introduction*, p. 177.

4. See, for example, Harald Krebs, "Third Relation and Dominant in Late 18th- and Early 19th-Century Music," Ph.D. dissertation, Yale University, 1980, pp. 138–42.

5. Heinrich Schenker, *Free Composition*, trans. and ed. Ernst Oster (New York: Longman, 1979), pp. 88–89.

6. Ibid., pp. 93–107. See also Charles Burkhart, "Schenker's Motivic Parallelisms," *Journal of Music Theory* 22, no. 2 (1978), pp. 145–75.

7. See, for example, the Fourth Ballade, measures 169–94, and the Mazurka, Op. 56, No. 1, measures 1–12, for related, though by no means identical, procedures.

8. Oswald Jonas, *Introduction to the Theory of Heinrich Schenker: The Nature of the Musical Work of Art*, trans. and ed. John Rothgeb (New York: Longman, 1982), pp. 73–74. The first German edition (which included Jonas's discussion of the Fantasy) was published in Vienna in 1934.

9. The larger metrical structure also shows a curious sort of overlap. The measure (or at least its downbeat) belongs metrically to the preceding four-measure group, to which it forms an appended downbeat measure. (Schenker illustrates such extra downbeats in *Free Composition*, figures 149/3, 4, and 5.) Simultaneously, the right-hand part forms an upbeat to the eight-measure group that begins the cycle.

10. Harald Krebs also recognizes the A♭ episode as a turning point. See Krebs, "Third Relation," p. 139.

11. Heinrich Schenker, "Mozart: Sinfonie G-Moll," in *Das Meisterwerk in der Musik*, 3 vols. (Munich: Drei Masken Verlag, 1925, 1926, 1930, reissued as 3 vols. in 1 in slightly reduced facsimile, Hildesheim: Georg Olms, 1974), vol. 2, p. 110, translated as "Mozart's Symphony in G Minor, K.550," trans. William Drabkin, in *The Masterwork in Music*, ed. William Drabkin, vol. 2 (Cambridge: Cambridge University Press, 1996), p. 62.

12. George Bernard Shaw, *Music in London* (London: Constable and Co., 1932), vol. 2, p. 209.

13. As in the First Scherzo, all of the Ballades except the third, and the Finale of the Third Sonata.

Carl Schachter

List of Publications

1967   "The Two Versions of Mozart's Rondo, K.494," (with Hans Neumann), *Music Forum* 1 (1967), pp. 3–34.

1968   "Schubert's Moment Musical, Op. 94, No. 1," *Journal of Music Theory* 12, no. 2 (1968), pp. 222–39, reprinted in *Readings in Schenker Analysis and Other Approaches*, ed. Maury Yeston (New Haven: Yale University Press, 1977), pp. 171–84.

1969   *Counterpoint in Composition: The Study of Voice Leading*, co-authored with Felix Salzer. New York: McGraw-Hill, 1969; reprint ed. New York: Columbia University Press, 1989.

        "More about Schubert's Op. 94, no. 1," *Journal of Music Theory* 13, no. 1 (1969), pp. 218–29, reprinted in *Readings in Schenker Analysis and Other Approaches*, ed. Maury Yeston (New Haven: Yale University Press, 1977), pp. 193–201.

1970   "Landini's Treatment of Consonance and Dissonance," *Music Forum* 2 (1970), pp. 130–86.

1973   "Bach's Fugue in B♭ Major, *Well-Tempered Clavier*, Book I, No. 21," *Music Forum* 3 (1973), pp. 239–67.

1975   "Introduction" to *Beethoven Piano Sonatas Nos. 1–32*. New York: Dover (1975).

1976   "Rhythm and Linear Analysis: A Preliminary Study," *Music Forum* 4 (1976), pp. 281–334.

1977   "Diversity and the Decline of Literacy in Music Theory," *College Music Symposium* 17 (1977), pp. 150–53.

1978   *Harmony and Voice Leading*, co-authored with Edward Aldwell. New York: Harcourt Brace Jovanovich, 1978–79; 2d ed., 1989.

1980   "Rhythm and Linear Analysis: Durational Reduction," *Music Forum* 5 (1980), pp. 197–232, reprinted in *The Garland Library of the History of Western Music*, vol. 14: *Approaches to Tonal Analysis* (New York: Garland, 1985), pp. 223–58.

1981   "A Commentary on Schenker's *Free Composition*," *Journal of Music Theory* 25, no. 1 (1981), pp. 115–42.

1982   "Beethoven's Sketches for the First Movement of His Piano Sonata, Op. 14, No. 1: A Study in Design," *Journal of Music Theory* 26, no. 1 (1982), pp. 1–21.

1983   "The First Movement of Brahms's Second Symphony; the Opening Theme and Its Consequences," *Music Analysis* 2, no. 1 (1983), pp. 55–68.

"Motive and Text in Four Schubert Songs," in *Aspects of Schenkerian Theory*, ed. David Beach (New Haven: Yale University Press, 1983), pp. 61–76.

1987   "Analysis by Key: Another Look at Modulation," *Music Analysis* 6, no. 3 (1987), pp. 289–318.

"The Gavotte en Rondeaux from J. S. Bach's Partita in E Major for Unaccompanied Violin," *Israel Studies in Musicology* 4 (1987), pp. 7–26.

"Mozart—the Five Violin Concertos: A Facsimile Edition of the Autographs," *Strad*, June 1987, pp. 448–49.

"Rhythm and Linear Analysis: Aspects of Meter," *Music Forum* 6 (1987), pp. 1–59.

1988   "Chopin's Fantasy, Op. 49: The Two-Key Scheme," in *Chopin Studies*, ed. Jim Samson (Cambridge: Cambridge University Press, 1988), pp. 221–53.

"Schenker's Counterpoint," *Musical Times* 129, no. 1748 (1988), pp. 524–29.

1989   "Mozart's *Das Veilchen*: An Analysis of the Music," *Musical Times* 130 (1989), pp. 151–55, reprinted in *Ostinato: Revue Internationale d'Études Musicales*, nos. 1–2 (1993), pp. 164–73.

"*The Music of Chopin* by Jim Samson and *The Music of Brahms* by Michael Musgrave," *Music Analysis* 8, nos. 1–2 (1989), pp. 187–97.

1990   "Either/Or," in *Schenker Studies*, ed. Hedi Siegel (Cambridge: Cambridge University Press, 1990), pp. 165–79.

1991   "The Adventures of an F♯: Tonal Narration and Exhortation in Donna Anna's First-Act Recitative and Aria," *Theory and Practice* 16 (1991), pp. 5–20.

"Mozart's Last and Beethoven's First: Echoes of K.551 in the First Movement of Op. 21," in *Mozart Studies*, ed. Cliff Eisen (Oxford: Oxford University Press, 1991), pp. 227–51.

"Twentieth-Century Analysis and Mozart Performance," *Early Music* 19 (1991), pp. 620–26.

1994   "Chopin's Prelude, Opus 28, No. 4: Autograph Sources and Interpretation," in *Chopin Studies 2*, ed. John Rink and Jim Samson (Cambridge: Cambridge University Press, 1994), pp. 161–82.

"Chopin's Prelude, Opus 28, No. 5: Analysis and Performance," *Journal of Music Theory Pedagogy* 8 (1994), pp. 27–45.

"The Sketches for Beethoven's Piano and Violin Sonata, Op. 24," *Beethoven Forum* 3 (1994), pp. 107–25.

"The Submerged Urlinie: The Prelude from Bach's Suite No. 4 for Violoncello Solo," *Current Musicology* 56 (1994), pp. 54–71.

1995   "The Triad as Place and Action," *Music Theory Spectrum* 17, no. 2 (1995), pp. 149–69.

1996   "Idiosyncratic Features of Three Mozart Slow Movements: The Piano Concertos, K.449, K.453, and K.467," in *Mozart's Piano Concertos: Text, Context, Interpretation*, ed. Neal Zaslaw (Ann Arbor: University of Michigan Press, 1996), pp. 315–33.

"Schoenberg's Hat and Lewis Carroll's Trousers," in *Aflame with Music: 100 Years of Music at the University of Melbourne*, ed. Brenton Broadstock et al. (Melbourne: Centre for Studies in Australian Music, 1996), pp. 327–41.

Index

Aldwell, Edward, 6

Bach, Carl Philipp Emanuel, 29, 143, 260
Bach, Johann Sebastian, 198–99, 258, 260
    Cantata "O Ewigkeit, du Donnerwort,"
        ex. 1.8
    French Suites: No. 4, 143–44, 146, 148, 154,
        ex. 5.9; No. 6, 194
    Musical Offering, 18–19, ex. 1.1
    Organ Prelude, 50, ex. 1.22
    Sonata for Unaccompanied Violin No. 3,
        127–28, 138, ex. 4.5
    Suite for Lute in E Minor, 44, ex. 1.17
    Suites for Unaccompanied Cello: No. 1, 5;
        No. 4, 10
    Two-Part Invention in F Major, 130
    Well-Tempered Klavier: Book I, A-Minor
        Prelude, 195; Book I, B♭-Major Fugue,
        239–59, exx. 10.1–18; Book I, C-Major
        Prelude, 105, 106–07, 135, 203, ex. 5.1;
        Book I, E-Minor Prelude, 137–38, 141,
        144, ex. 5.4; Book I, G-Major Prelude,
        200; Book II, B♭-Major Fugue, 47,
        ex. 1.20
Bartók, Béla, Bagatelle, Op. 6, No. 12,
    40
Beach, David, 142

Beethoven, Ludwig van, 83, 112, 202, 260
    Piano Concerto No. 4, Op. 58, 150–51
    Piano Fantasia, Op. 77, 261
    Piano Sonatas, 5: Op. 2, No. 1, 7, 55, ex. 2.3; Op.
        2, No. 3, 50, ex. 1.22; Op. 7, 142, 144–48, 149,
        150, 154, ex. 5.10; Op. 10, No. 2, 28, 142, 193;
        Op. 13 (*Pathétique*), 34, 148; Op. 14,
        No. 1, 13, 65–70, 75, 76, 83, 86, exx. 2.9–10;
        Op. 14, No. 2, 12, 45, ex. 1.18; Op. 26, 33; Op.
        27, No. 1 (*Sonata quasi una fantasia*), 83–86, 88,
        97, 109–12, exx. 3.1, 3.19–20; Op. 31, No. 1,
        152; Op. 31, No. 3, 265; Op. 53 (*Waldstein*), 55,
        152, 155, ex. 2.1; Op. 57 (*Appassionata*), 191,
        193; Op. 78, 41, ex. 1.15; Op. 79, 142; Op. 110,
        25, 38, 55, exx. 1.13, 2.2
    String Quartets: Op. 59, No. 1, 38, ex. 1.13;
        Op. 59, No. 3, 105–07; Op. 135, 25
    Symphonies: No. 3 (*Eroica*), Op. 55, 134;
        No. 6 (*Pastorale*), Op. 68, 170–82, 198, exx.
        6.8–11; No. 8, Op. 93, 33
    Violin Sonata (*Spring*), Op. 24, 142, ex. 3.8
Berlioz, Hector, 29
Berry, Wallace, 55
Bettelheim, Bruno, 11
Bizet, Georges, 12
    Jeux d'enfants, Op. 22, No. 7 "Les Bulles de
        savon," 41, ex. 1.15

291

Brahms, Johannes, 143
    German Requiem, Op. 45, 148–49
    Intermezzo, Op. 118, No. 1, 1, 9, 265
    String Quartet, Op. 51, No. 2, 25
    Violin Sonata No. 2, Op. 100, 139
    "Wie bist du, meine Königin," Op. 32,
        No. 9, 194
Bruckner, Anton, 12
Burkhart, Charles, 7
Busoni, Ferruccio, "Scales in Spirals," 37,
    ex. 1.10

Calvin, Italo, *Invisible Cities*, 121
Chopin, Frédéric, 139, 285
    Ballade No. 2, Op. 38, 139, 260
    Bolero, Op. 19, 260
    Etudes: Op. 10, No. 8, 35, 201; Op. 10, No. 12,
        30; Op. 25, No. 12 (Revolutionary), 30, 31,
        86, 88, ex. 3.2
    Fantasy, Op. 49, 9, 139, 260–87, exx. 11.1–16
    Impromptu, Op. 36, 198
    Mazurkas: Op. 33, No. 1, 1, 9, 123–24, 125,
        126, ex. 4.3; Op. 59, No. 2, 42
    Polonaise-Fantasy, Op. 61, 266
    Preludes: Op. 28, No. 1, 57–62, 63–64, 66,
        68, 72, 75, 76, exx. 2.4–7; Op. 28, No. 4,
        162–65, 168, 170, 200, exx. 6.1–2; Op. 28,
        No. 18, 135, 139, ex. 5.2; Op. 28,
        No. 24, 136
    Scherzo No. 2, Op. 31, 260
    Sonata No. 2, Op. 35, 139
Claudius, Matthias, 213
Collin, Matthäus von, 216
Cone, Edward, 31–32, 33, 36, 41, 54, 79,
    172
Cooper, Grovesnor, and Leonard Meyer,
    31, 34, 41, 55
    The Rhythmic Structure of Music, 32–33
Czerny, Carl, 260, 261

Eliot, T.S., 134
Emerson, Ralph Waldo, 268

Forte, Allen, 4, 7, 8, 63, 185, 186, 201
Fowler, H. W., 36
Fredrick the Great, 18–19
Freud, Sigmund, 11, 35
Fux, Johann Josef, 29, 41

Georgiades, Thrasybulos, 89
Gesualdo, Carlo, 148

Goethe, Johann Wolfgang von, 89
Gounod, Charles, 12

Handel, George Fredrick, 258
    Concerto Grosso, Op. 6, No. 7, 38, ex. 1.13
Haydn, Franz Joseph
    The Creation, Hob. XXI/2, 8
    "Emperor Hymn," 200
    Harmoniemesse, Hob. XXII/14, 141, 142, ex. 5.7
    Sonata, Hob. XVI/135, 50, ex. 1.22
    Symphonies: No. 99, 124–26, 127, ex. 4.4;
        No. 101 (*Clock*), 102, ex. 3.14; No. 104
        (*London*), 32
Hindemith, Paul, 30
Hoffman, E.T.A., 226

Jackendoff, Ray. *See* Fred Lerdahl
Jenner, Gustav, 143
Jonas, Oswald, 4, 184, 197, 269–72

Kirnberger, Johann Philipp, 42–43, 143
Komar, Arthur, 23, 25, 31, 35, 82
    Theory of Suspensions, 33–35
Körner, Klaus, 150

Laufer, Edward, 10
Lerdahl, Fred, and Ray Jackendoff, 7, 82, 83, 136
Lester, Joel, 7, 79
Levarie, Siegmund, 152, 155
Liszt, Franz, *Les Préludes*, 287
Lorenz, Alfred, 30
Lowinsky, Edward, 95

Mahler, Alma, 182
Mahler, Gustav, 182
Marx, Karl, 35
Mendelssohn, Felix
    "Songs without Words": Op. 62, No. 1, 165–
        70, exx. 6.3–7; Op. 102, No. 4, 112–15,
        exx. 3.21–23
    String Quartet, Op. 44, No. 2, 151
Meyer, Leonard. *See* Grovesnor Cooper
Mitchell, William, 4, 8
Morgan, Robert, 79
Mozart, Wolfgang Amadeus, 80, 83, 95, 152,
    221, 260, 285
    The Abduction from the Seraglio, K.384, 221, 222,
        ex. 9.1
    Don Giovanni, K.527, 222–33, exx. 9.2–8
    Eine kleine Nachtmusic K.525, 86, 97,
        ex. 3.2

The Marriage of Figaro, "Voi che sapete," 151–57, exx. 5.11–15
A Musical Joke, K.522, 204
Piano Concerto, K.491, 27, 128–30, ex. 4.6
Piano Fantasy, K.385g, 5, 261
Piano Sonatas, 5: Sonata, K.283, 20–21, ex. 1.3; Sonata, K.310, 27, 45, 47, 193, ex. 1.19; Sonata, K.331, 25, 79, 194, 195; Sonata, K.457, 48–51, ex. 1.21; Sonata, K.545, 21, ex. 1.4
Requiem, K.626, 94, ex. 3.7
String Quartets: K.499 (*Hoffmeister*), 34–35, 105, 107, ex. 3.16; K.590, 95–97, ex. 3.8
Symphonies: No. 35 (*Haffner*), K.385, 13, 62–65, 66, 68, 75, 76, 82–83, ex. 2.8; No. 40, K.550, 105, 278; No. 41 (*Jupiter*), K.551, ex. 1.15
Violin Sonata, K.378, 93, ex. 3.6

Novack, Saul, 7

Oster, Ernst, 9, 10, 12, 13, 184, 185, 190, 191, 194, 195, 197, 202

Palestrina, Giovanni Pierluigi da, 41
Ponte, Lorenzo da, 155
Puccini, Giacomo, 12
Purcell, Henry, *Dido and Aeneas*, 40

Rameau, Jean-Philippe, 29, 143
Riemann, Hugo, 31, 79, 80, 152
Rimsky-Korsakov, Nicolai, 29
Rosen, Charles, 18, 23, 35, 140–41, 150
Rossini, Gioachino, 12
Rothgeb, John, 184, 197
Rothstein, William, 7, 11, 104, 106
Rückert, Friedrich, 211

Salis-Seewis, Johann von, 209
Salzer, Felix, 4, 6, 7, 10, 12
Scarlatti, Domenico, 43, 178
Sonatas: K.78 (L.75), 107–09, exx. 3.17–18; K.545 (L.500), 22, 37, 45, ex. 1.5
Schenker, Heinrich, 3, 4, 7–8, 10–12, 13, 17–18, 19, 20, 21, 23, 25, 28–29, 30, 35, 36, 41, 54, 55–56, 59, 63, 64, 76, 79, 88–89, 93, 96, 103, 115–16, 121, 130, 134–35, 136–37, 138, 143, 144–48, 150, 151, 155, 157, 261, 263, 265, 278
Eroica analysis, 21, 28
Five Graphic Music Analyses, 28, 188–89, 198, 201, 202

Free Composition, 4, 10, 12, 28, 62, 63, 103, 104–07, 128–29, 130–31, 134, 149, 150, 184–205
Harmony, 18, 122, 144, 149, 150, 191, 204
Kontrapunkt, 185, 201, 204
Die Meisterwerk in der Musik, 7, 193
Tonwille, 7, 55, 56, 191, 200
Schindler, Anton, 54, 69
Schnabel, Artur, 55, 84–85
Schoenberg, Arnold, 30, 148, 149, 150, 153, 155, 157
Structural Functions of Harmony, 152
Schopenhauer, Arthur, 170
Schubert, Franz, 80
"Dass sie hier gewesen," D.755 (Op. 59, No. 2), 14, 209, 211–13, exx. 8.3–4
"Der Jüngling an der Quelle," D.300, 209–11, 212, exx. 8.1–2
"Der Tod und das Mädchen," D.531 (Op. 7, No. 3), 209, 213–16, exx. 8.5–7
"Erster Verlust," D.226 (Op.5, No. 4), 23–25, ex. 1.7
"Nacht und Träume," D.827 (Op. 43, No. 2), 13, 209, 216–19, exx. 8.8–10
Sonatas: Sonata, D.845 (Op. 42), 26, 43, 47, 139–40, 141, 151, exx. 1.9, 1.16, 5.6; Sonata, D.894 (Op. 78), 87, 88, ex. 3.3
String Quartet, D.804 (Op. 29, No. 1), 43
"Valse Sentimentale," Op. 50, No. 13, 70–74, 75, 76, exx. 2.12–14
"Wanderers Nachtlied," D.768 (Op. 96, No. 3), 89–92, 105, 200, exx. 3.4–5
Winterreise, D.911 (Op. 89): No. 7, "Auf dem Flusse," 131–32, ex. 4.8; No. 20, "Der Wegweiser," 103–04, ex. 3.15
Schumann, Robert
Album for the Young, Op. 63, No. 3, "Träller-liedchen," 203, ex. 7.1
Bunte Blätter, Op. 99, No. 5 "Albumblatt," 163, ex. 6.1
Davidsbundlertänze, Op. 6, No. 1, 97–102, exx. 3.9–13
Dichterliebe, 62, 152
Liederkreis, Op. 39, No. 1 "In der Fremde," 23–25, 27, ex. 1.6
Seeger, Charles, 94
Sessions, Roger, *Harmonic Practice*, 8
Shakespeare, William
Macbeth, 139
Titus Andronicus, 79
Shaw, George Bernard, 285
Smetana, Bedrich, 12

Strauss, Richard, 12, 29
  Tod und Verklärung, 287

Tchaikovsky, Peter Ilyich, 12
Tovey, Donald Francis, 11, 20, 30, 84, 137, 141,
    144, 247
  Essays in Musical Analysis, 12
Travis, Roy, 10, 55

Vengerova, Isabelle, 4
Verdi, Guiseppe, *Don Carlo*, 19, 104, 105, ex. 1.2

Wagner, Richard, *Tristan und Isolde*, 170
Webster, James, 7
Westergaard, Peter, 192
Wieck, Clara, 98, 99

Yeats, William Butler, 79
Yeston, Maury, 86, 94

Zarlino, Gioseffo, 192
Zuckerkandl, Victor, 36, 37